BURNING BODIES

BURNING BODIES

COMMUNITIES, ESCHATOLOGY, AND THE PUNISHMENT OF HERESY IN THE MIDDLE AGES

Michael D. Barbezat

CORNELL UNIVERSITY PRESS

Ithaca and London

First published 2018 by Cornell University Press
Printed in the United States of America

Library of Congress Cataloging-in-Publication Data

Names: Barbezat, Michael D., author.
Title: Burning bodies : communities, eschatology, and
    the punishment of heresy in the Middle Ages /
Michael D. Barbezat.
Description: 1st edition. | Ithaca [New York] :
    Cornell University Press, 2018. | Includes bibliographical
    references and index.
Identifiers: LCCN 2018017278 (print) | LCCN
    2018018164 (ebook) | ISBN 9781501716829 (pdf) |
    ISBN 9781501716812 (epub/mobi) | ISBN 9781501716805
    | ISBN 9781501716805 (cloth : alk. paper)
Subjects: LCSH: Human body—Religious aspects—
    Christianity—History of doctrines—Middle Ages,
    600–1500. | Flesh (Theology)—History of
    doctrines—Middle Ages, 600–1500. | Fire—Religious
    aspects—Christianity. | Christian heretics—Europe—
    History. | Europe—Church history—600–1500.
Classification: LCC BT741.3 (ebook) | LCC BT741.3 .B37
    2018 (print) | DDC 273/.6—dc22
LC record available at https://lccn.loc.gov/2018017278

For Mary, Michel, and Victor

Contents

Illustrations

Acknowledgments

I have incurred a number of debts, both personal and institutional, in the course of creating this book. The fellowship, insights, suggestions, assistance, and criticisms of many friends and colleagues were essential to the development of my ideas. I would especially like to thank Barbara Newman, Caroline Smith, Jill Ross, Joan Cadden, Joseph Goering, Kirk Essary, Mark Meyerson, Robert Sweetman, Robin Macdonald, and Suzanne Conklin Akbari. I would like to thank especially those who, at different stages, read and commented on portions of the manuscript: Alan Bernstein, Andrew Lynch, Anna Wilson, Daniel Price, Paul Megna, and two anonymous readers for Cornell University Press. The team members at the Australian Research Council (ARC) Centre for the History of Emotions at the University of Western Australia, and at the other nodes across the country, were pillars of support. Many members of the scholarly community at the Centre, through collaboratories, symposiums, and the everyday sharing of work and thoughts, aided me immensely. In particular, I need to acknowledge my deep debt to Katrina Tap and Pam Bond. The interlibrary loan staff at the University of Western Australia played a vital role in making this project possible, and they were extraordinarily graceful.

The research for this book has been supported by a fellowship through the Australian Research Council (project number CE110001011) at the Centre of Excellence for the History of Emotions in the University of Western Australia. The Arizona Center for Medieval and Renaissance Studies provided additional support. I also benefited immensely from access to the library of the Pontifical Institute of Mediaeval Studies in Toronto. I would like to thank the following publishers for allowing me to reproduce portions of previously published work in chapters 3 and 6: Taylor and Francis ("The Fires of Hell and the Burning of Heretics in the Accounts of the Executions at Orleans in 1022," *Journal of Medieval History* 40, no. 4 [2014]: 399–420) and the University of Texas Press ("Bodies of Spirit and Bodies of Flesh: The Significance of the Sexual Activities Attributed to Heretics from the Eleventh to the Fourteenth Century," *Journal of the History of Sexuality* 25, no. 3 [2016]: 387–419).

Earlier versions of some of the material in the following chapters were presented at a number of venues, including the International Medieval Society of Paris (2017), the Annual Meeting for the ARC Centre for the History of the Emotions (2016), the Perth Medieval and Renaissance Group (2016), the University of Sydney (2016), Arizona State University at Tempe (2015), the University of Colorado at Boulder (2015), Amherst College (2014), the American Catholic Historical Association (2014), and the International Congress on Medieval Studies at Kalamazoo (2012, 2013). Portions of the second chapter were delivered as a public lecture for the Institute of Advanced Studies at the University of Western Australia (2016). In contact with the diverse communities at all of these places, I have benefited from audience members' questions, comments, and camaraderie.

Outside of academia, many friends and family have continually supported me. I need to thank them all. This book is dedicated to Mary Ellen Barbezat, Michel P. Barbezat, and Victor Millete.

BURNING BODIES

Introduction
Burning Bodies and Medieval Human Communal Identity

The thirteenth-century Cistercian monk Caesarius of Heisterbach, in a chapter of his *Dialogus miraculorum* (*Dialogue on Miracles*), wrote what became a famous account of an earlier immolation of a group of heretics at Cologne in 1163. In this dialogue between a mature monk and a young monk, or novice, the older monk tells a series of stories designed to illustrate for the novice the dangers posed by demons and their temptations. Heretics, the monk explains, are Christians overthrown by these deceptions who have become knowing or unknowing servants of the Devil, like demons themselves. The monk recounts that under the authority of the archbishop of Cologne, a group of heretics, whose exact beliefs are left unexplained and who were led by a man named Arnold, was arrested. These people were then examined and convicted as heretics by "learned men," and, following their conviction, the secular authorities condemned them to death. After learning of their conviction and their sentence, the novice asks for a description of their deaths, and the monk replies with a short and striking account of judicial murder:

They were taken outside the town, and were together put into the fire near the Jewish cemetery. After the flames had taken hold of them, in the sight and hearing of a great crowd, Arnold placed his hand on the heads of his dying disciples, and exhorted them: "Stand fast in your faith, for this day you shall be with Laurence," and yet they were very far from the faith of Laurence. There was a maiden among them, beautiful though a heretic, and she was drawn from the fire by the compassion of some who promised that they would provide her with a husband, or if it seemed better, would place her in a nunnery. She consented to this in words, but when the heretics were now dead, she said to those who had charge of her: "Tell me, where does that seducer lie?" and when they pointed out to her where Master Arnold lay, she slipped from their hands, veiled her face with her robe, and threw herself upon the body of the dead man, and with him went down to burn forever in hell.[1]

Accounts like this one from Caesarius often perplex modern readers by their paradoxical combination of heartlessness and pity. How could people, who considered themselves good and righteous, end up burning human beings alive? How did they and their defenders, or "spinners of facts," describe and explain this atrocity? These questions occurred to me as I first read descriptions of medieval executions for heresy, and they proved remarkably persistent, demanding some kind of response. *Burning Bodies: Communities, Eschatology, and the Punishment of Heresy in the Middle Ages* replies to these questions by focusing on medieval accounts of the burning alive of Christian heretics from the eleventh to the early thirteenth century. In it, I analyze these descriptions of executions from the point of view of the executioners and their supporters, asking what the act of killing this type of criminal meant to them. As explained by these authors, the most threatening and traumatic image of exclusion from human community was deeply connected to the most fundamental and hopeful promises on which they thought their society was built. In other words, the justification of horrific atrocity mirrors in reverse the noblest of aspirations.

Burning alive, to these authors, formed a part of a collection of ideas about salvation, Christian community, and the role of love. Descriptions of burning supposed heretics alive are profoundly related to ideas of a redemptive Christian community based on a divine, unifying love, and medieval understandings of what these burnings could have meant to contemporaries cannot be fully appreciated outside of this discourse of communal love. For them, human communities were bodies on fire. Medieval theologians and academics often described the corporate identity of the Christian world as a body joined together by the love of God. This love was like a fire, melting individuals together into one whole. Those who did not spiritually burn with God's love were destined to burn literally in the fires of Hell or Purgatory, and the fires of execution were often described as an earthly extension of these fires. In this scheme, there were two burning bodies that defined human collective identity and destiny, and those who did not burn one way had to burn in another. Medieval authors recurrently saw the development of burning alive as the customary punishment for persistent heresy through their ideas regarding the larger significations of fire. In the form of the exclusionary fires of Hell and judicial execution, the purifying fire of postmortem purgation, and the unifying fire of God's love, medieval authors described processes of social inclusion and exclusion through the imagery of burning bodies.

In the accounts of burnings that they authored, medieval writers often depicted heresy and orthodoxy as coconstitutive, portraying heretics as the inverse of what they regarded mainstream Christianity to be. In the course of disavowing the heretical as everything the orthodox were not, these authors defined "Christian society by what it cast out to the margins," and in so doing they said a great deal about how they imagined themselves.[2] In this fashion, descriptions of executions, and the accounts of events that led to them, provided opportunities for particularly focused discourses on medieval ideas of religiously based community. In these sources, authors conjured up the presence of the heretic, put it to work, and then abjured it away.[3] The idea of the heretic conjured by these authors did important work, work on which developing concepts of orthodoxy depended. In their thinking with heretics, medieval writers portrayed exclusion that allowed integration and likeness that generated difference, and they explored the recurrent and unstable negotiations between such binaries in which they found themselves in different fires.[4]

In what follows, I offer a history of the ideas that orthodox authors of medieval historical and theological texts associated with the executions of heretics, from the earliest instances of burning alive as a punishment for heresy in the medieval West in the eleventh century until the advent of the internal crusades of the thirteenth. Out of necessity, I place what are often short accounts of executions in context, considering them alongside other sources. These other sources are either closely related to the actual events or describe the fundamental assumptions through which a medieval reader would have understood these often terse accounts of judicial murders.

My inquiry remains bound by the chains—sometimes explicitly golden—of orthodox polemic. By remaining in these confines, it leaves much essential work to be performed by other studies regarding heresy and its persecution in medieval worlds. Within orthodox polemic, the very real people who died in the events the sources describe were turned into instruments of the discourse that justified their murder. Any reality beneath such deliberate shaping is difficult, and sometimes impossible, to recover, but the deliberate shaping itself has a logic and a history that can be better understood. It was an essential component of what medieval persecutors thought they were doing, and modern attempts to understand their thought sincerely must grapple with it. In many ways, the attitudes and the arguments analyzed below are astonishingly ugly, but their foulness can only be completely appreciated in connection with a set of apparently noble, beautiful, and seductive promises. Without looking at the beauty, we cannot fully grasp the ugliness.

Questions and Issues in the Modern Study of Medieval Heresy

In part, my focus in *Burning Bodies* on the point of view inhabited by orthodox polemic arises in reaction to developments in the recent historiography of medieval heresy. These developments have problematized the relationship between orthodox polemic and what one might call objective reality. In their analyses of medieval heresy, medievalists have recently found themselves divided into two camps regarding the reality of the high medieval heresies described by traditional historiography. One group maintains a more "traditional" view, according to which organized heresies were, from the twelfth century onward, a historical reality. The other side argues that, up until the mid-thirteenth century, organized and systematic Christian heresies primarily existed as ideas in the minds of educated churchmen. The conversation between the two groups is often openly antagonistic and personal.[5] In the context of this debate, scholars are often grouped together by the general tenor of their conclusions while continuing to disagree with one another on many details.[6] In general, the traditionalists still adhere to familiar or conventional accounts of medieval heresy in which persecutors responded to phenomena that existed independently in their world. In the broadest outlines, many of these scholars would agree that heretical dissent, particularly Catharism, the most famous medieval heresy, first appeared in Western Europe during the twelfth century in the Rhineland, perhaps as an importation from the East, and then grew more prominent, especially in Italy and southern France, before the Albigensian Crusade.

In contrast to the conventional accounts of medieval heretical movements, the opposing side follows what Alessia Trivellone has termed a "new type of approach," which takes the attitudes of churchmen regarding heresy as its privileged object of study.[7] Scholars who have taken this focus have found that many so-called medieval heresies were intellectual inventions of the elite, and that these inventions were further elaborated and solidified by modern historians, particularly in the nineteenth century. For those who follow this approach, medieval heresy in the twelfth and early thirteenth centuries was primarily an idea, or set of ideas, that existed in the minds of those with power. As James Given summarizes, "In many cases those whom the rulers of society persecuted were phantoms of their own imagining rather than the real enemies of Christendom."[8]

The questioning of the difference between what medieval intellectuals constructed in their minds regarding heresy and what so-called heretics actually believed parallels, to some extent, the historiography of witchcraft. Once, historians read accounts of Witches' Sabbaths, consistently uniform across a long stretch of time and space, as an indication that something like them had to have actually happened and that historical authors described, often in garbled ways, this underlying reality.[9] This assumption came under withering assault in the second half of the twentieth century. Norman Cohn, in particular, turned the earlier assumption on its head. There was continuity, he argued, but it was in the learned tradition constituted by the literary descriptions of supposed events like the Witches' Sabbath. Outside of this literary tradition, the witch cult never actually existed. Cohn illustrated that the sex-filled nocturnal meetings ascribed to witches, heretics, early Christians, and similar groups formed a long-running trope in Western civilization. He tracked accounts of the supposed night-time meetings of various conspiratorial sects from the ancient world up to the Witches' Sabbaths of the early modern period. These meetings often featured sexual promiscuity, incest, demon worship, infanticide, cannibalism, and black magic. Cohn termed this trope "the nocturnal ritual fantasy."[10] The nocturnal ritual fantasy impacts the history of heresy as many of the sources that establish it in the geology of witchcraft are also important sources for medieval heretical sects, because medieval heretics were often reputed to perform the same acts at their meetings.

In English-language scholarship on medieval heresy, the move toward a fundamental reappraisal of the truth behind sources' claims regarding heretics began with the work of R. I. Moore. Moore's thesis in *The Formation of a Persecuting Society* argued that persecution itself in the Middle Ages did not arise and intensify as potential targets became more plentiful; rather, persecution was the result of the rise of central powers that could use the identification and exclusion of deviants as a way of justifying and expanding their authority.[11] The motivators of this process were the literate *clerici*, a newly emergent educated elite, who shared a way of viewing the world derived from their training at the schools. These learned men staffed the budding bureaucracies of centralizing powers, both secular and ecclesiastical, and advanced their interests and imposed their conceptions on their surroundings.[12] While Moore's work initially focused on the transformation of a culture, its analysis of that transformation, in the words of Carol Lansing, "stands the problem of heresy on its head: heresy becomes the result of the need to persecute."[13] In sharp contrast to the view of medieval persecution as an example of primitive delusion or sectarian backwardness, for Moore, persecution is a historical aspect of Western progress, if a regrettable one, and it arises from the self-interested rationalization of the world.

Scholars influenced by Moore, particularly Mark Gregory Pegg and Uwe Brunn, have taken his arguments further and indeed have influenced him to embrace some of the more radical possibilities that were implicit in his earlier work. Pegg, based on his research on early inquisitions around Toulouse and on the Albigensian Crusade, has argued that Catharism never existed in the Middle Ages.[14] The Cathar heresy, as it is often presented, is an invention of nineteenth-century historians.[15] Moore, for the twelfth century at least, now follows Pegg's argument.[16] This is not to say that medieval religious dissent did not exist, but that it did not take the form in which it is often presented. For Pegg, before the early thirteenth century, no one would have described themselves as a heretic or argued a suite of theological ideas consistent with the dualism ascribed to the Cathars by learned polemic. There was no shadow church confronted in the Albigensian Crusade, or hidden hierarchy linking heretical cells across medieval Europe. The persecutors of heresy only sometimes believed that there was, and they used different names, often drawn from antiquity, to describe it, repeating the tropes of a tradition rather than drawing from immediate observation. Modern scholarship often only amplifies this dynamic in the sources by laying the scholarly construct of the Cathar over the suite of heretical tropes found in the medieval sources, for example substituting "Cathar" where the original text has a more generic word such as "heretic," "good men," or "Manichaean."[17]

Uwe Brunn, in the words of Moore, delivered the coup de grâce to the traditional account of the emergence of the Cathar heresy in the twelfth-century Rhineland.[18] Brunn built on a recent French-language turn toward questioning the historical reality of the Cathars that began with Monique Zerner's *Inventer l'hérésie?*[19] He concludes that the term Cathar appeared in the twelfth-century Rhineland as a learned construct projected onto diverse dissident groups, particularly by Eckbert of Schönau.[20] This construct had a limited medieval circulation and is one of many ways authorities described dissent through the use of familiar tropes. Eckbert, a Benedictine monk, drew on literary concepts and historical figures he encountered in his clerical education to create his Cathars, including the works of Augustine, Manichaeism, and the decrees of early Church councils from which he took the term Cathar.[21] Brunn's work seriously challenges modern scholarly accounts that seek to link

Eckbert's Cathars with other dissident groups elsewhere and apply his Cathar theology to them. The arguments of Brunn and Pegg suggest that in the study of heresy there are two historiographical veils or *integumenta* that must be recognized. One arises from the filters used and assumptions held by the medieval authors of the sources. The other takes shape in modern scholarship regarding heresy, often building on select assumptions and generalizations present in some sources and projecting them onto others.

The scholars in the traditionalist camp largely concede that many elements of the sources, especially those from the twelfth century, must be read skeptically, but they maintain that this skepticism should not extend to the very reality of heresy itself. Accounts of medieval heresy written by orthodox intellectuals, they maintain, reflect a past reality that had actual heretics in it. In their arguments, a strong concern arises that the new approach to heresy goes too far, becoming a solvent to everything it touches. For John Arnold, "to make 'heresy' only the product of orthodox power is to impute to that power an overwhelming hegemony that is in danger of making the people subjected to it disappear."[22] Peter Biller, likewise, argues that the new approach to heresy threatens to render the actual lives and actual sufferings of real people nonexistent, a past reality cast aside in a scholarly quest to disbelieve the source.[23] To scholars like Biller, "there is a difficulty in seeing" medieval heretics, but "there is something to see."[24]

In the debate there is an important difference in the sources used by the two sides. Those who do not believe that medieval heretics existed as described specialize and largely focus on twelfth-century and early thirteenth-century sources, and the traditionalists, in contrast, focus on sources from the mid to late thirteenth century onward. As scholars who have positioned themselves in opposition to Pegg and Moore passionately argue, there is significant evidence from the mid-thirteenth century that heresy existed beyond the minds of orthodox intellectuals.[25] In response, opposing scholars do not deny the existence of this evidence, but instead disagree with the traditionalists about its significance, arguing that the existence of dualist heretics in the thirteenth century does not, by itself, prove their presence in the twelfth century. Moore, for example, agrees that thirteenth-century dualists do seem to exist beyond the minds of orthodox intellectuals, but he maintains that those who study these later dualists must now locate their origin outside the twelfth century.[26] Jean-Louis Biget has long argued for a similar process, although with differing dates, in which an initial evangelical dissent became anticlericalism, and then dualist heresy, shaped in large part by a dialectic between dissent and the preconceived schemas through which the elite characterized and rejected that dissent.[27] Julien Théry-Astruc suggests that actual dualists may have resulted from a century or so of intellectuals' well-publicized combat with phantoms in a Foucauldian pattern of "perverse implantation."[28] Moore himself points to the rise of modern witchcraft groups as an example of this kind of implantation in action.[29]

The scholarly controversy regarding medieval heresy centers on the usefulness and analytical limits of the skepticism we should have toward our medieval sources, but it also involves, and perhaps reveals, deeper principles held by the scholars involved. Tied to this conversation, in difficult and often nebulous ways, are individual scholars' convictions regarding the role of power and the extent of the role played by institutions and bureaucracies in shaping the world and the identities of the individuals in it with that power.[30]

It seems to me that the heresies described by the sources I examine are largely intellectual constructions that existed in the minds of the churchmen who described them. The deaths they narrate were often real, if not the particular details imputed to these deaths, but the sources as we have them are primarily written to narrate something else. While I believe that the "new type of approach" to twelfth-century heresy is the right one, I acknowledge that the fear expressed by scholars like Peter Biller is extremely perceptive. The kind of erasure Biller finds implicit within the new approach was in actuality exactly what orthodox polemic against heresy often was trying to do. In this polemic, the real suffering of real victims was transformed into a justification for victimization. Turning heretics into signs to be read by orthodox exegetes, signs that endlessly proclaimed the rightfulness of the actions undertaken by orthodox intellectuals who enjoyed the privilege to read them, was the goal behind the presentation of heretics on the pyres of the eleventh to early thirteenth centuries.[31] The reduction of the persecuted into sign is an essential window onto the persecutors' ethics and modes of interpreting their world.

The careful presentation of condemned heretics by hostile, orthodox authors aimed to defuse and to negate any supposed nobility in the choice to die for one's beliefs, while rendering what those beliefs were murky and often impossible to disentangle from hostile polemic. Unlike the confessional struggles of early modern Europe, for the eleventh to early twelfth centuries we have sources written largely from one perspective.[32] In this period, the real circumstances that may have led to the deaths of those condemned as heretics are often impossible to recover. A modern reader should wonder what convictions could have led the condemned to persevere and endure one of the most horrific punishments ever inflicted by human beings on each other. While the uncovering of these beliefs, despite the difficulties posed by the sources, is a worthy goal, my analysis is primarily aimed at a better understanding of how orthodox portrayals of the burning of heretics attempt to forestall an audience from even asking such a question. Early accounts of heresy and its punishments are carefully designed to discourage such interest and, paradoxically perhaps, to convert any inherent likeness between the heretic on the pyre and the supposed nobility of martyrdom into the service of those powerful enough to make martyrs.

I have approached the sources in the way that I have in order to better understand the complex of ideas that justified the persecutors' point of view. To realize this goal, I have taken seriously many of their claims that I do not regard as historical fact. To me, tales of demonic inspiration, orgiastic nocturnal rituals, and ceremonial cannibalism are obviously fallacious, but these shocking practices served as part of a unified complex of ideas for the medieval authors who attributed them to religious dissidents. For this reason, I have maintained their pairing with these dissidents' supposed theological positions, analyzing them together as parts of one whole. Even if the integument of medieval authors' topoi of the heretic could be penetrated to reveal the lived reality of religious dissent, these topoi themselves would remain important artifacts of the past that should not be discarded. Authors in the past often believed in these phantoms and put them to work, and, so employed, these specters did things. In particular, they served as a boundary marker for Christian community while also acting—or being made to act—as continuous participants in the creation of the community they came to demarcate.[33] In performing this function, the presence of actual heretics was not as important as their virtual presence within texts put into the service of orthodox self-definition and a developing understanding of the world tied to it.[34] Actors in the past carried these phantoms inside them and in this way one can say that what never existed was an integral part of what did. In understanding this complex of ideas, we can better see how and why particular heresies were created and how these creations served their creators. To orthodox authors, one of the key aspects of this service was a closer integration with their God in a community formed by love. In their arguments, it was this love that led to persecution, and this love was like a raging fire.

One final introductory point needs to be made about the exceptional and unusual nature of the subject matter of this study. While burning at the stake endures in the popular imagination as a major facet of the Middle Ages, it was actually a very unusual event. Burning alive was, compared to other methods of execution, rare in the medieval period, and burning alive for heresy even more so. Medieval secular authorities executed people regularly for many crimes, but they executed individuals for the crime of heresy only in extraordinary circumstances. The death penalty for theft, murder, or other crimes was relatively common in comparison with modern statistics. In fact, in the fourteenth century, where better records are available, the number of criminals executed per year in a large city could be roughly equivalent to the number of executions in the entire modern United States over the same period.[35] The vast majority of these executions were hangings.[36] Decapitation was less common, as it required a significantly skilled executioner, but it was still more frequently employed than immolation.[37] Depending on the region, burning alive was used as a punishment for different types of crimes and for different types of criminals. In France and in parts of Germany, custom forbade hanging women, and they were sometimes burned, buried alive, or drowned instead.[38] Burning alive was not a unique type of punishment reserved for heretics alone, but during the time period of this study it did become the customary punishment for unrepentant heretics before it became the official legal punishment in many jurisdictions.[39] Even in the thirteenth century and after, when burning alive was the official punishment for unrepentant heretics, it was rarely employed. For example, in the register of the famous fourteenth-century inquisitor Bernard Gui, out of 633 sentences only 41, or 6.5 percent, called for burning the condemned alive.[40]

The extraordinary symbolic power and larger cultural significance of burnings for heresy granted them a significance that far exceeded their frequency. Such executions were extraordinary, resulting from unusual circumstances, and their abnormality drew contemporaries' attention. As Paul Friedland has observed, medieval executions rarely attracted detailed written descriptions, especially in comparison to the attention lavished on the details of judicial spectacles after the sixteenth century.[41] Burnings for heresy are an exception to this tendency, an exception that mirrors, to some extent, the modern preoccupation with this form of punishment as emblematic of the medieval period as a whole. The unusual nature of the burnings for heresy examined in this book constitutes a large part of their value as historical sources. These executions represented an extraordinary exception to the everyday world of judicial violence. To contemporaries, they meant something; they set people to talking and writers to writing.

In the individual chapters that follow, I explore the meanings contemporary authors found in these unusual events. The chapters are divided into two main sections. The first section (chapters 1–2) sets the stage for the second by interrogating the foundational concepts that medieval authors used to understand and discuss executions for heresy. These authors expressed, explored, and elaborated on these concepts through imagery derived from scripture and its interpretations. This imagery is important in and of itself because it served as a tool through which medieval authors developed and debated their responses to heretics and the heresies they believed that they encountered. In other words, these images and metaphors were not simply used to explain and to rationalize the choices made by medieval authorities; they played a role in the making of these choices. The second section (chapters 3–7) examines the sources for specific burnings and their context. Each chapter focuses on one event or closely related group of events in a roughly chronological order. These chapters are not an exhaustive survey of all burnings in medieval Europe; rather, they question what meanings the authors of the sources for select events found in the act of killing heretics.

This book ends with the Albigensian Crusade for a number of reasons. More formalized processes against heresy, or inquisitions into heretical depravity, followed in the wake of that crusade. These practices saw an increased legal complexity and standardization of procedure. For this later period, other studies have examined both the punishment meted out to heretics and the portrayals of the heretic in the sources. In contrast, the episodes selected in *Burning Bodies* reveal the earlier, customary punishment of heresy and the presentation(s) of the heretic in relation to that punishment in a much messier period. These chapters illuminate some aspects of a process of becoming in which a set of central legal and symbolic assumptions was established that inform this later, and more studied, time.

CHAPTER 1

Our God Is Like a Consuming Fire
Burning Bodies and Christian Community

> It is written regarding the Creator of everything
> Himself: *Our God is a consuming fire* (Deut. 4:24; Heb.
> 12:29). God is called a fire because with the flames of
> His love he ignites the minds which He fills. For this
> reason, the Seraphim are called a raging fire, because
> the powers closest to Him in Heaven are set aflame by
> the unimaginable fire of His love. On earth, the hearts
> of the just burn, set on fire by this flame.[1]
>
> —Gregory the Great, *Homilies on the Prophet Ezekiel*,
> 1.8.28

For Gregory the Great, and Christian writers
who followed in the same tradition, fire was a tool to both describe the creation of community and enact exclusion from it. This chapter explores some
of the linked imagery and concepts that medieval theologians employed to
imagine Christian community as a body on fire. It also explains how these concepts of fiery unity relied on enduring divisions. This pairing is crucial and
deliberate. The very promises of radical love and social cohesion that I examine hold within them their opposites. These promises of an ardent unity in
love are also threats, and the tension created between these two poles propels
much of the discussion in not only this but also the following chapters. The
fiery images used to elaborate on and explain the ideology of Christian unity
had violent consequences.

In the work of many medieval authors, the presentation of heresy is intimately related to conceptions of orthodox community and how that community came about and grew. For these writers, heresy was part of a vast
complex of hostile forces that existed in opposition to orthodoxy. The members of this vast opposition were everything that faithful Christians were not,
and Christian community arose from the rejection of the foundational attri-

butes, motivations, and limitations of this opposition. In order to explain how medieval authors often presented heresy as an inverted image of orthodoxy, one must begin with an exploration of what these authors believed Christian community was, and a central image they used to describe the unity and nature of the Christian community was a body on fire.

Rather than offering a complete history of fire as a way to describe God's nature or the experience of otherworldly punishment, this chapter aims to provide a sketch of the central symbols and ideas regarding fire and community present by the twelfth and thirteenth centuries. I have chosen this period as a focus and as a terminus because of its relation to the specific instances of execution for heresy I examine in later chapters. This sketch will by necessity draw heavily from the Fathers, as later authors and scholars found continued inspiration in their works, but the emphasis will be on introducing concepts that will enliven and inspire specific engagements with fire and community in the later chapters. In particular, the discussion to follow sets the stage for how and in what ways eschatologically charged invocations of fire and violence were also explorations of fundamental notions of positive community and Christian identity.

While it is a quickly drawn picture, this chapter does tell a unified story. It regards three fires. One fire is spiritual, unifying, and divine. Another is material, divisive, and infernal. The third fire is somehow both spiritual and material, divine and infernal. As the work of theologians progressed into the twelfth century, these three fires worked together as thematically linked pieces of an increasingly systematized economy of salvation and human relationships.

As an image of unity, fire was like God. God's love, like His nature, could be spoken of as a fire, and this fire spread from believer to believer, uniting all in God's fiery love and fiery nature. This spiritual fire bound Christians together into one burning body with their God. God's love as *caritas*, or charity, was the foundation of community, and it set the parameters for both inclusion and exclusion from that body. Outside of the Christian body, there was only lack, and those without the fire of charity would burn another way.

While there was a fire of unity, there was also a fire of division. The fires of Hell existed to burn those human beings who remained outside the fiery ambit of God's love. These fires are likely more familiar to many modern readers and popular conceptions of the Middle Ages than the fires of love, but they can only be completely understood in the context of their divine counterparts. While God's flame was transformative, hellfire was not. It was a sterile, prisonlike thing in which the damned burned forever without any true change or consumption.

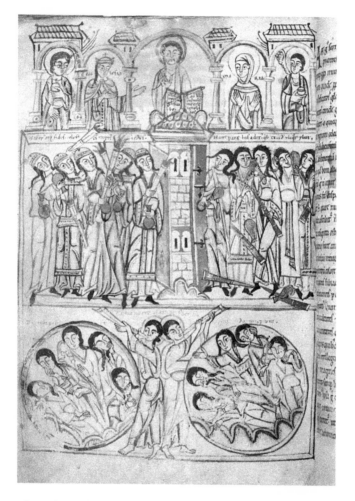

FIGURE 1. (*second register*) The wise virgins, who brought oil for their lamps, and the foolish virgins, who did not; (*top register*) Christ in judgment; (*bottom register*) angels blowing trumpets awakening the dead. © The British Library Board, Arundel, 44 f57v.

Finally, there was a third type of fire that functioned conceptually as a mixture of the other two. The fire of purgation burned those Christians who at their death bore with them minor sins. While this was a fire of punishment like that of Hell, this fire aimed to reform the less than perfect Christian, eventually opening the door to Heaven and the immediate presence of God. This fiery God could be reached through this avenue of fire, but the very passage was enabled, and in a sense made out of, His fiery nature. To burn in the purifying flames of Purgatory after death a Christian needed to also burn with the fire of God's love. Only with the two put together was postmortem reformation possible, and in this otherworldly flame, the threat and horror of Hell hybridized with the hope and spirit of God's unifying love.

The Fires of Love: Christian Community as a Body Burning with Love

In the theology of medieval Catholicism, there are two basic communities to which all rational creatures—human beings and angels—ultimately belong: the community of God and the community estranged from Him. As explained by Augustine of Hippo, these communities are founded on and directed toward opposed loves: "Two cities, then, have been created by two loves: that is, the earthly by the love of self extending even to the contempt of God, and the heavenly by love of God extending to contempt of self."[2] The earthly city is the community of people who loved themselves and the things of this world. The love that led this city was a small and selfish thing, the kind of desire that lay at the root of all suffering and cruelty.[3] In the earthly city, wealth and power made men great, and each was a unit by himself, seeking what was good to him and for him.[4] The politics of the earthly city remained clearly assigned "to the sphere of the appetites," rather than the love of God.[5]

In contrast to the desire at the base of the earthly city, there was another love. This love promised, beyond all else, to make many into one. This promise of unity between all people was divine, made out of God at the same time that it led human beings to Him. It was an impartial love without limit that not only transcended the bias of appearances but also existed, in a fashion, to reveal the falsity of divisive appearances. In contrast to the worldly desire to dominate and to victimize others, this love would lead the believer to feel that his neighbor was a part of him, and that we are all a part of each other. This love was a maker of community that promised to take what is worst in us and turn it into what is best, to build on the common resemblance between human beings while melting away the divisiveness at the heart of all violence, prejudice, and pain. The common resemblance between human beings, on which a union of all humanity can be built, was God's image. The image of the divine in man was distorted in the current world, and that deformation lay at the root of all vices and the suffering they caused. It followed logically that a harmonious human society could only be realized through the reparation of God's likeness in each individual through the transformative power of a unifying love.

This great unity could only come about if the object of love shifted to God away from the things of His creation. God had provided a method for this change in orientation through the Incarnation of Christ. Joined together in love of Christ, believers became united to their God and to each other in a shared body, as the Apostle Paul explains:

> For as the body is one, and hath many members; and all the members of the body, whereas they are many, yet are one body, so also is Christ. For in one Spirit were we all baptized into one body, whether Jews or Gentiles, whether bond or free; and in one Spirit we have all been made to drink. For the body is not one member but many. If the foot should say, because I am not the hand, I am not of the body; is it therefore not of the body? And if the ear should say, because I am not the eye, I am not of the body; is it therefore not of the body? If the whole body were the eye, where would be the hearing? If the whole were hearing, where would be the smelling? But God hath set the members every one of them in the body as it hath pleased Him.[6]

The unity of believers in God promised to dissolve the importance of many worldly differences: "There is neither Jew nor Greek: there is neither slave nor free: there is neither male nor female. For you are all one in Christ Jesus."[7] The corporate identity of the Christian community, imagined through the image of a united body, came about through the action of the Holy Spirit and the rest of the Trinity.[8] God created the love in each believer that brought about Christian community and Christian unity. Just as the way was the destination, this love that unites was the very object of that love.[9]

Medieval theologians imagined the unity of love through many images. They saw it in the body of Christ into which all Christians joined as limbs. They found it in the ark of Noah, which would carry its passengers through the destruction of the world into the future.[10] They described it as a city, a heavenly Jerusalem, where humanity would dwell with its creator in peace.[11] All of these images are coterminous with the Church on earth, and medieval authors used the linked images of city, ark, institutional Church on earth, and common body to refer to the same fundamental society that they viewed as their own.[12]

All of these images of redemptive unity coexisted with things outside this union, led on by a fallen love opposed to the love that created redemptive unity. Augustine had termed the fallen love of creation *cupiditas*, or worldly desire.[13] While God's community promised unity in one body composed by many members, fallen humanity had by its basic nature a unifying emptiness and shared doom. At birth, a person was not a member of the Church, but rather a sharer in the fallen nature of humanity.[14] This fallen nature was inherited from Adam and Eve, and all those who remained outside the Church belonged to it.[15] This fallen nature had within it the destructive love of self in contempt of God, which was the root of suffering and cruelty. In contrast to the fallen unity of humanity, membership in the Church must be acquired. One had to join, or be joined to, the body of Christ. The ark had to be boarded, and everything outside it would perish in the Flood. The City of God was like a pilgrim in the current world, surrounded by the earthly city and its citizens. The unity of God was in process, always growing but never in the current world complete, and the instrument of this reparative and expanding unity was a perfect love.

This love that united creator and creation was caritas, and this love in fact was God.[16] Often translated in the modern idiom as "love," caritas meant a specific kind of divine love.[17] While it was often used interchangeably with *amor*, in these cases the difference between this divine love and more earthly and physical loves was still clear.[18] Caritas is the virtue by which human beings love God and become united to Him.[19] It is a special, spiritualized kind of love, distinct from carnal affection. Union with God through caritas entailed a unity of believers with each other. As each Christian became united to God, they also became one with all other Christians, who were also part of that God. In this fashion, the command to "love your neighbor" could only truly come about through the power of caritas rather than worldly love and its physical expressions.[20] While theologians could, and in fact did, debate exactly how the virtue of caritas came about, there was broad agreement that it was a special virtue, enabled by the action of God in the human soul. Through caritas a human being could love God first and foremost, channeling their affections for the things of this world as tools by which to better enjoy Him rather than as goods in and of themselves. Christian community was fundamentally based on this coidentity of individuals with their God, and through their God with each other, brought about through the proper ordering of affections.

The caritas, or divine love, that joined humans to their God, repairing that God's image within them, was like a fire, and medieval theologians repeatedly had recourse to the imagery of fire to describe its effects and its nature; like God, it was "a consuming fire."[21] Repairing the divine likeness in humankind required humanity to become more like God's fire, or rather the fire that was God. Assimilation to this flame involved both violence and enlightenment; it was a purgative process of healing.   Hebrews

To Jerome, "our God is a consuming fire" had to be understood through the "double nature" of flame. Fire both illuminates and burns. The Lord consumes the figurative wood, hay, and straw that is built on the foundation of Christ. This fiery consumption, which would go on in the course of the Middle Ages to provide the theological foundations for the purgation of souls after death, removes the qualities that impede human reunion with the divine.[22] The flame that consumes wickedness provides the light by which humanity can see the way forward. "If we are sinners he burns; if we are just he shines for us."[23]

Ambrose of Milan emphasizes the purifying nature of charity. The Lord's charity, which unites humanity and God, has wings of fire.[24] Just as fire by its nature seeks the heavens, the wings of charity draw the Christian toward God.[25] This fiery charity flies into the breasts of the saints and "consumes whatever is material and earthly but tests whatever is pure and with its fire makes better whatever it has touched."[26] Its purification is like the refinement of precious metal as the flame draws away the dross. It is this fire that Jesus brought to set the world alight (Luke 12:49). It is on the fiery wings of charity that the Seraphim flew who purified the mouth of Isaiah with a burning coal (Isa. 6:6–7), and it is this fire that John the Baptist foresaw when he said of Jesus: "He will baptise you with the Spirit and with fire" (Matt. 3:11).[27]

The fire of charity purifies, protects, and leads the believer ever onward toward the goal of unity with God. This spiritual and figurative fire counteracts the gross carnality of the fallen world. Its mastery over fallen matter declares itself in the book of Daniel when the fire of charity cools the boys in the fiery furnace, shielding them from the corporeal flame.[28] Turning human love away from created things, the purifying flame of charity kindles a desire for God in the heart that continues to burn within, lifting the faithful up to Heaven as their inner nature conforms ever more to the nature of the heavens. Such desire, led on by charity, can bring humankind to its true homeland, the heavenly Jerusalem.[29]

The closer a creature was to God, the more it could be said to burn with the fire of His love, which joined created beings together as God's body. Gregory the Great explains that the Seraphim, the highest of the angelic hierarchies, who are the closest created beings to God, burn with this love. On earth, the "breath of the Holy Spirit" sets the souls of carnal men aflame with the desire for God.[30] Man and angel share a love for God, and this very love *is* God. In Heaven His limbs are the chosen angels and on earth they are converted humans. While the angels behold His divinity directly, God recalls men to the desire of His sacred flame through the humanity of the Incarnation.[31] While the approach to God is for living men less direct than for the angels, the access afforded to the object of love, through the object of love, is still real. While lovers may be many, "he is one who burns in the hearts of those who love."[32] Through this chain of love, God unites Heaven and earth.

Bernard of Clairvaux describes the Lord's consuming fire like that employed by a physician on a festering wound. The Holy Spirit is the physician of souls.

All good things proceed from its vast grace, but it comes with iron and flame to the sinner to arouse contrition in the heart and to drive the sinner to confession: "Contrition like a sharp stake stabs into the soil of our heart; like fire it burns the thorns and thistles of our sins, like a sharp sword it destroys and cuts off the enticements of the flesh."[33] Just as a physician burns away and cuts off putrid flesh, the Holy Spirit strikes at what is worst in humanity. To the sinner, it seems to leave the iron instrument of its moral surgery in the aching wound as the effect of its ongoing presence. This pain lasts until the very desire of removing the intrusive heated scalpel is itself taken away. It is "because of this effect that the Holy Spirit is called a fire."[34]

Such violence has a point; it is a step in a process toward the vision of God.[35] The pain of the physician drives the patient toward confession and to fear. This very fear caused by the presence of the Spirit is alleviated by it. Just as the shadow cast by a tree is drawn together by the motion of the sun at noon, so too does the "heat of charity" draw fear into itself until it is lightly surpassed.[36]

God's likeness to fire found particular expression in the charity that bound Him together with His faithful creatures. In response to the question, "What is God?" Peter the Chanter answers, "He is a consuming fire, hence Moses says: 'our God is a consuming fire'; he is love, hence John says: 'God is charity and he that abideth in charity, abideth in God, and God in him.'"[37] This charity is like a "fire kindled in our hearts by God."[38] God sets the heart of the Christian on fire through charity and as it burns this heart becomes more like Him. As in the prayer "Veni creator Spiritus," the faithful seek and require this fire, and its spread is the purpose of the Incarnation as in the words of Christ: "I am come to cast fire on the earth; and what will I, but that it burn?"[39]

For Hildegard of Bingen, God is fire. The brilliance of God's "burning charity" illuminates the universe.[40] The Holy Spirit, especially, "is a fire," not "an extinguishable fire that sometimes blazes up and sometimes is put out," but rather it is the unifying force that combines the "eternity" of the Father and the "equality" of the Son into the living Trinity. It is like the work of a smith who unifies copper and tin into bronze through immense heat.[41] The Spirit, the "fiery life" of the Trinity, suffuses all things that live. It is invisible and must be grasped by the human intellect rather than human eyes. Such a "fiery light" descended on Hildegard at the age of forty-two. This light inflamed her heart, not with a burning fire but with warmth, granting her the knowledge of the meaning of the scriptures.[42] Hildegard claimed that it is just such spiritual meanings underneath carnal appearances that those without God's fire cannot recognize. In their attention only to the things that they can see, the wicked "flee from the fire of the Holy Spirit," joining in the emptiness and death propagated by the Devil.[43]

This fire burns within the human believer and is the source of all virtues, proceeding from God "like sparks from a fire." Without this enlivening flame, all humans are only ashes.[44] The charity that unites human beings with their God and with each other is this fire. "Fiery charity which is God" moves believers to acts of compassion.[45] The fear of God, itself like the fire of God, extends charity like a spreading flame. Believers so moved serve "the inextinguishable fire that is life," becoming like the faithful angels "who are flames of fire."[46] The image of spreading flame describes the assimilation of the individual with the deity; touched by His fire, the individual becomes ever more like Him as he or she inwardly burns.

Those who lacked God's fire had a flame of their own. God willed that all the world burn with His flame, and this imperative to unity held significant repercussions for anyone who was conspicuously separate. The fire of the Holy Spirit played a role in an essential binary opposition, or rather a vivifying presence opposed to a crippling lack, as the twelfth-century theologian Hugh of St. Victor explained. Hugh took a special interest in fire, especially as an image of the spirit.[47] In a short work on the nature and signification of fire, Hugh identified eleven different types, or species, of flame in the natural world and what each could symbolize.[48] In the symbolism of flame, he found a corporeal similitude that through the process of human cognition could offer true access to a God that had no bodily shape. For Hugh, out of all things that provide a similitude of the invisible "fire alone has the highest place."[49] In fire, one finds a likeness for both virtue and vice. The image of flame, passing through the bodily senses to the imagination "returns inwardly for contemplating truth."[50] As Hugh explains: "For love is fire, and it is a good love, a good fire, namely the fire of charity. But there is a bad love, a bad fire, the fire of *cupiditas*. The good fire consumes guilt; the bad fire destroys nature. The good fire is kindled by the Holy Spirit; the bad fire is excited by the Devil. Charity, the good fire, is the source of virtues; the bad fire, *cupiditas*, is the root of vices."[51] All human beings burn with an inward fire. This fire is either the flame of terrestrial desires, cupiditas, or the fire that is both the desire for God and the very object of this desire.

Hugh explains that two artisans work within a human being, each using his own fire.[52] These fires are different, responding to individual dispositions and leading the person who inclines to them to different destinations. The fire excited by the Devil is already, in a sense, within us. The Devil simply blows into it like a bellows, puffing up what was just a smoldering ember into a raging flame.[53] The Holy Spirit, in contrast, is itself a fire. Those inflamed by it have caught its flame.[54] The human being before the Spirit is a flammable thing. This good fire, as God's charity and grace, is not present already in a man by his nature alone, but comes to him from outside, uniting him with its source.

That the bad fire is already present as a sleeping ember within the heart reflects the twisted image a human bears in the present life to God. Created in the likeness of God, humanity after sin resembles this model very imperfectly. Hugh explains that as a consequence the "Devil is not fire but is cold."[55] The living fire of the Spirit liquefies; it creates change.[56] The Devil's fire is fixed in place, subsisting on what is there and producing nothing; it is the permanence of a deformed image. Following this same logic regarding the Devil and change, Dante later had Satan frozen in ice up to his chest in the heart of Hell.[57] Hugh's image is the same; the heat of the flames of Hell, or of inner sin, is nothing compared to the true transformative fervor of the Holy Spirit, which like the Seraphim is "glowing hot."[58] The fires of Hell change nothing. They do not even consume what they burn as regular fire would.[59] In contrast to the fires of sin, that change nothing for the better, the fire of charity melts down the deformed image and casts it anew: "Just as a liquefied mass of metal poured through a tube takes on the shape of a coin, so the mind dissolved by the flame of love passes through the ray of contemplation all the way into the image of the divine likeness."[60] This reparation of the divine image is the restoration of human nature. The lack of the divine fire is a total failure for human teleology. It is the continuation of a harmful deformation, and this deformation is the material for the Devil's work, who, unlike God, wishes the human being to remain separate. The bad fire already present in man, like the Devil, is cold. It is the lack of heat, the lack of love; it is evil as a privation of good. God's fire, in contrast, repairs the image of God in the believer and in this reparation unites the believer to Him.[61] In this image, the realization of true human nature and Christian community were the same. Outside of Christian community, the human remained less than human, and in this conclusion the very theology of Christian unity offered a chilling threat to those outside its fervent embrace.

The good and bad loves or fires, outlined by Hugh, are the same as those that formed Augustine's two cities. Just as the divine fire works through the creation, or rather the realization of likeness, so too does the bad fire within. The bad love that joined together those who misunderstand the relationship between God and creation destroys what it touches. Augustine had explained this relationship through the imagery of Judges 15:4–5, in which Samson tied three hundred foxes together by their tails. Fastening torches between the foxes' tails, he set them loose on the fields, vineyards, and olive groves of the Philistines, burning them to ash. Following Origen's reading of Song of Songs 2:15, "Catch us the little foxes that destroy the vines," Augustine sees Samson's foxes especially as signifying heretics.[62] Samson, meanwhile, is Christ. These heretics, just like the makers of pagan idols, are caught up in the thoughts of terrestrial things, and these thoughts, led on by a bad love, unite them: "They combine with each other in worldly thoughts. Their belief is diverse; their vanity is one. . . . These people become one as a result of their vanity. As much as they disagree in their variety of opinions, they are tied together, nevertheless, by a similar vanity."[63] The faithful have left this vanity behind, and "forgetting those things which are behind" they have set their sights on the ultimate union with God through Jesus Christ (Phil. 3:13), becoming joined together by a similar love. The foxes, in contrast, trail a "corrupting fire" behind them setting alight the "fields of others," but not, as Augustine concludes, "our crops."[64]

The discordant unity at the heart of heresy was a powerful message conveyed by this influential exegesis. Innocent III cited it when he moved against heresies of all kinds, arguing that they are all expressions of the same divisive, fallen force.[65] This force existed in opposition to the unity through charity of which Innocent acted as the earthly head. While the opposition to God may have many names and many faces, the same vanity, the same meaning, existed inside these varied appearances, tying them together. They were all symbols or signs of the same thing.

This negative unity defined more than Christian heretics alone, extending to all groups identified in the medieval imagination by their essentially carnal orientation. Carnality as orientation constituted the one vanity underneath the diverse opinions of Christian heretics, Jews, Muslims, and the pagans of antiquity. Immersive love of created things was evil, and like evil it resulted from and further propagated a privation.[66] This lack at the heart of those outside the great body of Christ was the absence of the divine love of charity. Charity was the source of all good and was also the expression of divine participation in the thoughts of humankind. Frozen in unlikeness, those without charity suffered resultant cognitive disabilities that defined them as misinterpreters of symbolism and of texts.

From the twelfth-century perspective of John of Salisbury, the acquisition and enlargement of charity constituted the goals of a true philosopher. To John, whatever leads away from charity is not actual philosophical doctrine but rather "absurd, insipid, and stupid" babbling.[67] John's implication is that true philosophy can only be learned in charity.[68] The state of charity was the loving of God without limitation, and outside of this love the true life of the mind could not be lived.

The understanding of divine things, for Gerhoch of Reichersberg, depended on the assimilation of the believer and God as a spreading flame. To him, the likeness that a believer achieves to Christ is like the process in which a metal liquefied in a flame loses its earlier form to become more like the fire that heats it.[69] On a pilgrimage to the celestial Jerusalem, the Christian must become in-flamed with God's love, and having been so set aflame the Christian can never again be dissimilar to God.[70] This fire that makes the believer like God is a cleansing thing, "consuming blight and bringing out gold."[71]

This inward fire that creates likeness participates in and enables the pro-cess of understanding likenesses. The perfection promised to the elect will make men like angels. In particular, this angelic likeness will result in perfect understanding.[72] The route to this perfect understanding begins with charity. Charity comes before all virtues. As Paul states in 1 Corinthians 13, without charity no virtues or good works profit a man, and "if I hand my body over to be burned, but I have not charity, it profits me nothing."[73] Charity fills the heart of a Christian like oil poured into a vessel. Like the oil in the lamps of the five wise virgins of Matthew 25:1–13, when set aflame its light will illuminate the way to union with God through the darkness of the present night.[74]

Like the five foolish virgins, who brought no oil for their lamps, those without charity cannot see; they cannot understand likenesses as likenesses because they themselves are too imperfect a likeness. The faithless, like Jews, who miss the spiritual meanings of texts, have a "veil over their hearts." Unable to see through their hearts that lack the fulfillment of charity, they see only the surface meanings of things that meet the bodily eyes. The presence of this covering over their hearts and spiritual sense, which blocks their own understanding, transforms them into signs to be read by those who can un-derstand.[75] The Jews become the very texts they fail to interpret correctly, as Gerhoch explains by elaborating on a quotation from Augustine: "For the Jews are slaves who bear our texts, carrying books for us by whose testimony they themselves, pagans, and heretics are convicted of error."[76] The error of the Jews was one expression of a weakness shared by all the faithless. Those who lacked the illumination of fiery charity could not see spiritual meanings, and this limitation transformed them into an object for the very type of interpre-tation they could not perform. Put another way, those who did not become likenesses to God became different types of likenesses in the service of those who did.[77]

That the presence of God allows the recognition of God lies at the heart of what Karl Morrison has recognized as an interpretive tautology. As ex-plained by Gerhoch, the Christian, who understands correctly, can fill what he sees with divine meaning because he is already filled with grace.[78] The inter-preter sees the meaning that is already inside him, and in finding something of the divinity in an object of interpretation is again filled with the grace that was already present. This tautology is a form of an essential Augustinian paradox in which everything is taught by means of signs but nothing is really learned through them.[79] God's Wisdom as a teacher already inside the learner enlightens the mind, providing knowledge of the things signs signify. This a priori knowledge of reality provided by God comes as a result of faith in a sign that is at first not understood. Belief in the sign allows God's Wisdom, God's Word, or Jesus Christ into the soul. Once inside, Christ illuminates and allows the Christian to achieve cognition of heavenly things.[80] In this distinctly Christian modification of Platonic recollection, Christian community comes about through a dialectic between faith and knowledge, as the divinity whose presence creates unity grows within the individual through acts of belief that reveal its presence the more it is believed. The more present the God, the more accurate the cognition. The more accurate the cognition, the more present the God. As God's inner presence creates true community, it would logically follow that those visibly outside this community cannot achieve truly accurate understandings of heavenly things. It might also follow that those who espouse clearly divisive opinions are experiencing an inner privation of the divine presence. Another tautology develops: the separate are convicted of error by the evidence of their being separate.

Hell and Purgatory: Bodies Burning *ad Litteram*

The articulations of fiery Christian unity examined above gradually came to include considerations of enduring division not only as alternative models but also as necessary oppositional corollaries. In the course of outlining a process of unity that erased the differences between individuals, a definition and a form needed to be given to the enduring separation between them. The rendering down of the deformation in humankind's resemblance to God was an ongoing process. The work of God's fiery charity was in the present life forever incomplete, and this imperfection under repair constituted a tenaciously enduring lack that defined the basic nature of fallen humanity as a distorted image. For living believers, this lack had to be continually faced as a gap between what they currently were and the unfathomable object into which they had to be transformed eventually through love. The recognition of such an aporia is a violent discovery, and violence defines the imagery used to describe the persistence of this gap in the fiery imprisonment of Hell.

As there was a fire that united, there was a fire that imprisoned in difference. While the fire of charity was a spiritual expression of figurative allegory, the fires of Hell were literal material fires. The contrast between these flames is a revealing parallel with the love that brought individuals into contact with them. The material fires of Hell, as well as the (usually) material fires of purgation, were entered into as a result of succumbing to what Hugh of St. Victor termed the "bad fire" of cupiditas. In contrast, the spiritualizing love of God not only avoided this punishment but was also transformative. Just as in Augustine's two cities, the different ways an individual can burn were based fundamentally on two different loves.

The question of Hell offered a direct parallel to the familiar model of tension between the carnality of appearances and the spiritual signification behind them. As explained above, the essential issue returns again and again to reading and interpretation and the inner spiritual dispositions that facilitate successful signification through language. Hell is one part of the literalism that marks in the medieval imagination what I have termed an essentially carnal orientation. This orientation was a distinguishing feature of a web of enemies: Jews, pagans, Muslims, and heretics, who all existed outside of the Christian unity through charity.[81]

In Hell, those outside the redemptive spiritual unity of charity, often described as a fire, burned in literal material fires. This burning was a parallel to the immersion in corporeality and its loves, which condemned the damned in the first place. Those who cannot see spiritual meanings become slaves to the letter; those who cannot burn spiritually burn materially in the corporeal flames of Hell. While they burn in the fires of Hell, they can also suffer all kinds of other torments through the images of material things that they bring with them. They carry these images as a result of their worldly loves.[82] For theologians like Hugh of St. Victor or Aelred of Rievaulx, the soul encases itself in the images of the things it loves wrongly, and after death these very images become instruments for its torment.[83] The souls of the damned suffer through the images of corporeal things and through the corporeal flames of Hell as expressions of their permanent fall into worldly love.[84]

This neat symmetry took a great time to develop and even when its existence was clear, from the twelfth century onward, it was often left implicit. Nonetheless, it clearly emerged in certain times and places that called for implicit systems and relationships based on the similarities between ideas to be defined and distinguished. Many of these moments will be explored in future chapters, but none will equal the simplicity of expression of Eudes of Châteauroux in the thirteenth century. In one of his *ad status* crusade sermons, he explains that the Son of God came into the world not only so that people might love Him but also so they could burn with His love. Eudes warns: "Those who do not want to burn in this fire will burn in the fire of Hell in the future."[85]

The materiality of the fires of Hell was not a given in the Christian tradition, but a majority position supporting their materiality is clear for most of the medieval period. The exact particulars of their location or whether they were already present to torment disembodied spirits before the Resurrection were, likewise, subject to some variation and debate. By the twelfth century, there was a general consensus that the fires of Hell were material fires. These fires punished the souls of the dead before the resurrection even though the dead lacked bodies to burn.[86] Material fires were thought to affect immaterial souls in a number of ways, and this topic was the occasion for much acrimonious debate, which only underlined the importance given to the materiality of hellfire.[87] While Hell as conceived by medieval theologians doubtless housed a great multitude of torments, fire became Hell's preeminent punishment.

The fires of Hell were linked in a number of ways to another type of otherworldly flame that became increasingly prominent from the twelfth century onward: the fires of Purgatory. While those in Hell had no hope, those in Purgatory were promised an eventual entrance to Heaven. Through purgation after death, those who died less than perfect could still enter the heavenly Jerusalem. Purgatorial punishment was most commonly spoken of as a fire. While a purifying punishment that expunged sin after death was most certainly not a new idea in the twelfth century, otherworldly purification did become increasingly important in that century.[88] Noting this increased prominence and the increasing sophistication of theological discussions of purgation after death in that period, Jacques Le Goff argued that the twelfth century witnessed the "birth of Purgatory." Le Goff especially vested his argument in the emergence of Purgatory as a distinct "third place" alongside Heaven and Hell.[89] In the place of earlier phrases for purifying punishments after death, such as "purgatorial fire," he marked the first occurrence of the noun *purgatorium* as emblematic of the emergence of Purgatory as a third, separate destination for the souls of the dead.[90]

While Le Goff's argument has important limitations, it does illuminate central developments of the period. Some scholars have argued that Le Goff's "birth of Purgatory" focuses too much on novelty and rupture, rather than the evolution of doctrines and ideas over time.[91] Others took issue with his reliance on the supposed neologism *purgatorium* and his errors in its chronology.[92] The idea that certain sins could be removed after death was very old and did not require the noun *purgatorium*. To use the terminology of the High Middle Ages, these were venial or minor sins, and they formed a strong contrast to mortal sins, which would damn a human soul if they were not successfully expunged before death. While purification in the afterlife was an old idea, twelfth- and thirteenth-century intellectuals asked frequent questions about it and eventually achieved an increasing precision about how it might work and how sins could be expunged in life through confession and penance.[93] Likewise, the exact ways that suffrages offered by the living (prayers and offerings) could speed the purgation of the dead in the Other World were elaborated and repeatedly demonstrated through visions, ghost stories, and the sermons addressed to the laity.[94] It is in the description of this increasing precision that the enduring value of Le Goff's argument resides.

Purgatory as a place or state of punishment is conceptually close to Hell, and its proximity is reflected in the prominence of fire and the very geography of the afterlife in the descriptions of visionaries. The places of purgation visited by medieval visionaries were often Hell-like, creating the impression that Purgatory or the places of purgation were like antechambers to Hell itself.[95] Rather than Le Goff's "third place," readers of twelfth-century visions gain the impression of Purgatory as the other inferno. The voluminous *Liber revelationum* of Peter of Cornwall, written around the year 1200, contains the story of a visitation by a dead young man to a parish priest in Kent. When the priest asks him where he resides in the afterlife, the young man reveals that he suffers in "the inferno" for a crime left unconfessed. The priest, far from taking inferno to mean only Hell, immediately demands "again and again" which inferno it is: the one with hope of salvation or the one without. The young man replies that he burns "in the one without any hope of escape."[96] In this case, there are two infernos, but only one plays host to hope.

Fire held a central place in Purgatory, as it did in Hell, and these flames could be material or immaterial. The Cistercian monk who recorded the descent of the knight Owein into St. Patrick's Purgatory concluded that the knight's encounter with corporeal fire agreed with Gregory's account of otherworldly flame, suggesting that for him Purgatory's fires were as likely to be material as the flames of Hell.[97] Aelred of Rievaulx thought it possible that the fires of purgatory were incorporeal like the images of dreamers or the very image of the body carried by the soul itself.[98] These fires could affect the bodiless souls of the dead as the flames of Hell could, but their purpose was different. These fires were tools of unity, and they depended on the unifying spiritual fire of charity to do their work.

Prerequisites for Purgatory

In the work of many high medieval theologians, charity acted as the key to both Heaven and Purgatory after death. The bond of charity between the believer and God enabled purgation after death through otherworldly fire.

The purgative fire that consumed fault could do its work only because of the presence of the fire that transformed. In this way, the presence or absence of charity determined the destiny of the individual for either Heaven or Hell. The fire of charity that burned within the Christian provided the foundation of virtue that enabled redemption. The purgative fire burned the works of sin down to this foundation, and if it were absent there would be nothing present to save.

The centrality of charity for postmortem purgation, as it would have appeared to medieval theologians of the eleventh to thirteenth centuries, began with a group of passages in the works of Augustine. Augustine's ideas regarding postmortem purgation and charity took shape over a number of works, but one can find a clear and elegant summary in a passage from *De civitate Dei* (*The City of God*).[99] In his explanation of 1 Corinthians 3:10–15, Augustine interrogates what it is that will be tried by fire on the Day of the Lord. Following the imagery of the Epistle, the works of men can be thought of as a building. For Paul, the enduring foundation of the Christian is Christ Jesus, on which one can build in "gold, silver, precious stones, wood, hay, and straw." On the Day of the Lord, what sort of work each man has built on his foundation will be made manifest in fire. The work of those who have built with nonflammable materials will abide, while the works of wood, hay, and straw will be destroyed. The man who has built with flammable things will still be saved, but this salvation will only come through the loss brought about by a consuming fire.

In Augustine's reading, the foundation on which a person builds is really a question of love and the object(s) of that love.[100] Only the foundation of Christ is enduring; all else is transitory and, in the light of 1 Corinthians, flammable. Christ, as a foundation, is not universal. To Augustine, those who place temporal things foremost in everything do not have Christ as their foundation. For these, the fire will consume everything, creating no opportunity for salvation. Those who love Christ foremost but in their lives cleave to many carnal loves below Him, such as sexual lust for their spouse, have Christ as a foundation but build on it with flammable things. As Augustine promises, the "fires of tribulation will burn away all such delights and earthly loves."[101] This is the loss experienced by those "saved, yet so as by fire," whose love is burned down to the one enduring foundation. As this fire destroys the affection for worldly things, the Christian who is purged will suffer torment as he loses those "things in the enjoyment of which he rejoiced"—his worldly loves.[102]

Augustine considers and then rejects the possibility that the fire of 1 Corinthians 3:10–15 is the same as that of Matthew 25:41: "Then He shall say also unto them on the left hand, 'Depart from Me, ye cursed, into everlasting fire.'"

While those who suffer the loss of their earthly works might be cursed in a sense, the intention in the passage is stronger. There is a difference between the "everlasting fire" and the fire that will try the work of every man. The testing flame will try the works of those who will be saved, standing on the right of the last judge, either to their reward or to their loss. Both the very good and the not entirely good will encounter it.[103] Logically then, it cannot be the everlasting flame of the damned, who at the end will stand on the left and not the right.

Among those on the right, charity binds the individual to their foundation. The works of some, when they are tested, will not burn at all. "For others, it will be otherwise," Augustine writes: "The fire will burn what they have built, and they will suffer loss. They will still be saved, however, because they have held fast with surpassing charity, to the Christ Who is established as their sure foundation."[104] For those who die while still in love with the things of this earth, the presence of charity is the difference between Hell and an eventual entrance into Heaven.

Augustine is ambivalent regarding the timing of this purifying flame and whether it should be taken as a literal fire or something more like a figure of speech. Augustine suggests that Paul "calls tribulation 'fire,'" as suggested by Sirach 27:6: "The furnace trieth the potter's vessels, and the trial of affliction just men."[105] Likewise, in the *Enchiridion (Manual)* he links the fire of 1 Corinthians to "a sort of trial of affliction," like the furnace that tries a potter's vessels. A fire of this kind "works in the span of this life," as a man "burns with grief for the things he has loved and lost."[106] In these passages, Augustine portrays the fire as something like an internal process, but this is not the only possibility.[107]

This fire can be more literal and more clearly linked to the experience of the soul after death. The fire that tries the work of every man might refer to an ongoing process between the death of the individual and the Last Judgment. "Some say that during this interval, the spirits of the departed will suffer in fire."[108] This fire will be of a special kind that can only be felt by those who have built in wood, hay, and straw through their "morals and loves in this life." This fire can only consume works of this kind, and it might do so entirely in the world to come, both here and in the world to come, or only here. Augustine does not explicitly endorse this view, stating rather that he will not argue with it "for perhaps it is true." Death itself might be part of this tribulation, and "it may be that during the interval which follows death, each man undergoes an experience fitted to what he has built."[109]

The action of the purifying flame that consumes carnal love parallels the "conflagration of all the fires of the universe" that will end the current material world and usher in the new. At the end of the world, this conflagration will burn up the "qualities of the corruptible elements," resulting in a perfect corporeality and perfect human bodies that do not change.[110] This immunity to change addressed Augustine's recurrent association of natural processes with deterioration and decay.[111] The saints will not fear the flame that will consume the corruptibility of the current earth. Even the mortal bodies of Shadrach, Meshach, and Abednego defied the flames of the fiery furnace in the book of Daniel.[112] Following this example, the fires that will consume the old world cannot burn the immortal and "incorruptible" bodies of the saints.[113] All the matter of the world, not just human bodies, will pass through a purifying flame by the end.

Julian of Toledo included parts of this passage on the trying fire of Matthew in his influential *Prognosticum futuri saeculi* (*Foreknowledge of the World to Come*). Elected bishop in the late seventh century, Julian was a prolific author. His *Prognosticum* stands as the first systematic eschatological synthesis of the works of the Fathers, and enjoyed a wide circulation in the Middle Ages.[114] The influence of the work on medieval eschatology is difficult to overstate, and in the words of its most recent translator the text is "the common historical theological source of medieval eschatology" responsible for the "substantial homogeneity" found in most treatises of medieval eschatology.[115] Julian replicated Augustine's passage regarding the attachment to the foundation of Christ through "surpassing charity."[116] He also synthesized the works of the Fathers to establish a seemingly unified opinion on the materiality of hellfire.[117] A reader of the *Prognosticum* will gain the impression that hellfire is material both after the Resurrection and before, when only the bodiless souls of the damned are immersed within it. While Julian's position on the materiality of hellfire was very influential for intellectual authorities in the eleventh to thirteenth centuries (and beyond), the commonly cited explanation for the role played by charity in access to Purgatory and its fires came from a tradition arising from another text: the *Sententiae in IV libris distinctae* (*Four Books of Sentences*) of Peter Lombard.

In his *Four Books of Sentences*, written in the early to middle 1150s, Peter Lombard continued and expanded the logic found in Augustine regarding the role of charity in postmortem purgation. Peter was quite familiar with the work of Hugh of St. Victor and may have been his student while a resident of St. Victor.[118] It is no coincidence that his comments on fiery charity are reminiscent of those made by Hugh. The *Sentences* became, in the words of Richard Southern, "the immovable textbook of a scholastically united Christendom" for the next two centuries, acting as a sort of "door through which every aspiring theologian in the scholastic tradition had to enter," a staple of the classroom.[119] As it appears in the *Sentences*, charity not only secures the individual from the flames of Hell and allows access to the purifying flames of correction, but it also can do this work of purgation during life for the most pious. Drawing on quotations from Augustine, Peter explains that after death those who have built in wood, hay, and straw are exposed to the fire of purgation.[120] The wood, hay, and straw of 1 Corinthians 3:10–15 symbolize attachments to worldly things.[121] The stronger the attachment, the longer the "purgatorial fire" will take to remove it.[122] Those who build with these combustibles desire to please both God and world, although they place God foremost. If they did not so privilege God, their love of the world would not build on an enduring foundation but rather destroy it. This alignment of love allows the imperfect to possess charity, but the charity possessed by the perfect is a more spectacular thing.

Those who build in gold, silver, and precious stones love differently, and this difference in love means that they burn differently. They consider only how to please God rather than the world, and this correct alignment of love makes them secure from the fires of Hell and purgation.[123] Peter elaborates that even if such people sin venially, charity absorbs and ultimately consumes the sin: "The sin is absorbed in them by the fervor of charity like a drop of water in a fiery furnace, and so they never carry things to be burned with them."[124] Since the tremendous heat of fiery charity has already annihilated the sin, it does not remain to be burned by the fire that tries the work of every man after death. Those who build in nonflammables are already suffused with a consuming flame. This flame, in a sense, does the work of purgation in life, and those who do not burn with it while alive must burn after death in another way.

Even for those who bring with them combustible loves, charity has a central role to play. The charity that works within the imperfect does not consume all sin because the enduring love of the world that the imperfect still bear with them does not allow it. The presence of charity, instead, opens up the possibility that these sins will be "dissolved in fire" after death. If a man who "loves worldly goods with some attachment of cupidity" dies, he will be saved if he has charity and he has sincerely repented before his death.[125] The fires of purgation will consume his cupidity and he will become like those whose charity was in life comparable to a furnace of fire.

The implication in this passage is that the love that places Christ first before all worldly things is closely associated to, and perhaps synonymous with, charity. As Augustine maintained, the presence of this kind of love allowed access to postmortem purgation. This purification after death promised salvation to those who died less than perfect, those whose love for Christ coexisted with lesser loves for the created world. One can see a similar assumption underlying Peter's argument for suffrages for the dead, which again draws from an Augustinian exegesis of Galatians 5:6. The possession of a "faith that works through love," or charity, enabled Purgatory and its attendant suffrages from the living.[126] The foundation of Christ is the foundation of charity that binds the believer to Christ, and the purgatorial fires exist to destroy all love that is not like it.

Commentators on the *Sentences* continued to argue for the centrality of charity in access to Purgatory. Peter of Poitiers, a student of Peter Lombard and later chancellor of the University of Paris, maintains that only those who possessed charity can benefit from the suffrages of the living.[127] Those who died in charity but marked by the stain of sin (*mediocriter boni*) will endure Purgatory. Those who died in mortal sin (*mediocriter mali*) will experience a mitigation of their punishment. This alleviation comes through grace since, "all the good merits of the moderately evil, which they had while they were in charity, were destroyed by the mortal sins into which they fell."[128]

Charity not only opened the way to Purgatory and eventually Heaven, it also consumed the minor sins of the most faithful in life. Peter of Poitiers argues that the moderately good, who must pass through Purgatory, are those who built in wood, hay, and straw. These are flammable loves for worldly things that coexisted with a paramount love of God.[129] Those who built in gold, silver, and precious stones loved God perfectly. When they sinned venially in life, the fervor of their charity immediately destroyed the minor sin, "like a drop of water in a furnace."[130] Peter of Poitiers incorrectly attributes the image of venial sin dissolving in or being absorbed by the furnace of charity like a drop of water to Augustine.[131]

Likewise, for William of Auxerre, writing between 1215 and 1229, those who are in Purgatory possess charity, "the root and foundation of merit," while the dammed in Hell do not.[132] Without the foundation of charity, these suffrages for the dead cannot work, and those without charity are trapped forever in the likeness of the Devil.[133] Furthermore, these suffrages consume the flammable things that the dead bear with them in the way Peter Lombard described the consumption of the venial sins committed by those who build in gold, silver, and precious stones. William argues that suffrages do not, like a bellows, stoke the fires of purgatory to burn quicker and hotter; rather, suffrages burn away these flammable things "with the fire which is God, because as it is said in Deuteronomy: 'Our God is a consuming fire.'"[134]

Charity continued to enjoy an essential role in purgation. The image of the venial sins of the most faithful being consumed by the fire of charity, created in or popularized by the works of Peter Lombard, had a long life. It was used by Alan of Lille, Garnerius of Langres, Radulfus Ardens, perhaps Innocent III, Jacobus de Voragine, Thomas Aquinas, and Chaucer to name only a select few.[135] The uncertainty regarding its origin continued. In his commentary on the *Sentences*, Aquinas attributes it to Gregory the Great. For access to Purgatory, charity too remained central. In the late thirteenth century, Aquinas wrote in his own commentary on the *Sentences* that there are some who can be freed from sin after their deaths because they "have charity, without which the remission of sins cannot happen, for 'charity covereth all sins.'"[136]

In the fires of purgation, the divine, spiritual, unifying fire of charity comes together with the punitive fire of Hell. Both Hell and Purgatory were characteristically defined by their painful fires, and both were encountered by those who had loved imperfectly during life. In fact, all three types of flame issue out of different hierarchies of love. The lovers of the world in the place of God find themselves immersed in hellfire. The lovers of God above everything else burn with this love so ardently that what minor sins they do commit evaporate like water in a furnace. Those who love God but also the world burn in both ways. The presence of God's fiery charity saves them, while the fire of purgation punishes and consumes their improper loves. Like the position occupied by humanity itself, this fire holds a middle place. Purgatory is, at its heart, a very human thing.

The discussion above has created a sketch of how the corpus of Western theology by the twelfth and thirteenth centuries employed three different fires to imagine Christian community and its borders. To theologically literate authors of this period, the coming together of God and humanity was like a spreading flame or the liquefaction of metal in extreme heat. The form of fire was a possible way to imagine the divine nature, and humankind created in the divine image needed to conform to it. Joined in this burning body, Christians could realize a more perfect humanity and indeed redress the imperfections and disabilities that issued from the Fall and its perversion of human nature through the distortion of the divine image in humankind.

What about those human communities that did not burn in this fire? Jesus had come to set the whole world alight, but the horizons of the Christian world continued to testify to the imperfect spread of this flame. The orthodox body was a vehicle of charity in pilgrimage to its maker. In this pilgrimage, it traveled through what Augustine termed the "region of unlikeness."[137] This region of unlikeness was the mode of humanity's existence in the current world.[138] Created as an image of God, humankind was nonetheless a distorted image after sin, and this distortion colored almost all human experience in the current world. Only the union of human and God through charity could address this distortion, and those outside the community of charity could only remain distorted and imperfect.

Outside of the body on fire with charity, there was only a body of fallen humanity. This was a distorted and imperfect community, doomed to suffer eternally for its lack of the proper love. The vehicle of this torment that all unredeemed human beings would share was a fire that is in most respects the exact opposite of the unifying fire they refused. While the Christian community would pass through the region of unlikeness, the damned would be forever trapped within it. This imprisonment represented the failure of the human project.

In the passage through unlikeness, the burning body of Christendom co-existed with other social bodies fated to burn another way. While the ordering of the afterlife might be securely divided into three zones or classes that were in their basic ends really only two, the world of the living was a dangerously porous thing. In this blending and mixing lay a threat to the community of Christendom. What should be done about those bodies that refused to burn with charity, and what if these unkindled bodies could affect and maybe even reverse the spread of this divine flame?

CHAPTER 2

Fields and Bodies

Toleration and Threat in a Shared Space

> Then having sent away the multitudes, he came into
> the house, and his disciples came to him, saying:
> Expound to us the parable of the weeds of the field.
> Who made answer and said to them: He that soweth
> the good seed, is the Son of man. And the field, is
> the world. And the good seed are the children of
> the kingdom. And the weeds, are the children of the
> wicked one. And the enemy that sowed them, is the
> devil. But the harvest is the end of the world. And
> the reapers are the angels. Even as weeds therefore are
> gathered up, and burnt with fire: so shall it be at the
> end of the world. The Son of man shall send his
> angels, and they shall gather out of his kingdom all
> scandals, and them that work iniquity. And shall cast
> them into the furnace of fire: there shall be weeping
> and gnashing of teeth. Then shall the just shine as the
> sun, in the kingdom of their Father. He that hath ears
> to hear, let him hear.[1]
>
> —Matthew 13:36–43

As Jesus explains in the Parable of the Wheat
and the Weeds, or Tares, the wicked are destined to burn. For medieval authorities, this parable described the ultimate fate of those left outside the fires
of a love that reached only so far. In one aspect, the fires of love were bounded
by the non-Christian peoples on the edges of the Christian world. More immediately, even the entirety of Christendom was not yet alight. Non-Christians
existed within the apparent bounds of the body of Christ, and these neigh-
borly others, foreign and yet intimate, drew increasing attention, from the eleventh century onward. In addition to the Jews, long the most visible form of
religious difference for much of Latin Europe, authorities became ever more
concerned about the potential threat presented by supposed Christians who
were really not what they claimed to be. A spiritual union of many members
was a difficult thing to see with worldly eyes or police with carnal instruments,

FIGURE 2.   Miniature for the month of July showing laborers harvesting wheat. Courtesy of the Masters and Fellows of Trinity College, Cambridge.

and these difficulties sometimes made the maintenance of such a union an anxious thing. The possibility of Christian defection from the body of Christ to the other side of the damned became more prominent in the form of increased attention to Christian heresy, both actual and potential.

In this new attention to heresy, medieval authors grappled with questions that arose from their ideology of communal love. What should be done about those who refused the unity of Christian society, and what effect might these outsiders exert on the shared Christian social body? This was a moral discourse, interrogating the limits and possible repercussions of the toleration of internal difference. The stakes could not be higher; salvation or eternal damnation were both at stake. If the promise of total love and complete unity held within itself its own opposite, this promise might also suggest what should be done to the visible exemplars of that opposition.[2]

This chapter focuses on the logic and the imagery employed in theoretical discussions that orthodox authorities had with each other regarding the execution of heretics from late antiquity to the thirteenth century. In these discussions, authorities examined the question of whether or not unrepentant heretics should be killed. These authorities had diverse and nuanced opinions, and their internal discourse changed over time. Overall, the execution of unrepentant heretics became more theoretically acceptable, but this was not the case when executions for heresy began in the Middle Ages. These internal conversations witness a change in attitudes, and this change manifests in an evolving discourse of community. Biblical imagery and traditions of interpretation associated with this imagery were essential aspects of these conversations because they shaped not only the logic employed by medieval authorities but also the very language through which responses to heresy were debated.

Early conceptions of heresy and its effects on the larger body politic focus on two linked scriptural images. The first arises from agriculture, and compares those destined for salvation to wheat, and those destined for destruction, often interpreted as damnation, to weeds (or tares). This image privileges a reckoning to come only at the end of time, synonymous with the harvest. The second image draws on the body and disease, likening wicked human beings to an illness or a cancer assailing a body. This disease spreads within society like gangrene or a metastasizing cancer within a body, and if left unchecked it can kill. This possibility of uncontrolled and eventually fatal spread requires some kind of immediate action for the greater good of the shared social body. In the evolution toward the execution of unrepentant heretics by burning alive, authors used these sets of images both to argue for restraint and also to argue for the necessity of violent persecution. Both sets of images fundamentally rely on a discourse of love rather than hate and both have scriptural origins.

Spreading Weeds: Matthew and the Possibility of Toleration

The Parable of the Wheat and the Weeds can be found in Matthew 13:24–30 along with Jesus's eschatological interpretation of the parable in 13:36–43.[3] In this parable, a man sows good seeds in his field, but an enemy comes at night while his men are sleeping and scatters the seeds of weeds among them. When all the seeds sprout, the servants of the sower see the condition of the field: "Sir, didst thou not sow good seed in thy field? Whence then hath it weeds? And he said to them: An enemy hath done this. And the servants said to him: Wilt thou that we go and gather it up? And he said: No, lest perhaps gathering up the weeds, you root up the wheat also together with them. Suffer both to grow until the harvest, and in the time of the harvest I will say to the reapers: Gather up first the weeds, and bind it into bundles to burn, but the wheat gather ye into my barn."[4] Later that same day, when the crowds have gone away, the disciples ask Jesus to explain the parable's meaning. Jesus explains that the Son of Man is the sower and the field is the world. In this field grow both the wheat, who are the children of the kingdom, and the weeds, who are the children of the wicked one sown by the Devil. Angels will reap wheat and weeds in the harvest at the end of the world. After the reaping, the fate of the children of the wicked one will be terrible. The angels will separate the wicked and throw them into "the furnace of fire," where there will be "weeping and gnashing of teeth."[5]

The Parable of the Wheat and the Weeds would seem to advocate a degree of effective religious toleration on the part of Christians.[6] Not only does the ultimate harvest come at the hands of angels and not of men at the end of the world, but also a premature attempt to separate the good crop from the bad could result in the destruction of part of the harvest. That the ultimate fate of the wicked is to burn seems beyond doubt, but the choice of whom to burn and when lies with forces beyond the human.

The early Fathers interpreted the passage as a call for restraint in the use of force in attempts to cleanse the Church of sin during the present age. Cyprian maintained that those who felt that they were wheat should remain in the Church despite the presence of weeds among them because God in His final judgment would ensure that justice would be done. Jerome's exegesis of the parable was especially influential and shaped the interpretations of theologians after him.[7] He identified the weeds as the "doctrines of heretics" sown by the Devil while the leaders of the Church slept.[8] He argued that Jesus's admonition to leave the weeds in order to prevent harm to the wheat provides a "place of patience" and a warning "lest we amputate a brother too soon."[9] After all, those who are wicked today may not be tomorrow, and patience gives people the time to change. If eradication must wait until the harvest, what should be done about heretics now? Jerome warned that, especially in the earlier stages of growth, wheat and weeds look very similar. Because of this similarity, judgment should be reserved for the Lord. This judgment, nevertheless, will be terrible for the heretics and the hypocrites symbolized by the weeds. They "will burn in the fires of Gehenna" while the faithful are ushered into God's kingdom.[10] For Jerome, present violence against those who would likely be damned at the end of time represented a usurpation of the divine prerogative, leaving nothing for the Lord.[11] John Chrysostom, likewise, felt that premature action based on presumed eschatological destinies was too subject to error. Those who are currently weeds may in fact become wheat, and any attempt to weed the field of the current world would inevitably result in the unnecessary destruction of some wheat. Chrysostom adds that force can be used to suppress heretics' ability to subvert others; however, the force cannot be lethal.[12] For other authors, the necessity of containing the uncontrolled spread of the weeds would constitute a significant limitation of the logic of an eventual divine harvest.

In his *Quaestiones XVI in Matthaeum* (*Sixteen Questions on Matthew*), Augustine provided a detailed exegesis of the Parable of the Wheat and the Weeds that ties together many of these elements. He repeated the identification of the weeds with heretics and interpreted the field as the world.[13] While heretics, who believe falsehoods regarding God, are weeds, wicked Catholics, who believe the truth but fail to live up to their beliefs, are chaff. Pulling out the current weeds might destroy good grain because the wicked might themselves one day become good. There was another reason for forbearance, however, and this was the usefulness of the wicked for the good. Even in doing harm to the good, the wicked can unwillingly benefit them.[14] The good, "for whom the height of charity has been taken away as if it has withered after being plucked out," can be strengthened through the trials provided by wicked men.[15] In this way, the coexistence of the wicked and the good in the field is doubly useful, converting some weeds into grain and confirming the grain that already exists in its strength, because contact with the wicked can reinforce the charity that binds Christians together. Augustine's notion of the ultimate usefulness of heresy for orthodoxy would have a long future.

In his other works, Augustine largely reiterated the position that current Christians should wait for the Lord's harvest but placed a limit on this patience. The wheat and the weeds are mixed together in the current Church. In response to the question of why the righteous should "bear impatiently the mixture of the evil with the good," Augustine suggested that we must await the harvest. In the field of the current world, the evil are mixed in among the good, but it will be different in the barn at the end of time. Those who wish to eradicate the wicked now should "calm down."[16] Angels cannot make mistakes, but living men can, leading to the wheat being rooted up with the weeds.[17] Meanwhile, "the good should tolerate the bad."[18] Those who are weeds today may become grain tomorrow.[19] In this formulation, toleration of those who are wicked now provides time for the work of redemption in this life to run its course. In fact, the possibility of a sinner's redemption constituted an important part of the intercessory mission of Christian clergy, as opposed to the deadly and unredemptive punishments secular authorities visited on the body.[20] Precipitous human action intervenes in an individual's personal story, cutting short his or her own potential journey to salvation.

For Augustine, the patience shown to the current weeds should not extend to the toleration of a schism, and there comes a point where authority has to act against an offender. An individual guilty of a sin deserving anathema should be patiently corrected as long as there is no fear of schism. Those who refuse to be corrected or who do not recognize their fault place themselves outside Christian society and "will be cut off from the communion of the Church by their own will."[21] This purposeful separation will ensure their place among the weeds at the ultimate harvest, and pulling out the weeds in the present time can imperil some of the wheat. As Augustine explained, however, obvious and blatant weeds can reach a point where it is possible to act against them without danger to the rest of the crop: "When this fear [rooting out the wheat] is not present, and there is a firm security regarding the definite stability of the wheat, that is, when the crime is known and appears detestable to everyone to the extent that it has either no defenders at all or defenders through whom schism can occur, then the severity of discipline should not sleep, in which the more effective the correction of wickedness, the more diligent the preservation of charity."[22] As the reference to charity makes clear, there comes a time where "severe discipline" acts more to preserve charity, or Christian community, than to rupture it.

This discipline would most likely take the shape of an enforced complete social exclusion, putting pressure to bear on an offender to reform. This social distance, really a kind of quarantine, would follow Paul's suggestion in 1 Corinthians 5:11 that a Christian should not even eat with a "brother" who has fallen into extreme and obvious sin.[23] Experiencing this separation in life could be like a foretaste of the permanent exclusion awaiting those whom the angels consigned to the eternal fire, allowing the excommunicate time to reflect on their choices. While the guilty party experienced this chance at redemption, the larger Church would be protected from their crimes by distance. This "fraternal coercion" could remove the worst of the weeds, while preserving "peace and unity, without harm to the wheat."[24]

This model of fraternal coercion found employment in Augustine's own experience.[25] In fact, the model of excommunication imposed on Augustine himself by his mother had played a role in his own past conversion.[26] The campaign against the Donatist Church in North Africa also attempted to follow this pattern. Imperial legislation, as written, attempted to impose "inconveniences" on the Donatists that would make reasonable people rethink their allegiance.[27] These inconveniences increased to heavy fines and other exactions that made open membership in the Donatist Church and membership in civil society virtually mutually exclusive.[28] This was a type of coercion that aimed to create the conditions for the exercise of virtue that violence by itself could not create.[29] Despite this emphasis on nonviolent discipline, violence inevitably resulted from the criminalization of an entire sect. The problems faced in containing this violence highlighted the difficulties associated with nonlethal coercion or spiritual warfare as an act of love.[30]

Even with the emphasis on nonlethal force, Augustine recognized and accepted that some people would likely be killed as a result of these coercive measures, and that these select individuals would be damned. In response to Donatists who threatened to immolate themselves rather than surrender their basilica to the Catholics, he remarked that some were certainly predestined to Hell. It was just as well that these "perished in their own fires."[31] After all, without action all the Donatists would "burn in the eternal fires of Hell."[32] As a result of fraternal coercion, it would now be only these few.

The notion of charity is central to Augustine's ideas regarding the licit use of force, both in the persecution of heretics and also in waging a "just war."[33]

Augustine's justification for persecution rests on a notion of what has been called "charitable hatred."[34] He contended that punishment was an act of love if it was inflicted with the intention of preventing an evildoer from causing further harm or creating an opportunity for a malefactor to sincerely change their ways. Augustine's focus on the intention behind the use of deadly force is one of his distinctive contributions to the Christian tradition.[35] If the intention behind its use arose from charity, the love that united Christians with their God and therefore with each other, force became righteous, and its employment actually embodied and sought to preserve the model of restraint found in the Parable of the Wheat and the Weeds.

The presence of charity is what made the persecution performed by the orthodox quite different from the persecution done by non-Christians or heretical Christians. Suffering persecution was not itself meritorious, and persecuting was not in and of itself blameworthy. Augustine writes that when the good and the bad do the same things and suffer the same afflictions, "they are to be distinguished not by what they do or suffer but by the causes of each."[36] "The diverse intention therefore makes the things done diverse," and the presence of charity in the heart of an actor renders his actions just: "Such is the force of charity . . . it alone discriminates, it alone distinguishes the doings of men."[37] The good persecute out of love as a motivation; the wicked, who are outside the unity of the Church, act from the motivations native to the Earthly City in their rejection of that union. In this way, heretics persecute the Catholic Church harmfully, while the Church persecutes heretics beneficially in order "to compel them to come in."[38] Through this logic, Augustine maintained that he had persecuted the Donatists in North Africa in the way that "truth persecutes falsehood."[39] As Frederick Russell argues, Augustine's focus on the intention behind deadly force potentially justified "any hostile act" as long as "it was motivated by charity."[40] Of course, deadly force as employed in the Earthly City very often did not have charity as its clear motivation.

The logic of charity, and the union of many members in Christ charity enacted, defused for Augustine the essential circularity of his justifications for forceful persecution. In a sense, the just man employs force against others justly because he is just, but, for Augustine, the just man was constituted as just in the light of his relationship to the precepts and commands of authority. An individual could not himself employ deadly force by his own volition but only when commanded by a legitimate authority. In the secular sphere, the emphasis on authority took the form of the obedience owed to the emperor. In the religious sphere, the authority took the potentially amorphous shape of God's will as articulated by the hierarchy of the institutional Church on earth. The unity of this body was essential to Augustine's thought, and disobedience to the consensus of this institution that placed an individual outside it constituted a type of injury done against charity itself, which potentially justified "unlimited violent punishment."[41] This punishment still required a secular authority to carry it out. What an ecclesiastical authority could do was identify an injury of this type, allowing a secular power to take forceful action.

Augustine's exegesis of the Parable of the Wheat and the Weeds in the context of religious persecution depended on his notions of Christian unity. He argued that the call for patience and toleration in the parable was an exhortation to potential schismatics to remain within the Church, despite the current presence of the wicked within it. Until the end of time, when the weeds are plucked out or the wheat is separated from the chaff, the good should tolerate the bad within the Church.[42] In this deployment of the parable, Augustine, again, turned the persecution of contemporary heretics on its head. It is these heretics who have disregarded the parable, and become harmful persecutors; the orthodox simply act to re-create the unity, ruptured by heresy, which the parable enjoins.

Augustine's reading of the parable in this context accords well with his definition of the so-called just war, which proved very influential for centuries and did much to reorient Christianity toward militarism. "Just wars," Augustine says, "are accustomed to be defined as those which avenge injuries." He elaborates on what he means by "avenge," explaining that a just war can seek to punish "a people or a city" for a wrong it has neglected to punish, or seek to return what was taken away through injury.[43] Further, he argues that God commands some wars and that these are by nature just. As presented by Augustine, forceful responses to heresy and schism can accomplish the same two goals as the just war, punishing the act of departing from the faith and doing damage to it, as well as restoring what was taken away.

As an example of the readings possible in later centuries, Bede followed both Jerome and Augustine, insisting that both wheat and weeds be allowed to grow but that sometimes separation in the living field might be necessary. Allowing both wheat and weeds to grow is important because it provides a time for penance, "lest we amputate a brother too soon." This advice might appear contradictory to that offered by Paul in 1 Corinthians 5:11 to avoid notorious sinners. Bede reminds his readers that "as long as the plant exists the difference between wheat and weeds is either nonexistent or hard to discern." In this instance, God provides us with a warning so that we do not rush to judgment, but rather "reserve the end of judgment for the Lord."[44] It would seem that social isolation would be a judgment in a middle point, while execution or irrevocable amputation from the shared Christian body would be a final judgment. In these words, Bede reproduced Jerome's concern with similar and misleading appearances. Just as wheat and weeds may appear the same in the early stages of growth, so too could a heretic and an orthodox Christian appear the same in the present life.

In these discussions relating to Matthew 13, one can see recurrent calls to avoid deadly violence against apparent heretics while limiting the harm that they can cause to the faithful. The major harm that heretics threatened to inflict was schism, or rending the body of Christ by breaking the Church apart. While heretics threatened God's earthly form with violence, their ultimate damnation was not a foregone conclusion. Like all sinners, they could be redeemed, and an attempt at this redemption was in fact the duty of ecclesiastical authority. To muddy the waters even more, the identification of heresy was a fallible process, and orthodoxy could be mistaken for heresy. In light of the above, Jesus's caution that an attempt to weed the field will result in loss to the crop seemed particularly persuasive to these early Christian theologians. The fear of the harm heresy could cause, however, was only partially contained, and concerns regarding its potential damage defined the next strand of discourse that must be examined alongside the parable of Matthew.

Like a Cancer Creeping in the Body: Heresy and Social Hygiene

The scriptural origin of the image of heresy as a disease was more complex and was deeply connected to the unity of all Christian faithful in the body of Christ and therefore with each other. The faithful were all limbs of Christ's body.[45] This corporate identity as a whole constituted the Church. The unity of believers was enacted and celebrated when they partook in the Eucharist, structuring through that image the very self-conception through which the society of medieval Western Europe imagined itself.

Christ's body on earth was a shared body and its moral or spiritual hygiene was a public issue, since what one did with one's own body rebounded on other Christians as well as God.[46] Likewise, what one did spiritually or intellectually affected others through this common bond. Like a little yeast running through an entire loaf of bread, the wickedness of some could corrupt the entire corporate unit.[47] In this fashion, the imagery of disease provided a "comprehensive and systematic model" for the effect of heresy on Christian society.[48] For this reason, it was essential that malignant members of the shared body be removed.

Jerome, once again, set the stage for later exegetes, providing an influential example of the logic of bodily disease in his commentary on Galatians.[49] For Jerome, the yeast that corrupts the whole loaf was the same as the yeast of the Pharisees that Jesus instructed the disciples to purge and to avoid.[50] This leaven was their teaching, and this teaching was itself "the observance of the law according to the flesh."[51] Observing the law according to the flesh is to read only the surface of things, stopping at appearances at the expense of the spiritual meanings that might be obscured by carnal exteriors. This characterization of Jewish religious observance as essentially carnal accords with what has been called the long tradition of anti-Judaism in Western culture, but through Jerome's pen the observation was immediately extended to include heretical Christians by the use of Arius of Alexandria as an example.[52] In this conflation, Jerome suggested that the error and the corruption that runs through heretics and Jews was essentially one: an obsessive connection to carnality, and it was contagious.

Jerome explained that false, carnal teaching begins as a little thing but grows. A little bit of yeast, lightly spread, can change the nature of the loaf, and so "perverse teaching starting first from one man finds scarcely two or three listeners in the beginning," but spreads through the corporate unit just as a "cancer creeps in the body" (2 Tim. 2:17), or how "one scabrous sheep infects the entire flock."[53] The corruption of perverse teaching is not only like an infectious disease; it is also like a fire spreading out of control. "A spark is a little thing," but if given nourishment it quickly grows to consume whole cities and entire regions.[54]

Since perverse teaching is a contagious disease and a spreading fire, it should be contained in analogous ways. Jerome advised: "Therefore, a spark should be immediately extinguished as it appears, and yeast should be isolated from a neighboring lump of dough, putrid flesh should be cut off, and a scabrous animal should be driven away from the sheepfold, lest the entire house, lump of dough, body and heart, burn, be corrupted, putrefy, and perish."[55] Experience has taught the community the consequences that come from neglecting threats to its common health. Arius in Alexandria was just one man, "one spark," but as Jerome cautioned, "because he was not immediately stamped out, the entire world is now filled with his flame."[56]

Jerome's description of heresy as a spreading disease and uncontrolled flame caught the eye of later writers. This passage found its way into the *Decretum* of Gratian.[57] Peter Lombard reproduced it as an illustration of the way that a "little of the law [according to the flesh] corrupts the entire loaf."[58] Thomas Aquinas employed the passage to illustrate how the toleration of the heretic after the first and second admonition threatened the collective.[59] These later writers saw in these words the dangers posed by heresy to Christian society, and they also saw in them the suggestion that something has to be done to avert this danger.

The threat of contagion demanded an immediate response whose nature closely aligned with the practices of bodily medicine. These images, drawing on the language of amputation, have significant suggestions of violence within them, but they are not ipso facto endorsements of execution. They had the potential to agree with, and be used alongside, the responses to heresy that were outlined in discussions of the Parable of the Wheat and the Weeds, and, in fact, they were. For example, the exclusion of offenders from Christian society suggested by Augustine, as well as Paul, is the equivalent of driving the scabrous animal from the sheepfold. Even in this nonlethal approach, the ultimate threat of violence remains present. What happens to the sickly animal driven away? What becomes of diseased flesh after excision? All of these are destroyed, and this same fate awaits any and all who die outside the body of Christ. In the model of avoidance, this death remains outside human agency, and there always remains the possibility that the banished offender could be healed and return to the fold. This possibility, however, depends on the scabrous animal having somewhere to go where its present contagion is not dangerous.

Weeding the Field for the Common Health: Uniting the Two Strands

While the logic of removing offenders from the community could easily work in the atmosphere of early Christianity, what the removal of an offender would entail when the Church came to encompass all of licit public society was yet to be determined. In particular, in the era of the Peace Movements and in the region of the "Cluniac nebula," theories of difference took shape between 1000 and the mid-twelfth century that would ideally leave the spiritually diseased nowhere to be sent besides the Other World. Such ideas were first nurtured in monasteries and then exported to Western European society at large. As Dominique Iogna-Prat has argued, these responses to difference had at their heart a profound equivalence between society and institutional Church. This "logic of all or nothing and of the One for all" aimed to sacralize the entire world, and cast all opposition to this all-encompassing sanctity as a deviant and inverted "mirror image" of itself.[60]

To serve as the guide and vehicle for the sacralization of the world, the Church itself had to be purified, especially from the kinds of carnal entanglements that were emblematic of the world in its fallen state. The project of purification became a core element of the eleventh-century reform move-ment.[61] In the logic of the reformers, excommunication from the Church was theoretically tantamount to removal from all human institutions inhabited and composed by Christians. While theory and reality rarely align, the logic now existed that where ecclesiastical and secular authority agreed, those with no place in the Church had no place anywhere.

As R. I. Moore has argued, the continued impact of the eleventh-century reform and the contemporary rise of centralized secular states created not only the machinery to persecute and to punish but also the motivation to do so. The identification, persecution, and elimination of harmful forms of differ-ence provided new regimes opportunities for self-fashioning.[62] The process of self-realization on the part of authority that lay beneath the beginnings of a "persecuting society," suggested by Moore, suggests a radical sincerity regard-ing the claims of universality that provided its foundation. Attempts to purify a society by driving out "the 'impure' can be a witness to the values which hold society together."[63] The reification of a universal, corporate identity span-ning the distance between man and God could best articulate its sameness through its confrontations with difference. It was, in this early period, a sin-cere question how these confrontations should be resolved.

Heresy was certainly not the only type of difference that attracted increased attention from the eleventh century onward. Relations with Jews and Muslims, as well as spiritually and physically diseased Christians, became objects of in-tense concern. Calls for the reform of violence within Christian society in the eleventh century sought to limit warfare between Christians and redirect it against outside threats, influencing the advent of the Crusades against the exter-nal threat of Islam and helping to inspire the internal massacres of Jews.[64] In these clashes with forces outside the Christian body, the others Christendom confronted were useful for its own collective reimagining of itself.[65]

The concern with difference remained deeply and fundamentally tied to evolving models of Latin Christian identity. An enthusiasm for apostolic pov-erty and purity that was closely connected to the eleventh-century reform of the Church became a regular feature of the twelfth century, involving both learned prelates and also charismatic preachers with wide popular appeal. Some of these apostolic preachers became founders of religious orders, like Norbert of Xanten, while others never found accommodation within the in-stitutional Church. Inside this dynamic of accommodation, the line between heretic and reformer was razor thin, as both were often purportedly motivated by similar ideals.[66] The ideal of poverty, shared by supposed heretics and the reforming papacy alike, was expressed, in part, through the lens of the "simo-niac heresy."[67] In the context of the heresy of simony, "every call to reform [could be] a potential accusation of heresy, and every defence a counter-accusation against the reformers."[68] A good example of the proximity and potential interchangeability of reform and heresy depending on one's point of view is the history of the Milanese Pataria. It began as a reform movement reacting against the worldliness and corruption of the entrenched clergy, and initially enjoyed the support of Gregory VII.[69] By the twelfth and thirteenth centuries, however, with the original reform movement long gone, Patarene had become a catchall term applied to heretics that was functionally synonymous with Publican or Cathar.[70]

The close proximity and underlying similarity of orthodox reform and schismatic heresy are important factors through which to understand confrontations with heresy in the twelfth century. In making the differentiation between licit reform and heresy, authors utilized strategies of orthodox self-formation that emphasized both the banishment of the heretical enemy but also the somewhat paradoxical maintenance of what Steven Kruger has called its "spectral" presence. This spectral presence facilitated the maintenance of the identity established by the initial rejection of the so-called heretic.[71] While the suspicion against acting prelates of practicing, for example, the heresy of simony might fade, the threat of the heretical enemy of the Church could quite easily and profitably remain behind as a threat around which the faithful as well as their potentially sinful prelates could cohere.

The caution regarding the wholesale execution of heretics stemming from the exegesis of the Parable of the Wheat and the Weeds continued up until the first medieval executions in Western Europe for heresy in the eleventh century.[72] The first of these, at Orleans, occurred in 1022 under the auspices of King Robert the Pious of France.[73] A similar group became a center of attention at the Synod of Arras in 1025, but, instead of culminating in an execution, this episode ended in the conversion and readmittance of the supposed heretics into the Church.[74] In contrast, another burning occurred at Milan around 1028, under the influence of Archbishop Aribert of Milan, when the group in question refused to convert.[75]

The sources for these three early events all stress, to varying degrees, the role of the heretics' choice in their final execution or salvation. All the sources establish the heretics' unorthodox beliefs at length and feature attempts to convince them to abandon their teachings that stood clearly at variance with orthodox belief. The sources conjure up both crops, as it were, and place them side by side, making clear the difference between heresy and orthodoxy. In the shadow of this clear division, at Orleans and at Milan, many of the heretics refused to return to the fold and were burned. At Arras, the heretics were threatened with excommunication and damnation before their repentance and subsequent reentry into the larger society of the Christian faithful.[76] The clear demarcation between wheat and weeds was enough to fulfill the Augustinian requirements for forceful intervention, but it was insufficient to bring an untroubled endorsement of proactive execution from the authors of the accounts for Arras and Milan. In comparison the sources for the burnings at Orleans have a remarkably different tone, and will themselves serve as the focus for chapter 3, but the essential problem posed by heretics in all three episodes was similar. What should be done when the enemy is clearly and definitively exposed? In these early cases, the first recourse was to episcopal persuasion. At Orleans and Milan most of the heretics remained impenitent, and secular powers intervened violently.

In Landulf Senior's description of the executions at Milan, written around 1110, although the episode ends in an execution, the death of the heretics is never part of the leading ecclesiastic's plan. Also, although the heretics gain no real sympathy from Landulf in his telling of the story, he does not endorse what is ultimately done to them. After a frightening conversation with a member of the heretical sect, Aribert of Milan arrests the heretics at the castle of Monforte and labors in vain to convert them while suffering from a mounting fear: "When he had taken them to Milan and labored through many days, and through many of his priests, desiring to reintegrate them in the Catholic faith, he was terribly aggrieved lest the people of Italy be contaminated by this heresy."[77] Aribert's fear of a growing contagion is important and reflects the discourse surrounding heresy as a disease spreading through the social body. In light of this fear, the archbishop appears at an impasse in the face of stubborn heretics, unable to release them but unsure of what to do next.

The deadlock is resolved when "the leading laymen of the town" take the matter into their hands against the archbishop's wishes. After they learn of the situation, they give the heretics a simple choice: conversion or death. They set up a huge, burning pyre on one side and a cross on the other and instruct the heretics from Monforte to walk to the destination of their choice. Landulf related that "some coming to the cross of the Lord and acknowledging the Catholic faith were saved, but many with their hands placed before their faces leapt into the flames" and were reduced to ashes.[78] Landulf, himself a defender of the traditional way of life of the Milanese clergy, including clerical marriage, later associated the heretics at Monforte with the Pararene reform movement.[79] In drawing this connection, Landulf suggested that heretical rejections of marriage and procreation served as an inspiration for reformers' demands for clerical celibacy.[80]

The only other account of the burning of the Monforte heretics comes from the *Historiarum libri quinque* (*Histories*) of Ralph Glaber. While less informative about the sequence of events in comparison to Landulf, his version stresses the allegiance of the heretics to the Devil and the similarity of the heresy to the practices of pagans and of Jews.[81] He recorded that the population of the town was entirely "tainted by an evil heresy" and that these heretics preferred to die rather than to return to the "saving faith of Christ."[82] These heretics were like other groups outside the Church, worshipping idols like pagans and offering empty sacrifices like Jews. Glaber related that Manfred, the marquis of Turin, and Alric, the bishop of Asti, first defeated the heretics in battle and then "burnt them with fire" after they refused conversion.[83] After this brief summary, Glaber told a longer story of a visit by one of these heretics, a "noblewoman," to a dying knight. After the woman departs, the demon that inspires the heretics reveals itself, offering the knight continued life and earthly power. The pious knight refuses the demon's offer, and before he dies relates the truth about the heretics' patron. As Glaber concluded, "There can be no doubt that what he saw was for our benefit as well as his."[84]

The early clerical discomfort with executions for heresy continued into the mid-eleventh century, where it found its most famous expression in a letter written by Bishop Wazo of Liège, later reproduced by Anselm of Liège.[85] Between 1043 and 1048 Bishop Roger II of Châlons-sur-Marne sought Wazo's advice about what should be done regarding a group of heretics he had encountered in his diocese. According to Anselm, who paraphrased Roger's side of this exchange, Roger described to Wazo the doctrines of the heretics, including what would become familiar elements of supposed heretical sects: secret meetings, avoidance of marriage, refusal to eat meat, and baptism in the Spirit. This baptism came about through the imposition of hands that conveyed the Holy Spirit in a kind of apostolic succession from Mani of Persia as if he were the Holy Spirit itself.

These claims regarding the Holy Spirit suggested to Roger that these heretics could not be forgiven. In reference to Matthew 12:31, which states, "Blasphemy of the Spirit shall not be forgiven," Roger concluded that the heretics had fallen into "that blasphemy that according to the voice of Truth cannot be forgiven here or in the future."[86] The phrase "here or in the future" is significant because it contains a double suggestion. In the reference to the future, Roger indicated that for their false teachings regarding the Holy Spirit, the heretics would be damned at the end of time. Regarding the here and now, Roger suggested that their teachings also constituted an unforgivable crime in the present world, and implied that human authorities did not need to wait for God's eventual justice, or the final winnowing of the wheat from the weeds at the end of time. Something more proactive appeared called for than a tolerant quarantine or even conversion and readmittance to the faith after successful

persuasion as at Arras some twenty years earlier. If the heretics were ultimately and irrevocably damned, placed beyond God's possible forgiveness,
they were also beyond the possible forgiveness of man, and killing them in the
present was not only logical but beneficial and moral; it was the realization of
an inevitability. The immediate human response to heresy and God's ultimate response could directly align with each other.

Roger's logic suggests that not only could the human and divine responses
to heresy be mirror images of each other but also that violence might be necessary to prevent the harm that the heretics could cause to the Christian community. Roger, in fact, told Wazo that this harm was his principal concern
rather than the heretics' impending damnation. While the heretics were
doomed, they had the potential to drag others to Hell with them via the now-
familiar logic of heresy spreading like a disease in a body. Roger concluded
his letter by asking "whether the sword of terrestrial power should be turned
against them, lest the entire loaf be corrupted by a little leaven if they are not
exterminated."[87]

Wazo's response confirmed that he saw Roger to be arguing for the heretics' execution rather than enforced exile, and he vigorously disagreed. He did
agree that the group in question was certainly heretical; nonetheless, the clerical role in confrontations with heresy such as this should conform to the
model of Christ, as found in Matthew 11:29, who came not as a worldly war-
rior but instead to suffer for sinners. The "merciful and compassionate Lord,"
Wazo reminds Roger, "does not judge sinners immediately but looks forward
to their penance with equanimity."[88] In this formulation, a cleric should never
call for a heretic's death.

Wazo further illustrates the Lord's compassion and willingness to suffer for
the sake of sinners' eventual redemption through the Parable of the Wheat
and the Weeds. Not only is this parable an excellent illustration and source
for Wazo's point but it is also a kind of textual parry of Roger's earlier citation of the same Gospel while calling for the heretics' deaths. Using the familiar understanding of the parable, Wazo argues that the final differentiation
between the wheat and the weeds comes only at the end of the world. In fact,
he asks, what did the Lord show with these words if not that "it is possible
that those who are today weeds will tomorrow be converted and be wheat?"[89]

The rebuke to Roger gathers force as Wazo calls into question the possibility that the final fate of any present soul can ever be known during life, including Roger's own. In the pursuit of present weeds, the human gardener will
destroy good wheat. In fact, those who appear weeds today may not only become wheat, but may become even more meritorious than the clerics who
wish to condemn them. Wazo suggests the example of the Apostle Paul, who as

Saul of Tarsus was a persecutor of St. Stephen.[90] In contrast to Roger's earlier suggestion, the difference between now and the future is terribly significant, and the two cannot be collapsed into one. If such a conjunction between God's final justice and present human knowledge cannot be made, the execution of current heretics is no longer morally sure; it is a premature and potentially murderous harvest.

While Wazo rejected the execution of schismatics, he did argue that something must be done to contain the harm they could cause. What clerics could do followed from their role that was delegated to them from God. A bishop does not wield the sword of earthly power, and so he does not take life; he only gives it. Instead, the bishop could cut offenders off from the communion and unity of the Church as a kind of quarantine. Wazo suggests that heretics should be excommunicated and publicly denounced. So notified, the faithful could avoid them, "lest they touch their most unclean sect, because he who touches pitch will be stained by it."[91] The threat of contagion must always be addressed, but in Wazo's opinion this response should be nonlethal.

After copying Wazo's letter, Anselm of Liège added his own approval of the bishop's reply, emphasizing the deficiencies in current human knowledge that can lead the zealous gardener to kill good grain. Wazo's argument, Anselm tell us, follows the example of St. Martin of Tours, who opposed the execution of Priscillian for heresy in 385 and the identification of heretics by their pallid faces.[92] This "error and madness" had doubtless led to the death of good Catholics.[93]

Anselm elaborated with a reference to recent events, suggesting that just as the errors of the early Christian past prove an enduring model for heresy's reemergence in the present, so too do the errors in the authorities' response. At Goslar in 1052, Emperor Henry III hanged a group of "Manichaeans" brought before him by Duke Godfrey of Upper Lorraine. Another source for this event provides the familiar justification of social hygiene, saying that the emperor killed them "lest the heretical infection, creeping widely, infect more."[94] Anselm, for his part, found this execution unjustified. Doubtless, he reasoned, the group at Goslar were true heretics, but this status did not justify their deaths. Instead of some great outrage or lengthy process of deliberation, to the best of Anselm's knowledge, the death sentence was passed when the heretics refused their bishop's order to kill a chicken. In conclusion, Anselm feels compelled to say that "had Wazo lived to see it, he would not have agreed."[95]

When Ramihrdus of Cambrai was burned for heresy in 1076, Wazo's words regarding the ambiguity of heresy and the difficulty in identifying the heretic appeared prophetic. Gerhard II, the bishop of Cambrai, ordered Ramihrdus to appear before him after hearing that the man had attracted quite an audience "preaching against the faith." After Ramihrdus refused communion from the bishop and his clerks, citing their sin of simony, "certain of the bishop's servants" took him outside and burned him in a hut. The condemned died well, and "his followers" collected his bones and ashes like relics.[96] Gregory VII denounced Ramihrdus's execution and suggested the latter's objections to simony (at least as they had reached the pope) were not heretical.[97] Bishop Gerard later confessed the sin of simony and was reinstated by Gregory.[98] In this episode, the positions of heretic and martyr possess blurry boundaries, and their vague borders underscore the perils in executions for heresy. The authority of the pope, moreover, far from endorsing such action, had condemned it.

The evolving *Glossa ordinaria* (*Ordinary Gloss*) of the Bible, compiled in the early twelfth century at the School of Laon, transmitted the Fathers' interpretations of the Parable of the Wheat and the Weeds in a form close to that found in the letter of Wazo. The widely available *Patrologia Latina* edition stressed that through this parable Jesus taught "good will, caution, patience, discernment, forbearance, and justice."[99] The gloss repeated the familiar themes of avoiding premature amputation, because the bad may become good, and living human beings may make mistakes that God and His angels will not. The gloss amplified Augustine's point regarding the usefulness of heresy, borrowing some phrasing from his *Sixteen Questions on Matthew*.[100] It summarized Augustine's point succinctly: "The evil should be patiently tolerated where some of them are found who can help the good."[101] Later in the twelfth century, other commentators would develop the theme of heretical usefulness further.

In the long trajectory of history, Wazo's argument calling for significant restraint in authority's response to cases of manifest heresy did not carry the day. Later discussions of the execution of heretics reflect two possible reasons. Heresy represented a threat to the shared Christian community, which demanded some kind of forceful response; such a response could itself be useful for strengthening the very foundations of Christian community that heresy threatened. While medieval executions for heresy remained infrequent and closely associated with exceptional events, the following centuries saw far more incidents like that at Goslar than calls for patience and forbearance as eloquent as that of Wazo. Uses of the Parable of the Wheat and the Weeds as well as the employment of the imagery of disease reflected a growing consensus that death was an appropriate punishment for pernicious heresy.

Around 1140 Gratian, in the *Decretum*, explored the question of the just war through a hypothetical infestation of heresy. Gratian used this particular scenario as an ideal case to explore when and for what causes and for what goals a Christian may rightfully go to war. He posited a situation in which an entire region had succumbed to heresy, including both common people and bishops, and its heretical inhabitants had begun to encroach on their neighboring Catholics. In such a scenario, Gratian asked, can a war be waged legitimately to defend the faith and force the heretics to return to the fold?[102] He cited a long list of biblical passages, including the Parable of the Wheat and the Weeds, which might suggest that it is always a sin to wage war.[103] Gratian rejected this interpretation, arguing that arriving at such a blanket conclusion, according to the literally apparent meanings of the text, would be an interpretive error.[104]

In Gratian's argument, the figurative meaning of these injunctions against violence and war arrived at a more nuanced conclusion. Through an excerpt from Augustine, Gratian argued that these passages seek to shape the intention behind violence that the good Christian should possess.[105] The Christian should act out of patience, not repaying evil for evil but rather acting for the greater good of the whole, including the wicked. Following the logic pioneered by Augustine, a war waged justly by Christian combatants opens up space for the spiritual realignment of the vanquished by removing the impediments to their reform. In short, the focus should be on the spiritual health and eventual salvation of all those concerned rather than on glory or worldly wealth. Bodily combat should reflect a more significant spiritual struggle.[106] The violent persuasion or removal of entrenched heretics is licit.

What the argument of the *Decretum* suggests is that a strict reading of the Parable of the Wheat and the Weeds, or any apparent total condemnation of violence in the Bible, is a form of literalism, a letter that kills rather than gives life. Its spiritual understanding will mean something other than its immediate appearance. An appropriate exegetical understanding, rooted in a specifically Christian spiritual interpretation of the text, recognizes that violence has its place, especially in response to manifest heresy. A just war then, as presented by Gratian, better fits military action against heresy, such as the Albigensian Crusades, than crusades against Islam.[107] The type of existential and eschatological threat posed by heresy to the Christian social body demands some kind of response, and this threat is the ideal justification for such a response to involve violence.

An influential commentary on the Gospel of Matthew from c. 1140–50, once ascribed to Anselm of Laon, reveals how the execution of convicted heretics could be made to fit within the long-standing exegesis of the Parable of the Wheat and the Weeds.[108] It also reflects a growing uniformity of procedure in prosecutions against suspected heretics. The commentary borrows portions of Augustine's exegesis of the parable from the *Sixteen Questions on Matthew*. It repeated the familiar argument that weeds can become wheat and that the wicked can be useful for the good. To these Augustinian excerpts it adds a question drawn from its medieval context: "Why are some heretics, after being excommunicated by bishops and separated from the Church, killed by secular rulers?"[109] The author addressed this question by stressing the separation between the spiritual and secular powers. Excommunication is not in itself a death sentence; rather, it is designed to facilitate the correction of men. Bishops cannot effect a general separation from the field that is the world. That is, they ought not to kill.[110] The ability to kill lies in the secular sphere. Nonetheless, the execution of heretics is a reality, and the author suggested that this fact of life be understood not as the violation of a long-standing interpretation of the parable but rather the setting of a limited example: "And if certain people, having been judged, convicted, and handed over, are killed by the secular power for the correction of others; nevertheless, a general separation of the wicked should not be done, because few of the good would remain and this is the time of change, and who are today evil may tomorrow be good."[111] Those who reform before the final harvest will be together taken into the Lord's barn because "they loved the unity of charity."[112]

The author of the commentary, in his consideration of the Parable of the Wheat and the Weeds, saw the execution of some wicked people as an exemplary deterrent that aimed at the reform of others. It was not a general slaughter of all the wicked, because, as he says, human beings are by their nature so wicked that there would be few people left. Instead, limited executions carried out by secular rulers were useful. The usefulness of capital punishment was a common argument found in medieval Europe. Execution as a deterrent, a commonplace of Roman law and the medieval reforming papacy, was used as the justification for the execution of common criminals, such as thieves, and these executions outnumbered those for heresy by an enormous margin.[113] In the argument of this commentary, the discourse about the execution of heretics moved closer to the quotidian realities of medieval capital punishment.

Twelfth-century schoolmen continued to offer warnings regarding the execution of heretics but they increasingly accepted the deaths of particular individuals in extreme circumstances. Peter Comestor, working with the *Ordinary Gloss* and the commentary on Matthew examined above, worried about possible miscarriages of justice that would ensue from hasty procedure. Like the commentary on Matthew, Comestor accepted the execution of some individual heretics by secular authorities. Peter the Chanter, meanwhile, shared the concern with potential injustice. He stressed, like the commentary on Matthew, that a general removal of all the wicked would eliminate almost everyone. He approved, however, of the removal of particular diseased members of the flock in order the save the rest from infection. The nature of this removal seemed to trouble the Chanter more than Comestor or the author of the commentary on Matthew. The Chanter stressed that given time even an apparently impenitent heretic might reform, rendering execution premature. To this worry, the Chanter added another long-standing concern: misleading appearances. For example, a good Catholic might become pale from fasting and be mistaken for a heretic who refused to consume all products of earthly procreation, while the healthy glow of a glutton might be judged a sign of perfect orthodoxy.[114] In the work of these two men, appearances needed to be interrogated carefully before the increasingly potent arsenal of potential penalties could be applied.

Papal pronouncements on the subject reflected the hardening of attitudes. The Third Lateran Council in 1179 acknowledged that the "discipline of the Church should be satisfied with the judgment of the priest and should not cause the shedding of blood," while conceding that the threat of "bodily punishment" at the hands of the secular power provides the main incentive for many, judged to be sinners, to abandon their sin.[115] This council saw the excommunication of a number of supposed heretical sects, as well as encouragements and rewards for those who took up arms against them.[116] In 1184 Pope Lucius III, in cooperation with Frederick Barbarossa, renewed these excommunications, and stipulated that unrepentant heretics, whether clerics or laymen, would be handed over to a secular judge "to receive due punishment." Likewise, those who had repented and then relapsed into error would be handed over to the secular authority.[117] The nature of the punishment this authority would inflict is strongly implied. Unlike the ecclesiastical courts, the secular judiciary could shed blood and put offenders to death. Additionally, for those placed outside the Church, this authority was the only logical one left.

Innocent III advanced the consensus in the direction of execution while not clearly advocating such a position himself. In his response to heresy, Innocent continued to stress the potential danger precipitous action against heresy posed to the faithful, along the lines of the traditional interpretation of the Parable of the Wheat and the Weeds. He observed that in the field of the Father weeds often sprout among the wheat, and moths often appear in the vineyard of the Lord. In response to these threats, a prudent farmers and winemakers must take care lest they destroy good grain and vines.[118] In the struggle with heresy, Innocent suggested that this care take the form of the careful examination of individual cases, particularly the willingness of potential heretics to submit to the institutional authority of the Church.[119]

In Innocent III's work, a refusal to submit to the corporate authority of the Church took on grave consequences. He explained these consequences as a response to the threat such disobedience represented for the collective through the imagery of spreading weeds, little foxes uprooting vines, or a spreading cancer.[120] In 1199 Innocent connected heresy to lèse-majesté, paving the way for responses to it along the lines of Roman law, including the penalty of death. In the decretal *Vergentis in senium*, Innocent appeared to place heresy on the same footing as treason against a temporal lord.[121] The logic in this decretal relied on the corporate identity of Christian society as the body of Christ and the place of the papacy as the earthly governor of that body.[122] Innocent reasoned that since in Roman law *laesa maiestatis*, or treason, is a capital crime that allows the seizure of offenders' goods, the possessions of heretics could also be confiscated because departing from the faith offends Christ. Leaving the mystical body is an assault, of a kind, on the spiritual union that constitutes it. Since Christ is the head of the Church as the body of Christ and the ultimate authority over that body, offending His eternal majesty is certainly "far graver" than an injury to the majesty of a temporal lord.[123] Following the logic of the decretal, the pope as Christ's earthly representative was the most sensible authority to identify what constituted a departure from the faith that offended Christ's majesty.[124] Importantly, although treason was a capital crime, Innocent III did not call specifically for heretics' deaths in this decretal; instead, he ordered the seizure of their goods and their excommunication.[125]

The exact scope of the penalties Innocent III wished to be applied to heretics remained unclear, but the pope's words increasingly suggested the possibility of deadly force. In a decretal of 1207, Innocent commanded that heretics in the territories under temporal papal jurisdiction should be handed over to secular courts for due punishment, and reiterated that heretics' goods should be seized.[126] What this punishment should or could be the decretal suggestively did not say.[127] In 1208, Innocent launched the Albigensian Crusade, which was from the pope's point of view a holy war of the type outlined as the ideal just war by Gratian. As Innocent saw it, this defensive war clearly legitimated the deaths of the heretics and their supporters whose assaults on Christendom necessitated it.[128] At the Fourth Lateran Council of 1215, Innocent enlarged the procedures he had outlined earlier for the Papal States to the entirety of Europe. He condemned all heretics of any type, since they, like the foxes of Samson, were joined together at the tail by the same vanity.[129] Whatever name heretics might have, they are essentially the same kind of criminal, and all so condemned were to be handed over to the secular power for "due punishment." What this punishment should be remained somewhat ambiguous, as Innocent admonished the secular powers to "exterminate" (*exterminare*) all those designated as heretics by the Church from their jurisdictions.[130] This wording does not preclude confiscation of goods followed by exile, but it certainly does not strongly preclude execution either.[131]

Around this time, secular authorities began to make the first official and systematic connections between heresy and the penalty of death. In 1198 Peter II of Aragon became the first European ruler in the Middle Ages to decree the penalty of burning alive for heretics by law. Peter declared that Waldensians and all other heretics "anathematized by the holy Church" should be expelled from his territories. Those who remained after a period of thirty days would have their goods confiscated and their "bodies destroyed by fire." Peter added that any who provide any assistance to heretics of any kind would lose their goods in punishment for the crime of lèse-majesté.[132] In 1231, Frederick II connected the Patarene heresy to treason (lèse-majesté) as well as its penalties "in the ancient laws."[133] The emperor condemned those who persevered in their error "to the death for which they strive." This death was "the judgment of the flames," and the emperor ordered that pernicious heretics should be "burned alive in the sight of the people."[134]

William of Auvergne provided a concise and powerful example of what work the parable of Matthew and the fears of contagion could do in the growing consensus regarding responses to heresy, especially in the years after the Albigensian Crusade. William, a master of theology at the University of Paris and then bishop of Paris from 1228 until his death in 1249, argued that execution was a necessary penalty for heresy. In making this argument, he combined the imagery of the Parable of the Wheat and the Weeds with that of a spreading infection. In contrast to Wazo, through William's pen the parable of Matthew was not a call for present restraint but an argument for immediate action.

In his *De fide et legibus* (*On faith and Laws*), a section of his voluminous *Magisterium divinale et sapientiale* (*Teaching on God in the Mode of Wisdom*) written between 1231 and 1240, William of Auvergne observed that regarding the executions of heretics some commentators are accustomed to object, citing the Gospel of Matthew. In this Gospel, Christ advised that the weeds be allowed to grow until the harvest, "lest by chance the wheat be destroyed at the same time."[135] William's response was simple; for him it was obvious that Christ made this suggestion for the sake of the wheat: "He did not want to spare the weeds, but only the wheat, hence He did not want to spare the weeds to the detriment of the wheat."[136] It follows that in cases where it is not possible to spare the weeds without harm to the wheat, Christ "does not want them to be spared."[137] Where heresy grows "at the expense or diminution" of the Christian community, heretics "should be eradicated, and through a corporeal death, when it is not possible to eradicate them in another way."[138]

In William's argument, everything now rests on how often it is possible, if it is possible at all, to spare the weeds without harm to the wheat, and the bishop's words do not paint an optimistic picture. Heresy seeks to grow, and every moment of its presence is a threat to the crop. Following this logic, "incorrigible and stubborn" heretics, who cannot be eradicated in any other way, "have to be killed out of necessity."[139] In response to arguments like that of Wazo, that those who are now weeds may become good grain, William offered a utilitarian argument, suffused with the logic of communal hygiene:

> If anyone says that the very ones who are now weeds can become wheat because they can be converted to a life of truth, they certainly speak truly, but that these will be converted and become wheat, especially those who are obstinate and pernicious in their error, is not certain. It is obviously certain, however, that through them those who are wheat become weeds. For the simple and unlearned are subverted by their cunning with great ease, and a few weeds easily corrupt and suffocate a great field of wheat. We see with great difficulty the rare conversion of heretics, but we see constantly the easiest subversion of the faithful. Whence the good of the conversion of errors of this kind is both small and rare as well as difficult, and entirely uncertain, to such an extent that it is not apparent how it can rightly succeed.[140]

While the destruction of a present weed may be tantamount to the destruction of some wheat here or there, this harm is justified by the protection it offers to those who are good grain now. Furthermore, the execution of the heretic is actually an act of mercy, taking from them the opportunity to commit further crimes that would certainly increase their ultimate sufferings in Hell. While confirmed heretics will still be damned, the faithful can spare them some increase in their tortures, and so it can be said "they therefore profit from the death of their bodies."[141]

In this argument from the second quarter of the thirteenth century, one can see a significant transformation of the use of the parable of Matthew in the discourse surrounding executions for heresy. Rather than a call for patience and restraint, it is now patience itself that is immoral. Sparing the heretic is harmful to the faithful and to the heretic himself, and a violent response is a pious duty. This duty articulates itself against the backdrop of communal welfare and an alignment between God's ultimate punishment of the damned and the human response to criminality strongly associated with damnation. In certain circumstances, the difference between wheat and weeds is obvious, as Augustine suggested. In such apparent cases, following Gratian, the parable should not be read too literally. According to William, when this difference can be easily seen, the potential spread of these weeds justifies their immediate removal. Finally, in William's day the fate of the weeds at human hands was becoming by law, as well as by custom, identical to the final fate in fire promised to them by God.

This chapter has followed the creation, enduring influence, and implementation of two models for responding to heresy. The first is the Parable of the Wheat and the Weeds from the Gospel of Matthew. This model might suggest present toleration of some religious plurality in anticipation of a future judgment from God. The second is the concept of heresy as a spreading infection or disease that can potentially corrupt the shared Christian body. This model might more strongly recommend active responses in the present to prevent the infection's spread. Taken together, these two conceptions provide a number of possibilities for thinking through responses to heresy and the kinds of threats heresy posed, as well as the stakes at hand for inadequate responses to heresy.

In practice, of course, both models traveled together, and early medieval engagements with the possibility of heresy called on them both. Rather than a foregone conclusion, the execution of unrepentant heretics for the crime of heresy divided learned opinion and took time to become commonly accepted, and the circumstances under which it could occur remained situational and debated. This gradual acceptance took place in a wider context, amenable to a clearer alignment between the actions of human authorities and the eschatological judgments of God. While in the time of Wazo weeding the fields of Christendom could be seen as precipitous, by the time of the Albigensian Crusades the attitudes of authorities appear to have changed. In fact, in Gratian's examination of the just war and in the interpretation of the Parable of the Wheat and the Weeds offered by William of Auvergne, the apparent call for present toleration, long found by exegetes in the parable of Matthew, became reversed. Instead of a call for forbearance, to William the parable called for the immediate bodily death of the revealed heretic. Some explanations for how such a reversal became established will be the subject of the next five chapters, which examine the sources for specific executions for heresy in the eleventh, twelfth, and early thirteenth centuries.

The reversal of apparent meanings found in Gratian and William of Auvergne resonated with Christian traditions of spiritual exegesis. Jerome had cautioned that the leaven that corrupts the entire loaf was the carnal reading of the sacred text, a kind of interpretation led on by the worldly appearances of things. Christian reading, in contrast, was thought to proceed from a different source. It arose, as explored in chapter 1, from the love that joined together the Church as the body of Christ; this shared love suffused the language and the logic medieval authorities used with each other when they discussed the threat of heresy. As presented by medieval authors who pondered how to respond to heresy, the persecution of heresy became more severe out of love. When medieval authors justified persecution to themselves, they framed it as a defense of those they loved as part of the shared body of their society and their Church. What executions for heresy could mean from the point of view of the instigators depends on this fundamental asymmetry in the attribution of motives.[142] Heretics by their nature diminished and assaulted the body of Christ, and in this nature they were an outside force based on hatred. The orthodox collective, in contrast, was an identity and ideology based on love.

In the discussions analyzed above, three central issues have returned again and again to influence the debate: the centrality of love as the organizing principle of orthodox identity; the misleading appearances of people and of words; and the unintended usefulness of the evil of heresy to the good of orthodoxy. Orthodox discourses on heresy recognized the problem of misleading appearances and argued that the essential mendacity of appearances could only be resolved correctly in the context of Christian community. In the logic of wheat and weeds, or the body and disease, the recognition and labeling of a threat is the essential moment. To orthodox authors, this recognition could only occur within a society joined together by a divine presence that alone allowed the passage from an "outer shell of seeming to the inner kernel of reality."[143] The divine presence that allowed meanings to be read in spite of appearances created out of itself a union of love. Those who existed outside this union were not only a threat to it but also themselves an object of figurative reading, presenting to orthodox exegetes a useful object to be interpreted. What meanings supposed heretics—or all non-Christians—might have within them, meanings that they themselves by their very carnal natures could not recognize, will be the subjects of the coming chapters: accounts of heretics' executions were excellent opportunities for medieval authors to find and to develop ideas regarding the usefulness of heresy.

CHAPTER 3

The Beginning at Orleans in 1022
Heretics and Hellfire

The first burning of Christians for heresy in the medieval West occurred outside Orleans in 1022. According to the French chronicler Ralph Glaber, the heretics approached the pyre willingly and without any fear. The thirteen condemned entered the flames on their own, but as they began to burn their demeanor changed. They cried out from the middle of the fire that they had been deceived by the Devil, and that everything they had taught was a lie. Finally, they described the full extent of their punishment to the crowd, declaring that for their blasphemy they would suffer not only the temporary flames of execution but also the eternal agonies of Hell. The witnesses of this first burning, Glaber says, were so overwhelmed with pity that they rushed up to the pyre and attempted to pull the condemned out of the fire, but it was too late. The heretics were already dust and their souls were already in Hell.[1]

As Glaber portrayed it, the audience of this burning learned a lot from what they saw and what they heard. At the touch of the flames, the condemned became public confessors of truths, unambiguously instructing the crowd about what their deaths meant and what their deaths could prove. Glaber did not describe a crowd that received these revelations with eager satisfaction, but instead depicted one that came together in shared pity for the damned. This pity did nothing for the heretics because repentance in Hell cannot help the damned; instead, it provided yet another service for the crowd that watched them die. These onlookers received moral and theological edification, all the while remaining not implicated in and excused from the act of killing themselves, shielded by a unifying wall of pity that was itself constructed in reaction to the eternal agony of a few.

Like Glaber's account, the other sources for the first burning of Christian heretics in the medieval West tend to stress how the good community of Christians, composed of both actual witnesses to the event and also witnesses created at a distance through the medium of written accounts, was well served by seeing living men and women burned alive. These sources used the ideas of Hell and hellfire to make sense of the burning of the heretics, portraying the fires of execution as a likeness or extension of the fires of Hell. In this way contemporary authors recounted the first burning of heretics in the Middle Ages as foreshadowing eschatological destinies.[2] Beyond mere foreshadowing, the sources for the burning stressed the necessity and acceptability of immediate human activity based on eschatological assumptions. While those who would be saved at the end of time could not be perfectly known, those who refused to take their place in a Christian society progressing toward possible salvation could be excluded before the end. Such a separation was essential to the common good, and the major accounts of these executions focused on the necessity of just such a proactive anticipation of God's ultimate justice.

There are five principal sources for the burnings at Orleans, written at various distances from the event. These sources range from letters, acta, and hagiography to chronicles. The sources, in order of composition, are a letter from John of Ripoll, a monk at Fleury, to Bishop Oliba of Vic; a paragraph in the *Chronicon* of Ademar de Chabannes; a chapter from the *Histories* of Ralph Glaber; a section from the *Vita Gauzlini* (*Life of Gauzlin*) by Andreas of Fleury; and finally an account by Paul of St. Père de Chartres.[3] The chapter will examine these sources in their probable order of composition, rather than in order of their reliability or direct access to the event itself. As a result, the account written by Andreas will come next to last, even though his was likely an eyewitness description. This organization is justified by the argument's focus on the immediate historiography of the events at Orleans in 1022.

All of the authors are distinguished by their own positions, prejudices, and contexts, but they all share some common attributes. Each was a cleric, and associated with the regions of Burgundy and Aquitaine, and all of them were, to various degrees, concerned with eschatological preparations. Their concerns with the final fate of the world and the individuals in it need not be as pronounced, or contentious, as the association of Ralph Glaber with an expected apocalypse around the year 1000. Indeed, a hopeful, invigorated, and newly assertive Latin Christian world could just as powerfully raise the issue of the collective progress of Christian society toward its eventual goal as a Christendom haunted by an immediate apocalypse. Tied into this heightened sense of mission was a new engagement with enemies both near and far.

What really happened outside Orleans in 1022, and what had the condemned really done or said? A definitive answer is impossible to provide, but there is no shortage of suggestions.[4] In that year, King Robert the Pious ordered a group of people, numbering between ten and fourteen, burned alive after they were revealed as unrepentant heretics at a special synod.[5] Burning alive, in later centuries, became the customary and often official punishment for unrepentant or relapsed heretics, but in 1022 there was no immediate precedent for the king's actions.[6] According to Robert-Henri Bautier, a political power struggle between royal appointees and the circle of Odo II of Blois may lie behind the synod and its dramatic conclusion.[7] In response to this possibility, Thomas Head and Malcolm Lambert have stressed that very real religious concerns may likely have been at play, however much the sources might misrepresent them.[8]

Whatever the truth behind the event, close attention to its portrayal by contemporaries reveals more about the significance of the method of execution chosen for the condemned. These descriptions illustrate how contemporaries understood what we today call the "formation of a persecuting society" in Europe and the appearance of one of its signature punishments and images.[9] The immediate sources for the executions at Orleans also illustrate how apocalyptic or eschatological expectations, especially around the year 1000, could shape the contemporary expression of these origins.[10] In fact, as Norman Cohn stressed, many of the accusations made against the condemned at Orleans fit neatly into a long genealogy of wild accusations leveled against supposedly deviant groups with striking consistency from the ancient world to the witch trials of the early modern period, which he calls the "nocturnal ritual fantasy."[11] Rather than a study of what actually occurred at Orleans, or what the supposed heretics actually believed, what follows below is an analysis of "ideas of heresy" and how these ideas made sense of burning as heresy's punishment.[12]

John of Ripoll and the Novelty of Burning Heretics

Compared to most of the other sources, the letter written by John of Ripoll, a monk at Fleury, to Abbot Oliba of Vic is rather short: a description of the heretics, their heresy, and their punishment, which in the modern edition amounts to one paragraph. It seems that John wrote within one year of the burnings and while rumors were still rife. In John's description of the heresy he appears to assume that Oliba may not have believed any rumors he had already heard of the event: "Meanwhile, I want you to know about the heresy that happened on the day of the Holy Innocents in Orleans, for if you heard something about it, it was true. King Robert burned alive around fourteen of the better clerics or of the more noble laypeople of that city."[13] John continues, describing the doctrines the heretics held. They denied baptism, the consecration of the body and blood, the clerical remission of sins, and marriage. They also abstained from meat as if it were by its nature corrupt. John concludes his recapitulation by urging Oliba to inquire diligently about this matter in his diocese or abbeys, lest "anybody lie hidden in this crime under the guise of empty religion."[14]

John's brief description introduces themes that found considerable development in the other accounts of the heretics' execution. His phrasing seems to stress surprise at the events, the victims, and the punishment. To Julian Havet, John's wording underscores the unprecedented nature of the punishment for this particular crime.[15] Likewise, John takes these events as a call to further action, leading some to suggest that more executions may have followed of which we have no record. In particular, he regards the burning of the heretics as bringing about the revelation of a hidden truth. In the events surrounding their immolation, apparently model Christians are revealed for the frauds that they really are. This concern with false appearances also characterizes the later accounts, and fire plays an important role in the performance of this revelation.

Burning living human beings alive, of course, was itself not new in 1022. Secular authorities had long held this punishment as one option in their arsenals. Burning alive appears as one form of capital punishment in Roman law, along with hanging and decapitation. In the *Digest of Justinian* it is seen as secondary to hanging, since it was supposedly devised after it.[16] This punishment appears particularly suitable for those who are enemies of the state or deserters to the enemy, slaves who conspire against their masters, and arsonists in urban areas.[17] Burning alive is also a possible response to sacrilege.[18] Of more immediate relevance in 1022 would be burning alive in early "Germanic" law codes and early eleventh-century practice. The Salic Law (Lex Salica) lists burning alive as a punishment for poisoning through magical potions.[19] Immolation was a spectacular punishment and lent itself to theatrics, and if there were reservations over hanging women along with a group of men, burning alive was gender-neutral.[20] Beyond its appearances in written codes, burning alive was certainly employed by authorities in the eleventh century, and the chronicle sources for the burnings at Orleans themselves described other instances of malefactors being burned alive for their crimes. While burning alive itself was not novel, what was new, and indeed surprising, in John's account of execution by fire was the crime it punished in this particular case.

Moreover, specific instances of this punishment could take on their own meaning. The other four sources for the burnings at Orleans assigned an infernal significance to the events, and developed at some length two other elements found in John's description. The same concern that John expressed regarding false appearances and the possibility of a pernicious fifth column hidden inside the Christian society of Aquitaine would fascinate and engage the other authors who recorded the same events.

Ademar of Chabannes: Community, Eschatology, and the Struggle for Homogeneity

The account of the heresy at Orleans written by Ademar of Chabannes can be found in the third book of his *Chronicon*.[21] In his version, there are ten heretics and they are all canons of the Holy Cross at Orleans. Ademar's account of the heresy relies on the logic of oppositional eschatological communities, a binary division between the saved and the damned. In the current world, this division articulates itself most clearly between those who are members of the Christian Church and those who remain intentionally separate from it. Individuals who take their place in a properly ordered Christian Church and society form the party of God, while all of those who separate themselves from this Church and society constitute the servants of the Devil.

Ademar of Chabannes has a two-sided reputation. Compared to his contemporary Ralph Glaber, he might appear as a somewhat sensible historian. In contrast, he is also regarded as a brazen liar, especially for his apostolic forgeries promoting St. Martial. Born into the minor aristocracy in 989, Ademar entered monastic life around the age of seven, where he acquired his education and undertook his literary and historical work. After putting the finishing touches on the last version of his *Chronicon*, he went on a pilgrimage to Jerusalem where he died in 1034. Ademar likely wrote his account of the heresy at Orleans between the years 1027–28.[22] In his origin, career, and even in the place of his death, Ademar's life encapsulates the transformations, ambitions, and fears of the Latin West.

While Ademar's style is often viewed as the complete antithesis of the millennial anxieties expressed by Glaber regarding the year 1000, his work is actually alive with eschatological expectations, prefigurations, and concerns.[23] Ademar had a good grasp of the fundamental eschatological ideas of his time through the *Prognosticum futuri saeculi* of Julian of Toledo. Ademar's uncle had this work copied and additions made to it, a project on which Ademar was very likely involved.[24] The *Prognosticum* provided a selection and synthesis of the ideas of the Fathers regarding the end of time that proved to be enormously influential throughout the medieval period.[25] In fact, the essential similarity of Western eschatological ideas in the Middle Ages can be directly attributed to the impact of this fundamental text.[26] In particular, the *Prognosticum*, taken as a whole, amounted to "a primer for identifying the millennial kingdom with the church which will spread the word of God until the Last Judgment."[27] The centrality of the Church as the vehicle and shared body of human redemption would prove essential to Ademar's account of the heretics and their punishment, particularly as their punishment prefigured the fate of all those who separate themselves from the Church.

Among the ideas regarding the fate of human beings that Ademar encountered in the *Prognosticum* was the centrality and materiality of fire in the punishment of the wicked. The *Prognosticum* informs its readers that the damned will suffer in flame, among other torments, and that this punishment will begin immediately after death, while a human being exists as a soul without a body, as was the case in the story of the rich man and Lazarus found in Luke 16. The text suggests that even before the Resurrection the punitive flames of the Other World will be corporeal flames, even though they torment bodiless spirits.[28] There will also be purgatorial fires to purge the sin of those destined for eventual salvation, but unlike the fires of Hell these flames will be finite.[29] Fire awaits the majority of human beings, but for the damned it will be eternal, beginning immediately after death and continuing without end. If a damned individual leaves this world through the medium of a material fire, another equally material flame awaits to receive him in the Other World.

Ademar's account of the heretics and their punishment centers on their separation. He describes the heretics as secret schismatics, who, when they are revealed for what they are, steadfastly refuse to be reintegrated into the larger body of believers. Ademar stresses that King Robert burned the heretics only after they had refused "to return to the faith," and after he had ordered them stripped of their holy orders and "taken out of the church."[30] In this imposition of a liminal status, the king reifies visibly the separate spiritual state these clerics have chosen for themselves.[31] Due to their beliefs, the canons are not really part of the true Christian community, and before they are burned alive they are publicly removed from the offices and premises of that community. The logic underlying these actions suggests that outside of this sacred community there is only one ultimate destiny that will be shared by all the damned, and this destiny lies in Hell and its fires.

Just as the true Christian community shares a ritual meal that underlines their unity in the form of the Eucharist, so too do the heretics. According to Ademar, the "certain rustic" who began the heresy used to carry with him the ashes of dead children, and if anyone received these ashes (*communicare*) they quickly became a manichee, or a sharer in the heresy. This ritual, a clear antithesis to the sacramental meal at the heart of the Christian mass, articulates the heretical community around it. That this community, outside of and opposed to the Christian community, is the same as that of the Devil cannot be doubted. Indeed, the heretics knowingly worship the Devil, who appears as both an Ethiopian and as an angel of light. That the Devil appears in both forms to the heretics highlights that they knew full well what he really was and with full insight chose to follow him. Once again, the choice is between binary positions that divide the world into those with God and those against Him. The challenge to the faithful is separating one from the other, in short the recognition of an enemy who can appear as an expression of both oppositional forces: demon and angel of light.

What is most insidious about the heretics at Orleans is that they appear to be members of the faithful community seeking God; like their master the Devil they can appear as angels. The heretics know that they are not really members of this sacralized community, having rejected Christ at the instigation of the Devil; however, in public they lie and claim to be "true Christians."[32] The heretics' misleading appearance, like that of their master, constitutes a fulfillment of Paul's warning regarding "false apostles" in 2 Corinthians 11:13–15.[33] This fifth column chips away at the City of God from the inside, attempting to subvert any men and women they can.[34] Ademar points out how difficult it can be to detect the enemy in one's midst by reference to the character of the dead cantor Theodatus, who in life had been one of the heretics while at the same time falsely renowned for his apparent sanctity. When the events at the synod revealed Theodatus for what he really was, his body is exhumed and cast out of the cemetery. The community, or social body, of the Christian dead awaiting together the day of resurrection will not have this traitor and cancerous contaminant in its midst.[35] The dead cantor, who seemed like an angel of light, is really more like a dark Ethiopian.

After establishing the logic of oppositional communities and the necessity of discerning between them, Ademar's narrative comes to the burning itself. The king orders the ten canons to the fire, even Lisoius, the precentor of the cathedral, whom the king had once loved for his apparent sanctity, continuing the development of the trope of the Devil as an angel of light. Rather than fearing their sentence, the canons claim that the fire will not harm them. Their boastful promise is essential. To an audience, these canons may still seem like holy men. There must be a test that reveals them for what they are, and their promise to leave the flames unscathed provides just this necessary proof.[36] Laughing as they are tied to the stake, the men are "without delay completely reduced to ashes." Their destruction is so complete it is miraculous as not even "the remains of their bones can be found."[37] The heretics have failed the test, or ordeal, that they themselves volunteered to undertake. The notion of an ordeal through flame for the heretics at Orleans will return in the descriptions offered by other writers, particularly Andreas of Fleury.[38] The heretics are, through their very susceptibility to fire, identified as members of the Devil's community, with a common destiny in fire awaiting it.

The logic underlying Ademar's account of the affair at Orleans had at its heart the clear articulation of oppositional eschatological communities, and the need to demarcate between the two as much as possible in the present. The heretics were confirmed as devoted members of the community opposed to the Church. In the common figurative understanding of the Church as Noah's Ark, they were those who refused to board the ship, preferring to perish outside it. Nonetheless, for all appearances in the present world they had seemed to be aboard and their actual status had be clarified for the safety of others. The dangerous mixture of the City of God and the Earthly City needed to be filtered, making those who remained a faithful part of a well-ordered Christian society clearly separate from those who were not progressing toward the same ultimate destiny.

This drive to separate the Christian community from its opposites, as both a prefiguration and an anticipation of the eschaton, appears in confrontations with Jews and Muslims elsewhere in the *Chronicon*. In the third book, the bishop of Limoges commands the city's Jews either to convert or to leave the city. After a month, "only three or four" Jews convert, with the others preferring flight to other places.[39] In this action, not only is the Christian community of the city rendered homogenous, but also the eventual conversion at the eschaton of some of the Jews to the truth of Christianity is prefigured.[40] Just before the expulsion of the Jews from Limoges, Ademar recounts the destruction of the Church of the Holy Sepulcher in Jerusalem at the instigation of a strange alliance between the Jews of the West and the Muslims of Spain. At their suggestion, the caliph orders the destruction of the Holy Sepulcher and the forced conversion of the Christians in his domains, similar to the bishop of Limoges's demand to the Jews of his city. The remains of those Christians who die in this persecution as martyrs work miracles, and so too do the remains of the Holy Sepulcher. While the Muslims destroy most of the building, they find that they cannot destroy its most sacred heart. The caliph's servants "heap copious fire" on the stone of the monument, but "it remains immobile and solid like adamant."[41] After a vast famine ravages the Muslim lands as punishment, the caliph himself is captured by his enemies and with his "belly cut open and his intestines pulled out, casts his impious soul into Hell."[42]

In the story of the destruction of the Holy Sepulcher, the binary division of the world clearly articulates itself. Jews and Spanish Muslims are the closest and most intermingled enemies of Christian society that can be found, and their collusion with other non-Christian powers farther afield appears to underscore the essential unity of all opposition to Christendom. At the end, all this opposition is doomed and will be consigned like the caliph to the prison of Hell; in contrast, the Christian faithful will literally be reborn to glory from their remains at the Resurrection. The martyrs and the Sepulcher are united in their ultimate resistance to the forces of destruction like the relics of the saints, and this resistance contrasts remarkably with the fate awaiting the wicked.[43]

Ralph Glaber: Renewal, Division, and Apocalypse in Miniature

The account of the affair at Orleans written by Ralph Glaber in his *Histories* is not generally held to be a very accurate account of the actual events. His version does not appear to be derived from a particularly well-informed source, and has been discounted by a number of experts as a source for the real goings on at Orleans in 1022.[44] However, Glaber's description of the heresy, the heretics, and their punishment can reveal a great deal about what the heresy at Orleans meant to near-contemporaries. In particular, his story illustrates how the episode at Orleans took part in the drawing of boundaries between Christian society and all of those excluded from it. In the process of establishing this separation between an assertive *Christianitas* and its enemies, these enemies are associated in their most spectacular incarnations with fire as both punishment and destiny.

Glaber's personality has in large part defined historians' approach to him and his work. Born around the year 980, Glaber lived as a monk at an impressive number of monasteries, including Cluny. Leaving one house due to his apparently querulous nature, he always found himself welcomed at another due to his literary talents. He likely wrote the majority of his *Histories* in the 1030s at Saint-Germain d'Auxerre, where he died around 1046. Once hailed as a nearly hysterical harbinger of the millennium, this appraisal of his state of mind has cooled. Rather than seeing him as a proponent of an immediate apocalypse, many modern scholars, such as John France, now believe that the "anxiety and tension" so evident in his writing arises not from the expectation of the imminent end of the world but rather an awareness of the transformations in motion all around him, particularly the assertion of the Latin world as a great power.[45] One result of this necessary reappraisal has been a certain embarrassment about the discussion of apocalyptic themes in his work.[46]

While the notion of a hysterical, millennialist Glaber is outmoded, the importance in his work of the apocalypse and its anticipation cannot be ignored. Richard Landes, for example, argues that Glaber was perfectly capable of realizing he lived in a time of great changes while at the same time associating these changes with the millennium and thoughts of the eventual end of the world, whenever it might be.[47] In this appraisal, Glaber took the year 1000 "as a turning point in history" and "a new dawn for Christendom," while trying to make sense of his earlier apocalyptic expectations for that date.[48] Christian renewal and self-assertion can still have room in it for the apocalyptic.

The heresy in Orleans has an important role to play in the story of Christian renewal Glaber presents in his *Histories*, and this role becomes clearer through a consideration of the episode's context in the larger work. In the second book, Glaber connects the rise of heresy to the loosing of the Devil foretold in Revelation 20:2–3, and hints that some of the heretical followers of Vilgard of Ravenna were burned.[49] Glaber places the rise of the Devil and his heretics in a larger context when, after a gloomy and eschatologically charged second book, he apparently changes his tone in book three, offering one of the most famous appraisals of the emergent piety and wealth of the Christian West in the early eleventh century: "Just before the third year of the millennium, throughout the whole world, but most especially in Italy and Gaul, men began to reconstruct churches. . . . It was as if the whole world were shaking itself free, shrugging off the burden of the past, and cladding itself everywhere in a white mantle of churches."[50] Select parts of the past, however, took a prominent place in this renewed world. In particular, relics of the saints began to come to light around this time in enormous numbers, "as though the saints had been waiting for a brilliant resurrection."[51] Like a mirror of the end of the world, the events of Glaber's time galvanize the Church and the hopes of its faithful members, but this articulation of the Church triumphant brings its opposite with it.

The renewal of the faithful brings with it a surge of opposition. Glaber paves the way for this opposition right after his description of the reappearance of the saints' relics. In the city of Sens, where these discoveries began, a series of misfortunes occur as a result of the worldly greed that arises from the great wealth the new relics caused: "As so often happens when something good occurs which at the start is good for men, the vice of cupidity flourishes and in the usual way disaster strikes."[52] This disaster takes the shape of Ray-nard, "the Judaizer," the new count of Sens. Glaber gave him this name from the unusual favor he supposedly showed to the Jews. In addition to question-able friendships, Raynard proves himself to be an enemy to the people he rules. Eventually, the king takes action against the Judaizing count, seizing the city and "destroying quite a large part of it by fire."[53]

The opposition to the renewed Christian world intensifies in the form of an old enemy: the Jews themselves. After the account of Raynard the Juda-izer, Glaber's readers are already well prepared to associate Jews with the forces against which the renewed world articulates itself. The Jews of Orleans, in-spired by the Devil, bribe a fugitive serf, named Robert, to travel as a pilgrim to Egypt. There he delivers Hebrew letters to the caliph, instructing him to destroy the Church of the Holy Sepulcher. This action inspires Christians the world over to take action against the Jews, but the most spectacular punish-ment awaits their Christian confederate. After his return and continued asso-ciation with the Jews, Robert is taken by the "royal officers" outside the city and burned alive.[54]

There is a clear symmetry between these two accounts that foreshadows the events to happen at Orleans. In both cases, a Christian departs from his own community in action and in spirit to join forces with the other outside it, leaving the community of the faithful for its opposite. This opposite com-munity literally consists of all non-Christian forces, Jewish and Muslim, in a natural alliance in service to the Devil. In response, the king of France takes action, either directly or through his officials, to punish the offender, and in both cases this punishment involves fire. The faithful are themselves defined through this removal and punishment of the unfaithful. The punishment of the wicked and the identification of the good are two sides of the same coin. Glaber's account of the heresy at Orleans follows this model exactly.

The motif of royal power suggests how the performance of justice with an eschatological coloring could also work in the service of the authorities that inflicted punishment. Burning malefactors on earth could draw a parallel be-tween the earthly authority giving the command and the God who also uti-lized fire as a form of punishment. As Philippa C. Maddern has argued, when the world is viewed through a paradigm in which God has ordained certain expressions of violence as if they were forces of nature, types of violence per-formed by actors "in a right relationship with authority" are legitimized so much that they are "not simply just but justifying."[55] In an eleventh-century atmosphere colored by a "craving for order" in response to the erosion of old authorities, the performance of a type of justice that drew a direct line between God and king would have been most welcome.[56] Robert's actions could, likewise, fit neatly into the tradition of support for and authority over the Church in France exercised by the Carolingians and earlier Capetians.[57] It is in this atmosphere that the burning of heretics by the secular arm appears in Glaber's work: as the action of an authority, defined by its potential for violence, in contrast to an ecclesiastical authority in need of its strength. Like the Peace Movements, in this case the use of force is in service to the wider Christian community; it is divine.

Glaber's description of the heresy has at its heart the division of humanity into two groups based on the actions of this life. In Glaber's account, the origin and nature of the heresy is very similar to that found in Ademar. The founder is an Italian woman, who could seduce both laymen and high-ranking clergy by her lies.[58] King Robert learns of the heresy and calls the leading heretics, Herbert and Lisoius, before him and they explain the basic attributes of their doctrine. Glaber's narrative displays its unique traits in a lengthy refutation of the heresy that follows the initial setup. In the eyes of some modern readers, this refutation seems to run out of control, away from the matter at hand into general doctrinal, theological, and anthropological reflections. These reflections, however, have a point. Glaber emphasizes first the necessity of heresy. Its existence, following the words of Paul (1 Cor. 11:19), is a kind of test that will prove the faithful.[59] Mankind alone has the opportunity to suffer this ordeal due to its middle position as a being of both flesh and spirit, high and low, which can choose to incline either toward God or downward away from him. Those who make the choice to diverge from God and incline away from him have a role to play for the faithful, as they "serve as a warning to those who stick to the narrow path of righteousness."[60] The existence of heretics, and especially their description to audiences, helps to define the faithful.

The ultimate fate of the faithless, against whom the faithful can define themselves, is eternal torment. Again, alone of all animals mankind has the choice between two extremes. Just as he can incline toward or away from the spirit that is his maker, so too can he enjoy eternal happiness or eternal agony. As Glaber explains, "For he alone before all other living things is able to obtain the blessedness of eternity, but beyond him no corporeal animal will feel the eternal punishment of his own mistakes and shame."[61] Eternal blessedness assimilates the believer to God through the restoration of the divine image inherent in humanity. Conversely, those who make the active choice to forsake this likeness are rendered "worse than animals" through their eternal separation from their maker and their model.[62] Indeed, all the heresies and the perverse sects on the earth make this choice in the face of God's incarnation as Jesus Christ. If they do not convert, their fate will be so terrible it would be better if they had "not existed."[63]

Only when this lengthy explanation of the significance of division is finished does Glaber resume the story of the actual heretics at Orleans, and it is an illustration of the points he has made above. The king makes every effort possible to make them return to the faith, including showing them the large pyre constructed outside the city, but the heretics are unmoved and do not fear the flames. Thirteen willingly go into the fire, but once they are set alight, their tone changes immediately. While they burn before their audience, the heretics declare their errors and proclaim that they will suffer both "a temporal and an eternal retribution."[64] Onlookers, moved to pity by their cries, tried to pull them from the flames, but the "avenging flame consumed them and reduced them straight away to dust."[65]

In Glaber's description, it is almost as if this world and the next, or the current moment and the end of the world, briefly overlap in the immolation of these heretics. As they burned, the heretics reversed all their positions, reifying all of the ideas they had challenged and rendering their expulsion from the society of the living also a reaffirmation of the central tenets of the united Christian society which they had challenged. The burning of these heretics takes its place alongside the "white mantle of churches" in the context of Glaber's renewal of the Christian world. Indeed, just as the sacralization of the world and the quasi-resurrection of the saints foreshadow the blessedness to come, so too does the fate of the heretics at Orleans foreshadow the damnation of those outside the Church or the sacralized world. If the apocalypse failed to occur in 1000 or 1033, it could at least be played out in miniature through the events at Orleans.

The burnings at Orleans have an especially direct meaning for Glaber in contrast to some other examples of burning alive in the *Histories*. He mentions in passing the burning of many heretics at Monteforte, who worshiped idols like pagans and made vain sacrifices like Jews.[66] Elsewhere, Glaber describes that during the famine of 1033 three people were burned alive for the crime of cannibalism.[67] The last of these was a wild man near Mâcon, who ate passersby, and was burned alive by the count of Mâcon after he was found with forty-eight severed heads. Glaber states that he watched this execution himself.[68] While Glaber comments on the horror of these actions, nothing like his refutation of the heresy at Orleans suggesting the penalty of damnation for a life lived poorly accompanies these episodes.

In different episodes, Glaber describes burning alive as both an emulation of Hell and also a horrific punishment utilized in response to horrific crimes. He constructs the punishment that awaited the serf who betrayed all of Christendom in the destruction of the Holy Sepulcher as a parallel to the burnings at Orleans. The fate of the cannibals, in contrast, appears to demonstrate a less infernally inflected use of burning alive as a punishment. Nevertheless, Glaber's own experience of the burning of living human beings arose in part from witnessing the punishment of one of these cannibals, the wild man of Mâcon. It is hard to imagine that his memory of the wild man did not color his thoughts regarding the earlier burnings at Orleans, which he did not see.

Andreas of Fleury: Present Fires and Eternal Fires

While Andreas of Fleury wrote his account of the heresy at Orleans at some distance from the actual events, there is good reason to suspect that his may be an eyewitness account. Andreas could very well have been a member of the entourage of Gauzlin, the abbot of Fleury, who was present at the synod and execution in 1022.[69] Even if Andreas was not present, his account is at the most secondhand, as he doubtless consulted with those who had been with the abbot when he wrote the *Life of Gauzlin* sometime later.

Andreas of Fleury actually wrote his story of the burnings at Orleans twice. The two versions are largely identical, but their different endings illustrate the clear alignment in Andreas's mind between the fires of earthly execution and the eternal fires of Hell. His first account of the affair appears in the *Miracula Sancti Benedicti* (*Miracles of Saint Benedict*) written between 1041 and 1043.[70] As an introduction to a vision of Benedict seen by one of his brethren, Andreas recounts the heresy at Orleans. He outlines the heretics' doctrines, particularly their apparent opposition to the mediating role of the institutional Church on earth. When he comes to their actual punishment he states: "The venerable prelate, Gauzlin, turning his attention to the matter came to a place in Orleans with the wiser men of Fleury, and with the enemies convicted by the testimony of the divine books, they were ordered by the above-said king to be handed over to the fire."[71] Following this brief account, Andreas then recounts the aforementioned vision.

One of the monks at Fleury saw in a vision at night an illustration of both the threat posed by the heretics and their infernal punishment. The brother watched the heretics emerge from the latrines, as Andreas explains, "a fitting lodging for their merits."[72] Almost immediately, the heretics rushed down in an attack on the dormitory filled with the sleeping monks. The heretics inspected the cots "one by one" until St. Benedict came on them from the direction of the monastery's church.[73] Wielding a staff, the saint drove them all to the north gate, where a pack of demons waited to drag them to fitting torments. Andreas concludes by observing that this episode reveals how potent Saint Benedict is in the defense of his monks.[74]

Andreas's second, and more familiar, account of the heretics at Orleans is in his *Life of Gauzlin*, composed around 1042. In the conclusion to that version he makes one very significant addition.[75] He largely recopies his description of the heretics from the *Miracles of Saint Benedict*, including his description of their deaths at the hands of the king, but in the place of the earlier vision he adds just one clause: "They were ordered by the above-said king to be handed over to the fire *in order to be received by the everlasting fires*."[76] The drama found in the nighttime vision of the monk of Fleury, in this retelling, is found in the spectacle of the execution itself.

The handing over of the heretics to their due punishments in the Other World, seen in greater detail through a vision by the monk at Fleury, is here signified through the flames of execution alone. In Andreas's second telling, the flames used to punish unrepentant heretics are a worldly extension of the fires of Hell. Like the emergence of the heretics from the latrines in his brother's vision, or the punishments to which a multitude of demons takes them after they are expelled by a saint, execution by fire fits their crimes. It prefigures their ultimate punishment both immediately after death and for eternity in the company of the rest of the damned in Hell.

Gauzlin's statement of faith, which follows the description of the execution, explains that the damnation of these heretics is the logical outcome of their choices. Andreas writes out the profession of faith which Gauzlin recited at the synod in detail. It lays out an orthodox understanding of the Trinity, the Incarnation, the Resurrection, the origin of sin, and the remission of sin. The profession ends with the statement: "I confess that outside of the Catholic Church no one is saved."[77] Andreas's account repeats the now familiar logic that one is either a member of the one Christian community or its opposite. Membership in one or the other community will have major eschatological repercussions as those within the Church have the potential of salvation, while those outside do not. The heretics have chosen to separate themselves and their damnation appears almost certain as a result; of course, this damnation will involve fire.

Thomas Head has remarked on the ways that the fires of execution in Andreas's accounts of the heresy at Orleans functioned as "an extension of the fires of Hell," and may very well be likened to Gauzlin's use of the ordeal by fire to test dubious relics.[78] Head has tracked accounts, beginning in the late tenth century, of relics being exposed to sources of heat, like hot coals, to test their authenticity. Following the words of Paul 1 Corinthians 3:13 that "fire shall try every man's work," those who utilized this technique expected the bodies and personal effects of the saints to prove invulnerable to fire.[79] Gauzlin likely heard about this kind of test while at Monte Cassino and used it himself to test a piece of Christ's shroud shortly before the synod at Orleans.[80]

Head's suggestion of a basic similarity between the ordeal through fire and execution through fire brings new significance to the boasts put in the mouths of the heretics by Ademar and Glaber. In both their accounts, the heretics initially have no fear of the flames, willingly entering them and even laughing as they are tied to the pyre, and in both cases this confidence is revealed as illusory when the heretics burn away to nothing. The heretical canons, "who appeared more religious than the others," attempted to prove themselves through fire, just as Abbot Gauzlin proved the cloth of Christ's shroud, or the stone on the Holy Sepulcher proved itself to the caliph's servants.[81] In all of these accounts, a shared assumption arises: objects and people associated with divine power have a particular resilience against fire, while the wicked have a pronounced susceptibility to it.

Belief in the fire that would try the work of every man gave the burning of living human beings the potential to be always both justice and prefiguration for its witnesses. As Mitchell B. Merback observes for a much later period, the audience at such an execution would have the opportunity to reflect on their own likely encounter with fire in either the form of the flames of purgation or the flames of Hell.[82] Since fire would try the works of every man at the end of time, the majority of medieval people could expect to burn someday. If Andreas of Fleury did in fact watch the executions in 1022, he saw them as a literal handing-off between two linked fires: the temporary fires of this world and the eternal fires of the next. Beyond a simple exchange, the agony of the heretics provided an illustration of the pains awaiting the sinful in the Other World. While the faithful could look forward to their works being tried by fire in a test that would have a finite duration, the damned would have no such release. The goal was to pass through the possibility of destruction into a rebirth, but the possibility of a lasting death always remained.[83] The heretics at Orleans, in the opinion of Andreas of Fleury, presented just such an example of destruction, and in the manner of their deaths Hell appeared, if only for a brief time, to the eyes of the living.

Paul of St. Père de Chartres

The account of the heresy offered by Paul of St. Père is the fullest of the five and the most cited in studies of medieval heresy. Paul, a monk at St. Père de Chartres, wrote his account in the course of reconstructing the cartulary of his house after a fire in 1078.[84] It elaborates considerably on the uncovering of the heresy and the lurid details of the group's nocturnal rituals. In the development of both of these points, Paul utilizes and amplifies prominent themes found in the earlier accounts of events. In particular, the articulation of the heresy as an image in reverse of the Christian community plays a central role in Paul's presentation.

The heresy is revealed through the undercover work of a knight named Arefast. After hearing through a friend of the doctrines promoted by Stephen and Lisois, Arefast informs his lord, Richard of Normandy, of the heretics' existence. Alarmed, Richard forwards the information to the king who commands Arefast to infiltrate the organization. As he prepares for his assignment, Arefast seeks out spiritual advice so that he can avoid falling prey to the heretics' arguments. A "certain wise cleric" named Ebrard gives him the following advice: "Daily he should devoutly enter the church first thing in the morning to ask for the help of the All-Powerful. He should bow in prayer and fortify himself with the sacred communion of the body and blood of Christ. Then, protected by the sign of the cross, he should proceed to listen to the heretical depravity. He should contradict none of the things that he may hear from them, but with the feigned expression of a student he should quietly tuck away everything in his heart."[85] Thus fortified, Arefast was able to infiltrate the heretics' circle and earn their trust. In short order Arefast informs the king that the trap is prepared, and King Robert calls a synod. As Paul's account develops, Arefast's daily communion, as well as his adoption of a misleading appearance, will develop into important counterpoints to the heretics' own practices.

After briefly setting the stage of the confrontation with the heretics at the synod, Paul pauses to describe the heretics' anticommunion. This meal, which they called "celestial," is made from the ashes of dead children, as in the account of Ademar, but here the tale is more lurid. The heretics have their meetings in a house. Before they begin, they summon a demon by invoking demonic names. After it appears in the form of an animal, they extinguish the lights and have sex with the nearest woman at hand without respect for status or kinship. If a child results from this union, it is thrown into a fire "in the manner of the pagans" and burned to ashes.[86] They venerate these ashes just as "Christian religiosity ought to guard the body of Christ, to be given to the sick about to leave this world as the viaticum."[87]

The ashes of these dead children bond the heretics together, just as Christian communion binds the Christian community together with its God, but this heretical communion celebrates only death. Paul states that these ashes have "such a great power of diabolic deception" in them that whoever eats of them "can scarcely ever after direct the pace of his mind away from that heresy to the way of truth."[88] Not only does this ritual establish the heretics as the members of a community in opposition to Christian society, but it reveals the essentially hollow and deadly nature of that oppositional community. In the place of the meal that gives life and unites human beings with their God, the heretics eat only ashes; rather than life, they eat worldly death.

In light of the heretics' "celestial" food, Arefast's daily communion takes on the trappings of an antidote that reaffirms his membership in the Christian community. Immersed in the enemies of Christian society, Arefast is daily reunited with the larger body of faithful Christian believers. It is through the opposition of these two meals that the basic opposition of the heretics and orthodoxy, or the body of Christ on earth and the company of the Devil, appears.[89] Paul's account vividly articulates the logic of two binary communities that has proven so important to the other historiographers of the same events. Arefast's deception, likewise, acts as a counterpoint to the heretic's own deception. While the demonically aligned fraud of the heretics does not hold up under scrutiny, Arefast finds himself perfectly capable of fooling them. Even in the game of false appearances, so often associated with the demonic as an angel of light, the power of God and of His servants triumphs.

The heretics, in choosing to remove themselves from the Church as the vehicle of human salvation, place themselves within the Devil's community and subject themselves to the torments that this community will endure. When they confirm their beliefs at the synod, Paul remarks that the heretics "have a mansion prepared with the Devil in Hell."[90] As if in response to this conclusion, the heretics are taken out of the Christian city of Orleans and burned alive in a "large cottage." In this method of execution one can see their dwelling with the Devil reified and performed. The heretics are literally removed from the Christian community and placed in a house to burn together.[91] Two of the condemned, a cleric and a nun, are saved when they repent at the last minute.[92] The last-minute reprieve given to these two people underscores that burning with the Devil in Hell rests on their choices made in life. The punishment handed out by the king to these heretics appears completely appropriate as long as they go to their deaths shouting their separation from the rest of the community, a separation which can mean nothing other than a determination to possess a mansion with the Devil in Hell. If, however, they rejoin the body of believers, as the cleric and the nun did by repenting, burning them alive no longer fits, because their particular eschatological destiny becomes just as obscure as that of any other Christian.

In the accounts of the heresy at Orleans, fire as the punishment and destination of individuals placed outside of Christian society constitutes a central message. The separation of the heretics from the true Church results in their membership in its demonic counterpart. Outside, of the Church as the City of God, Noah's Ark, or Christ's body, there is only the community of the Devil. This infernal community counts heretics, Muslims, and Jews among its members, and as Christendom grows so too do the assaults of these spiritually united enemies. The punishments of Hell await this opposition and events in this world can and do foreshadow this ultimate justice and retribution.

The logic these sources use in the descriptions of the heresy at Orleans and its spectacular punishment articulates a fundamental division of great importance. This division is the separation of humanity into two major communities based on expected fates after death and at the end of time. Members of the Christian Church in a right relationship to its doctrines and authorities constitute one of these bodies, while all non-Christians or unorthodox Christians make up the other. In the presentation offered by the authors of these sources, the possibility of salvation is extended only to the former rather than the latter. For the authors who recorded events at Orleans in 1022, Hell offered a paradigm of exclusion based on righteous punishment and segregation, which could be brought to bear on human events in the current world. The consignment of the heretics to a fire that visibly enacted the punishments promised at the hands of God constituted one way in which medieval culture represented itself.[93] This kind of representation serves as one example of a case where the more outlandish claims found in texts regarding heresy have an important story to tell. Furthermore, such an enactment of the final fate of the dammed was useful in the present. As Glaber argued in his account of the heresy at Orleans, witnessing the fate of those who chose to depart from the Church could function as a warning for others, a negative example against which they could fashion themselves.[94] As the Apostle Paul said, "There must be heresies" so that those "who are approved may be made manifest among you."[95]

In later centuries, when burnings for heresy would become more common and even customary, the meanings found in these sources at the tradition's point of origin by contemporary historians provided an important foundation for future representations. Looking to the future, one remarkable aspect of the fires glimpsed at Orleans is their almost completely infernal signification. These fires tested claims of sanctity and punished those who failed forever. There was no element of redemption through suffering or contrition ascribed to them. The idea that fire could be reformative and perhaps even redeeming for those it burned became apparent only in descriptions of the executions of supposed heretics from later centuries.

Following the executions at Orleans, there was a brief spate of recorded confrontations with heresy that involved execution, or the threat of execution, in the eleventh century. As explored in the last chapter, the threats made to supposed heretics and the punishments handed out to them aroused mixed feelings among clerical authorities. At the synod of Arras in 1025 Gerard of Cambrai confronted a group of heretics who did not end up dying. In this confrontation, Gerard employed logic that was much the same as that expressed in the sources for the execution at Orleans a few years earlier. While the heretics at Arras were peacefully reconciled with orthodox doctrines and episcopal authority, they were threatened with excommunication and with damnation as a result of this excommunication if they died in that state.[96] The Arras story ends with the heretics' repentance and reentry into the Christian camp; the story of Orleans features the reintegration of only a few, if any, of the heretics.[97] While the death toll is different in these two cases, the logic of inclusion and exclusion as well as the consequences of this inclusion or exclusion are the same.

After the early executions at Orleans, Milan, and Goslar, executions for heresy did not attract enough attention from authors to receive long and detailed descriptions until the mid-twelfth century. Among these twelfth-century sources is a group from the Rhineland near Cologne of great importance for medieval discourses regarding heresy. In the 1140s and again in the 1160s, this region's authorities burned groups of heretics after a series of remarkable confrontations. It is from the sources associated with these events that the term Cathar arose as a name applied to medieval heretics, and the myriad meanings and uses that authors of these sources found in these heretics in the Rhineland witness a significant development from the simpler messages and themes present in the sources for the first medieval burning of heretics at Orleans.

CHAPTER 4

Likeness in Difference
Three Burnings in the Twelfth-Century Rhineland

Eckbert of Schönau, the first medieval author to describe a heretical sect who called themselves "Cathars," assured his Catholic readers that they, too, one day would burn. This burning would be merciful, and it would come after death, consuming terrestrial desires and ushering the faithful into God's own city. Eckbert argued that John the Baptist described these purgatorial fires when he spoke of a coming baptism with the Holy Spirit and with fire. Good Catholics could find evidence for his interpretation by considering the recent burning of heretics at Cologne. The Cathars, he explained, did not understand John's meaning and took a reference to a spiritual fire literally. If they were correct, they surely should not have burned but instead become one with the Spirit. Those who saw them die, however, watched them pass from terrestrial to eternal fires.[1] As Eckbert described them, these two baptisms in fire explained their difference through their likeness.

A series of burnings occurred in and around Cologne in the mid-twelfth century separated by a span of about twenty years, of which Eckbert's baptism in fire was one. The first occurred in 1143 or 1144 and involved the deaths of three people. The second, in 1147 or 1148, saw two burned to death. The third, in 1163, featured the deaths of up to six. The accounts of these burnings illustrate the meanings and possibilities medieval authors saw in executions by fire, and in their treatments of these events, spanning into the thirteenth century, medieval historians and clerics developed a strikingly consistent set of basic themes and methods of interpretation, highlighting the deep connections between processes of exclusion and inclusion and the profound usefulness of the profane to the sacred.

In the sources for the burnings at Cologne, the "boundaries of the established community" are drawn through the removal of the heretic.[2] My reading of the sources for these events at Cologne takes the form of a "hermeneutic circle," a kind of dynamic play that allows the "knower to assimilate the known." The ultimate focus of this drama is not the spectacle but rather the spectator.[3] The recording of these executions invokes a mimetic process that focuses, by necessity, on one side of a relationship, returning again and again to the mind and identity of the viewer.[4] In this tautology, human bonding is effected through a discourse of intimate hatred and love, and the sources themselves note how strangely close the two emotions become. In its strongest expression, this way of reading takes expulsion enacted in a moment of mutual resemblance between opposites as an opportunity for integration.

The war on heresy in the Rhineland took place in an atmosphere marked by confusions and mixtures of categories in which orthodox identity was itself at stake. In the eyes of many contemporaries, the clergy of Cologne were mired in corruption of many kinds, such as the "heresy" of simony, the soul-deadening pursuit and accumulation of material wealth, and a crippling entwinement with secular politics.[5] The troubling mixture of Church and world involved both bishops who presided over the see during the executions examined here. Arnold I, archbishop from 1138–51, was suspended for simony by Eugene III in 1149. Rainald of Dassel, archbishop from 1159–67, was chancellor to Frederick Barbarossa during his long struggle with Alexander III, and as a consequence was excommunicated by the Roman pontiff in 1163.[6] Depending on one's side in these conflicts, the legitimacy of established authority itself was often in question.[7]

In this climate of dissatisfaction with the established clergy, the motives attributed to orthodox reformers and supposed heretics were largely the same. Reports of a widespread heretical infection appear with some regularity in the mid-twelfth century in an area stretching from Cologne and Bonn in the east to Ypres, Lille, and Arras in the west and to Nevers in the south; however, the number of supposed heretics does not seem to have ever been very large.[8] These heretics often appear, especially in the Rhineland, linked to post-Gregorian dissident groups, frustrated with the continued corruption of the ecclesiastical hierarchy.[9] Some of these often-frustrated reformers found accommodation within a developing orthodoxy as licit reformers while others did not.[10] It is only in the process of accommodation that a decisive separation between the two was made, and the strong creation of such a separation helped the process of accommodation along. As Uwe Brunn has decisively shown, reformers in the twelfth-century Rhineland who found their place within the ecclesiastical hierarchy were quite eager to describe other would-be reformers as heretics and to ascribe a vast range of theological beliefs and religious practices to them that they very likely lacked.[11] In portraying heretical reformers in these ways, orthodox reformers assured established authorities that their would-be reforms belonged within the larger body of the Church, unlike so-called heretics from whom they strove to be differentiated. In summary, there is very little space between the reformer and the heretic; often it is no more than a name.

The authors of many of the accounts of the mid-twelfth-century burnings in the Rhineland were reformers. Men and women like Eberwin of Steinfeld, Bernard of Clairvaux, Elisabeth of Schönau and her brother Eckbert, and Hildegard of Bingen desired to effect the regeneration of "the moral life of the clergy."[12] Finding a resolution to the coexistence of the seemingly incompatible opposition between sacred and profane, reform and revolution, was central to this regeneration, and these authors' accounts of the immolation of living heretics enact a similar synthesis of incompatible positions and assertions.

From the point of view offered by orthodox activists, heretics acted as a dark mirror of licit ecclesiastical reform, illustrating the bounds beyond which licit reform could not pass and leaving themselves clearly on the side of orthodoxy. Heretics supposedly entered into the moral vacuum created by a corrupt religious hierarchy, offering criticisms of the established leadership very similar to the reformers' own.[13] What supposed heretics did with these criticisms was different and they failed to find a point of rapprochement with the established Church. The recurrent errors ascribed to these dissidents—denial of the Eucharist, baptism, marriage, and prayers for the dead—are all concerned with the social functions of the Church hierarchy in the lives of the laity.[14] These heretics, at least as they were presented by Catholic authors, lived what they regarded as an apostolic life, eschewing property and the delights of the flesh. This type of life would eventually find, perhaps, its fullest orthodox accommodation in the form of the mendicant friars, representing what Andrew Roach has called the use of "nails to drive out nails."[15] This image illuminates a reality that was far more complicated than the salubrious imitation of already existing heresy by a newly attentive orthodoxy. It can instead describe a process in which individuals who are fundamentally alike identify and enact essential differences between one another through acts of expulsion. It can describe the development of a subtly altered orthodox identity itself.

Little Foxes with Burning Tails: Eberwin of Steinfeld and Bernard of Clairvaux on the Burnings of 1143

In the 1140s two groups of heretics were burned in or near Cologne and Bonn. Our two main sources likely refer to two separate incidents in Bonn in 1143 and in Cologne in 1147 or 1148; however, past scholarship has most often taken both sources to refer to the same underlying incident.[16] One source locates the execution at Cologne and its description bears strong similarities to earlier events at Milan over a century earlier. The other account specifies that the burning occurred at Bonn after a considerably different process. Both Milan in 1028 and Cologne in the 1140s were mob actions, in which a group of prisoners were taken by a group of laymen against the wishes of the clergy and given an immediate choice between conversion and death. In contrast, the execution at Bonn involved a process that would become familiar: the heretics were first identified by an ecclesiastical authority and then later killed by a secular one. The identification of the heretics came about through a somewhat organized judicial process in the form of an ordeal, and once identified they were executed by a secular ruler only after they refused to believe the Catholic faith.

The *Annales Brunwilarenses* records that in 1143 "an indictment was made against heretics in the Church of St. Peter at Cologne in the presence of Archbishop Arnold."[17] Many of the accused, after being captured and put in chains, purged themselves through the ordeal of water.[18] Others, however, fled, "troubled by their guilt." At Bonn, Count Otto presided over the burning of three of these after they refused to convert, "preferring to die rather than to believe the holy Catholic faith."[19] This sequence of events loosely followed a model that would become a normal sequence for accusations of heresy resulting in an execution for the later Middle Ages.

Eberwin of Steinfeld provides his account of the 1147–48 executions at Cologne in a letter addressed to St. Bernard of Clairvaux.[20] Recent scholarship has clarified our image of Eberwin and his place in the reforming discourses of his era. Eberwin was the first provost of the Premonstratensian canons at Steinfeld. His house, which took the place of an older Benedictine establishment, was the product of a reforming zeal that had been accommodated to the structures of the institutional Church.[21] The Premonstratensians originated in the preaching of the hermit Norbert of Xanten, who had been a fierce proponent of apostolic poverty and the inclusion of women in the apostolic life. In becoming an order within the Church as institution, some of his followers had compromised on poverty and on the inclusion of women in ways that broke apart the initial movement. As both Brunn and R. I. Moore have suggested, the picture Eberwin paints of his heretical enemies has many unaccommodated elements of Norbert's reform in it, and it is easy to see followers of Norbert of Xanten, who refused to compromise, among the supposed heretics Eberwin confronted.[22]

Eberwin and Bernard were well acquainted, and the former accompanied the latter on his journey to Germany in 1147.[23] Eberwin wrote to the abbot of Clairvaux requesting arguments and authorities from the Catholic faith against the heretics of his day that he believed were appearing "on every side" and "in every church." Reminding Bernard of the traditional exegesis of verse 2:15 from the Song of Songs: "Catch us the little foxes that destroy the vines," Eberwin suggested that just such a broadside against modern heresy would fit perfectly into Bernard's interest in the exegesis of the Song of Songs.[24]

Eberwin tells Bernard that recently a group of these modern heretics had been uncovered near Cologne. Some of these, once uncovered, readily returned to the Church, but two of them resisted. These men, a "bishop" and his companion, defended their views in a meeting of clerics and laymen that apparently included Eberwin himself. The two heretics used scriptural examples and quotations, drawn from the New Testament, in their defense. As Eberwin suggests, they felt that the debate was not going in their favor, and requested that they be given time to produce other members of their sect who could better argue their case. If these masters could be defeated, they would rejoin the Church, otherwise they preferred to die.

Rather than engage the heretics further in debate, the authorities admonished them for three days "to come back to their senses," but they steadfastly refused, and this refusal led to their fiery deaths. At this apparent impasse, Eberwin tells us, the laity intervened: "They were seized by the people, stirred up by a great zeal, placed into a fire and burned against our wishes."[25] As Eberwin describes it, these two heretics had multiple chances to come to their senses, but by holding out for three days they essentially signed their own death warrant. The number three recalls the advice of Titus 3:10–11, which enjoins the faithful to avoid the heretic after the first and second admonition.[26] One may wonder how the Christian faithful, in the intimate communities of the twelfth century, could avoid an unrepentant heretic outside of a violent expulsion. In fact, Henry II of England enacted just such an expulsion in 1166 when he branded a group of heretics on their foreheads and left them outside in the winter to die of exposure.[27] In this case, the question was resolved by a mob action that took the situation out of the clergy's hands.

The personal conduct of the two condemned men on the pyre disturbed Eberwin, recalling in his mind patterns of behavior associated with the ancient Christian martyrs. As Eberwin relates to Bernard: "And, what is more astonishing, they entered into and endured the torment of the flame not only calmly but with happiness. In these circumstances, Holy Father, if I were there with you I would like to know your explanation as to where a great firmness arises in these limbs of the Devil in their heresy such that can scarcely be found in the most devout in the faith of Christ."[28] Such composure befits only Christians, and members of the Devil's body should not be able to exhibit it. Eberwin suggests that in his mind he has difficulty imagining the current Christian faithful, perhaps including himself, conducting themselves so well in the face of death for their beliefs. Eberwin's discomfort is all the more pointed in light of the generally low opinion both he and Bernard shared of the secular clergy of Cologne, whom they denounced for soft living and corruption.[29]

In Eberwin's description of the heretics' deaths, the impression arises that he found two mutually exclusive genres colliding with each other, and that he asked Bernard to resolve the contradiction. The contradiction involved a terrifying confusion of categories. The heretics in their firmness had acted as Eberwin would wish saints to act. At the very moment of exclusion, where divisions should be logically most clear, the categories of Christian and heretic, sacred and profane, body of Christ and the body of the Devil have collapsed into each other. Eberwin's real request to Bernard is the reaffirmation of a system of classification by the rhetorical incarnation of a shared body of belief. Eberwin does not need to know that the two men murdered at Cologne were heretics. He follows the description of the heretics' deaths by a detailed list of their erroneous beliefs for Bernard to use as ammunition against those like them. What he needs is Bernard's eloquence in service of what he already knows. Bernard is here tasked with the curation of an assimilation between knower and known. This is a textual look in the mirror that will by necessity go beyond the actual doctrines supposedly espoused by the heretics themselves into a reaffirmation of the identity of Eberwin as Catholic reformer in the face of illicit reform.

Bernard's reply to Eberwin's letter, as well as to the problem of heresy more generally, took the form of his sixty-fifth and sixty-sixth sermons on the Song of Songs.[30] This response is carefully crafted to make the case that the heretics' composure on the pyre is not at all equivalent to the behavior of Christian martyrs. Indeed, it cannot be, because of its source. The heretics are outside of the Church, and by this exclusion they are, as Eberwin suggested, "limbs of the Devil." For both Bernard and Eberwin, the heretics fall under the image of "the little foxes that destroy the vines." On this exegetical stage, defined by negotiations between signs and symbols, the orthodox community can best articulate its advantage. The little foxes become lost in the gap between things and their symbols, or in the movement between sign and the signified, embodying the potential for misunderstanding in attempts to bridge the distance between God's speech and human hearers. In their error, they become symbols for the orthodox to read.

"What should we do with these foxes?" Bernard asks. In a line of logic filled with the need for exclusion backed with force, but adverse to outright slaughter, the abbot of Clairvaux argues that the heretics must be removed from the Church for the common good, but that this removal should not be accomplished through violence. If a heretic, once identified, remains obdurate, the Church has an obligation to remove him from its body, just as Jesus suggested that an offending eye, hand, or foot be removed.[31] A heretic allowed to remain in the Church is a poisonous element, turning the communion and fellowship of sharing Christ's body in the Eucharist into an opportunity for corruption. Their talk spreads like a cancer.[32] For this reason, Bernard states that he himself will reject a heretic after the first and second admonition "without hesitation," as suggested by Titus 3:10.[33]

In Bernard's view, these heretics are a tool of the Devil and each of their doctrines is actually carefully crafted to inflict maximum damage on the spiritual health of the community. These foxes work in secret, looking to work harm rather than win an open victory.[34] The heretics themselves do not know the origin of their doctrines because demons are the actual authors.[35] The rhetorical battle versus heresy is really a conflict with demonic wiles. What one could call demonic writing has a certain ironic way of dissolving under orthodox scrutiny. It is full of hypocrisies and double meanings that to an experienced exegete declare its true identity. For example, the heretics despise all things that result from copulation and do not eat meat. They hold all matter to be by nature polluted and unclean and so spit out the flesh that God has created for them. In fact, it is the heretics themselves who are spat out "by the body of Christ, which is the Church" because of their pollution.[36]

As a result of demonic creativity, it is impossible to respond to every possible error, and it is also pointless to engage intellectually with those who have been willingly under diabolic influence for extended periods. As Bernard argues, "These men are not to be convinced by logical reasoning, which they do not understand, nor prevailed on by references to authority, which they do not accept, nor can they be won over by persuasive arguments, for they have been subverted. This is indisputable, for they prefer death to conversion."[37] The utter perversion of the heretics makes them steadfast in their errors, and it is no wonder that they accept death, for they have in fact embraced eternal destruction. This destruction takes the form of an eternal punishment.

Those who join the demons by heading their arguments and being spat out by the body of Christ are doomed to burn. "The end of these men is destruction, fire awaits them at the last."[38] This fiery end has been prefigured in scripture, when Samson, in action against the Philistines, set fire to the tails of foxes.[39] The proper interpretation of the verse shows that their end is already written. The foxes, once identified, have one destiny. When the heretics burned at Cologne, they entered into the fire that was their ultimate destination.

Nevertheless, Bernard cannot endorse such a proactive damnation at human hands. This destiny in fire is God's plan, but men should not enact it prematurely. Bernard acknowledges that the people have attacked revealed heretics and in doing so "made new martyrs for the cause of Godless heresy." While he applauds the zeal, he does not recommend the action. Faith, says Bernard, is "a matter of persuasion, not of force."[40] Of course, since, as he has already argued, the heretics are beyond persuasion, an authority with the potential for violence must restrain them. Rather than allow the heretics to infect others, one "who bears not the sword in vain" should stand ready to punish a wrongdoer as a "servant of God."[41]

In the light of all these arguments, the heretics' conduct on the pyre that so disquieted Eberwin was not a sign of meritorious tenacity; rather, it was a demonic madness. Once the Devil has been admitted to the hearts of men, he takes possession. From there he can inspire men to harm or kill themselves, like Judas after the betrayal of the Lord.[42] Eberwin should not remember the burning at Cologne as a martyrdom, but rather as a suicide.[43] Bernard's explanations craft a logic for the event that makes the burning of these men into the burning of the Devil through effigy. The heretics' "bishop" and his associate were men who chose to make of themselves puppets held by the Devil's strings.

This account of the work of the Devil in heretics' hearts forms a parallel with Bernard's ideas regarding the workings of grace. Both involve a process that operates inside individuals through a greater force. This force inclines human beings in the direction indicated by their own will, growing far beyond the initial act of free consent.[44] For the faithful, the inward action by God facilitates the reparation of the divine image in humanity.[45] For the wicked, consent to the Devil allows wickedness to bloom and thrive within to the detriment of the divine grace that alone allows a human being to desire good, what Bernard calls *liberum consilium*. Reading Bernard's concept of grace, the impression arises that if the assimilation of others to God by preaching and argument required that they already be inhabited by the Holy Spirit, the replacement of this Spirit by the Devil, along with an individual's separation from the corporate structure through which grace could flow, rendered a return from wickedness almost impossibly difficult. As Bernard argues, for a person subverted by evil the regret felt in the flames of Hell is really the loss of the ability to enjoy self-indulgence, not repentance for the act of willing evil.[46] Logically, this same limitation would render purgatorial fire useless; those filled with the Devil can only burn in one way.[47]

The act of consent to the Devil deserves punishment, but it also renders the intentionally wicked into tools for God to try the faithful. Bernard explains that God makes of the rational but ill-willed creature "a rod of discipline which when his child has been corrected, he will cast into the fire as a useless twig."[48] What the will initiates, superhuman forces amplify and consummate in keeping with a predetermined purpose and narrative plan. In this formation, once individuals are consigned to the ranks of the truly wicked they are fashioned into symbols and lessons for the rest. In fact, when the orthodox identify one of the little foxes, this very identification comes about through the help of God through inner illumination or an outward sign that is itself interpreted by the illuminated mind.[49] In this way the recognition of a heretic by authority is self-justifying and an exercise in a fundamentally circular logic.[50]

In all the accounts for the burnings in 1143, the question of what to do with unrepentant heretics has been central. Bernard's question, "What do we do with these foxes?" echoes through all of them. First, how do we confirm our suspicions regarding the identity of possible heretics? In response, the sources offer a combination of conversation, ordeal, and divine illumination to answer this question. Second, once heretics are identified without doubt, what do we do? As strangers to the body of Christ, they are destined for damnation, but eschatological destiny does not grant license for immediate human action. As Bernard argues, we should not, as yet, light their tails on fire. As had occurred for centuries in Christian discourse, both Eberwin and Bernard express displeasure with immediate attempts to weed the fields of Western Christendom. Nonetheless, Bernard does articulate a logic that necessitates the use of violence—within limits.

The logic of demonic inspiration also subtly undermines one of the most persuasive elements of delay found in the Parable of the Wheat and the Weeds. In the interpretations of the parable that we have encountered up to now, if believers take immediate action against the wicked they deny these individuals the chance for redemption. Weeds can, with time, become wheat. Bernard's rhetoric does not deny this possibility, but it certainly minimizes it. Heretics are so conditioned by the Devil that it is not even worth one's time to argue with them. Since their redemption is so terribly unlikely, the ultimate punishment of damnation can be safely ascribed to them even while living as an eschatological destiny recognizable in the present for specific individuals. A delay in killing such condemned people takes on the air of a courtesy to God's prerogatives rather than a possibly redemptive act of Christian mercy.

To Bernard's question of what we should do with these foxes, I would suggest adding another: What should we make of these foxes? In the logic of suicide Barnard ascribes to them they become symbols to be read. The body of the heretic and its destruction signify the presence of the Devil. This presence takes root in the heart of a person like the meaning inside the form of a word. Whatever the body does should be read through our knowledge of the presence of this meaning and its foreknown relationship to the orthodox social body. The circle of interpretation and understanding is complete.

A Baptism in Fire: The Burnings at Cologne in 1163

The burnings at Cologne in 1163 and our sources for them hold a position of great historiographical importance in the study of medieval heresy. The Cathars as a named medieval heresy first appeared in these sources, and descriptions of supposed Cathars written later in the Middle Ages looked back to this first appearance. Our earliest sources for these burnings are a short description by Dietrich of Deutz, written very soon after the event, and even shorter identical notices in a number of annals. Influencing Dietrich's account are the ideas of Eckbert of Schönau, the brother of the famous female visionary Elisabeth of Schönau.[51] Eckbert discusses these executions in his "Thirteen Sermons against the Cathars," alternatively titled "Against the Heresies of the Cathars," written between 1163 and 1167.[52] After these rather immediate sources are a group of much later thirteenth-century accounts, including that of Caesarius of Heisterbach, which embroider and refine select elements of the event for deliberate rhetorical effect.

Scholars often associate the group destroyed in 1163 with the heretics uncovered at Cologne sixteen to twenty years earlier who so concerned Eberwin.[53] Some of their reported beliefs sound similar; however, there is good reason to be cautious. The earlier sources do not label the heretics as Cathars, and Bernard in fact stressed that they were not Manichaeans. The heretics in 1163, in contrast, are called Cathars and Manichaeans. The description of the Cathars and their beliefs offered by Eckbert of Schönau has been hugely influential in modern historiography regarding their supposed spread, and his treatise is often taken as the first systematic explication of the sect's beliefs.

A concern with the bravery shown by the condemned as they went to their deaths represents one point of continuity between the sources for the burnings in 1143 and 1163. This attention to the heretics' final moments again betrays some level of anxiety that observers might see the public execution of criminals as martyrdom. Like the earlier sermons offered by Bernard, the rhetorical strategy of the sources describing these executions attempts to undermine some possibilities, likening the heretics' embrace of death to suicide and damnation.

The annalistic sources from the twelfth century offer very little detail, recording that a group of heretics were burned in Cologne and that the conduct of one woman among them was remarkable. This woman "consigned herself headlong into the fire with no one forcing her."[54] The impression made by her behavior on the pyre runs through all the sources for this event even if it is not consistently associated with her or indeed with one individual heretic at all. This woman's action becomes an essential part of the larger messages regarding choice, baptism, and fire that this group of sources was particularly concerned to present.

Dietrich records that in August 1163 a group of "Cathars," consisting of six men, two women, and their leaders (heresiarchs) Arnold, Marsilius, and Theodoric, were detained in the city of Cologne. The group were "judged and anathematized" as heretics by the city's clerics. When they refused to return to the Catholic faith, the "judges and people of the city" burned them alive on "Jew Hill" near the Jewish cemetery. As they met their death, Dietrich records that the heretics' conduct was extraordinary: "They had made use of the Devil's inspiration in their way of life with such persistence that some of them even threw themselves into the furious flames."[55] For Dietrich, multiple heretics willingly met the flames rather than one woman.

This first version of the events at Cologne in 1163 involves now familiar themes, particularly the connection of the heretics to Jews and to the Devil, based on their freely made choices. This infernal connection is a logical outgrowth of their conscious decision to separate themselves from the Catholic faith. Their fate is one that they have chosen, in both this world and in the next. In this world they have every opportunity to return to the fold. Their refusal, even in the face of death, indicates their damnation, since dying as unrepentant heretics almost certainly precludes any possible entrance into Heaven. Even more dramatically, they chose to die, throwing themselves into the fire. If their allegiance was not enough to damn them, their suicide clearly is.

The description of their willing entry into the flames is revealing regarding their otherworldly fate. Dietrich says that they were so used and susceptible to the Devil's influence that they jumped into the fire. Like an athlete at the end of a race with the finish line in sight, they rush to their final destination. This end is Hell and its fires that they will share with the Devil and his angels. In characterizations like Dietrich's, in contrast to a Christian, who sets his eyes on the goal of Heaven, "forgetting those things that are behind," a heretic thinks only backward, fixed on his final damnation.[56] The heretics' rush into the fire functions to forestall and defuse other possibilities in their remarkable conduct on the pyre.

Inside Dietrich's account, it is easy for a modern eye to see suggestions of a different story regarding the heretics' composure at their deaths, suggestive not of damnation but rather of martyrdom. Like the burning at Cologne only twenty years before that so disturbed Eberwin of Steinfeld, the bravery of the heretics may have been genuinely moving to witnesses.[57] Condemned to death, members of this small community may have calmly walked into the flames, conducting themselves like the Christian martyrs of old. That reading, however, is deliberately denied by Dietrich's short text. Just as Bernard of Clairvaux suggested in reply to Eberwin, the disturbing composure of condemned heretics on the pyre is nothing more than the Devil's madness; it is a form of suicide.[58]

Closely associated with Dietrich's description of the heretics as Cathars are the series of sermons written by Eckbert of Schönau with whom Dietrich had collaborated in the publication of the revised version of the St. Ursula legend, occasioned by the discovery of the remains of the eleven thousand martyrs at Cologne in 1155.[59] Eckbert's sermons provide a vital context for how Dietrich and later authors conceived of the heretics' beliefs and the punishment these beliefs deserved. These sermons are also very significant for the development of a conception of dualist heresy in the course of the twelfth century for both medieval thinkers and for modern historians.[60] Eckbert's heretics belong to a single widely spread sect that is devoted to secrecy in opposition to the open evangelization of Catholicism. This Cathar Church espouses a radical theological dualism, arguing that all matter is the work of the Devil, Jesus Christ could never have taken on a real fleshy body, and that human beings are really fallen angels trapped in the prison of the flesh.

Eckbert claims no small amount of direct knowledge regarding the heretics' beliefs. He says that when he lived as a secular canon at Saint Cassius in Bonn he often argued with these people and that he even held some of these disputes in his own home.[61] He also says that he heard some doctrines of the heretical sect explained by a former member in the presence of Arnold the archbishop of Cologne, perhaps placing Eckbert in direct contact with the executions sixteen to twenty years earlier.[62] While Eckbert certainly had contact with real individuals whose theological ideas he found strange and offensive, likely real dissident groups in the form of semireligious communities and urban confraternites, there is good reason to believe that the shape and coherence he gives to them are his own.[63]

Eckbert wrote his sermons very soon after the event in 1163, and they are extremely revealing regarding the messages sent and received as a result of the method of execution used against the heretics.[64] They are also an informative source for what an educated cleric in his place and time would have taken intentional opposition to and separation from the institutional Church to entail. Eckbert, under his sister's influence, left the soft life of a secular canon behind and became a Benedictine monk in 1155, and thereafter was a changed man, eventually becoming abbot of Schönau. The heretics he denounced were often people who wanted an increase in the clergy's rigor similar to the one he himself enacted, but where Eckbert had followed the proper channels, moving from secular canon to cloistered monk, the heretics he fought left all authority behind.

What Eckbert's sermons inform a modern reader of less well are the actual beliefs of the condemned. While he claimed direct access to the Cathars, modern scholars have been cautious at taking Eckbert completely at his word. Moore has argued that Eckbert appears to conflate different dissenting groups into one heresy, acknowledging different beliefs held by the heretics he has met while insisting they are all essentially one group.[65] Instead, the existence of these dissenting groups provides Eckbert with an opportunity to systematically expound the essentials of the Catholic faith by rebutting propositions contrary to them, as he had been taught as a student.[66] Eckbert's heretics have a conceptual unity, an "internal coherence," which he prioritizes as a foil to the conceptual unity at the heart of the legitimate Church.[67]

The name Eckbert uses for the heretics was also one he had learned in the schools. Eckbert acknowledges this modeling, to a certain extent, remarking on the etymology of the term Cathar, meaning "cleansed" or "pure," as used for the heretics of late antiquity, such as those found in a canon of the First Council of Nicaea.[68] He argues they are ultimately Manichaeans, and appends excerpts from Augustine regarding Manichaeans and *Catharistae* to his treatise.[69] He also had a pattern of looking to past histories and their sources for useful modern inventions in support of St. Ursula and the eleven thousand virgins, and St. Potentin, the patron saint of Steinfeld. The Cathars that Eckbert presents, modeled on a heresy from the fourth and fifth centuries, fit this pattern perfectly.[70] Eckbert's details are likely very inaccurate. The reality behind his Cathars is almost certainly not a secret sect that had survived from antiquity and been reintroduced from the East, but rather a "covering of local evangelical dissidents with the costumes of antiquity."[71] Eckbert's use of familiar scholarly conventions and his conflation of different groups of dissenters, both modern and historical, also makes perfect sense when one considers what he took persistent theological dissent to entail. In the logic Eckbert lays out in his sermons, one either takes the entire body of faith or none of it; one is either a member of Christ's body or a limb of the Devil's, and the Devil's nature is stable.

For Eckbert, the heretics represent an impediment to the desire for union with God, and an object deserving mockery. They are part of a cluster of contemporary threats against the Church, including widespread clerical negligence that leads God to take action in the world.[72] Their doctrines deny believers hope, and twist the nature of love. The Cathars hate the body that should be loved, and this hatred blinds them to the role played by corporeality in human redemption. Where the body of the faithful can burn with hope, the heretics can only burn in vain despair. The Cathars by their choices cut themselves off from a redemptive spiritual unity in the body of Christ, becoming extensions of the Devil. As a face of this enemy, Eckbert accords them no sympathy.

Further, the Cathars are like a poison or a disease seeping through the body of the Church. Catholics come together through their faith, becoming limbs of a shared body.[73] In contrast, the Cathars are not true sharers in this body united by faith; they have, in fact, attached themselves to another. As a malignant fifth column, their doctrines and their presence act "like an airborne leprosy running far and wide contaminating the precious limbs of Christ."[74] The disease they represent arises from their ultimate spiritual allegiance to the Devil that places them outside of the Church and outside of licit society. The Catholic Church draws its practices and builds its faith on the foundation of Peter who himself based his doctrines on God in the form of Christ.[75] The heretics instead build their spiritual genealogy on Mani of Persia.[76] These "doctrines of the Manichaeans" are "not of God but of the Devil, not of Christ but of the Antichrist."[77] Mani himself is with the Devil in Hell, and Hell is where the Cathars are destined to go.[78]

The heretics' malignancy toward the body of Christ and their lack of a proper fit within it reflects their misunderstanding of the very nature, functions, and origins of bodies. According to Eckbert, they say that all corporeality is evil and that God originally created human beings as bodiless angels. Since all matter is evil, procreation is a wicked act, the creation of a new prison for a soul. Eckbert argues that in these beliefs the heretics were displaying a now-familiar narrow mindedness, an inability to grapple successfully with symbolism that relates the immediate appearance of things to spiritual meanings. Sex between a married couple is just this kind of symbolic relationship, a joining together of two human beings by means of their bodies that points toward the spiritual unity of all Christians and the potential of redemption in that union.[79] As Eckbert explains, relating the creation of human beings to that of angels, "For [God] created all angelic spirits at the same time, so that no angel would be born from another. The human race, however, He ordained to create in such a way that humans would succeed each other in turn and that some would be born from others, to the end that the union of charity [caritas] would be stronger between them because of their shared blood. He wanted them all to have the first man as one head and one origin so that the entire human race would be clearly propagated from him and that he would be in this a likeness with God, who is the head and the beginning of all creation."[80] The basic corporeal unity of all human beings is here made a method of cultivating the spiritual unity of charity that provides the possibility of redemption through a unity with God.[81] The multiplication of Adam's body, likewise, functions as a sign of the unity of all things in God. Once again, the heretics, just like Jews, cannot read symbolism.[82]

This treatment of humanity's unity in Adam also recalls explanations for why fallen humanity can be redeemed through God's grace while fallen angels cannot.[83] According to Anselm of Canterbury, for example, it is the presence of bodies that allows redemption. Since humanity is one genus it can be redeemed at once through the Incarnation of Christ as one man. As mankind is one in Adam and in Adam's sin, mankind is one in Christ and his redemption. Each angel, in contrast, is its own genus, and its redemption would require an angelic messiah custom-made for it alone.[84] Alternatively, the weakness of the body provides an excuse or a mitigating explanation for humanity's propensity to error. A spirit, free from this weakness, bears its entire fault as a deliberate intellectual choice, made from a position of full knowledge and self-control.[85] Such a chosen sin deserves no chance at redemption.

The material unity of all human beings in Adam becomes a redemptive spiritual unity in Christ through baptism and the Eucharist.[86] Baptism makes a Christian a limb of Christ's body.[87] The Eucharist, once consumed, further enacts this union, "crossing into the soul" where it "comforts, illuminates, and leads it to eternal life."[88] The different elements of the heretics' theology disrupt the opportunities for this spiritual unity as part of a deliberate attempt by the Devil to ensnare as many souls as he can.[89] The heretics place themselves outside of the redemptive unity of human beings and their God. Like demons they make redemption impossible by their pernicious and perverse will.

The sermons stress that the conduct of the Cathars in no way conforms to the apostolic norms of Catholicism and, as a result, when they are captured and killed their fate is not a kind of martyrdom. Unlike the founders of the Roman Church, the Cathars preach in secret. If they were correct that their faith is the only way to salvation, they would condemn all who by chance never learn their doctrines because of this secrecy. When they do openly profess their beliefs, it is a result of being caught and trapped. Such is not the witness of a martyr, but rather "the confession of a thief."[90] In their theology and in their deaths the heretics can only imitate the trappings of true holiness, and this imitation dissolves under intelligent scrutiny, testifying to its falsity by its very incoherence.

Eckbert dedicates his eighth sermon to a refutation of the heretics' belief in a baptism by the Holy Spirit and by fire, which calls on the pyre at Cologne as one of its central images. He suggests that the destruction of the Cathars in the flames should be read as a failed ordeal, perhaps something like that prescribed by the Council of Reims in 1157, but with a far more dramatic staging and far higher stakes.[91] In fact, not only does their manner of death highlight their damnation, but it again establishes that the heretics' own theology, if read correctly, perhaps with the aid of the Holy Spirit, proclaims their doom.

The heretics rejected baptism by water, citing John the Baptist's words in Matthew 3:11: "I indeed baptize you in the water unto penance, but he that shall come after me, is mightier than I. . . . He shall baptize you in the Holy Spirit and fire."[92] As a result, heretical baptism does not involve water, but rather takes place in the center of a ring of lamps. When a "novice" joins the sect, or is "Catharized," he is placed in the center of this ring and the "arch-cathar" then holds a book in one hand while laying the other on the head of the candidate, passing on the blessing of the Holy Spirit. They call this a baptism in fire "on account of the fire of the lamps that burn in the circle."[93]

Eckbert argues that this ritual is yet another example of heretical misreading in both the literal and allegorical senses. A baptism of this kind, in fact, makes the initiate "a son of Gehenna" rather than of the kingdom of God.[94] It amounts to the exchange of a redemptive fire for the flames of Hell. On the literal level of grammar, Eckbert points out that the verse reads "in fire" (*in igne*) not "next to fire" (*juxta ignem*), as the heretics understand it.[95] This problem with prepositions highlights the more serious errors encoded in the poor exegesis of this verse. These errors all result from the incorrect interpretation of signs, particularly the signs of a written text, and the literal enactment of signs and gestures that should be read symbolically.

Eckbert argues that if the heretics wanted to read the Bible literally, as they seem intent to do in this case, they would have to actually place the candidate *inside* a raging flame. This kind of baptism would be tantamount to the most strenuous of ordeals, the kind of test only the greatest of saints could hope to survive. Eckbert provides the choreography for exactly this kind of event, suggesting how the heretics should proceed: "Set up a large fire in the middle of your synagogue and take your novice, whom you want to Catharize, and place him in the middle of the fire. And then, you, archcathar, place your hand on his head as you ought, and thus bless him. Then, if you do not burn your claws and if he escapes unhurt, I will certainly admit that your Cathar has been baptized well."[96] But what if the novice does not emerge unharmed from the flames? Maybe, Eckbert mocks, he is "so inflamed he's gone to Heaven."[97] However vicious Eckbert's suggestion may seem, all the truly faithful will survive just such a test, as he goes on to explain.

In fact, Eckbert writes, such a baptism in fire, or trial by fire, has recently occurred, and its results were conclusive. He asks if lately at Cologne the archcathar, Arnold, and his accomplices flew from their pyre into Heaven. Similarly, at Bonn did Theodoric and his companions so escape?[98] No, Eckbert answers, the agony and bodily destruction of the Cathars leaves no doubt as to where the fires took them: "Nay, as it should be more truly said, they descended into the depths of Hell, from a temporary fire to the burning of an eternal fire. And indeed quite rightly, just as they despoiled the baptism of water, established by the Lord Savior himself, teaching that baptism should be in flame, so did it happen that by the most righteous judgment of God that they were baptized in fire so that they were irrevocably consumed."[99] Rather than a divine flame that flies unto Heaven, the fires of execution handed these heretics off to the fires of Hell.

This was a fitting and "most righteous" punishment that places the actions of the people at Cologne in context with the timeless. Those who commanded and who watched the executions at Cologne can be assured that in this act the present order and that sacred came together for one instant, placing the proper ordering of authorities both earthly and divine in one continuous line. In the expulsion of the heretical cancer, the temporal and the timeless met and overlapped, and in the terrible agony of these flames, acting as a literal highway to the eternal inferno, a spectator could not only see the terrors awaiting the damned but also find confirmation of a shared identity opposed to that of the condemned. One can see how for Eckbert the heretics' destruction in the fire could constitute a revelation of a kind akin to those he so eagerly sought from his sister, regarding the hidden world of the spirit and the judgments of God.[100] The faithful are a body that aims to burn differently, that wishes to escape the horrible and endless moment without hope in which Arnold, Theodoric, and the others are forever imprisoned. As those who were present at the event or those who read Eckbert's sermons could imagine, the Cathars at Cologne are still burning.

How the faithful will experience baptism by fire further compounds the irony surrounding the heretics' faulty exegesis and the punishment this perniciously defended error deserves. As Eckbert explains, John's promised baptism by fire is real, and its true form is another type of fire misunderstood by the Cathars: the fires of Purgatory. According to Eckbert, the Cathars argue that immediately after death the souls of the dead go either to Heaven or to Hell, spending no time in between. This rejection of Purgatory and all the ecclesiastical observances associated with it is monstrous. As Eckbert asks, who outside of the greatest saints would be worthy to travel straight from this world into the very presence of God?[101] In this argument, Eckbert finds yet another example of how the heretics' theology is actually a hopeless nightmare that would allow salvation to only a very select few. This false theology places terrible limits on the hope that the faithful can nurture that their desire for union with God will be attained.

Punishment after death through a purgatorial fire provides an opportunity for salvation to those who die with the stain of minor sins on their souls.[102] It is an avenue of hope. This possibility is open only to those who remain within the Church and who have made confession for "criminal sins" before their deaths.[103] The pain from this fire will be considerable, but unlike the fires of Hell it is a temporary pain. For this reason its agony should be considered "nothing compared to that of the eternal punishment" suffered in Hell.[104]

It is this burning to which John the Baptist referred when he spoke of a baptism by fire. Eckbert explains that our Savior first baptizes us outwardly by the visible ministers of the Church through the baptism of water. Inwardly, we are baptized by the Holy Spirit through this ritual, which grants us remission for all our sins. "But in fire he baptizes us, when after this life he purifies our souls from the stains of our sins in purgatorial punishments, which they [our souls] take with them from the dwelling of the corruptible flesh, because he wishes to welcome nothing in his purest city that is not cleansed from all filth."[105] This fire will burn away our excessive love for the things of this world. This love that distracts from the love of the things of God is a flammable thing, like the "wood, hay, and straw" of 1 Corinthians 3:10–15.[106] Most, in order to see God and to love him correctly, must burn.

Both the damned and the majority of the faithful will burn in the fires of a corporeal flame.[107] The differences primarily lie in the fire's length and in the fire's purpose. The flames of true baptism are a hopeful thing. Heated by these, unlike the fires of execution or the fires of Hell, the soul can indeed fly up to Heaven. The faithful will burn only for a set time and then they will be released. It is their punishment that is in fact a single, limited event. In contrast, the fires of the heretics are an eternal prison; they are an eternal trap of carnality for those who failed to comprehend the carnal. And so, even though the spectacle of execution possessed a limited duration it provided a window onto the timeless. For spectators, such a sight may have reinforced a desire to burn like the condemned for as short a time as possible. Those who were still limbs of Christ could aim to burn with hope.

The Maiden Who Cannot Be Saved: Later Accounts of the 1163 Burnings

The next accounts of the burnings at Cologne in 1163, written after those of Dietrich and Eckbert, come from over five decades later. They develop the messages already identified in the event, but use different images to focus the reader's attention and pathos. In particular, the desire of the audience concentrated on the pyre for a redemptive rather than eternal and retributive fire finds a new and poignant focus in the form of a doomed maiden. The audience's desire to save the maiden becomes an image of a kind for the tragedy of heresy and damnation, evoking a loss of innocence and human failure on the path to redemption. The maiden's tragedy is all the more poignant when read through the desire of the audience to burn better themselves.

The descriptions from the 1220s in the *Chronica regia Coloniensis* (*Cologne Royal Chronicle*) provide a slightly different picture, modifying the memory of the heretics' composure at their deaths to better control the message. There are two different recensions of this execution in the modern edition of the chronicle, and they both manage to say and suggest very different things. The first version records clerical anxieties about the staging and popular reception of such an execution, and the second abandons such concerns altogether to craft a far more effective and focused account of the event as a regrettable but unavoidable tragedy. Both replace Dietrich's multiple heretics who willingly entered the flames with a single maiden, as in the annals.

The first recension records that "heretics from the sect of the Cathars" came from the area of Flanders to Cologne "where they were seized and consumed by fire outside the city." The number of the condemned decreases as does the account of heretical conduct on the pyre. The burned included "four men and a maiden, who threw herself into the fire against the wishes of the people."[108] In addition, a wholly different and potentially unstable element in the staging of such an execution appears in the form of a sudden rainstorm in the city that made the clerics who remained there very afraid that the executioners' fires would be dramatically extinguished.[109] Evidently no rain fell outside the city to douse the executioner's flames, further suggesting the divine sanction of the event. The clerics' fears about the rain illustrate how at such a spectacle any unexpected element could become suffused with meaning. This element is like a rogue signifier, difficult to place in an explanatory framework, and it is no surprise that the rain does not appear again.

The second recension develops the tragedy of the maiden, while dropping the fears about the rain. This version also provides an explanation for how the heretics came to the attention of the authorities in the first place. The heretics are still Cathars from Flanders. They take up residence secretly in a barn, but the secret seems to have been a poorly guarded one because they are "seized and detected" when they fail to attend church on Sunday. Questioning by representatives of the Catholic Church is enough to confirm their heresy. The group is then urged to abandon their beliefs, but they stubbornly refuse to convert. In the face of their persistence, they are "cast out from the Church and handed over into the hands of the laity, who, taking them outside the city, hand them over to the flames." The victims remain the same: "four men and one maiden."[110] Finally, the attempt of the crowd to redeem the maiden finds more detail: "[The maiden], while she might have been saved by the efforts of the people, if by chance she had been frightened by the destruction of the others and consented to more sensible advice, suddenly slipped out of the hands of those holding her and willingly threw herself into the flames and died."[111] The maiden's story becomes the center of attention in this version, which seemingly attempts to draw on the reader's pathos. In the second recension the story has been significantly altered from Dietrich's version, investing more of its power in the tragedy of the maiden and elaborating the process whereby the heretics are discovered and condemned to die.

The version of the Cologne burnings offered by Caesarius of Heisterbach, also from the 1220s, presents the story of the maiden in its most moving form while also engaging with the personal conduct of the condemned in the fire.[112] Caesarius records that the burning took place "near the Jewish cemetery," and that on their way to the site Arnold and his followers were denied bread and water because of fears they might attempt to conduct their own viaticum. As they burn, Caesarius describes Arnold's attempts to comfort his disciples in a way that recalls Eckbert's mocking outline for a heretical baptism in fire: "As the flames had taken strong hold of them, in the sight and hearing of a great crowd, Arnold placed his hand on the heads of his dying disciples, and exhorted them: 'Stand fast in your faith, for this day you shall be with Laurence.'"[113] Caesarius adds, however, "yet they were very far from the faith of Laurence."

Arnold's words and gesture inject this scene forcefully into the stream of possibilities seen in the earlier sources, such as a literal baptism in fire.

St. Laurence was a martyr saint, supposedly grilled alive by Emperor Valerian in the mid-third century.[114] His invocation here, again, likens the fate of the condemned at Cologne to the Christian martyrs of old. Caesarius's immediate aside defuses this possibility, reminding the reader that the Roman Church, of which Laurence was a deacon, is still here, and the heretics are not members of it. Likewise, the closeness of Caesarius's description of Arnold's final gesture to the baptism in fire suggestion made by Eckbert is striking. As in a heretical baptism, Arnold places his hand on the head of his disciples, and as Eckbert suggested he does so while they are consumed by flame. As in Eckbert's sermon, here the result is the same: the destruction and death of the

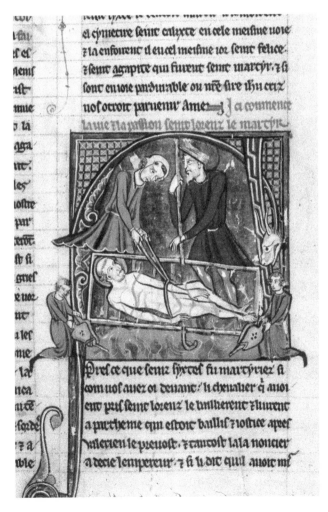

FIGURE 3.   The Martyrdom of St. Laurence. © The British Library Board, Royal 29 D. VI f84.

heretics. In fact, Arnold and his followers all still burn together in Hell, a fact made clear through the tragedy of the maiden.

Caesarius's account of the maiden dwells on her beauty, the salvation she rejects, and the compassion of the audience who attempts to save her. The maiden is "very beautiful, though a heretic," he cautions. He states that "she was drawn from the fire by the compassion" of members of the crowd. These unnamed bystanders offer to provide her with a husband or place her in a nunnery if she would prefer. At first the maiden appears to consent—to marriage or to the nunnery Caesarius does not say—but when her would-be saviors let down their guard she acts on her true intentions. She asks, "Tell me, where does that seducer lie?" In response, she is shown where the body of Arnold still burns. Immediately, the maiden slips from their grasp, veils her face with her robe, and throws herself on the burning body, and, as Caesarius concludes "with him went down to burn forever in Hell."[115]

In the midst of the horror, the maiden becomes the focus of the crowd's compassion, literally their shared suffering and their shared hope. While expelling the heretics, the community attempts to bring one back. The choice of the heretic to bring back along with the choices she is given remind us of the charity Eckbert found in the multiplication of the body of Adam. The enlargement of charity undergirds the attempts to redeem the maiden through offers of marriage with either male bystanders or with God. The last-minute efforts to place the woman back into the community are very close indeed to the later custom of reprieves on the scaffold in response to marriage proposals.[116] According to this mainly French custom first recorded in 1274, a young man could be pardoned if a woman in the crowd asked for him in marriage.[117] While the custom was most commonly seen as a way to pardon men, there is at least one example in which a man in the crowd saved a condemned woman by proposing marriage.[118] Proposals on the scaffold also unite desire for community with human sexual desire, focused on the spectacle of the beautiful body of the condemned.[119] This custom provided an opportunity for mercy, reformation, and reintegration into community.[120]

The logic of salvation through integration and assimilation found within the customary pardon through marriage is the same as that which Caesarius suggests in his imagining of the doomed maiden of Cologne. In fact, he might have had an 1198 decretal of Innocent III in mind as he told the story.[121] "Among the works of charity" modeled in the scriptures that the faithful should imitate, Innocent placed the redemption of prostitutes through marriage.[122] Men who took these women as wives, freeing them as sinners from the way of their sin, performed an act of penance for their own faults. The joining of two penitent sinners into one flesh facilitated a more meaningful incorporation into the body of Christ as the shared society of the faithful united to God. This joining is both unifying and expulsive. Likewise, the option of becoming a nun was a contemporary avenue of reform suggested for prostitutes.[123] Like a secular marriage, this option united the individual to God, extending the boundaries of Christian charity while ejecting sin. It is this generative and redemptive unity with man and God that the maiden rejects, opting instead for spiritual and reproductive barrenness and death.

For a moment, the maiden is a symbol of hope and the potential for redemption at the very gates of Hell. In this role, a multitude of desires focus on her character and on her body. She is an opportunity for the enlargement of community and the charity that creates and sustains community. Twelfth-century Christians watching the heretics burn before them likely hoped for a similar redemption when they burned, wanting their fire to lead to something more than fruitless damnation. As Eckbert argued, fire could be a baptism that prepared the faithful for Heaven, removing sin and uniting the one burning to God. The audience's hopes for the maiden are dashed, however, when she chooses to perish with her spiritual seducer and burn with him without hope forever.

The phenomena in search of a meaning described by Eberwin have now been replaced with a much more focused story and image in the form of the maiden. Instead of a confusion of categories between sacred and profane, there is now a single object of desire whom the community tries to save. That this beautiful heretic destroys herself illustrates the utter perversity of the power that works through her. The message was clear. Bravery at the pyre can move us and at the same time be an unambiguous symptom of impending damnation. The apparent human that we want to save and unite with us can be a puppet of the Devil, if read well.

Even in defeat the maiden remains an object of desire, and this desire is essentially purgative. In each of the iterations of the Cologne story, the girl serves as a symbol of the tragic consequences of the exclusion brought about by rooting out the weeds from the fields of the twelfth-century Rhineland. In wanting to save the maiden, the authors of these accounts and the readers of them assure themselves of their own goodwill. Their impulse is the image of God's will, which desires not the destruction of sinners but their reformation.[124] In the midst of a discourse so strongly defined by its apparent callousness, the maiden is a point of compassion on which a modern and medieval reader can converge, as both readers share the same desire, forever frustrated, that she be saved.

Hildegard of Bingen and Salvific Resemblance in Opposition

This desire to pull something of value from the flames, from the jaws of Hell and its eternal death, shaped the contribution of the famous author and mystic Hildegard of Bingen. Hildegard played a significant role in the events associated with the burnings at Cologne in 1163, and the larger campaign against heresy in the Rhineland of which it formed a part. Hildegard herself addressed the clergy of Cologne, likely in the same year that the burnings took place, and at the request of Philip of Heinsberg, the dean of the cathedral and later archbishop of Cologne, who was certainly involved in the executions, she provided a written copy of her words.[125] She urged the clergy to reform their lifestyles and combat heresy.[126] Through her own combat with the Devil, she uncovered Cathar heretics, leading to the direct involvement of Eckbert of Schönau, and she corresponded regarding the Cathar threat with his sister, Elisabeth.[127]

Hildegard placed God's spiritual fire at the center of her call for an evangelical renewal to the clergy of Cologne. Addressing this audience, she switched between her own voice and the voice of God Himself, lamenting that the clerics of the city have forsaken the proper care of souls, allowing the heretics to flourish. The clerics' works "do not shine before men with the fire of the Holy Spirit" providing good examples for the flock.[128] This fire should fall on and illuminate the faithful, but at present it does not. Using "the teaching of the scriptures, which were composed through the fire of the Holy Spirit," these clerics should be the very pillars of the earth supporting the Church, but they have left this duty for their own leisure, turning their subordinates into windblown ashes.[129] Rather than acting as a guiding pillar of fire, the leaders of the Church have left their faithful to wander alone.

In this moral vacuum, the heretics appear to be what Hildegard wished the Catholics to become. They are poor, lack all greed, and are truly chaste. These men apparently enact the sanctity the Catholic clergy has forsaken, but it is really a demonic ruse. Hildegard warns that the Devil "is within these men," working through the spirits of the air. These spirits permit the heretics' desire to be chaste in order to better deceive.[130] Like Bernard's reading of the brave conduct on the pyre that troubled Eberwin, what seems the most praiseworthy in heretics is actually a sign of what is most wicked. For Hildegard, however, this resemblance itself is fertile.

Like many authors before, Hildegard maintains that these people "seduced by the Devil" will become a scourge to discipline the faithful. God will make of them an "iniquity which will purge iniquity."[131] In Hildegard's eloquent joining of iniquities, God will make a point of convergence into a salvific opportunity. This expulsive meeting of similarities is a step beyond the familiar proverb of driving out nails with nails.[132] It is rather more akin to the purifying and purgative joining of "like with like" in the Incarnation.[133] In this case, wickedness paired with wickedness creates an opportunity for redemption, as the heretic turned into a divine instrument purges the clergy like the very purgative fire these same heretics will likely never have the opportunity to know. The wickedness of both orthodox and heretic allows the salvation of one while requiring the destruction of the other. The very resemblance of heretic and orthodox in this miraculous about-face creates a possibility for purgation.

Hildegard's prolonged confrontation with a demon-possessed noblewoman some six years later in 1169 further illustrates the possibilities of resemblance and integration between the sacred and the profane. This woman, named Sigewize, first came to Hildegard's attention through Abbot Gedolphus of Brauweiler.[134] The abbot wrote to Hildegard telling her about the case of a woman who had struggled with a demon for eight years. This demon, after being conjured, confessed that only Hildegard could expel the demon.[135] In response, Hildegard advises a complex exorcism that involves seven priests taking on the personae of Abel, Noah, Abraham, Melchisedech, Jacob, Aaron, and Christ to represent the seven gifts of the Holy Spirit. These biblical figures should lightly strike Sigewize with rods while offering conjurations until the spirit departs.[136] The abbot later wrote to Hildegard informing her that the exorcism worked briefly but that the demon has now returned and will only be permanently exorcised in Hildegard's presence.[137]

In a series of escalating efforts to free Sigewize, Abbot Gedolphus sent her to live in Hildegard's community. The demon attempted to disrupt the unity of Rupertsberg, offering mockery, foul language, and terrible smells to its hosts, but the sisters kept Sigewize with them. The sisters, along with the men associated with the community, struggled with her, offering "fasts, prayers, alms, and mortifications of their bodies" on her behalf from the Purification of the Virgin Mary until the Saturday before Easter, a span of almost two months.[138] This relentless inclusion in a community with God eventually transforms the demon into a divine tool.

As a result of the conviviality between the sisters and the demon, iniquity purges iniquity, and the demon, like a captured prisoner of war, informs on the Cathar heretics who are its compatriots. While living in Hildegard's community, Sigewize's demon finds itself forced by divine power against its will to confess before large audiences, "many things regarding baptism, the sacrament of the body of Christ, the danger of excommunication, the perdition of the Cathars, and similar things." These true facts strengthen the faith of many people and lead them to make amends for their sins.[139] These recitations of spiritual truths are similar to Hildegard's own sermons, and both women draw their knowledge from supernatural sources.[140] In fact, the topics the demon covers sound so much like Hildegard that it is almost as if she is speaking to herself.[141] This moment of resemblance between supposed opposites, holding a profound circularity at its heart, prompts sincere reformation and redemption, signaling again the fruitfulness of contraries' participation in each other. This useful joining of difference rendered into similarity happens only in an explanatory field illuminated by God's action, allowing a self-repeating closed circle to grow with each repetition.

According to Eckbert's brief vita, included within the facts regarding the perdition of the Cathars that the demon offered to audiences at Bingen were a list of around forty of their names, where they lived in the city of Mainz, and where they buried their dead.[142] When investigation verified the truth behind these claims, Eckbert of Schönau, as a local expert, sprung into action, heading off to Mainz in order to make the heretics' error and heresy manifest in spite of their clever and evasive answers to questioning.

Eckbert's mission, set in motion by Hildegard's cohabitation with a demon, was a success, driving out the majority of the heretics while saving one. It appears that Eckbert was able to convict the heretics publicly and as a result "those who were in Mainz were all thrown out of the city, except one." This one had been their heresiarch and their master or teacher for many years. Repudiating and "detesting" his former error the heretics' former leader returned to the Church, "giving thanks to God for the liberation of his soul from death."[143]

The identity of the heretic who is saved is important. He was the one most like Eckbert. In this resolution, one religious leader and scholar saves another, and this salvation is only possible due to the resemblance between them. Trained at Bonn through long hours in the presence of heretics, including in his own home, Eckbert knew them. This knowledge of their beliefs allowed Eckbert to identify and exclude but also enabled the assimilation of the object of knowledge most like himself. Unlike the case of the maiden at Cologne, this attempt to save the doomed heretic, who tugs most poignantly at the heart of the observer, is successful.

Eckbert's feat of integration through exclusion at Mainz mirrors the final result of Hildegard's struggles with Sigewize and her demon. After prolonged prayers, alms, and offerings on her behalf, on Easter vigil, as the priest blesses the baptismal font, the demon finally gives up its hold on Sigewize.[144] In Hildegard's description, it is literally squeezed from her body as an ejection of corrupt fluids from the woman's private parts, corresponding to the flight of Satan from the temple of the woman's heart, into which enters the Holy Spirit.[145] Free at last, Sigewize remains with the sisters as one of them.[146] The presence of the demon and the drama of its departure bring the noblewoman into contact with the sacred. What began as an artificial and performative mimesis in Hildegard's first exorcism has ended in a true and transformative mimesis in her own community of nuns.

Both Hildegard's efforts for Sigewize and Eckbert's conversion of the heresiarch represent acts of integration through exclusion. Unlike the doomed maiden of Cologne, these accounts manage to save the human object of desire and assimilate it. These two accounts highlight one of the more unexpected functions of medieval discourse regarding heresy. In both cases, integration depends on expulsion enacted in a moment of mutual resemblance between opposites. In performing such a feat, Hildegard and Eckbert managed the kind of happy conclusion that was so wanted and so distant in the field of ecclesiastical reform, where sacred and secular could not seem to meld gainfully into one another in the moment of their separation.

This chapter has focused on the linked sources for a few burnings for heresy in the mid-twelfth-century Rhineland as objects of interpretation for contemporaries, or near contemporaries, of the fact. I have argued that the basic hermeneutic these contemporaries used to make sense of these events constituted a circle, with a focus on themselves as spectator rather than the spectacle. In a sense, this way of looking for meaning in death finds a center of attention and explanation for murder in the murderer, who through the continued ability to speak and endlessly to confess—or through creative retellings be made continually to confess—dominates the discourse surrounding killing to the exclusion of the victims. But in this kind of circular search for meaning, the viewer or the speaker has the opportunity to articulate what they see as the truth about themselves.

The acts of understanding described in the sources depend on moments of mimetic resemblance between the knower and the immediate object of knowledge. The gateway to these mimetic processes is formed through what initially appear to be different types of category confusions. All of the authors confronted different types of these confusions, and through their work of interpretation turn these mixtures into opportunities for self-knowledge or self-enlargement. The circle begins with what the viewer is and what the viewer knows. The closing of the circle involves the affirmation and enlargement of both elements. In particular, moments of resemblance between sacred and profane, Catholic and heretic open up the possibility of interpretation and from this interpretive opening something resembling the interpreter is taken as a meaning or a prize from the interpretive episode. For Eberwin, with the aid of Bernard, the apparent resemblance between heretic and martyr-saint comes to declare how dissimilar the two categories actually are. For Eckbert, the prize is literally the heretic most like himself, turned into a Christian man. Through mirror-like self-reflections, the fashioning of the heretical subject is also an opportunity for self-fashioning.[147]

Like a knotty verse pondered by an exegete, the heretics could become symbols, words, or tools of a divine order, holding within them a transformative message for the orthodox viewer. Eckbert's sermons focused on correct reading. He found in the heretics' errors an opportunity to explain the hopes of Christian community and the way that that community could burn with hope rather than in damnation. This purgatorial burning is what would allow the majority of the faithful to reach the God from whom they were currently separated. The horror of the heretics' deaths is in this case the inability to recognize, or to read for, this promised emersion in fire. In their failure they become an object lesson and means of purgation for the faithful. The tragedy of the maiden reflects on these linked elements of desire for the unattained and the human potential for error. For Hildegard, acts of mimesis between demon and human religious lead to the enlargement of community in the process of the diminution of community. These uses of heretics as tools of a divine order require their eventual disposal once their function is accomplished, like Bernard's rod of discipline cast into the fire. In all of these sources for events in and around Cologne, an essential paradox finds constant enactment: integration comes about through exclusion.

In the transformation of the heretics' lives, identities, and deaths into an object of knowledge and interpretation, the orthodox interpreter draws closer to a desired moment of personal integration. This longed-for assimilation is equivalent to the possession of God as the ultimate object of knowledge. The expulsion of heretics, through the thought processes outlined in these episodes, facilitates the assimilation of the orthodox with their God. In this process, the bodily reality of the burning heretic ceases to exist outside the act of interpretation, completing the act of annihilation to leave only the refashioned interpreter behind.

CHAPTER 5

Like Rejoices in Like

Recognition and Differentiation in Descriptions of Heresy

Between 1160 and 1178 an anonymous Cistercian in the Rhineland told the story of how an accused heretic had demanded a trial by fire. This supposed heretic, a dissatisfied parish priest named Albero, believed that the flames would not burn him, proving the truth behind his claims regarding the incorrigible corruption of the institutional Church. The Cistercian explained that this was a heretic whom the authorities refused to burn, even though he asked for it. They refused because they believed that Albero would use demonic magic to escape the flames in an apparent miracle. The anonymous monk dismissed Albero's demand, concluding that he burned on the inside with wickedness and so desired to burn on the outside too, because "like rejoices in like." While explaining that similar things seek each other out, the Cistercian author described his own hatred of ecclesiastical corruption in terms that were very similar to those of Albero. This author was drawn to Albero, and his attraction resulted from the fundamental similarity between the reforming heretic and the reforming churchman who persecuted him. As the Cistercian explained, Albero was a reforming zealot, who like many others made himself into a heretic in frustration with ecclesiastical resistance to reform.

The treatise against Albero attempts to understand and to exorcise the likeness between persecutor and persecuted through the conceit of a heretic who would not burn. Sources like the treatise against Albero inverted the familiar narratives of the burnings of heretics around Cologne between 1143 and 1163, imagining heretics who appeared immune to fire. Such immunity would, of course, be itself superficially like that of the saints, distinguished not by appearance but instead by the inner qualities behind appearances. Heretics who could not burn were a way of exploring fundamental hermeneutic questions connected to the larger reparative project of the Christian faith in the context of persecution. As Augustine had suggested, "contrariety and similarity" together formed "the basic principle of Christian healing."[1] In considering interactions between things that were superficially similar but essentially different, the interpreter grew through the discovery of disguised meanings, and this discovery was ultimately enabled by the orientation of love. Love guided the process of interpretation, divided into two basic types: a carnal love associated with misleading appearances and a spiritual love whose meaning transcends appearances. The revelation of this deceptively simple-looking binary of loves was messy; in effect, both sides needed each other.

Beginning with the revealing declaration that like rejoices in like from the treatise against Albero, the argument below will follow an eclectic course through a range of sources joined by place, time, subject, and method. The description of Albero's desire to burn resonates with contemporary accounts of the role of fire in human anthropology and of the usefulness of evil. From Albero and the many fiery images connected to the description of him the focus of the chapter will shift to the hermeneutical questions posed by another example of apparent heretical immunity to fire from the *Dialogue on Miracles* of the Cistercian monk Caesarius of Heisterbach as read in the light of Augustine's *De doctrina christiana*. The analysis of these diverse associations seeks to place a seemingly strange trope in context, illuminating the kinds of connections that occurred in the minds of educated, twelfth-century churchmen whenever the burning of human beings arose as a subject of discussion or rumination. These associations, as they appear in the sources examined below, served the worldview and the sense of self of orthodox polemicists, defusing their frequent attractions to supposedly heretical ideas by attributing them to others. Beyond mere projection, these acts of attribution allowed for the retention of some elements of heterodox polemic, bringing them fully into the service of a reformed orthodoxy.

Burning on Both Sides: Albero of Mercke and the Likeness of Difference

An anonymous treatise, *Libellus adversus errores Alberonis sacerdotis merkensis* (*Against the Errors of Albero the Priest of Mercke*), is a neglected source for the history of heresy in the twelfth-century Rhineland. Uwe Brunn suggests that it helps especially to establish how religious dissent in the Rhineland did not uniformly follow the Cathar model that originated with Eckbert of Schönau.[2] Albero appears to have served as a priest for a parish dependent on the Cistercian monastery of Altenberg near Cologne, and the author may have been a member of that house.[3] As noted above, our record of the charges brought against Albero comes from the years between 1160 and 1178.[4] Like our earlier sources for the burnings at Cologne, the accusations against Albero take place in an atmosphere of deep dissatisfaction with clerical corruption. Rather than a member of a continent-spanning heretical sect, Albero appears as an exasperated would-be Gregorian reformer who finally broke with the institutional Church.[5] In the eyes of the author, it is this intentional separation from the collective body of Christianity that turned a reformer into a heretic.

The anonymous Cistercian labels Albero as one of the foxes uprooting the vines in the Lord's vineyard, hiding his inner depravity by an appealing veneer of sanctity.[6] Albero's depravity originates from his desire for purity, particularly for a clergy freed from the corruption that he saw all around him. According to the author, Albero's major heretical teachings all suggested that the moral status of a priest directly impacted the efficacy of the sacraments he offered on behalf of the faithful. In Albero's opinion, so many priests were wicked that the mass was more often accompanied by demons than angels.[7] He taught that corrupt priests were unable to confect the sacrament.[8] If, in consideration of the faithful who had no knowledge of the priests' sins, God did allow wicked priests to confect, these sacraments would still be without any virtue for those faithful who knew of these priests' criminality, including suffrages offered for the dead.[9] The writer of the treatise marshals a host of authorities against these opinions, drawn from the canons of the *Decretum* and the Church Fathers, particularly Augustine. In the course of this refutation, the impression develops that Albero has allowed his desire for purity to get the better of him, becoming himself impure.

The author recognizes the possibility of a ready transference between opposites while sustaining an emphasis on the human responsibility for the maintenance of the divisions between them. This awareness takes the form of a paraphrase from Horace offered in the course of explaining the nature of Albero's theological mistakes regarding sinful priests' ability to confect the sacrament: "But because very many when they flee vices fall into their opposites, for the flight of error leads to vice if it lacks skill, it should be examined closely how what we say can be true."[10] The dangers inherent in strident criticism apparently threaten both the author of the treatise and its target, Albero. The writer realizes that his refutation of Albero could slip into a defense of criminal priests. Finding fault with Albero, the author himself might become impure. Likewise, Albero's readiness to find fault with the institutional clergy has itself led to a grave moral failing in the form of his desertion of the Church that is the sole vehicle for human salvation.

In the face of this barrage of authorities, the author reveals how Albero asked to be tested through the ordeal of fire. Albero offered to undergo this ordeal to prove the truth of his teaching and to demonstrate his sanctity against his corrupt opponents. In the opinion of the writer of the treatise, Albero's request sprung, in fact, from his inner disposition, in the form of an attraction between similarities enabled by an earlier transference between opposites: "Because it is written that like rejoices in like, just as he was badly aflame inwardly, he sought the flames outwardly, asking to be tested through fire so that the truth of his defense could become known to all."[11] Albero, the heretic, sought his natural complement, fire, but as the author explains, this relationship with flame is complex and potentially misleading to observers; it needs interpretation.

Albero's heretical nature that seeks fire, as like is drawn to like, may itself affect the natural virtue of the flame. As the author points out, if Albero had undergone the ordeal and "passed through the fire without burning," this would have been due, not to his holiness, but to demonic power. "Some kind of sorcery (*maleficium*)" could cause the element of fire "to let go of its own power."[12] Albero's request for the ordeal is denied for this reason, and through fear that the ordeal in general is a form of testing God.[13] The idea that a supernatural event, something between a sacrament and a miracle, could be called up on demand by human action and by human will appears in this treatise as both offensive and closer to magic than to licit religiosity.[14] The author's sentiment is a symptom of the orthodox reform, which sought to diminish clerical involvement in the judicial ordeal in the twelfth century, and the author cites a letter of Gregory the Great criticizing the ordeal found in the *Decretum*.[15] In the refusal of the ordeal and the demonization of those who seek it as a sign of legitimacy, an orthodox reformer asserts his identity against the figure of Albero as an illicit reformer.

A comparison with St. Laurence further underlines the disparity between Albero's desire for the flames and the desire of the saints to suffer and to witness for God. The heretic's experience of fire is not the same as that of Laurence, as Caesarius likewise stresses in his account of the 1163 executions at Cologne. Albero eagerly looks forward to the flames, while "Laurence did not seek the flames, but having been brought to them patiently suffered them."[16] Both the saint and the heretic might burn, but the meaning is different and this difference originates in an inner disposition that must be inferred through an interpretive process. Correct interpretation allows an observer to recognize that what might appear as two identical objects are actually contraries, and in the treatise this awareness of contrariety allows a new round of association based on likeness.

The author's observation that "like rejoices in like" leads to further associations between Albero and the demonic. The author claims that Albero asserted that a "new gospel" had been communicated to him "through visions and dreams or through angels from Heaven." In fact, Albero's instructors were not angels but demons. "His vision is not prophetic but fantastic, or rather a frantic deceit" created by demons. While Albero claims that demons accompany the sacrifice of the altar offered by wicked priests, it is he, in fact, who is a regular companion of the demonic.[17] Their companionship comes from the fact that they are very much alike, because they are both a force outside the community of God.

Albero's association with the Devil and his legions is a natural result of his break with the institutional Church. His desire for reform has been enacted badly, and in this unskilled attempt at realizing holiness he has himself become the opposite of the holy. Outside of the Church, there is only its opposite, so by logic all reform must be internal. The author writes: "Your faith is not only new, but it is also solitary. As such, it is not the Catholic faith. If you were Catholic, that is universal, you would strive to realize a singular life in the common faith. Your voice is dissonant with the universal harmony, and thus in the great concord of our faith the voice of a lone man is the voice of no one."[18] Separation is both destruction and defection to the opposite side. Christ is with the Catholics, and "who is not of Christ is of the Antichrist."[19] Having rendered Albero the man into "no one," the writer shifts his attention and the object of his address to those who had been Albero's own targets. This change as it grows and elaborates becomes a deliberate replacement or refashioning of the destroyed heretical voice.

With Albero annihilated and his discordant voice drowned out by the orthodox harmony, the treatise ends by switching the target of its denunciation to the wicked priests who inspired his heresy. In a sense, the treatise has become the purifying instrument that Albero should have been. This transformation has only been made possible through Albero's rhetorical destruction and the opportunity this deconstruction has afforded for reflection on the nature of reform within a still united and universal Church. Like has again been drawn to like, as the author's desire for reform takes the place of Albero's own desire. The author warns the wicked priests that they should not smile at Albero's defeat as his banishment does not equate to an endorsement of their sins. In fact, it is the opposite. In their wickedness, they will be with him in

Hell. Like Albero, they hide evil under a veneer of good. "Under the figure of light" they are really "the princes of shadows." Rather than "soldiers of Christ," they are "accomplices of the Antichrist."[20] The study of Albero has also been a study in the wickedness of the secular clergy for both are so similar as to be essentially the same, and ultimately they will be.

The author argues that the wickedness of the local Christian clergy has in fact created Albero and other heretics like him.[21] With an eloquence that seeks to channel the universal harmony, the treatise's author explains: "Lovers of virtue (*zelatores*) have made themselves heretics by comparing the sanctity of the sacrament and the perversity of those carrying it out, thinking that such an opposition in the same thing at the same time ought not to be nor can be."[22] This origin story is an important addition to the discourse regarding heresy, so often concerned with stories of heretical genealogies reaching back to antiquity.[23] The author of this treatise links heresy's origin with the reforming zeal of his time and the opposition that it poses to the failings of the established clergy. Here the desire for a purified orthodoxy generates heresy out of itself. The very zeal that creates heretics is much like the zeal that leads to the refutation and destruction of heretics, recalling the words of Bernard of Clairvaux who praised the zeal of the mob at Cologne while withholding his commendation from their act of murder. One gets the impression that both the author and Albero are lovers of virtue. What is different is their enactment of their impulse and their interpretation of apparent oppositions.

The author's observation that Albero sought out the flames of an ordeal because "like rejoices in like" might at first appear clumsy. The author observes that "badly aflame inwardly," Albero "sought the flames outwardly." This seemingly simple demonization of the heretic through an association with fire is more complicated than it seems.[24] On close examination its immediate Cistercian context opens up a set of associations between likeness and difference that extends the kinds of linkages and transferences between binaries, noted above, to include the basic structure of the divine and worldly orders.

The adage "like rejoices in like" has a long history.[25] Similar expressions often originate from the exegetical tradition around Sirach 13:19.[26] Erasmus in his *Adages* attributes it to Aristotle's *Ethica Nicomachea* (*Nicomachean Ethics*).[27] This portion of the *Ethics*, however, may not have been available in Latin translation until around the year 1200.[28] Even if the entire *Ethics* was available through the translation of Bernardo of Pisa, it is likely that the author of the treatise against Albero drew the phrase from another source.[29] This source cannot be identified with absolute certainty, but I will argue that the author's use of the phrase is most likely influenced by the *Epistola de anima* (*Letter on the Soul*) of Isaac of Stella.[30] Isaac was a Cistercian monk and abbot of Stella near

Poitiers.[31] In this context, the appearance of "like rejoices in like" in the treatise against Albero invokes a particularly Cistercian human anthropology.[32] Even if my attribution is mistaken, a consideration of the work done by this adage in Isaac's *Letter* and others closely linked to it will illuminate the wider meanings signified by this phrase among Cistercians in the twelfth century.

Isaac wrote his *Letter on the Soul* to Alcher of Clairvaux in 1162.[33] Alcher had asked Isaac to describe the soul's nature and its powers, and in reply Isaac classifies the powers of the soul, the nature of its ascent to God, and how it relates to the body. Isaac's work found a significant avenue of dissemination when the anonymous compiler of the *Liber de spiritu et anima* (*Book on the Spirit*

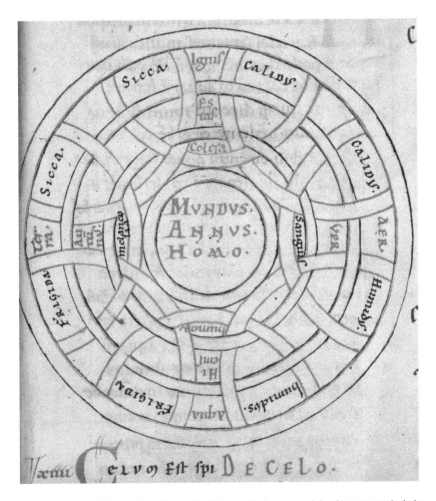

FIGURE 4. The ordering and the relationships between the humors and the elements, particularly how the elements are joined together by their qualities. The rounded depiction emphasizes the connections and interactions between them. © The British Library Board, Harley 2660 f37.

and the Soul) included much of it, including the section in which he describes the tendency of like to rejoice in like.[34] The *Book* was a very influential and widely disseminated text. Falsely attributed to Augustine, it played a role in thirteenth-century debates regarding the anthropology of man. The *Book* likely took shape around 1170, and because of that date the author of the treatise against Albero might have encountered "like rejoices in like" through this intermediary. The date of the text, however, would place it at the extreme edge of the possible composition dates for the treatise, making Isaac's *Letter* the more likely possibility.

In Isaac's view, the universe is joined into a hierarchical whole by a great chain of being, and the links of this chain are formed through the attraction of like to like. Such a great chain can be found in the process of human sense perception and cognition. Isaac explains that the unity of the spiritual and corporeal parts of man occurs at the extremities of each, where they are most like each other. The sensory capability of the body is almost spiritual, and the likenesses in the imagination of those things apprehended by the senses are almost corporeal. Nevertheless, "There are some things similar to both [the body and the spirit], namely the highest part of the body and the lowest part of the spirit, in which, without a confusion of natures, they can be easily tied together in an individual union. For like rejoices in like and those things that do not recoil due to unlikeness easily adhere in connection. And so the soul, which is truly a spirit and not a body, and the flesh, which is truly a body and

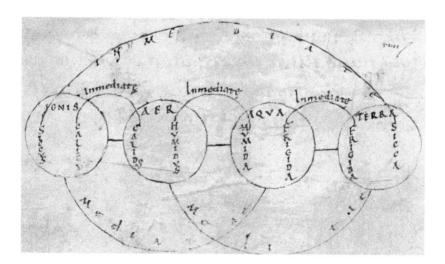

FIGURE 5. The four elements in a hierarchically ordered chain, from the lowest (*right*) to the highest (*left*). Fire is the highest of the four terrestrial elements. Einsiedeln, Stiftsbibliothek, Cod. 149(558), p. 172 (www.e-codices.unifr.ch).

not a spirit, are united easily and fittingly at their extremities, that is, in the phantasm of the soul, which is almost a body, and the sensuality of the flesh, which is almost a spirit."[35] This meeting point, Isaac explains, is fire.

The essential resemblance at this point of likeness, the lynchpin between humankind's physical and spiritual natures, is fiery. "The faculty of sensation in the flesh" is "mostly fire" and "the imaginative faculty of the spirit is said to be a fiery force." Such is the meaning hidden under the involucrum of poetic language in the *Aeneid*, when Virgil says regarding souls: "Fiery is the strength in them and heavenly its origin."[36] The order of cognition and perception in humankind is joined together in an ordered progression just as the four elements are linked in the field of natural philosophy, creating a great unity between matter and spirit. Fire is the highest body, and as Isaac has explained it is joined by "a certain similitude" to the lowest part of the spirit.[37] Moving in the opposite direction, fire is joined by a similitude to air, and air to water, and water to earth. Through these links "the lowest realities hang down from the highest" like the "golden chain of the poet."[38]

Like's attraction to like describes not only the unity of the spiritual and corporeal parts of humanity, but, through humanity as microcosm, the unity of all things with the God that is their source. Human beings are made in the image of God, and although this union of like with like was once broken by sin it was repaired through the Incarnation of Christ as the central link in a chain reunited through God's love. God's love as grace descends this chain, enlightening the mind and "igniting" the rational spirit "with its heat." In this way what is below participates in what is above, allowing the soul, through a five-step process that mirrors the ordering of the terrestrial elements, to journey upward to the source of everything, to the fullness of wisdom and the "pyre of charity."[39]

In the light of this reading of Isaac's *Letter on the Soul*, the reference made by the author of the treatise against Albero in the context of fire to "like rejoices in like" takes on new significance. The author is suggesting that Albero is finding his place in the great chain of being. Badly aflame inwardly, he seeks not the consuming pyre of charity but rather material flames. Albero is not on a journey to Heaven; he is moving toward Hell, drawn there as like is drawn to like. His journey to Hell is really a failure to climb, an arresting of the human journey to God through the love of God. Albero does not burn with this love but burns instead with what Hugh of St. Victor termed the bad fire of *cupiditas*.[40] Burning badly, he is drawn to burning infernally.

What the wickedness that Albero has come to embody through his unmoderated desire for good could mean for the orthodox becomes even clearer through a consideration of a possible influence on Isaac of Stella's own use of "like rejoices in like." This possible influence is a passage from the *Senten-tiae de divinitate* (*Opinions on Divinity*) of Hugh of St. Victor.[41] Isaac of Stella was familiar with Hugh's work and some scholars have wondered if he might have had direct familiarity with the school at St. Victor, but any such links re-main speculative.[42] Nonetheless, the Victorines influenced Cistercian anthro-pological writing, like the *Letter on the Soul*, and Hugh's work is a noted source for the *Letter* and an influence on Isaac's work more generally.[43]

In the *Opinions on Divinity* of Hugh of St. Victor, the joy like finds in like explicitly leaves room for the usefulness of unlikeness. Hugh's use of the phrase "like rejoices in like" occurs in the context of a discussion of the beneficence of God. In considering the goodness of the divine will, Hugh questions how it could be that something displeasing to God, such as evil, could possibly exist. He explains that God is the highest good, and so all good resembles God. Evil, in contrast, is unlike God; it is dissimilar to Him. Hugh says: "God wills every good; every good is pleasing to God, because God is of such a nature that every good agrees with his will, which is the greatest good, because like rejoices in like. And so just as every good agrees with the nature of God, so too every evil disagrees with his nature, because its unlikeness is hateful and contrary."[44] God wills the good, but willing the good is not the same as will-ing only the good to exist. Hugh explains this distinction through the exam-ple of the human desire for fire. As Hugh explains, there is a difference between saying "I want fire" and "I want fire to exist." Saying "I want fire" is the same as "I love fire," or "I want to be heated." Saying "I want fire to exist," in con-trast, equates to saying, "I wish that fire were present where it is not," in order for its heat to be useful, even if I myself have not kindled and tended a fire. This kind of distinction is the difference between "God wills the good and God wills good to exist," or "God does not will evil and God does not will evil to exist."[45] When God wills evil to exist, it is because it is useful, not because he loves it.

Evil, in its unlikeness to God, is a privation, a defect in the good, but its very existence makes the good more apparent and more beautiful.[46] God has no defect, but His creatures can and indeed do. This potential lack in created things creates an important contrast: "Insofar as a defect of a particular good in some part becomes apparent," Hugh tells us, "everything stands out more beautifully."[47] Through the recognition of this difference better things are judged more beautiful, and this is the good that comes from the defect of the good called evil.

God is pleased by those things that are like Himself, but what is unlike Him has its uses, and in this way God does not will evil, but He does will that some types of evil exist, because these will, eventually, produce even more good that is like Him. Here unlikeness is the servant of likeness, creating similarity out of its dissonance. As Hugh says, "He [God] wants evil to exist because its result is useful for everything."[48] In willing the existence of certain expressions of evil, God ultimately wills the good that is the very image of Him. It is this transformative encounter with difference that is enacted in the treatise against Albero. In his fall, Albero is, nevertheless, an instrument of reform.

In the treatise against Albero, a set of complex interactions between similarity and opposition is developed. At the heart of these interactions lies the delicate balancing on the part of an interpreter that allows a harmonious resolution to be reached through the employment of difference. At different points Albero has been described as very similar to demons, the fires of judgment, and the wicked priests he despises. Additionally, I have argued that as the treatise develops he is also somehow made like the author of the treatise himself. His evil and his error originate from his good; what is worst in him not only comes from the desire for what is best, but it recurrently appears as identical to it. Similarity consistently coexists with difference in the process of self-definition and self-fashioning. The recognition of this difference within a moment of attraction between apparent similarities allows the eventual banishment of difference, and this expulsion reifies the true shape and mission of the self, which necessarily must exist within the logic of binary communities. There are only two human societies. These communities, while separate in their fundamental natures and their final destinies, are in the present almost inextricably mixed. The task of the orthodox lover of virtue is to manage the acts of reading and interpretation, the recognition of the weeds from the wheat, which allow effective negotiation between them and an eventual secure admittance to the community of God.

Contracts between Worlds: Reading under Heretics' Skins and Christian Interpretation

Caesarius of Heisterbach, another Cistercian in the Rhineland, tells the story of a group of heretics who actually did, if only for a time, defy the flames. They did so in just the way the author of the treatise against Albero suggested: calling on demonic power, or *maleficium*.[49] Like Albero, the presence of this power must be read from the inside out, because outwardly it appears the same as a miracle. This likeness comes about through a contractual interaction between humans and the Devil.[50] This contract, pact, or agreement is initially difficult to see, but becomes apparent through a series of interactions between extremes.

Writing in 1220, Caesarius described how, about the same time as the burnings at Cologne in 1163, two supposed holy men came to Besançon.[51] They lived lives of the greatest apparent sanctity, and having caught the attention of the laity began to preach "unheard of heresies." To prove the truth of their novel doctrines, they seemed to work miracles. The two men walked on flour without leaving footsteps, strode over water without sinking, and had wooden huts burned down around them. These flames could not harm them, and, as such wonders continued to sway the people, the bishop felt compelled to consult expert advice.

The advice that the bishop sought against these heretics was from the very demons who provided their power. The bishop ordered a clerk, skilled in the art of necromancy, to summon the Devil and ask him, "by what power these great and stupendous miracles are being wrought."[52] The bishop knows that these are not true miracles by the content of the heretics' preaching. The foreknowledge of what the heretics are guides the bishop's own process of interpretation and his actions. The dissemination and realization in action of this foreknowledge forms the prelate's main goal. The common people do not have his learning or his discernment, and lacking these traits they are unable to interpret successfully the apparent wonders the heretics work before them. When the clerk objects that he had long ago given up the sinful practice of necromancy, the bishop responds that without definite answers the people will surely kill him. If the clerk obediently summons the Devil, this act will be an expiation for his past sins, rather than a new one. False miracles, here, cause recourse to a forbidden art in the service of God; like is joined with like in the service of their contrariety. Indeed, the truth of the contrariety is demonstrated through the pairing.

Once summoned, the Devil informs the clerk that the two men are his vassals and that they preach what he has "put in their mouths." They cannot be injured because the contracts, by which they became his vassals, have been "sewn under their armpits just beneath the skin." If these texts were ever taken from them, their powers would leave them, and "they would become weak like other men."[53] The heretics' written contracts of vassalage recall the legend of Theophilus, translated into Latin in the eighth century.[54] This legend is the origin in the Christian West of the pact with the Devil that would become synonymous with later witchcraft. Theophilus sold his soul to the Devil through a written contract, and this story would later inspire a set of legends surrounding Gerbert of Aurillac (Pope Silvester II) and Faust.[55]

The contracts are described as *cyrographa* (chirographs), and their specific form, paired with their literal insertion into the heretics' bodies, creates a powerful connection between the heretics and the demonic. A chirograph is a particular type of written contract that is split into parts along a curving line. Only by bringing two or more portions together can one part be validated as an original copy.[56] By implication, another part of the contract is in the hands of the Devil. These texts are therefore direct connections with the demonic. Their insertion under the heretics' skin is a parallel with the power of the Devil that works within them to such an extent that they are almost puppets, speaking the Devil's words and working his false wonders.

The removal of these contracts equates to the unmasking of the demonic power at the heart of the heretic, dissolving the apparent likeness between false wonder and miracle or saint and heretic.[57] The heretics are like the allegorical *integumenta* (veils) or *involucra* (wrappings) of the classical pagan authors, under which these authors chose to hide moral and scientific truths.[58] Pagan tales of apparent immorality, as read by medieval Christian interpreters, had to be taken to mean things other than the literal reading of the words would suggest. In this fashion, the literal level is never an appropriate meaning and halting the act of interpretation there is actively harmful. These stories must be interpreted to make the invisible meanings held inside them visible. The heretics, likewise, must have their hidden meaning extracted from them. This meaning is an actual hidden text from inside their bodies that exists as an antecedent to them. The retrieval of the text from the heretical human body that encases it is a recovery of this anteriority. Filled with the Devil's writing, the heretics in this story are really "container[s] for the contained," and, just as in the case of pagan allegory, the act of interpretation that follows the recognition of this text "is itself an act of placing a veil over the visible meanings (*visibilia*) of the text."[59] The surface meaning of the pagan allegory is submerged within its moralized meaning, and the heretic, as human individual, is destroyed by his unmasking. In his destruction, he dissolves into the fires of the Devil that existed before his individual life.

The clerk-necromancer informs the bishop of the heretics' vulnerability and the bishop forms a plan that will ensure their destruction. He proclaims to the people that he will follow the heretics' teachings if they work one of their miracles before him. He has a large fire prepared in the middle of town, and before the heretics enter it the bishop springs his trap. Asking to examine their persons for "charms" (*maleficia*), the bishop's men discover small scars under their arms.[60] With the help of knives, the contracts are drawn out of them.[61] The heretics, now overwhelmed with panic, no longer wish to enter the flames, at which point the bishop exhibits the chirographs to the crowd. Enraged, the people "hurled the servants of the Devil into the fire prepared for them, that they might go to be tormented with the Devil in fire eternal."[62] Caesarius concludes the story by remarking that the bishop's swift action completely extinguished this particular heresy.

Caesarius's story of the heretics at Besançon is a model for a hermeneutical process guided by an authority that can direct its subordinate members in the literal piercing of misleading appearances. The bishop's servants, under his direction, cut open the heretics' skin with knives. This corporeal pulling back of the veil completes the hermeneutic circle at the heart of the reader's awareness of this episode. As the heretics in the exemplum enter the flames, the reader resolves the integument of the story in fire as well. Remembering the Cistercian anthropology of Isaac of Stella, the meeting point between signs to be interpreted and the immaterial soul of man is itself made of fire. The two condemned men are signs for something else. The heretics and their apparent wonders must be rendered into a form within "a process on the way to its completion."[63] The shape of this process is clear because of the application of a foreknowledge that places the piece in a dialectical relationship with the whole. Appropriate to a setting riven by a desire for reform and a concern for the maintenance of a hierarchically organized community, this dialectic can only be achieved through the guidance of legitimate authority.

The heretics in this episode represent in microcosm the larger and more basic rhetorical combat between God and the Devil that imperils all acts of interpretation undertaken by living human beings.[64] Such danger occurs particularly in the process of representation and its recognition as representation. According to the fundamental doctrine of Christian teaching as laid out by Augustine, all things are learned via signs.[65] Augustine defines a sign as a thing which of itself makes some other thing come to mind.[66] Some signs are natural, and other signs are given, existing by convention, either through an understanding between God and His creatures or between His creatures and each other. These given signs are used to convey what is in one person's mind to another.[67]

Signs point to things, and an ignorance of this relationship can derail the process of understanding. A failure in understanding a text comes about through unknown or ambiguous signs that veil its meaning.[68] A sign can be mistaken for the thing it represents rather than a representation, or what a sign represents can be misunderstood. Misreading a sign as an object of signification in and of itself reflects the fundamental problem of love in Augustinian theology. Human interpretation is led by love, and a love of created things in the place of their creator is the equivalent of mistaking a sign for a signified. Things can either be used or enjoyed, and only God is to be enjoyed or loved. The things He has created are to be used to learn more about the God that created them and to return to that God.[69] In this idea of use and enjoy-

ment lies the suggestion that the created things encountered by human beings in their lives should be appreciated as signs. All of creation, when read
correctly, testifies to the existence and goodness of God.[70] If creation is understood and enjoyed as a good in and of itself, the interpreter errs, mistaking a sign for the thing it signifies. The joy a created thing finds solely in
another created thing is problematic.[71]

Like's tendency to rejoice in like is at the root of the problem in human
signification and understanding, and this problem is exploited by demons in
the creation of signs that point to nothing. This mistake comes from and results in misplaced love, where creation becomes the object of delight that its
creator should be.[72] With the creator marginalized, the proper ordering and
even existence of signs becomes obscure. Some signs are unknown or difficult
to recognize due to limitations in an individual's experience and the ever-present
misplacement of human attachment in the fallen world. Other signs, however, are carefully crafted frauds, designed to play on this weakness.

Some fraudulent signs, or superstitions, are made by demons to deceive
human beings. These signs constituted the majority of the religious and ceremonial practices of the entire human race before the birth of Christ. Demonic
signs are made to order, designed to appeal to the "speculations and conventions" each individual accepts.[73] In short, they will look very much like the
things one expects to see; apparent similarity lies at the core of the realization
of their mission. This mission is to continue the human estrangement from
God through the displacement of love.[74] Whether a human is a willing participant or not in this distraction, these signs "establish certain secret or even
overt meanings" in the form of "consultations or contracts about meaning
arranged and ratified with demons, such as the enterprises involved in the art
of magic."[75] In this fashion, a person who uses these signs enters into a kind
of contractual relationship, or implicit pact, with demons. Augustine's idea of
the implicit pact entered into the standard medieval literature on magic, appearing in the work of Burchard of Worms, Ivo of Chartres, and Gratian.[76]
Over the course of the medieval period, such an idea of a demonic pact, linked
to apostasy, became an important element not only of some heresies but also
of the idea of witchcraft as an act of lèse-majesté against God.[77] Caesarius's
heretics, literally encasing their magical contracts of vassalage by their per-
sonhood, enact precisely this role. The contracts have their origin in the misplacement of human love, and they fix this displacement like words recorded
on the page.

Such misleading signs can only function due to a condition in an individual existing before their exposure to them. The victims of demonic deceit are
misled according to "what their wills deserve."[78] In an interpretive process

guided by "faith, hope and charity," the lack of these virtues opens the door to mistake and deception.[79] These virtues, particularly charity, or love, arise through the action of God within an individual.[80] The Augustinian system deeply relies on a recognition of what is already there, guided by the very thing that is revealed. The terrible difficulty held within this relationship has inspired millennia of debate, especially regarding predestination. In the case of Caesarius's heretics, the anteriority that they represent as signs of the Devil and his evil also indicates a preexisting wickedness on their part that only becomes apparent through the act of interpretation in the present. Just as the illumination of God allows the correct interpretation of signs, the guidance of the bishop reveals to the people the true signification inside the heretics at Besançon.

The problem of love held within like's tendency to rejoice in like was turned on its head by God's decisive rhetorical intervention in the form of the Incarnation of Christ. The Incarnation of the Word shattered a world largely held in slavery to empty demonic signs that pointed to nothing.[81] The light of God's true sign promises the ability to finally read all signs in the face of demonic interference. This improved reading begins on the level of the love that inspires and enables misreading. When God became man, He took on the human form of His creation. The love that could be directed to God as man, from like to like, became also love directed to the divine. In this miraculous reversal of force, the very expression of the problem becomes the vehicle for its resolution, and likeness and contrariety work gainfully together in the process of "Christian healing." Joined to God as man, humanity could then approach God as God through faith, repairing in this advance the currently distorted divine likeness, becoming ever more alike God and in turn knowing Him ever more, because like knows like.[82]

The restoration of like's joy in like was also a contractual exchange. In his commentary on Psalm 144, Augustine explained that the promise of human redemption, as enacted in the Incarnation and recorded in the scriptures, constituted "a certain chirograph of God."[83] For Augustine, chirograph likely meant a general written contract, and this particular agreement recorded what God promised to those who believe.[84] God's contract invalidated the earlier "chirograph of our death," destroyed by Jesus's blood.[85] To any who doubt the coming rewards of the just or the punishment of the wicked in "eternal fire," God says, "Read everything that I have promised in my chirograph."[86] Those who could read and understand this contract know that God would pay out everything He owed.

Caesarius's heretics with contracts hidden under their skin and the Augustinian implicit pact and chirograph of God involve processes of discovery led by inner dispositions. In such contexts, likeness and difference are here navigated by inner faculties and seem themselves to be created out of each other. These stories continually draw attention to the self-reflective assertion of "the basic symbolic pact between the communicating subjects."[87] It is this pact that allows entities beyond the human to intervene in the navigation between outward appearances and inner realities. Such fruitful dialectic is the exclusive domain of the Christian who loves correctly. This love joins the Christian interpreter to a foreknowledge that cuts through appearances like a knife, while at the same time transforming and delivering the interpreter, who requires such cutting, from the carnality imputed to them through their inability to interpret alone.

The Cistercian sources examined above all combine likeness and difference in a search for meaning. The discovery of meaning, as well as its creation, was enabled through the orientation of love. The existence of a bad love, a thing that generates as well as fixates on appearances at the expense of spiritual meanings, was essential to the articulation and recognition of a good love that spun true meaning out of itself. The role of the heretic was to embody the misleading and entrapping love, to become a symbol of it to be read. In reading this symbol, the orthodox could see themselves as reaching a fulfillment that the heretic lacked. In the process of interpretation, the resemblance between orthodox and heretic, divine and demonic, was essential, since each depended on the other for its narrative generation.

Demonic power could perform many of the same functions as divine power. The essential differentiation lay in the narrative purpose served by the diabolical. It existed for its own unmasking; its power flourished so that it might more dramatically fail. The power of the Devil, just like the existence of the heretic, came into being as the result of a successful process of interpretation. Outside of this process and the divine assistance that enables it, the diabolical could not be found anywhere, because it was in no way distinguished from the divine to which it remained recurrently similar and alike. As Steven Kruger has observed for medieval presentations of Jewish voices, "Such figures are, in other words, conjured up only to be put to rest."[88] It is no coincidence that the accounts analyzed above place such an emphasis on literal conjurations. These formulae encapsulate the intentions, the guiding desires, that created the very categories sought.

In such accounts, the revelation of evil as evil entailed a corresponding revelation of the deity that constituted not its opposite but the fullness that it lacked. It was an illustration of the way to consummation in the face of arrested development. The reparation of apparent privation organized the narrative frameworks that situated the, presumably, orthodox reader at the their center. Through investment in the heretic and the heretic's destruction, the orthodox can ruminate on and then redress their own lack of fit within an idealized orthodoxy. The enemy revealed is not the reader but someone else; through regarding this revelation the likeness between the faithful observer and perceived enemy can be exorcised through the simple action of its observation.

The observation of the heretic created the need for an erasure, but the heretic's removal was haunted. In the accounts of heresy above, the heretic as well as the particular, carnal love at the core of the heretic were conjured up to be banished away. The unmaking of the individual heretic was a generative act, productive of meaning. Both the occurrence of this destruction and the maintenance of its memory were essential. The remaining specter of heresy enabled the vibrant life of the good Christian.

CHAPTER 6

Witches and Orgiastic Rituals

Heresy, Sex, and Reading in the Late Twelfth
and Early Thirteenth Centuries

According to the *Chronicon Anglicarum* (*Chroni-
cle of English Affairs*), of Ralph of Coggeshall, a young Gervase of Tilbury, in
a vineyard outside Rheims, very righteously brought about the death of a beautiful woman who refused to have sex with him. Gervase recognized that her
refusal was born out of heresy rather than any actual virtue or respectable
choice, and his accusation was proven completely correct after the woman fell
into the hands of his employer, the archbishop of Rheims. The archbishop and
his assembled clerics convinced the maiden to reveal an ugly old woman as
the origin of her heresy, which, among other things, held that sexual intercourse irreversibly stained the soul. Both women refused to abandon their
false beliefs and were sentenced to burn. In the end, the old woman escaped
by flying through an open window while the young maiden, left behind, was
burned alive.[1]

Peter the Chanter had alleged that in the same region angry churchmen
falsely labeled women who spurned their sexual advances as heretics, and
Ralph's telling of this curious episode disarms contemporary allegations such
as these by turning a formula regarding clerical corruption and sexual desire
into something else.[2] Through the abuse and eventual destruction of the
maiden, Ralph's story transforms a young churchman's desire to sin into a
shared triumph for educated, male discernment, substituting a hermeneutical
victory for a sexual conquest. The interpretive victory in place of sex requires

the overcoming of appearances. As in the process of spiritual exegesis, a reader could only know the true signification of a text by surpassing the carnality of the letter.[3] Accordingly, sources like Ralph's reduce heretics into gendered texts whose appearances must be overcome. In the examples that follow, the carnality of the letter is connected to the carnality of women's bodies, and the conquest of this carnality in the process of interpretation provides a pleasure akin to that of sexual intercourse.

By rejecting the unabashed carnality and sensuality of the heretic, orthodox authors and readers cultivated a type of pleasure opposite to and also founded on that initial rejection. This pleasure was intellectual and spiritual and stood in opposition to the carnal pleasure orthodox authors recurrently ascribed to supposed heretics. In other words, the ability to experience this intellective pleasure was an essential element of the common identity of the learned clerical class, making its discovery in accounts of heresy a unifying event; in interpreting the initially misleading heretic correctly, the educated Catholic could gain a better sense of himself.

The argument of this chapter proceeds in two main sections. The first examines the story of Gervase and the maiden as told by the Cistercian abbot Ralph of Coggeshall. The second section interrogates the recurrent trope of indiscriminate sexuality ascribed by orthodox authors to heretical sects, and how these authors utilized accounts of scandalous nocturnal orgies as yet another way to portray heresy as a negative, carnal image of orthodoxy and orthodox modes of reading.

Gender and Reading in the "Witch of Rheims"

While the first story examined in this chapter, from Ralph's *Chronicle*, is about two women, it is often referred to, especially in older scholarship, as the story of the "Witch of Rheims," as if there were only one.[4] While more recent surveys of medieval heresy have been more attentive to detail in naming, this scholarly shorthand actually arises from the structure of the story itself. Ralph's tale has attracted attention in histories of witchcraft as well as heresy because it illustrates vividly the conceptual foundations both topics shared in the twelfth century.[5] Ralph's story of the two women casts the discovery of heresy in gendered terms, suggesting that the recognition of heresy is related to the masculine domains of scriptural reading and interpretation exercised on a surface that is feminine. In this mode, masculine, clerical reading breaks through carnal appearances to apprehend spiritual truths, turning the ravishment of the letter into a spiritual parallel to the worldly seduction or rape of a woman.

The story of the Witch of Rheims is actually an account of learned interpretation as gang rape.

Ralph of Coggeshall and his *Chronicle* are major sources for English events during the reigns of Richard I and John, as well as for the Third and the Fourth Crusades. It covers the period 1066–1224, but its richest contents derive from the period of Ralph's authorship between 1187 and 1224. Little is known of Ralph himself, especially in comparison to many of his contemporaries. He was a Cistercian monk and abbot of Coggeshall from 1207 to 1218, when he resigned the abbacy because of poor health.[6] His house was not very rich or important, but it was well positioned for collecting information across the British Isles and among fellow Cistercians visiting from the continent. In some ways, Ralph wrote in a traditional annalistic mode, but he set himself apart by the inclusion of well-told and lively stories drawn mostly from oral sources.[7] His storytelling was deeply influenced by a number of contemporary literary and historical conventions, such as romance, filtered through the "conventional Christian ethic of his day," lending him a voice that often comes across as "doctrinaire, even cruel" to modern readers.[8] He had an interest in the extraordinary and the supernatural, particularly visions or revelations regarding the spiritual world.[9]

Ralph's account of the so-called Witch of Rheims is the fifth in a series of six anecdotes of wonders and miracles inserted into the *Chronicle* in the midst of the preparations for the Fourth Crusade between the years 1200 and 1201.[10] The dates for the composition of the *Chronicle* are debated, but it is likely that Ralph wrote the wonder stories in the early thirteenth century, perhaps between 1201 and 1205, or in the 1220s.[11] The stories themselves are set earlier in the reigns of Henry II, Richard, and Louis VII. The first four stories involve wondrous bodies: a man dragged from the sea; green children; the discovery of giants' bones; and a girl named Malekin, who became a spirit or changeling after being abducted from a field. The final two stories focus on heresy and orthodoxy in the juxtaposition of the Witch of Rheims and the saintly Alpais.

Scholars have suggested that these six tales should be considered together as offering commentary on the events around them in the *Chronicle*. Elizabeth Freeman argues that Ralph's attention to "unusual and bizarre" bodies in this section provides "a metaphor for the broader Christian body of believers" under the threat of disintegration.[12] The six wonder stories are united by the threat to the unity of the Christian community posed by those outside it, and Ralph presents this unifying theme through "the metaphor of bodily integrity and transformation."[13] Christine Neufeld, likewise, believes that a concern for the integrity of the Christian body in the form of "imaginative exercises in distinguishing the self from the other" unites the six stories. The imagining of self and other invests itself in the symbolics of the female body.[14] In this group of stories, identity is explored and constructed through women's bodies by exclusionary means.

Ralph cites his source for the Witch of Rheims story as Gervase of Tilbury, himself a major medieval author, cleric, and courtier. Gervase is best known for his *Otia imperialia* (*Recreation for an Emperor*), a large and complex collection of stories purporting to provide entertainment and edification for Emperor Otto IV.[15] Master Gervase was a highly educated cleric, who may have become a Premonstratensian canon very late in life.[16] Gervase is not only the source for the story but also a major character in it. Comparing the dates for his life with the reign of Louis VII and Archbishop William of Rheims, who is also a character in the story, the Witch of Rheims tale must be set between 1176 and 1180.[17]

Ralph recounts that in the time of Louis VII of France a prodigy occurred in the city of Rheims regarding a certain old woman infected with the illness of the Publican heresy. While the story, at least according to Ralph's introduction, ostensibly regards this old woman, the story itself begins not with her but instead with a beautiful maiden. One day, Archbishop William "White Hands" of Rheims and his clerics were riding outside the city.[18] One of William's clerics, Master Gervase of Tilbury, saw a young woman walking alone in a vineyard, and "led on by the curiosity of slippery (*lubricae*) youth," he left the archbishop's company and went to her.[19]

Two elements of this setting would have particularly shaped the expectations of contemporary readers: the initial similarity of the plot to a pastourelle and the location of the encounter in a vineyard.[20] In the medieval poetic genre of the pastourelle a knight recounts his chance encounter with a shepherdess to an audience. This encounter proceeds in stages. The central part is the *débat amoureux*, an attempted seduction in the shape of a verbal duel between the man and the woman. The man begins with flattery and becomes bolder, even violent, as the poem progresses. The poem ends in one of three ways: the woman's consent to sex, the man leaving in disappointment, or with rape.[21] The pastourelle structure shapes the account of the Witch of Rheims, but it primarily serves to raise expectations that the plot will subvert. It is the first of many misleading appearances.

The location of this encounter in a vineyard sets a complicated stage for what follows, and the predatory curiosity of a young cleric finds in this pastoral setting a different kind of predator. The setting of the vineyard placed the interaction between the young Master Gervase and the maiden within a set of associations regarding heresy and privileged male self-fashioning that was intimately familiar to contemporary Cistercians. These associations had already served a prominent role in the earlier polemics surrounding burnings for heresy in the Rhineland. Traditionally, the vineyard had long served as a scriptural symbol for the people of God, somewhat like the field of grain in the Parable of the Wheat and the Weeds.[22] In this tradition, the vineyard took on something like a double signification. Its vines are the people of God, growing to a harvest, and it is also a space in which the people of God can labor, earning by their work a share in the harvest. For example, Augustine explained that each Christian should see himself as a vineyard: "We are the vineyard of the Lord, because He cultivates us to fruition. We are the building of God because He who cultivates us dwells within us."[23] Augustine, following what was in his time an established tradition, saw the vineyard of the self as under threat from heretics, symbolized by the "little foxes that destroy the vines" described in the Song of Songs, and centuries later Bernard of Clairvaux also followed in this tradition.[24]

Bernard's familiar sermons on the Song of Songs help to illuminate the power of the associations between the vineyard and heresy present in this story, just as they did for the Rhineland executions around 1143. In fact, many of dynamics present in the earlier instance are replicated in this later story from Ralph of Coggeshall. In the tale of the Witch of Rheims, however, the associations between the interior lives of religious men, as the vineyard, and the threat posed by heretics, as the little foxes, take on stronger gendered connotations. Bernard argued that the vineyard is an interior domain of effort for the wise man.[25] The cultivated man is a virtuous man, and the effort to produce virtue and wisdom is the tending of the vineyard. In this spiritual signification of the biblical vineyard only a wise man can be said to possess, or better *be*, a vineyard: "These spiritual vineyards signify spiritual men within whom all things are cultivated, all things are germinating, bearing fruit and bringing forth the spirit of salvation."[26] The interior of the religious man is a vineyard, but so too is the larger Christian world, made up of many individual believers as vines. In fact, when Bernard left the cloister to preach against heresy, he shifted his attention from this internal domain of effort to an external one, explaining that he moved from the interior vineyard of the monastery to the larger exterior vineyard of the world.[27] His use of these images indicates a conviction that the internal cultivation undertaken by spiritual men in the homosocial monastery offered a model for the policing of the larger world by educated, clerical men, particularly in the identification and eradication of the threat posed by the little foxes. Many other authors in the period, especially Cistercians, made similar associations between foxes, heresy, and hunting.[28] Importantly, in Latin the gender of the word for fox, *vulpes*, is feminine. In this exegetical framework, especially vivid to Cistercians of the mid-twelfth century like Ralph of Coggeshall, the interaction between Gervase and the maiden in a vineyard becomes deeply evocative.

In the space of the vineyard outside Rheims, things turn out to mean the opposite of what their appearances might initially suggest. Gervase should be a worker in the vineyard, but here he seems a hunter within it. Led on by the "slippery" or "dangerous" curiosity of a young man, Master Gervase stalks the young woman whom he should protect, telling her of the joys of sex in a manner befitting the courtiers of secular lords rather than the stewards of God. At first it would seem that Gervase is destroying the vines of his own vocation as one of the archbishop's clerks and those of the laity entrusted with their care. As a momentary predator in the vineyard, however, Gervase finds another hidden predator in the form of the young woman, hiding under the guise of apparent prey. Master Gervase has caught a fox.

At first Gervase makes small talk, asking about her origin, her parents, and why she was in the vineyard alone. Eventually, "when he had closely observed her beauty for some time," Gervase gets to the point, speaking to her in the manner of a courtier (*curialiter*) about lustful love.[29] The young woman decisively rebuffs the young master's advances in a manner that has terrible consequences: "God preserve me, young man, from ever becoming your mistress, or anyone else's, for if I lost my virginity and my flesh were corrupted even one time, I would without doubt be subject to eternal damnation with no remedy."[30] To the ear of Master Gervase, the young woman's defense of her virginity is clearly heretical. Some modern commentators have argued that the maiden's words are in no way heretical, reflecting the high status of virginity and an abhorrence of the sin of fornication.[31] Seen from the point of view of an educated cleric on the forefront of contemporary penitential theology, however, the young woman's insistence that no remedy could cleanse her if her flesh were even one time corrupted is heretical. The girl suggests that this sin cannot be repented. Perceiving this logic in her words, Gervase knows "at once" that she is one of the Publicans, pursued all over France and exiled to freeze alone in the snow at Oxford by Henry II of England.[32] Obliged to defend her opinions on virginity and salvation, the beautiful woman's ability to speak for herself remains limited. Overhearing the argument between Gervase and the maiden, Archbishop William orders the girl arrested and taken back into the city, where he and his household attempt to convince her of her error. The young woman admits that she cannot respond to their objections, but says that she has an "instructress (*magistra*)" that could answer them.

The young woman's instructress is the old woman with whom the tale began, and she engages the clerics in a theological debate in place of the worldly débat amoureux. With the young woman's help, the authorities seek out this "instructrix of wicked error," and she proves to be as proficient as her student said she would be, perverting all the authorities the clerics cite with "subtle interpretations" and moving effortlessly between the New and the Old Testaments.[33] The old woman is clearly well practiced in theological debate, and there is something monstrous in her intrusion into the masculine sphere of textual and spiritual interpretation. She mixes "truth with falsehood" in a sense, multiplying the veils or carnal appearances of the letter to endlessly obscure the spiritual meanings hidden by them, distorting "the true interpretation of our faith with a kind of perverted insight."[34] Ralph concludes that "it was obvious to everyone that the spirit of all error was speaking through her mouth."[35] The encounter with the old woman, who has been revealed only through the diligent pursuit of the beautiful maiden, is an encounter with evil itself.

That the interrogation of a beautiful woman who has a limited ability to speak leads to the revelation of an old woman who speaks wickedly well, accounts for the common tendency to call the female objects of this story the Witch of Rheims.[36] Even though the story is literally about two women, this scholarly naming convention refers to both women as one. The act of gendered occlusion arises from the text itself. The beautiful woman that attracts Master Gervase in the vineyard is only a misleading appearance; the old witch is the inner truth that hides behind it. The Witch of Rheims tale achieves this effect through what Barbara Spackman calls the "enchantress-turned-hag" topos. The beautiful enchantress first encountered by a male hero (woman as lie) is eventually revealed as an "ugly, toothless old hag hidden beneath her artifice (woman as truth)." For Spackman, this topos is a hermeneutic figure symbolizing the revelation of "truth beneath falsehood, plain speech beneath cosmetic rhetoric, essence beneath appearance."[37] The search for spiritual signification embodied within the enchantress-turned-hag topos refers to a fundamental method of spiritual reading that existed as the intimate domain of educated male clerics.

In the revelation of the witch beneath the maiden, the clerics move from the carnality of the letter to the spiritual truth behind it. This process mirrors the essential elements of literary activity, and as Carolyn Dinshaw has shown, this literary activity is often structured, explored, or understood in gendered terms. The acts of writing, signifying, allegorizing, interpreting, glossing are associated with the masculine, meanwhile the surface on which these acts are performed are identified as feminine.[38] The text as it appears has to be stripped naked, penetrated, and its hidden meaning seized and carried off by the interpreter. This spiritual or allegorical reading, as Dinshaw stresses, generates pleasure in the exegete.[39] The interaction between Gervase and the maiden first casts pleasure in carnal terms but finds its resolution by relocating pleasure from physical intercourse to literary and hermeneutical conquest, and this conquest is the rejection of the letter in favor of its meaning. As a result, the beautiful young heretic is doomed.

As all attempts to convince both women to renounce heresy fail, "common council" decides to burn them alive. Before this moment is reached, the women are given the rest of the day to think over their errors after the first encounter. When this waiting period is over, they are then engaged in debate a second time before all the archbishop's clerics as well as noble laymen. They both stand firm in this more public confrontation, leading to their condemnation, but only one woman suffers the penalty.[40]

As the flames are lit in the city, the old woman makes her escape. Imprisoned in the upper story of a building while awaiting execution, the old woman waits for the archbishop's servants to arrive. Before they can drag her away, she calls them all madmen and unjust judges. She asks, "Do you think that you can burn me on your fire? I neither respect your judgment nor fear the fire which you have prepared."[41] As she speaks, she takes a ball of thread from her bosom. The old woman keeps one end in her hand and throws the other into the air shouting "Catch!" In response, she lifts into the air, flies through the open window, and is never seen again. "We believe," Ralph says, "that she was taken aloft through the aid of the vengeful spirits who long ago lifted Simon Magus in the air."[42] In conclusion, Ralph states that what happened to "the old witch (*malefica*)" or where she went none of the onlookers ever knew.[43]

The old woman's escape is a final revelation of the timeless evil she represents. It validates all the clerical convictions regarding her, and places her within the context of a great heretical genealogy reaching back to the time of the apostles. In Acts 8:9–24, the magician Simon Magus of Samaria offers money to the apostles to receive the power of the Holy Spirit. Enraged by the offer, Peter replies that such power cannot be bought.[44] In the Middle Ages, the sin and heresy of simony, or the buying and selling of ecclesiastical appointments with money, took its name from this episode.[45] The reference to the spirits that lifted Simon Magus points to a story that originated in the apocryphal Acts of Peter, elaborating on the exchange in Acts. In this apocryphal story, Simon engages in a miracle contest with the apostle. Frustrated after Peter brings a dead man back to life, Simon announces that he will fly up to God. Simon does indeed fly, but at the prayer of Peter he comes crashing down.[46] In the version of the story prevalent at the time Ralph wrote, Simon flew only through the aid of demons. These demons lifted the anti-apostle into the air before they were banished by Peter's prayer.[47] By Ralph's time, Simon Magus, the magician, served as the anti-apostle from whom heresies descended in an inverted image of the apostolic succession.[48] The old woman clearly represents this poisoned lineage.

With the old woman gone, the focus returns to the young one, like closing a circle. "No reason, no promise of wealth" can convince her to abandon her heresy, and she is burned alive. Appealing in life, many find her admirable in death, as she dies without sighs, tears, or wailing, "enduring to the end the torment of the consuming fire steadily and eagerly." In this performance she was "like the martyrs of Christ . . . who once upon a time were slaughtered by the pagans for the sake of the Christian religion."[49] This is yet another false appearance, as Ralph tells the reader. One must understand the different intentions that lie behind similar behavior. Her death might look like a Christian martyrdom, but it is, in fact, for a "separate cause." There is no similarity, moreover, in this impious sect to the constancy and steadfastness of real martyrs, whose contempt for death arises from piety. The young woman, in contrast, chooses to die, Ralph insists, because of hardness of heart. As Bernard of Clairvaux argued in his sermon referring to the executions in the Rhineland, the death of the beautiful heretic is a suicide and not an act of admirable faith.[50] As in the discernment of spirits, one must know how to read appearances for the truth behind them. As Nancy Caciola has shown, such discernment takes its often female objects as ciphers to be interpreted according to observers' ideologies, self-interest, and the exigencies of the power they wield.[51]

In his glossing, Ralph invites learned readers like himself to join the interpretive conquest at the heart of this spiritualizing pastourelle. The carnality of the maiden's body can now be fully seen through, and what lies obscured behind it is, in the form of the old woman, an eternal wickedness that runs in a line back through time to Simon Magus and the Devil behind him. With this meaning grasped and made off with, the obscuring veil of the beautiful woman can be "cast into the fire as a useless twig," to quote Bernard's explanation for the usefulness of evil beings.[52] The inversion of the secular genre of the pastourelle in this tale was particularly appealing to Ralph and his immediate audience, which was composed of men experienced in both *saeculum* and *sacerdotium*, courtly service to the world and clerical service to God.[53] Cistercians, recruited from the higher social classes and from repentant courtiers, not unlike Gervase of Tilbury, lived in their own lives a similar inversion of roles, exchanging active sexual masculinity for spiritual virility invested heavily in particular modes of reading.[54]

In this interpretation of the Witch of Rheims story, successful hermeneutics is like a sexual conquest. The clerical interpreters in this tale seize meaning from the misleading feminine veil that obscures it. This revelation of the woman's truth is parallel to the sexual conquest attempted by Gervase at the story's opening. This conquest is, at least rightfully, denied to him as an unmarried man moving in the circles of celibate ecclesiastics, but something like it can be legitimately accomplished through spiritual interpretation. Gervase does, however, manage the rape of the maiden as an object of interpretation. Her appearance is penetrated, pierced to reveal the truth inside. This truth is a timeless thing, literally flying off to join the literary list of wickedness to which it now belongs, and the carnality of the letter, the beautiful maiden, is given over with contempt to the fire.

After the description of the maiden's death and how it should be read, Ralph continues the glossing through a summary of the beliefs held by the Publicans. They deny infant baptism, prayer for the dead, and the intercession of the saints. They condemn marriage and advocate virginity "as a cover for their indecency."[55] They despise any food that comes about as the result of procreation. They do not believe in the fire of Purgatory but instead hold that the souls of the dead either go to Heaven or to Hell immediately after death. Finally, they only accept the Gospels and the canonical epistles as legitimate authoritative texts.

Ralph complicates this list of their beliefs immediately through evidence brought to light by "those who have investigated their secrets."[56] These investigators have uncovered that the heretics believe an apostate angel, named Luzabel, rules the entire material world. Human bodies were formed by the Devil, "but the soul was created by God and poured into bodies." The existence of two creators creates a battle between spirit and matter, which is really a conflict between inside and outside: "Hence it comes about that a kind of stubborn battle will always be waged between the body and the soul."[57] In the opinions of the heretics the combat between good and evil is a fight between inner spirit and outer covering. This erroneous theology is the mirror image of the orthodox hermeneutic at the heart of Ralph's Witch of Rheims story. Ralph presents this fallen image of his own way of reading as a monstrous distortion held by "rustic people."[58] Rustics are the very opposite of the clerical, a category on whose repudiation the self-identity of the cleric takes shape.[59] As rustics they do not respect rational arguments, proper authorities, and clerical eloquence. The heretical explanation for the war between the letter and the spirit lacks all subtlety. In the consideration of its failures juxtaposed with the edifice of orthodoxy, the orthodox reader can find that his methods, his authorities, his very identity, all stand out more beautifully.[60] The spiritual interpretation that brings this beautiful contrast to the fore continues to generate pleasure in the interpreter as it does so. Heresy may be ugly but its revelation clothes orthodoxy in beauty and in pleasure.

The next and last of Ralph's wonder stories provides an orthodox contrast to the heretical femininity of the Witch of Rheims. Ralph recounts that around the same time as the burning at Rheims there was a most sacred virgin, named Alpais, who survived on the Eucharist alone.[61] Alpais lived in the diocese of Sens in the late twelfth century.[62] When Ralph wrote Alpais still lived, existing as a kind of font of divine information for ecclesiastical magnates, princes, and laymen alike. Alpais died in 1211, and a later hand in the manuscript of the *Chronicle* adds that her fast has now lasted more than thirty years.[63] After the composition of her vita in 1180 at the Cistercian monastery of Echarlis, Alpais of Cudot attracted the attention of a number of medieval chroniclers and historians, including Robert of Auxerre, Caesarius of Heisterbach, Jacques de Vitry, and Stephen of Bourbon.[64] Ralph's account of her ability to survive without conventional nourishment, or *inedia*, while recounting many of the same incidents, is independent of all of these other sources.[65]

Ralph's account of the virgin Alpais constructs her as the positive opposite to the heretical women narrated before her. As Freeman argues, "Every bad practice in the heresy tale is remedied by its equivalent good practice in the Alpais' description."[66] In contrast to the heretical maiden at Rheims, whose pleasing integument had to be pierced through force, Alpais not only readily submits to clerical interpretation but also repeatedly proclaims that submission. The learned men who interpret her submissive body find in it a revelation of the Holy Spirit to which they sought to unite themselves. Alpais is a virgin and abstains from food for the right reasons. The saintly Alpais suffers immense pain, but does so in the spirit of patience, like a true martyr, in contrast to the women at Rheims. While the old witch was eager to speak, Alpais avoids speaking, and defers to ecclesiastical authority until she is vindicated by providence. Finally, Alpais engages in a test and debate with William White Hands, just as the two heretical women did, but with very different results.[67]

As a young woman, Alpais was struck by a terrible illness, leaving her paralyzed. At first she was also covered with stinking sores, which other sources specify as leprosy and Ralph calls ulcers, but these marks disappear after she sees the Virgin Mary in a vision.[68] The foulness of Alpais's body is a cover for her sanctity, and the Mother of God removes this veil so she can more easily be read. Mary praises the young woman's patience and promises her that she would now be as desirable to everyone as she had been despicable before in the eyes of the world.

This interaction repeats the negotiation between outside and inside, letter and spirit, initiated earlier, and Alpais too becomes an object of interrogation and interpretation for Archbishop William. Hearing of her miraculous fast, William at first does not believe. He sends "a multitude of honest and rich women" to test the paralytic. Alpais sees through all their ploys with mild laughter, while accepting from them no food or drink. Intrigued, William comes himself, speaks to her "sweetly (*suaviter*)" and promises to build a church there with regular canons to see after her and celebrate the mass.[69] While this plan would grant her easier access to the Eucharist, Alpais objects. Filled with the Holy Spirit, she clings to her inborn poverty, rejects worldly glory, and "humbly" contradicts the archbishop. William is unmoved by this objection, and Alpais suffers his decision until she is again directly consoled by God. She remains, humble and faithful, offering visions and revelations to the grandees that come to see her. Alpais is a passive body that shores up the larger body of the Christian community around her. While the "spirit of all error" spoke through the witch, the very Holy Spirit itself makes use of Alpais's body, illustrating as it does so the communion between the flesh and the spirit so easily misunderstood by supposed heretics.

Heretics and Ritual Sex

At the end of his account of the Witch of Rheims, Ralph provides a hint regarding another way in which the supposed Publican heretics misunderstood the proper divine relationship between matter and spirit. After Ralph shares the secrets uncovered by orthodox investigators of the sect, such as their belief in the demonic creation and continued governance of the terrestrial world, he adds that these heretics gather together to perform sinister nocturnal rituals: "Some also say that in their underground lairs they carry out foul sacrifices to their Lucifer at appointed times, and that they perform certain sacrilegious indecencies at the same time."[70] In Ralph's description, the heretics regard the entire material world as impure, and at the same time worship its overlord. This apparently glaring contradiction again suggests that what holds together the accusations lobbied against the heretics in Ralph's text is not a coherent set of ideas held by actual heretics but a set of associations set up as a kind of dark mirror of orthodoxy. How these Publican heretics functioned as an inverted image of orthodoxy will become clearer through an examination of Ralph's suggestion that the heretics provide something much darker than simple offerings to Lucifer in the form of "sacrilegious indecencies."

The convoluted wording "sacrilegious indecencies" refers to a long-running idea regarding deviant sexual behavior at the secret meetings of heretics and other aberrant groups. Deviant ritual sex forms an essential part of what Norman Cohn termed the literary tradition of the "nocturnal ritual fantasy."[71] From the ancient Mediterranean up to the Witches' Sabbaths of the early modern period, various conspiratorial sects supposedly met at night to plot against the larger community and to engage in sexual promiscuity, incest, demon worship, infanticide, cannibalism, and black magic. Earlier, hostile Roman pagans levied such accusations against early Christians. Hostile medieval accounts of heretical sects followed the model of the nocturnal ritual fantasy in describing ritualized sexual activity as a part of the heretics' practice of worship. In suggesting these sexual rites at the end of his account of the Rheims episode, Ralph further nullifies the maiden's claims to purity. How could a member of a deviant cult renowned for carnal excess truly be pure?

Augustine, in his *De haeresibus* (*On Heresies*), had alleged that Manichaeans secretly consumed human seed, gathered from both men and women, in their rituals. One source claimed that those who followed such rituals were most properly called "Catharistae," or "purifiers," a specific Manichean subsect. The eating of human seed was also connected, Augustine alleged, to passages in the "books of Mani" describing the transformation of males into females in order to excite sexually the princes of darkness and extract the divine substance trapped within them.[72] Augustine's allegations rely on what has been called the Manichaean "metabolism of salvation" taken to a logical extreme, in which corrupted matter is separated from divine particles in the bodies of the elect through the process of digestion.[73] For later ideas about heretical sexual depravity, Augustine's *De haeresibus* provided a model that potentially connected three elements: gender instability, ritual sex, and the communal consumption of the products of that sex. In the twelfth century, Eckbert of Schönau reproduced Augustine's allegations regarding the eating of human seed in his *Sermones contra Catharos*.[74]

As medieval orthodox authors described them, the sex acts supposedly performed by heretics constituted a kind of negative image of the liturgical practices through which orthodox Christians underscored their union in the body of Christ.[75] The orthodox came together in open worship, and through ingesting the Eucharist directly encountered their God. In this encounter, the individual believer reaffirmed and strengthened the union of redeeming love, or charity (*caritas*), between God and His fallen creature. Through union with this God, Christians also became united to each other as fellow members of Christ's earthly body. Heretics, in contrast, remained completely in the fallen human state, meeting in secret to reject by their choices and their actions the unity of divine charity that alone promised salvation. Their union consisted in this fallen human state and its stubborn continuance. *Cupiditas*, or the desire for earthly things and their pleasures, is emblematic of the fallen state, and heretical worship becomes a celebration of this cupidity in opposition to divine love.

Sexual indecencies as a clear inversion of orthodox worship were a standard part of medieval descriptions of heretical sects, beginning with the sources for the very first burning for heresy in the medieval West at Orleans in 1022. For example, Paul of St. Père in his record of the Orleans sect wrote: "They gathered together on certain nights in an assigned house. Each, holding lights in their hands at the beginning of their litany intoned the names of demons until suddenly they saw a demon in the guise of some small animal descend among them. Immediately, as they saw that sight, they would extinguish all the lights and every man who could seized whatever woman came into hand for sex, with no thought given to sin, whether they were their mother or their sister, or a nun. They considered their coitus sacred and an act of worship."[76] If any children result from these unions, they are thrown into a fire, like pagan offerings, and burned to ashes. The heretics venerate these ashes just as "Christian religiosity ought to guard the body of Christ, to be given to the sick about to leave this world as the viaticum."[77] Indeed, Paul informs the reader that they called this meal "celestial." These ashes have "such a great power of diabolic deception" in them that whoever eats of them "can scarcely ever after direct the pace of his mind away from that heresy to the way of truth."[78] In this account, the nocturnal rites of the heretics are a clear parody or deformed copy of the liturgical practices of legitimate contemporary Catholicism. The inverted copying is particularly apparent in their cannibalistic Eucharist, which rather than an encounter between human and God is the literal ingestion of a dead child.

Nocturnal orgies, like those described by Paul of St. Père, became a recurrent element in descriptions of medieval heresies. Such shocking sexual escapades appear in the autobiography of Guibert of Nogent (1114), the influential papal bull *Vox in Rama* (1233), and the accusations against the Templars (1307), to chose only a few examples.[79] In these sources there is a remarkable continuity in the kinds of behaviors and specific sexual acts attributed to different deviant sects. The continuity does not arise in most cases through clear influences between texts. In fact, some of the more lurid examples had a very limited circulation, and the authors of some of these texts were most certainly unaware of similar descriptions offered by earlier authors. What is clearly apparent, however, is a continuity of message and the ways in which sexual behaviors could be used to articulate this message.

Decades before Ralph of Coggeshall recorded the story of the fateful encounter between the Publican maiden and Gervase outside Rheims, the satirist Walter Map had described the nocturnal rituals of another group of Publicans or Paterenes.[80] Walter Map was a courtier from the Welsh marches in the service of Henry II of England, who is mostly known today for his fascinating but difficult *De nugis curialium* (*Courtiers' Trifles*).[81] This long work, which appears to have evolved over a long period in different sections, is in its attention to the grotesque, lurid, and fantastic, "a kind of thermometer of [its] age."[82] In his day, Walter appears to have possessed a reputation for devastating wit, and his commentary on heresy puts this quality on bold display.[83] Writing in the 1180s, Walter described the origins and the nocturnal rituals of the Publicans or Paterenes, claiming that they originated from those disciples described in John 6:54–67 who rejected Christ's command to eat his flesh and drink his blood, objecting that "this is a hard saying." In Walter's description, this origin specifically points to an interpretive misunderstanding based on an inability to move beyond carnal appearances to spiritual significations. The unnamed followers who deserted Christ after he described the foundation of the Eucharist placed all their faith in the flesh at the expense of the Spirit that gives life (John 6:64). These deserters have lain hidden among Christians ever after, and to this day they do not believe in the Eucharist or the Gospel of John. As Walter paints them, this group remains as an enduring opposition to Christian hermeneutics, and they represent a way of interacting with the world whose rejection was fundamental in the establishment of orthodox Christianity itself.

Walter emphasizes the inability of these heretics to understand the spiritual union of charity enacted in the Eucharist through his description of the heretics' indiscriminate sex. Former heretics, who have returned to the Catholic side, relate that at the first watch the heretics shut all their windows and doors and wait for a cat to descend by a rope. When the heretics see this cat, they extinguish the lights and grope after it in the dark while humming through clenched teeth. When they find it, they kiss it and "the hotter their feelings, the lower their aim," often ending up on its anus or sexual organs. Following the kiss, "Each seizes the nearest man or woman and they join together as much as each can endure the mockery. Their masters also say and teach their novices that it is perfect charity to either perform or endure (*pati*) what a brother or sister desires, as if in turn extinguishing each other's fires, and it is from enduring (*paciendo*) that they are called Paterenes."[84] This fanciful etymology for the Paterenes ties the heretics' name to the passive role in sexual intercourse.[85] In fact, the Paterenes originated as a reform group in Milan opposed to clerical simony, but by the time Walter wrote they had become synonymous with the Publicans or the Cathars as a general catchall term for heretic.[86] In Walter's description, the indiscriminate and often bisexual sexual behavior of these heretics is a deliberate mockery of Christian charity. In the place of the suffering of martyrs or Christ himself, the heretics suffer sexual penetration as an act of mutual charity between them. This sexuality as mockery of charity naturally has no regard for bodily sex. It is mutual and freely shared between the heretics just as spiritual charity, or love, is ideally shared between all members of the Church: man or woman, rich or poor.[87]

After the description of the heretical orgy, Walter shares a story told to him by William White Hands that, once again, centers around misleading appearances.[88] Walter explains that these heretics often entrap others through magically altered food. Those who unknowingly eat the food ensorcelled by the heretics become like them. William White Hands once told Walter that a nobleman from Vienne always carried consecrated salt with him to add to any food that he was served in order to avoid such a poisoning. Sprinkling this salt on what looked like a whole mullet served to him by his nephew changed the appearance of the fish to little pellets like rabbit's dung. In a clear parody of the Eucharist, this meal that would transform a Catholic into a heretic relies on a false appearance that disguises the food's putrid substance under a false seeming of wholesomeness. The touch of the divine removes this false appearance to reveal the inner truth. Taking the dynamic of appearance and reality further, William told Walter that this nobleman seized the heretics who had converted his nephew and ordered them burned alive in a hut. After the hut burned to nothing, the heretics were untouched, and the archbishop of Vienne ordered the heretics burned again, but in a larger building. The archbishop sprinkled this structure with holy water to defeat the heretics' charms. Touched by the consecrated water, the house did not burn, but inside the structure the situation was different. The heretics, in contrast to the blessed material of the large house, had been burned into ash, including even their bones.

Walter Map ends his short excursus on heresy with another story about the interpretation of ambiguous appearances.[89] At the Third Lateran Council of 1179, which Walter attended as part of the delegation of King Henry II, a group of Waldensians, "simple illiterate men," requested the right to preach from Pope Alexander III.[90] Walter argues that such men were hardly fit to interpret the sacred text, and that he played a role in exposing the limits of these unlearned rubes.[91] At the council, a leading prelate summoned Walter to dispute with the Waldensians. Walter defeated these men through misleading questioning that would be immediately recognizable to anyone with theological and liturgical training, but quite perilous for anyone else. Running through the Creed (I believe in God the Father, the Son, and the Holy Spirit), he asked them first if they believed in God the Father, and they replied that they did.

Next, he asked if they believed in the Son, and they replied that they did. Then he asked if they believed in the Holy Spirit, and they again eagerly said that they did. Finally, he asked if they believed in the mother of Christ, and they again affirmed that they did—to peals of laughter from the assembled prelates. In this exchange, the illiterate Waldensians were fooled by a misleading appearance, simply answering the question posed to them. The learned, in contrast, could see the meaning underneath the appearance: that Walter's questions paralleled the Creed. In answering that they believed in the mother of Christ, the Waldensians seemed to elevate her into the Trinity, creating a kind of "quaternity."[92] In this anecdote, once again, heretics distinguish themselves by their inability to read spiritually, underscoring the basic carnality that defines them.

One final example of the way orthodox authors ascribed ritualized sex to heretics as a kind of commentary on the nature of their theological errors comes from the eve of the Albigensian Crusade. In 1181, Henry of Marcy, cardinal bishop of Albano and papal legate, laid siege to the castrum of Lavaur near Toulouse. Henry attacked Lavaur as part of a limited "not quite holy war" against Roger II Trencavel. Roger II Trencavel, the viscount of Carcassonne, had crossed Henry three years earlier over the imprisonment of the bishop of Albi and the violation of the peace, including the employment of mercenaries.[93] In this earlier episode, Henry had become involved in events in the region at the request of Raymond V of Toulouse. Raymond wrote to the pope requesting help in his struggle against heretics and their patrons. The heretics Raymond likely identified were his opponents in an ongoing regional power struggle between the counts of Toulouse and the Crown of Aragon. Roger II, who repudiated an earlier marriage alliance with Toulouse to join a regional alliance under Aragonese influence in 1177, was one of these opponents.[94] In this war, imported mercenaries were an essential and infamously brutal component. Witnessing the devastation caused by these troops, the papal representatives who responded to Raymond's call in 1178 had sought to mitigate the destruction particularly associated with this kind of warfare, and in doing so they assimilated the employment of foreign mercenaries to the idea of heresy.[95] Henry of Marcy's 1178 mission ended with the excommunication of Roger II Trencavel as a "traitor, a heretic, and an oath-breaker regarding the violation of a bishop."[96] The 1181 attack on Lavaur continued what this earlier mission started.

Although Henry justified his 1181 attack on Lavaur as an attempt to rein in the devastation caused by combatants who were so disrespectful of the Church and so brutal that they must be heretics, Mark Gregory Pegg has suggested that the legate's attack is better seen in the context of that very kind of regular warfare. Rather than a small crusade, Henry's attack occurred in the local political context of ongoing hostilities.[97] Of course, that a papal legate, rather than a secular lord, had directly commanded an army set an important precedent for future events.[98]

The account of Henry's 1181 siege of Lavaur written by Geoffrey of Vigeois pays a great deal of attention to the sexual activities of the supposed heretics, focusing on details which Jean-Louis Biget has argued are drawn completely from "the Cistercian imaginary."[99] Geoffrey is the first to call the heretics in the region "Albigensians," and a large part of his account of the siege is copied from a now lost letter written by Henry himself.[100] Geoffrey reports that Adelaide, Roger's wife and the daughter of Raymond of Toulouse, surrendered the castrum to the legate. Following the surrender, Roger along with other leading men, forswore heresy. The leading heretics present inside the fortress then openly confessed the teachings of the sect, and Geoffrey includes Henry's own account of the content of these confessions. The heretics did not believe that God became man, arguing that Jesus never actually ate or drank or performed any base bodily functions. Jesus, likewise, did not truly die and rise from the dead. All these claims in the Gospels the heretics described as "fantasies," and they condemned all the liturgical practices based on them, including the Eucharist, the baptism of children, marriage, and other sacraments. Furthermore, the heretics asserted that Satan created Heaven and earth and later gave the law to Moses.[101]

Following this list of heretical theological positions immediately comes a catalogue of sexual perversity. Henry states: "They say that there is an equal crime in sexual intercourse between any man and any woman, either parents or brothers, either shared mothers, or any kind of blood relation or other kind of affinity in which the women might be. The women among them who become pregnant kill the baby; nevertheless, it is said by the more experienced of them that it should be avoided, since it would be obvious that among them many women had become pregnant, but no offspring are evident."[102] Henry adds that the heresiarchs confessed to these practices openly before the prelates and the people. To Henry's account, Geoffrey adds a more lurid and suggestive detail purportedly drawn from Archbishop Guarinus of Bourges. A local noblewoman, Vienna, the wife of a Sicard de Boissezon, openly confessed to the archbishop that she had sex with fifty "of the more religious men of that same sect" in one night. Vienna supposedly explained that "she scorned her husband's bed and joined with these men for the cause of a holier life."[103] This wording suggests that Vienna's sexual initiation into the sect was not only like an antibaptism but also like a literal coming together of the heretical community. In the description of the bishop of Berry, the entrance into the heretical community occurred through the medium of sex in a manner parallel to the spiritual union of orthodox Christians enacted through the Eucharist as the body of Christ. To become one of the heretics, Vienna rejects the spiritual union in the body of Christ through baptism and the Eucharist, opting instead for a literal carnal unity by becoming consanguineous with all the heretics through intercourse. In medieval canon law, coitus created an affinity between partners, meaning that both partners became relatives, of a kind, through the act of sharing blood.[104] This mixture of blood equated to a unity of flesh; the affinity it created was an impediment to marriage with previous sexual partners or their near relatives.[105] In the carnal sphere ascribed to the medieval heretic, it was this kind of union through blood that formed the basis of human community. The spiritual union of Christians into one body formed through the fire of charity was its opposite. In the extraordinary debauchery of Vienna, an orthodox reader could find yet another example of heretical literalism as an inverted image of orthodox spiritual interpretation.

In the sources interrogated in this chapter, three essential elements have emerged repeatedly. The first is the construction of heresy as an opposing image of orthodoxy. The second is the insistence on orthodox, Christian hermeneutics as the piercing of misleading appearances in the context of an interpretive progression from the carnal letter to its spiritual signification. The final element is the communal context for the Christian hermeneutical progression from letter to spirit and how this community is formed and vivified by a unifying spiritual power that the heretics lack.

In these examples the contexts of gender and sex, along with heresy, were particularly powerful discursive fields for medieval authors to emphasize and explore these ideas. Ralph of Coggeshall in his account of the maiden in the vineyard outside Rheims utilized the hidden truth of woman as object to not only explore perceptive and authoritative reading in alliance to authority but also to investigate and to experience the intellective pleasure of the learned celibate provoked by the interrogation of women's hidden truth. For authors such as Paul of St. Père, Walter Map, Geoffrey of Vigeois, and Henry of Marcy, the hidden sexual deviance of heretics provided an opportunity for the better appreciation of the spiritual, as opposed to carnal, community of orthodox Christianity. In accounts such as these, orthodox authors found occasions to describe an enemy through which they could better see themselves.

CHAPTER 7

Leaping from the Flames
Love, Redemption, and Holy War in the Albigensian Crusade

Few episodes of internal religious persecution in European history are as infamous as the Albigensian Crusades. Their infamy stems, in part, from the lasting significance these events still bear into the present. This internal crusade, launched from Christian Europe against a target within Christian Europe, altered the course of Western history.[1] Historians have keenly felt its importance, straining to capture it in words and images. Joseph Strayer described the Albigensian Crusades as a "gaping wound" in the history of both France and of the Church.[2] Beverly Mayne Kienzle labeled them "one of the cruellest medieval wars."[3] Malcolm Lambert likened the crusades to a kind of spirit, which once conjured could not be fully controlled.[4] Most recently, Mark Gregory Pegg has argued that this conflict served as the entry point through which a "homicidal ethic" "ushered genocide into the West."[5]

This chapter interrogates the ethic of the crusade, particularly how it embodies the kinds of formative interactions between self and other that have preoccupied past chapters. The Albigensian Crusades—or crusade, with reference to the main fighting between 1209 and 1218—made an important contribution to the history of Western ideas about the enactment of violence, but this contribution had a significant genealogy behind it, particularly regarding execution by fire. Pegg argues that the crusade linked "divine salvation to mass murder, by making slaughter as loving an act as [Jesus's] sacrifice on the cross.

This ethos of homicide is what separates the crusade massacres from other great killings before the thirteenth century."[6] Although the moral justification of killing that Pegg identifies may not have been present in mass killings before the thirteenth century, it certainly echoes ideas found in the more modest burnings for heresy that occurred in the eleventh and twelfth centuries, as illustrated in earlier chapters. That partial continuity of thought is especially prominent in the role played by ideas of love. In leaving their homes to fight the enemies of Christendom, crusaders performed a service of love. Through the act of killing, they experienced and cultivated charity, and this charity, in turn, cultivated them.

In the course of these wars, more spectacular burnings for heresy occurred than during the entire period before.[7] In Minerve, during the summer of 1210, around 140 supposed heretics were burned together in one event.[8] At Lavaur, on May 3, 1211, "an innumerable number" of townspeople, perhaps as many as three or four hundred, were burned as heretics.[9] Soon afterward, in the summer of 1211, after the surrender of the garrison of Les Cassés, the crusaders burned around sixty unrepentant heretics.[10] In the summer of 1214, after the siege of Morlhon, the victorious crusaders burned seven Waldensians. One of the best-known burnings, at Montségur, actually occurred after the main period of the crusade. In March of 1244 the fortress was finally captured after a difficult siege that began as a result of the assassination of two inquisitors. After its fall, around two hundred defenders were burned as unrepentant heretics.[11]

Our knowledge of the Albigensian Crusade largely comes from three contemporary sources: The *Hystoria Albigensis* (*History of the Albigensian Crusade*) by Peter of les Vaux-de-Cernay, the *Chronicle of William of Puylaurens*, and the *Chanson de la croisade albigeoise* (*Song of the Albigensian Crusade*) by William of Tudela and an anonymous successor.[12] Peter and William of Puylaurens were both monks who wrote in Latin prose from the crusaders' side. The Provençal *Song* is more complicated. It was begun by William of Tudela, "a clerk in holy orders," who supported the crusaders' cause but expressed qualms about particular acts of violence. After William's death, an anonymous poet continued the work. The anonymous poet hated the crusaders and the crusade, providing a southern account intensely critical of the entire enterprise, eager to point out the many hypocrisies of the supposedly holy war.

The attitude of the anonymous poet is closer to modern appraisals of the crusade, but the task of this chapter is to understand the "homicidal ethic" of his enemies. After the death of Simon de Montfort, the leader of the crusade, outside Toulouse in 1218, the poet records this stinging commentary on the count's epitaph:

The epitaph says, for those who can read it, that he is a saint and a martyr who shall breathe again and shall in wondrous joy inherit and flourish, shall wear a crown and be seated in the kingdom. And I have heard it said that this must be so—if by killing men and shedding blood, by damning souls and causing deaths, by trusting evil counsels, by setting fires, destroying men, dishonoring *paratge*, seizing lands and encouraging pride, by kindling evil and quenching good, by killing women and slaughtering children, a man can in this world win Jesus Christ, certainly Count Simon wears the crown and shines in Heaven above.[13]

The sympathies of a modern reader easily align with this suggestion of Simon's wickedness and hypocrisy, but this chapter seeks to understand the positive content rejected by the commentary of the anonymous poet. How could one win the crown of Heaven by killing men, women, and children, sending souls to Hell, and setting fires?

My search for possible answers to these questions falls into three sections. The first provides a brief overview of the course of the crusade, focusing on the events between 1209 and 1218. The second section outlines how the sources from the crusaders' side portray the crusade as a necessary war. Beyond its necessity, the war was presented as an opportunity for redemption through love that could avoid the flames of Hell and perform the work of Purgatory during life. The third and longest portion of the chapter focuses on burnings for heresy as described in the *History of the Albigensian Crusade* of Peter of les Vaux-de-Cernay. I focus on this text because of its strong proximity to the crusaders' point of view. Peter has been described as "in effect the official historian of the Albigensian Crusade," and he was personally present at many of the events he describes.[14] Beyond his proximity, however, Peter most clearly and consistently articulates the message of slaughter as an act of love.

The Course of the Struggle

The Albigensian Crusade began officially in 1209, but events before that time were essential in bringing the crusade into existence. The north and the south of France were very different places, home to dissimilar ways of life.[15] The south was more urban and lived by different codes of law and of custom. Its patterns of landholding and lordship were different, and the expectations held by northerners regarding the power a lord could exert on his vassals were unrealistic and indeed foreign to the specific political situation of Occitania.[16] In fact, an ongoing struggle between the counts of Toulouse and the Crown of

Aragon rendered who was the actual overlord for many parts of the region contested and difficult to tell.[17]

Concerns about heresy, doubtless heightened by these cultural peculiarities and coming to prominence in the context of regional political struggles, had clustered around the south of France, or the Languedoc, for some time by the turn of the thirteenth century. Ecclesiastical leaders had long decried the use of mercenaries by the rulers of the area, equating the practice to heresy.[18] Bernard of Clairvaux had toured the region in 1145, preaching against what he, and others like him, regarded to be a spreading infection in Christendom.[19] Bernard's efforts aided the growing stigmatization of the region as a hotbed of heresy as reflected in canons of the Council of Reims (1148), the Council of Tours (1163), and the Third Lateran Council (1179).[20] In 1177 Count Raymond V of Toulouse, in the context of an ongoing conflict with the city of Toulouse, some of his leading vassals, and the Crown of Aragon made an appeal to Pope Alexander III and the French king to help root out heresy, and this appeal had serious future consequences for his son and his dynasty. The heresy of which Raymond complained conveniently implicated his local enemies. This appeal led to a papal mission in 1178.[21] One of the leaders of this mission, Henry of Marcy, the papal legate and former abbot of Clairvaux, organized an attack on the fortress of Lavaur in 1181 that in hindsight appears to presage later events.[22] In these earlier attributions of rampant heresy to the Languedoc, clerical concepts of heresy acted as an "almost paranoid" and largely "imaginary vision" which added fuel to the fire of existing regional political struggles.[23]

Ultimately, the consolidating strength of the international papacy, especially under the guidance of Innocent III, came into fatal contact with this local world. With his attention drawn increasingly to the region through the actions of William VIII of Montpellier and Peter II of Aragon, Innocent's legatine representative, Peter of Castelnau, urged Raymond VI of Toulouse, who had succeeded his father Raymond V, again and again to pursue heretics and rectify abuses in ways that were beyond, and in some ways contradictory, to his powers. Finally, in April 1207, Peter excommunicated Count Raymond, appealing to the count's overlord, Philip Augustus of France, to take action against him. Connected to this appeal to Philip was another call for others to take up arms and dispossess the count of Toulouse independently of his technical overlord. Such excommunications were not exactly rare in the period, but the events that followed created a unique situation.

On January 8, 1208, Peter of Castelnau, the representative of Innocent III, was cut down while crossing the Rhône River. The murder of the papal legate occasioned a renewed and more strident call for a crusade against Raymond.

Innocent III held Count Raymond responsible for the murder, calling for a crusade and offering an indulgence to those who took the cross against the count of Toulouse and the heretics he supposedly protected. The northern lords of France took up arms and marched on the south, assembling in 1209 under the command of the new papal legate, Arnold Amalric, the abbot of Cîteaux. In the face of this armed intervention, Raymond himself took up the cross and offered to compromise or capitulate on most points of long-standing contention between himself and the representatives of the Holy See. The crusade then turned against some of the other lords of the south, especially Raymond-Roger Trencavel, the viscount of Carcassonne, a lord long hostile to Raymond. The crusaders turned their attention to the Trencavel and their lands for a number of reasons. The Trencavel were not conspicuous patrons of Cistercian monasteries and had relatively recently run afoul of Henry of Marcy, a former abbot of Cîteaux, in a context involving heresy. Furthermore, they were politically isolated, and their position with their own vassals was perhaps insecure.[24] Despite this redirection, Arnold Amalric never trusted the count of Toulouse and strove to redirect the crusade back against him.

During the conquest of the Trencavel lands, the crusade found a leader of surpassing qualities in Simon de Montfort. A minor lord from the north of France, Simon's ability as a leader helped sustain the crusade. Most crusaders served for a period of forty days, according to their oaths, before departing for home. As a result of these brief periods of service, Simon was often short of soldiers and supplies, and his strength fluctuated widely between winter and summer. This changing strength accounts for what became a regular rhythm to the crusade: Simon's holdings would surge in summer, with castra and local lords submitting to him, only for these same fortifications and lords to rebel as soon as his position weakened.

Despite repeated attempts to fully placate the crusaders and the pope, Raymond never managed to quell their animosity to him, and the crusade eventually turned back onto him. After the conquest of all the Trencavel lands, Simon began to attack Raymond's territories after the summer siege of Lavaur in 1211. Over time, and with repeated reversals, Simon overcame most of his opposition. After his defeat of Peter of Aragon, who had come to Raymond's defense, at the battle of Muret in 1213, Simon held almost the entire County of Toulouse in his grasp. At the Fourth Lateran Council in 1215, Simon was confirmed as Raymond's successor.

The southerners still did not accept Montfort regardless of Simon's successes on the battlefield or at the Fourth Lateran Council, and they rallied to the side of Raymond VI and his son, Raymond the Younger, when they renewed the struggle in 1216. It was during this resurgence of resistance to Simon and his army of northerners that Montfort's position disintegrated. While besieging the city of Toulouse, which had turned against him, Simon was killed by a stone on June 25, 1218. Following Montfort's death, the two Raymonds retook most of their lands by 1222.

The restoration of the southern lords did not last, since the claims of Simon de Montfort and his son passed to the French royal family. In the face of renewed action from the north, Raymond the Younger, now Raymond VII, who had taken over from his father, came to terms with the crown in 1229. Following the terms of this treaty, when he died with no direct male heir in 1249 his titles passed to his son-in-law Alphonse of Poitiers, the brother of the French king, Louis IX. When Alphonse died without any heirs in 1271, Toulouse passed directly to the French crown. The conquest of the south by the north was complete.

It was in the period of relative calm after the reconquest of Raymond VII that the inquisitorial investigations against heresy, which are now often synonymous with the crusade in popular conception, began. These inquisitions of heretical depravity were largely the projects of individual mendicant friars, operating under the authority of the pope or local bishops.[25] The first papal inquisitors in the Languedoc were appointed in 1233 under Gregory IX. Two such inquisitors, Bernard de Caux and Jean de Saint-Pierre, conducted an inquisition at Saint-Sernin in 1245–46 that involved almost six thousand witnesses.[26] Proceedings of a more modest scale continued into the fourteenth century, including those of the famous inquisitor Bernard Gui.[27] In these forms, decades of later scrutiny built on the foundations of the crusade in the south.

A Necessary War

Both Peter of les Vaux-de-Cernay and William of Puylaurens describe the origin of the heresy of the southerners by appealing to the Parable of the Wheat and the Weeds (Matt. 13:24–30), and through the imagery of a spreading disease. Peter likens heresy to the infectious illness of leprosy.[28] This disease had begun where the true faith once flourished in the province of Narbonne when "the enemy of the faith began to sow weeds."[29] These weeds took deep root and could not be easily dislodged. The infection of false belief spread in the same way that one scabrous animal infects the entire flock.[30] "Impaired and infected," the people refused to return to the faith, becoming no longer participants in the body of Christ but rather "limbs of the anti-Christ."[31] William explains that the negligence of the southern prelates had allowed heresy to flourish. The teachings of the heretics spread through the land like a cancer (Tim. 2:17), infecting and seducing those it touched. In this way the Devil took control of most of the land, holding it as if it were "his own house."[32]

For these authors, the Albigensian Crusade is a response to a spreading infection. It is an attempt to save the body from the malignancy that has taken hold in one limb, or an attempt to save the crop from an invasive species. As Peter and William present it, the crusade is not an offensive war; it is a defensive action, a duty taken on through love. In this vein, William chides the prelates of the region to take more seriously their care of souls in future so that never again will the "enemy sow weeds among the good seed." "Seed," William adds, "sown in a field that has been cultivated with such labor, at such great cost, and with such an effusion of human blood."[33] Such an effusion of blood is foreshadowed in Peter's *History* when heretical peasants, harvesting wheat on a feast day near Carcassonne, find their harvest covered in blood.[34] In events to come, human hands will weed the living field of the world, renewing its purity by destroying human weeds.[35]

The sources that were written from the point of view of the crusaders portray support for the crusade and allegiance to God as synonymous. In the light of this equivalence, opposition to the crusade is opposition to God, effectively a kind of treason; it is a choice to separate from the body of Christ and take up arms in the service of the Devil.[36] William of Puylaurens describes the preparations for the great battle of Muret in just these terms: Simon de Montfort is the champion of the "cause of God and of the faith," and those who fight him, led by Peter II of Aragon, are pursuers of "the opposite side."[37] Peter's own accomplishments, including the defeat of the Almohads at Las Navas de Tolosa and becoming the first Christian ruler to decree death by fire to heretics as official policy, did not prevent his hostility to the crusade equating to hostility to Christ.[38] The theologies attributed to the heretics stress the inversion of Catholic understandings and practices.[39] To follow these teachings, one must leave the Church and pour scorn on it. Likewise, only a traitor to God would defend his enemies. To resist the crusade, in this rigid logic, is a shifting of allegiance.

In their own words, the heresy the crusaders faced was not Catharism; rather, it was the multifaceted doctrines of the Devil. As Pegg argues, no heretic is called a Cathar by the main contemporary accounts of the crusade.[40] Peter of les Vaux-de-Cernay calls most of the heretics "Albigensians," since that is the term for them used by outsiders, but he knows they actually belong to different sects.[41] He also distinguishes Waldensians as a different group.[42] For William of Puylaurens, the heretics were of diverse sorts, including Arians, Manichaeans, and Waldensians. In essence, it is opposition to the Church that unites the disparate strands of heresy. They all conspire "against the Catholic faith to the ruin of souls."[43] In this effort, they are tools of the Devil. In William's words, rather than by a doctrinal or bureaucratic unity, the heretics are united through the force that moves through them and which they serve, like foxes bound together by their burning tails.[44]

In the face of this threat the shared body of Christ must come together in an enactment of the love that creates that very body. Nothing less than the salvation of one's brethren is at stake, and there is no greater love than the willingness to die for the welfare of one's friends.[45] This defense of others is also self-defense. Joined together in the love of God, the protection of neighbor, of self, and of God is one action, pulling together creation and creator like an act of worship. Described in this way, as it often was by medieval authors, crusading is an expression of Christian charity, an act undertaken by those who burned in its fire.[46] It is just such an ideal of the crusading enterprise that was articulated by Innocent III, and this ideal suffuses the *History* of Peter of les Vaux-de-Cernay.

After the murder of Peter of Castelnau, Innocent III proclaimed the crusade in a letter on March 10, 1208, as a vehicle for Christian unity, self-defense, and the forgiveness of sin. Peter of les Vaux-de-Cernay includes this letter in his *History*, and its rhetoric is an important preface to how Peter will describe the actual conduct of the war that follows.[47] The pope assured those who took up the cross that they would have their sins forgiven if they were truly repentant and confessed their sins. The vague reference to a remission of sins likely built on an earlier letter Innocent had dispatched in November that directly stipulated that those who took up arms against Christian heretics in Languedoc would enjoy an indulgence equal to that enjoyed by those who took up arms against the Saracens.[48] Surviving documentary evidence shows that participants took the spiritual benefits of a crusade in Languedoc, on par with that of an armed pilgrimage to Jerusalem, seriously.[49] Innocent stressed that the southern heretics were worse than Saracens.[50] They threatened the totality of Christian society, menacing far more than mere property, and souls as well as bodies. These "corrupters of souls and despoilers of lives" had to be faced, and in such a struggle the Christian should not fear death, but rather the consignment of both body and soul to Gehenna. The death of Peter of Castelnau should not only fail to instill fear, but rather succeed in "kindling love."[51] This love, once ignited, will allow others to copy the legate's example, earning a place in Heaven. The crusade is an "opportunity."[52]

In the context of crusade, fighting was an act of penance, and, as was the case for Purgatory, successful penance required the presence of love. In Purgatory, those who die with the stains of lesser sins on their souls, but who still possess charity, will be purified and reformed. The crusade too purifies. It replaces the experience of otherworldly purgation, and just as otherworldly purgation requires the presence of charity, so too does the redemption promised by the crusade. When one takes the cross, becoming a *crusignatus*, or one signed by the cross, one becomes identified as a lover, a bearer of a badge of love, affixed through love. In the words of Jacques de Vity, who preached the crusade to the population of northern France, the sign of the cross is attached to the crusader by the thread of God's love. The crusade is an opportunity for the redemption of sinners, and this is the reason the evil of heresy even exists.[53] Through the wickedness of the heretic, God creates an opportunity for the faithful to purge themselves by fighting against heresy. The crusade is a way for purification of sins in life, much like the consuming charity of the perfect, which burns like a furnace of fire dissolving sin.[54]

Snatched from the Flames: Community and Appearance for Peter of les Vaux-de-Cernay

The *History of the Albigensian Crusade* of Peter of les Vaux-de-Cernay is a major contemporary source with which all historians' accounts of the events it records must necessarily grapple. Its general tenor is challenging, and Peter's authorial voice has been described as "simplistic and naïve," or like that of a "second-rate spin doctor" taking up the unenviable task of "defending the indefensible."[55] What such characterizations agree on is the extent to which Peter's way of viewing the world was a product of his environment. The idealized conceptions of Christian unity and the wickedness of those who would oppose this unity were foundational truths to him. Peter's intellectual horizons were shaped by the monastic library at Vaux-de-Cernay, filled with the works of ecclesiastical rather than classical authors.[56] Peter took the idealized conceptions regarding heresy and society available to him and used them to build a work that was not a simple list of events but rather a structured narrative of the crusade.[57]

We know very little definitively about Peter's life beyond its barest outlines. He was a Cistercian monk at the Abbey of les Vaux-de-Cernay. He was the nephew of its abbot, Guy. Alongside his uncle, Peter took part in the Fourth Crusade, going as far as Zara before turning back when the crusade turned against fellow Christians.[58] In this brief bout of crusading, he first met Simon de Montfort and other figures who took part in later events. He arrived in the south in the middle of 1212 with his uncle, who soon became the bishop of Carcassonne. Experts are unsure of his dates. He was able to read complex

Latin in Venice in 1202. He was a monk when he arrived in the south during the summer of 1212, and he describes himself as a *puer*, or boy, in the *History*, perhaps suggesting that he was still quite young when he wrote. W. A. and M. D. Sibly suggest that these elements yield a likely birth date around 1190, putting him in his early twenties when he wrote the *History*, but he may have been older.[59] The date of his death is, likewise, debatable. Since the *History* ends in 1218, many scholars have assumed that he died around that date, but the course of the war and the death of Simon de Montfort may also explain why Peter could have abandoned the work while still living.

The structure of the *History* reflects the course of both its evolving narrative and its composition. The work covers the events from 1203 to 1218, with a clear focus on the period 1208–18. The modern edition of the work is divided into 620 sections, but these divisions are not original.[60] Peter himself divided the *History* into three main parts: "On the Heretics," "On the Preachers," and "On the Crusaders."[61] This last section is by far the longest. Peter likely wrote most of the *History* in 1213, soon after his arrival in the south, and made his last additions sometime in 1218. As a result, the contents of sections 5–398 are completely secondhand. Peter's sources for this material seem to be some of the highest-ranking personages in the crusade: his uncle Guy, Arnold Amalric, and Bishop Fulk. In the preface, Peter dedicated the work to Innocent III.[62]

The story Peter tells begins as a history of the crusade, but many readers have found that as the narrative progresses the focus appears to narrow ever more on the character of Simon de Montfort. In fact, the *History* ends very soon after Simon's death, as if its purpose had been lost. Readers have advanced various reasons for the work's sudden termination. The oldest explanation simply is that Peter died in or around 1218, and that his death is the reason why the account does not cover the entire period treated by William of Puylaurens.[63] Christopher Kurpiewski argues, to the contrary, that Peter lost the reason to write. For Kurpiewski, the gritty realities of war pushed an idealistic young Cistercian monk to invest more and more purpose into Simon de Montfort the man, who could embody the values and ideals that events themselves simply could not. When Simon died, his death frustrated what had become the core idea of the project, and it could not move forward.[64]

There is something attractive in the idea that reality somehow escaped the confines of Peter's narrative. Congruous with reality or not, his narrative can reveal how the perpetrators of the crusade could view their actions, or at least attempt to view them. An appreciation of this point of view, so different from most modern accounts of the crusade, is particularly important for understanding Peter's retelling of the first burnings for heresy during the crusade.

Redemption and Condemnation: Burnings at Castres and Minerve

Soon after the election of Simon de Montfort as leader of the crusade, the count traveled to Castres to take possession of the castrum there.[65] The townsmen had invited Simon to Castres, and its strategic location made the offer irresistible.[66] Arriving with a small force sometime after mid-August 1209, Simon accepted the townsmen's homage. The count appeared to be aware that, separated from the main army, his position at Castres was particularly vulnerable, and this awareness appears clearly in his interaction with a group of knights from Lombers. While at the castrum, these men offered to submit to Simon under identical terms to the men of Castres. Despite the important position of Lombers, Simon refused to travel there, wanting to return to the main army as quickly as possible. The count officially took possession of Lombers perhaps a month later with a larger force behind him. Simon's earlier reticence was, in fact, very wise, as the knights of Lombers planned to betray him during this visit and only gave up on their plot out of fear.[67]

Peter recalls that while Simon was at Castres between late August and the beginning of September two heretics were brought before him.[68] Pressed for time and in a difficult position, Simon may have felt pressure to resolve the issue quickly. In addition to issues regarding strategy, the count may also have seen this situation as an important moment in his new leadership over the crusading enterprise in the south. After taking counsel, with whom we do not know, Simon decides to burn the heretics alive. In Peter's *History*, this is the first instance of burning heretics, and it is the earliest in any of the main accounts of the Albigensian Crusade to be recorded in much detail.[69] Far from a simple execution, like so many of those to follow in the different accounts of the crusade, this first burning is a complex event that does not follow Simon's expectations and is not fully under any one person's control.

The comportment of one of the heretics immediately complicates the attempted execution. Outwardly the two heretics conform to a familiar pattern. One, the oldest, is a "perfectus," and the other is a younger "novice" under the senior's tutelage. After the death sentence is pronounced, the novice repents and promises to return to the Roman Church. The "heartfelt grief" that the novice displays immediately divides the crusaders.[70] In the opinions of some, the young man's reversal is exactly "what we had told him to do."[71] If the heretic follows the crusaders' demands and returns to the Church, he should not be killed. Others argued the contrary, saying that a conversion in the face of death cannot be a true conversion, prompted more by fear than "by his love of heeding the Christian religion."[72] In other words, the young man only looks repentant, but in his heart he cannot be.

This "great debate" captures in miniature a central dilemma faced by the crusaders.[73] In the face of an organized and armed attempt to confront heresy, could heretics be truly redeemed? Was the point of the crusade to weed the fields of Latin Christendom, or could it bring about the conversion of weeds into wheat? These questions about the purification of community versus the enlargement of community also involve problems of interpretation. The youth's apparent repentance raises the issue of misleading appearances that so often accompanied discussions of heresy. How could the difference between wheat and weeds, or the Devil and an angel of light, be known when they look the same? In summary, how could the crusaders discern the boundaries of Christian community at the point of the sword?

Simon's resolution to the crusaders' internal debate attempts to steer a middle course between these possibilities through the logic of postmortem purgation. The count decides that the young man should be burned with his master, but if the contrition he had outwardly displayed was genuine "the fire would serve to expiate his sins." On the other hand, "If he was lying, he would receive a just reward for his perfidy."[74] This middle course is lined with persistent ambiguities that cannot be escaped. In fact, its very viability relies on them. For those watching, it would be unclear if they were viewing a purgation or an initiation into Hell, as both are a dying man's body in flames. Simon's logic relies on the existence of an inner truth known only to God, and the justice God will mete out based on that truth. The fire will change, becoming punitive or reparative to suit the one it burns. Despite these uncertainties, for Simon the act of execution will benefit the society of Christians by removing a diseased limb or purifying a penitent.

The young man's comportment continues to challenge Simon's stage directions, by threatening the present ambiguity on which the count's resolution depends. Like a martyr, the novice accepts his death. The two heretics are fastened to stakes, tied with string chains by their legs, their middle, and their necks, and finally their hands are tied behind them. While he is being fastened to the stake, the crusaders ask the young man a highly leading question and his response proves decisive: "The man who appeared to be repenting was then asked in what faith he wished to meet his death. He said: 'I foreswear the evil of heresy. I wish to die in the faith of the Holy Roman Church, and I pray that this fire will serve for me instead of Purgatory.'"[75] The young man's acceptance of his punishment is a revelation of a set of truths. It is a declaration of his true repentance as well as an acknowledgment of the weight of the sins he has committed through his former heresy and way of life. These sins necessitate penance and pain. In fact, if the pain of burning alive on earth serves instead for the purgatorial fire, the overall pain experienced by the young man will actually be lessened. The pains of Purgatory, as commentaries on the *Sentences* of Peter Lombard were accustomed to say, would be worse than any pain possible in this life.[76] Burning in life, however terrible, is an easier punishment, as would be any willing penance undertaken by the living, including answering the call to crusade.

The opportunity given to the young man is much the same as the promise later made to the crusaders themselves before the battle of Muret. As Simon's army prepared to fight the combined forces of the count of Toulouse and the Crown of Aragon, the bishop of Toulouse began to bless the crusaders one by one. Unhappy with the delay, Garcia, the bishop of Comminges, took the crucifix out of his hand and blessed the entire force at once, giving them a simple promise: "Go forth in the name of Jesus Christ! I am your witness, and will stand surety on the Day of Judgment, that whosoever shall fall in this glorious battle will instantly gain his eternal reward and the glory of martyrdom, free of the punishment of Purgatory, so long as he is repentant and has made confession, or at least has the firm intention of presenting himself to a priest as soon as the battle is over for absolution from any sins he has not yet confessed."[77]

In this efficient summary of holy warfare as an act of penance, dying on crusade takes the place of the purgatorial fire. The judgment given to the young man at Castres is a close parallel to the opportunity the crusaders faced themselves.

The novice's acceptance of Simon's decree of death in short order becomes an escape from it. In the face of the apparent division within the crusaders' ranks regarding the young man's execution, such a response can only invoke compassion. The young man apparently has nothing worldly to gain by stating his desire to die a Catholic; regardless of his answer, he is going to die. In the face of death he can speak his truth, and this truth is akin to the statement "I am one of you." Within the body of Christ, as the Church, such a statement also implies "I am you."[78]

That the young man is a part of those who condemn him transforms his burning into a foretaste of the fire that would try the work of every man.[79] This purgatorial fire awaited the vast majority of Christians, who would escape eternal damnation but nonetheless likely die with the stain of their sins still present on their souls. Rather than the punitive flames of Hell, the imperfect expected this flame to expunge their remaining sins after their deaths, rendering a passage through flame an ordeal that awaited the vast majority of medieval men. The young man prays that the fire set by the crusaders will act as this flame, inflicting on him not only pain that he deserves, but also pain that he ultimately cannot avoid. As he accepts the verdict of Simon, he accepts the justice of God. As the spectators watch him burn, they can see themselves burn with him.[80] Like the young novice, most of the men at Castres expected to one day find themselves in fire. For the Christian, this fire is ideally purgative, and just as the crusaders hoped to emerge from the purifying flames triumphant, so too does the young novice at Castres. The fire kindled around him tries the young man's work of repentance and reveals it to be true.

As the fire burns vigorously around the two men, the repentant youth breaks the "strong chains" that bind him and escapes from the flames. The older perfectus, however, is "consumed by the flames instantly." In contrast to this destruction, the young man is unharmed except for the tips of his fingers which are "lightly scorched."[81]

This miracle resolves the problem of misleading appearances. The initial difficulty that faces the crusaders is the inability to tell the difference between Catholic and heretic. The sequence of events recounted by Peter in this story removes this ambiguity by revealing how the signs presented by the young man's outward words and comportment can be read to indicate his inner, spiritual disposition. This reading relies on the rule of charity.

The spiritual bond between Christians is decisive in enabling the young man's behavior to be read like a text. The miracle of the young man is about Christian community, and acts of interpretation within this community. The Christian reading of the young man's behavior involves removing the veil of ambiguity around appearances to reveal the spirit within. This successful reading relies on the charity between God and men. When the young man articulates this bond, the fire that touches him becomes of a different type than that which engulfs his former master. The one fire does the work of both Hell and Purgatory.

The apparent miracle of the young man's escape is also a spectacular enactment of Christian confession and penance, nestled within the outer spectacle of an ordeal. As Talal Asad has argued, in the face of the pain awaiting souls in Purgatory penance was "the effect of a choice about the condition of one's soul which presupposed that in one way or another one would have to face up to the truth." The admission of guilt by penitents in confession was the admission of the truth about themselves. This truth would be made manifest in pain if the choice to recognize it freely in life were overlooked. It was a "collaborative activity that sustained the relationship between priest and penitent."[82] In this case, the collaboration was markedly different. It is not the regular verbal dialectic between cleric and layman; instead, it is a salvific drama enacted between laymen of violence. This drama reifies, heals, and structures its participants and builds the community in which they participate. It is a kind of self-formation.

Charity and compassion also inform another reading that a modern eye can perhaps see in this text. An ahistorical and somewhat cynical interpretation could easily find in the crusaders' internal divisions and their leading questions a test to see if the young man should be let free and then an action taken as the result of that test. Since the young man correctly answered the questions put to him, perhaps his half-hearted executioners left his bonds half-taut, facilitating the miracle of his escape. This possibility, appealing to the modern sensibility for its purgation of the supernatural, would deny the miraculous element so important to the original text, but the emotional and spiritual power in it would remain the same as in the original. The drawing of Christian community unites the crusaders together with one of their victims, and this union recalls this victim from the flames.

Peter's account of the first burning of the crusade embodies the complexities of the homicidal ethic that proceeded from the crusaders' realization of their eschatology. Simon's logic in the decision to burn both heretics is the same as that attributed to Arnold Amalric by Caesarius of Heisterbach in his account of the fall of Béziers from the 1220s.[83] Béziers fell on July 22, 1209, before the events at Castres, and much of the population of the town was killed in what became an infamous massacre.[84] Peter justifies the slaughter of "up to seven thousand" of the inhabitants inside the church of La Madeleine as God's vengeance for their heresy and the earlier murder of their viscount.[85] In the version written by Caesarius, after the fall of the town the crusaders found it impossible to tell the difference between heretics and Catholics. Confused, they asked the legate what they should do with the townspeople, and Arnold's purported response has been infamous for centuries: "Kill them. God knows his own." The legate's reply is born out of the fear that heretics will escape by feigning orthodoxy, living to infect more good Catholics and damn more souls.[86]

The reasoning in this exemplum from Caesarius rests on the ultimate justice of God beyond this life to resolve ambiguities that human powers cannot, just as in Simon's judgment at Castres. While the truth of Caesarius's account has been debated, and none of the contemporary sources for the crusade include these words from the legate, Peter's story of the two heretics relies on the same logic, finding in it not pointless killing but a truthful reckoning.[87] It is a meeting in miniature between man and the justice of God that must be faced by everyone. This kind of meeting builds the community of orthodox Christians as it also demarcates this community's limits, and these limits are drawn through the damnation of some and the purgation of others enabled by a salvific love.

Peter's crusaders face another similar set of questions regarding the purpose of the crusade and its place in Christian community at the siege of Minerve.[88] The siege resulted in the first of the mass burnings that are so often associated with the crusade. In the summer of 1210, Simon laid siege to the castrum at the urging of the citizens of Narbonne.[89] After Minerve had been besieged for some time and had its defenses seriously weakened, the defenders sought terms of surrender. As Peter tells us, the discussions for a peaceful surrender were then complicated by the arrival of Arnold Amalric, the abbot of Cîteaux.[90]

In contemplating the peaceful surrender of the stronghold filled with heretics, the abbot and the other crusaders faced a set of dilemmas similar to those encountered at Castres. Simon and William named the abbot as arbitrator for the negotiations, but the abbot certainly did not prove to be enthusiastic about a diplomatic settlement. Peter recalls that the abbot found himself in an anxious position since he wanted the heretics to die but as a churchman was unable to condemn them to death. Named as arbitrator, he immediately tried to find "some means of inducing either the count or William . . . to break their agreement to seek arbitration."[91]

Arnold's first attempt at sabotaging the negotiations draws on strategies first used in theological debates against heretics and later against Jews. He commands both sides to write down their terms and present them to each other. This method of conducting debate privileged the side with the balance of power who sought to find in an opponent the slightest weakness or error with which to take issue.[92] With the give and take of oral negotiation or debate absent, a written offer takes on the logic "of all for one and one for all."[93] Either one accepts the entirety of what is written or rejects it wholesale. Before the crusade, Diego of Osma had used this same strategy in the debate at Montréal, requiring that both sides exchange written depositions before a chosen set of arbitrators.[94] The abbot's plan almost works when Simon finds the terms as written unacceptable. In a last-minute effort to save his life, William offers to surrender without conditions. Simon finds himself unable to refuse an unconditional surrender and accepts.

The written negotiation strategy also underscores the divine sanction for the crusaders' actions. Earlier in Peter's *History*, the papal legate Milo and his assistant Thedisius used a similar method to illustrate the unity of Christian prelates in the confrontation with Raymond VI. At Montélimar the two men called together a "large number of archbishops and bishops" to discuss the "business of peace and the faith, especially in connection to the count of

Toulouse."[95] The way Milo seeks the advice of these prelates parallels Arnold Amalric's later actions at Minerve. He asks "each prelate individually to give him, in writing and under seal, their views on the specific points laid down by the abbot of Cîteaux." "Incredibly," the prelates' views agreed "on all points without exception," in a concurrence so remarkable that Peter reminds the reader: "Surely this was the Lord's doing."[96] The unity of these written opinions underscores the total alignment that the crusaders possess with God's will and through that will with each other. The very fact that at Minerve William's terms of surrender fail to accord with Simon's illustrates William's discord with righteousness, and that the actions undertaken by Arnold Amalric, based on his conviction that this discordance exists, are appropriate. As events play out, the abbot's convictions will indeed be proven correct.

Despite the frustrations presented by Minerve's surrender, the crusaders continue to maneuver toward what Peter portrays as a necessary massacre. Both the abbot and now Simon had been seemingly thwarted, but matters come to a head when the heretics are given a choice. The abbot orders that William and all the inhabitants of the town, including the heretical believers and their leaders, would be spared on condition that they agree "to be reconciled and obey the orders of the Church."[97]

Hearing that all the townspeople, Catholic and heretic alike, could be spared, one of the crusaders immediately protests, citing his understanding of the purpose of the crusade itself. Robert Mauvoisin, as Peter pointedly reminds us, "a noble and dedicated Catholic," becomes concerned that the heretics will say anything to avoid their deaths.[98] The purpose of the crusade was to destroy heresy, so allowing half-hearted conversions on pain of death threatened to betray that purpose. Robert warns that the soldiers would never allow such a betrayal, regardless of what the crusade's leaders decide.

Robert's objection, so often portrayed as an example of bloodlust, is logical and based on moral convictions. In Peter's *History* it is recognized as an insistence that the point of this war was the eradication of heresy, an attempt to arrest the spread of an infection for the common good of the rest of the body. In the face of this purpose, false or misleading appearances are the great threat. Deceived by heretics who really remain the opposites of what they claim to be, the crusaders' own actions could be transformed into the opposite of what they intend. An apparent act of mercy could itself become a moral betrayal of the rest of Christendom. Heretics left alive will damn more Christians as they inevitably spread their spiritual disease. Robert reminds the crusaders, and the reader of the *History*, that sparing the heretics of Minerve is the immoral act. In this example, true Christians, joined together into the body of Christ, must kill as an expression of the love between them. This love allows the crusaders to resist the impulse toward deceitful mercy. Sparing the heretics of Minerve would be the indulgence of a false appearance, and the crusaders realize moral virtue through the rejection of this false appearance. As written by Peter of les Vaux-de-Cernay, Robert is not the bloodthirsty man; he is the layman most filled with a sense of Christian community.

The abbot recognizes the validity of Robert's objection, and assures him that the heretics will not lie to save their lives. He replies, "Do not be afraid. I think that very few will be converted."[99] Things work out as the abbot foresaw, as group after group of captured heretics refuse conversion. Abbot Guy of les Vaux-de-Cernay enters the town, traveling first to a group of male heretics and then their women. All refuse to convert, insisting that "neither death nor life can separate us from the beliefs we hold."[100] After Abbot Guy, Simon himself enters the town as a secular lord and again urges the heretics to convert. After they again refuse, Simon takes them, "at least a hundred and forty" in all, outside the town and burns them alive.[101]

The heretics' conduct on the pyre is remarkable, emphasizing both the wickedness of their choices and their inability in the face of the crusading enterprise to disguise this wickedness. As Peter records: "A huge pyre was made ready, and all were thrown on it—indeed there was no need for our soldiers to throw them on, since they were so hardened in their wickedness that they rushed into the fire of their own accord."[102] Far from pretending conversion to live and sin another day, as Robert logically expects, the heretics rush to their deaths. The illogic of this action, the madness of it, highlights what the heretics truly are against the backdrop of Christian sanity and right-minded alignment with God's justice. In the face of the crusade, as before the very judgment of God, people are revealed for what they truly are.[103]

Even here, before the vengeance of the flames, there is still redemption. While most of the heretics die, three women are "snatched from the flames and reconciled with the Church" through Christian intercession. This intercessor takes the form of the "noble lady" Matilda of Garlande, the mother of Bouchard de Marly.[104] Peter does not record what prompted her to save these three, or how these three were moved to accept the offer of salvation. Perhaps, like the attempts to save the maiden of Cologne over half a century before, there was something moving in their beauty, or maybe, like the young man at Castres, they repented.

In any event, these women represent the persistence of a self-reflective and redemptive impulse alongside the most graphic descriptions of executions for heresy in Peter's History. "Snatched from the flames," these three women were in miniature the embodiment of what the crusaders were ideally attempting for the whole of the Church. As the creeping cancer of heresy threatened the entire body of Christ and the Christian society with which it was synonymous, crusaders like Robert Mauvoisin saw themselves as snatching their own community from the flames. The act of pulling themselves from that fire involved persistent negotiations between mercy and severity, appearance and inner reality, self and other. In the examples examined above, the success of these negotiations rests on the very Christian community they reify and police.

In the pairing of these two episodes from the early phases of Simon's campaigns, there is an interesting coupling of logical reversals that tells a modern reader a great deal about the ethical world inhabited by the crusaders. In the case of the young man, the acceptance of death is the defeat of death. At the fall of Minerve, the indulgence of mercy is a fall into immortality. Both examples frustrate immediate expectations; their recognition and understanding require thought. The success of this interpretive process relies on the place of the individual in community and the hierarchical structures that organize and delineate that community. So situated, the skillful reader can see through illusory facades to reveal the truth, just as the Lord's fire will make the truth unambiguously manifest for everyone after death and at the end of the world.

Crosses and Fire: Miracles and Signs in Peter of les Vaux-de-Cernay

In the *History*, two miracles are closely connected with events at Minerve that illustrate two essential motifs of Peter's account of the crusade.[105] After the capture of the city and the burning of the unrepentant heretics, Simon prepares to leave Minerve with his army. As the foot soldiers depart, they set fire to the huts that they had made for shelter during the siege. Peter tells us that these huts were made of dry branches and leaves that caught fire with great speed, filling the whole valley with flames "as if a great city was burning," yet out of all these huts in the burning valley, one was different.[106]

There was one hut, exactly like the others in its state and its construction, that did not burn. In fact, while all the others were completely destroyed, this hut showed no sign of any damage from the flames. It was not saved by its location, standing "half a foot" away on all sides from the others that were consumed. It was saved because a priest had worshipped within it during the siege. This brush with the divine was enough to make a tinder-built shack immune to the fire. This miracle located so close in time, place, and in the order of the *History* itself to the burnings of "at least 140" human beings makes a statement. The touch of God delivers from the flame, while its absence dooms. Looking on the burning valley in the crusade's wake, one can see the fate of the entire undelivered and unredeemed world. This great city of the world, in contrast to the City of God, will end in flame.[107] The miraculous survival of this siege hut is an illustration in microcosm of the crusade as an attempt at salvation. The crusaders' struggle for redemption is an act of worship done in concert with God. The service of God is all the more compelling because around it everything is burning; redemption and condemnation bring out the fullness of each other's qualities, and in the contrast one can see something of the Lord.

While Simon besieged Minerve, another miracle happened at Toulouse. Great numbers of silvery crosses began to appear on the freshly whitewashed walls of Notre Dame de la Dalbade. These crosses were in constant motion, appearing and vanishing so quickly that astonished onlookers did not even have the time to point toward them. The miracle lasted for almost fifteen days, and most of the people in Toulouse were able to see it, including the main ecclesiastics involved in the crusade: Fulk, bishop of Toulouse, Arnold Amalric, and Master Thedisius.

The miraculous crosses at Toulouse echo those worn by the crusaders as a sign of their commitment to holy warfare, and are emblematic of the crusading enterprise as a whole. As noted above, *crucesignati*, or "those signed by the cross," was the term used by the crusaders and their chronicles to identify themselves.[108] More than the equivalent of a uniform, the sign of the cross was part of the identity it marked. The cross of the crusade, called by Jacques de Vitry the "sign of the living God," miraculously appears here at the very time that the violence of the crusade accelerated. The moving crosses at Dalbade demonstrate the powerful alignment between the crusade, its leaders, and the will of God, in an illustration of a continued congruence much like that found in the miraculous agreement of the prelates at Montélimar. The crusade is a harmony between faithful creatures and their creator, like the singing of a mass.

A similar pairing of burning heretical bodies and nonflammable matter touched by the divine occurred at Lavaur. Simon's assault on Lavaur took place at an important juncture for the crusade, when the focus of the crusaders' aggression shifted onto the holdings of Raymond himself.[109] After a difficult siege, Lavaur fell on May 3, 1211. Aimery, the commander of the defenders and the former lord of Montréal, and eighty knights were put to death.[110] This execution was messy as the gibbets, built in haste, collapsed under their victims' weight, and the crusaders finished the task with their swords. The crusaders also killed Geralda, the Lady of Lavaur and sister of Aimery, by throwing her into a pit and heaping stones on her. In contrast to other accounts of Geralda's death, Peter finds no fault in it, saying only that she was "a heretic of the worst sort." Peter concludes his account of the killing at Lavaur with the burning of "innumerable heretics with great rejoicing."[111] With the phrase "with great rejoicing" Peter drew a connection between this burning of heretics and liturgical offerings given to God in the likeness of burned sacrifices at the temple in Jerusalem.[112] Peter's use of the abstract descriptor "innumerable" suggests that the number killed at Lavaur was greater than those killed at Minerve, and the other accounts of this event suggest this assumption may be true. William of Puylaurens says three hundred were burned, and William of Tudela suggests the number was around four hundred.[113]

The mass burning at Lavaur is accompanied by another tale of miraculous immunity to fire. Peter tells the reader that at Lavaur the cloak of a crusader "by some mischance" caught fire. The cloak burned except for the part where the cross was stitched on it. This part, "by God's miraculous judgment," was left untouched by the flames.[114] This miracle repeats the essential elements already seen in the survival of the siege hut at Minerve and the moving crosses at Dalbade. Fire, which consumes heretics and their works, does not touch those things in contact with the divine. The preeminent symbol of that divine contact is the cross, as an emblem of the crusade and the identity of the crusaders. Peter's association of God's touch, the symbol of the cross, and the crusade is also a statement of alignment between the conduct of the crusade and God's judgment. In the slaughter of captured knights or the throwing of a noblewoman in a pit the reader should not find a moral failing in the crusading venture. Each pairing of burning heretical bodies and unburned symbolic ephemera of the crusade is a testament of ongoing righteousness.

Unlike the other descriptions of burnings for heresy in Peter's *History* examined so far, there is apparently no attempt at Lavaur to redeem anyone. A partial explanation for this difference may be found in Peter's description of the lengthy siege itself. Lavaur is a place synonymous with heresy, and Peter calls it "the source and origin of every form of heresy."[115] Defense of this place is an open declaration of hostility to God, and in this episode Peter's recurrent conflation of opposition to the crusade with enmity to God is in full force. The account of the siege reads as a crescendo of outrages. Raymond of Toulouse withdraws the support for the siege that he promised and in fact aids the defenders. A group of nearby crusaders is massacred, and a priest is killed beside the altar of a church after he identifies himself as both a crusader and a priest.[116] The bishop of Toulouse is forced out of the city.[117] Finally, the defenders of Lavaur celebrate the breaking of a cross affixed to a siege engine, disrespecting all it symbolizes. When the city falls on the Feast of the Cross, what happens afterward is the revenge of the cross, and Peter suggests that it be read that way.[118] In a similar vein, William of Puylaurens, in his account of the burnings at Lavaur, finds a direct alignment between the crusaders' actions and the judgment of God, arguing that all of those burned at Lavaur were taken from the flames of this world directly to the "everlasting fire."[119]

These testimonies through susceptibility or immunity to fire follow a model established early in Peter's *History*. Peter recounts that at Montréal in 1206 Dominic Guzman, later St. Dominic, the founder of the Dominican Friars, defeated a group of heretics in a debate.[120] Afterward, Dominic put in writing the authorities he had cited and gave the paper to the heretics so they could study it.[121] When the heretics again convened together in private they resolved to test the manuscript by throwing it in the fire. If it burned, the destruction of Dominic's text would prove the faith of the heretics, but if it remained untouched by the fire they would admit that the faith preached by Dominic and his fellows was true. The heretics threw the paper into the fire and after but a moment it jumped out on its own accord. Unmoved, the most hardened of the heretics demanded that it be thrown in again. When the paper leapt from the flames a second time, this heretic insisted that it be tossed in yet again. True to form, the paper jumped, unharmed, from the fire a third and final time. Nevertheless, even in the face of such unambiguously miraculous testimony the heretics refused to convert, insisting that the story be kept a secret, especially from the supporters of the Church. Their containment strategy failed, and the miracle of the Catholic authorities' leap from the flames got out through a witness sympathetic to the Church. Peter concludes by saying that he heard this story from Dominic himself.

While the miracle does not move the hard-hearted heretics who witnessed it, it serves the orthodox as yet another testimony to the righteousness of their cause. This miracle is ultimately for the benefit of the orthodox rather than the heretics, whose stubbornness has led them to disregard its meaning.[122] In this function, the miracle is quite like later tales of host desecration at the hands of Jews.[123] In both cases, a miracle clearly declares the truth of orthodox doctrines to an immediate audience that, at least initially, chooses not to appreciate it. The audience who benefits from this divine sign is the one among whom the story is retold. As illustrated by the hostility of the Jews, who tortured the Eucharist long after its miraculous nature had become glaringly apparent, or the heretics' similar repeated attempts to burn Dominic's authorities, the true wickedness of the enemies of Christendom originates from a position of understanding. These enemies know that the teachings of the Church are true and willingly reject them.[124] Miracles that enact this essential trope are part of an eternal and universal story that brings the present world into constant contact with the tropology of biblical events. In a sense, the present and the past dissolve in the context of this truth, leaving only a timeless battle between good and evil. The living Christian is by necessity a participant in this struggle.

In this simple story one can find the blueprint for Peter's account of the crusade. The enemies of the faith are doomed to be destroyed in fire, and through their annihilation the true faith will leap away from the flames of destruction. This conception of the struggle against heresy reached far beyond Peter's account of the crusade. In the version of Dominic's debate with the heretics told by Jordan of Saxony in the early 1230s, the event is like a contest between book-length written arguments. The judges, unable to decide between Dominic's book or the book of the heretics, throw them both into a fire. The heretical book is immediately consumed, but the one written by Dominic leaps from the flames unharmed three times.[125] In the account of the crusade written by Peter, its so-called official historian, such a leap from the flames was the ideal purpose and point for the entire enterprise. The struggle against heresy was another opportunity for orthodox self-realization and perfection.

The homicidal ethic articulated in the sources for the Albigensian Crusade is profoundly related to the discourse surrounding earlier medieval executions

FIGURE 6. Dominic's book leaping from the flames during his debate with heretics. © The British Library Board, Harley 2449 f160.

for heresy. These previous burnings provided opportunities for formative interactions between self and other in which the orthodox identity of medieval Latin Christendom took better shape through the exclusion of the condemned. The major sources for the Albigensian Crusade, likewise, take processes of expulsion and exclusion as opportunities for self-realization and improvement. The enhancement of the orthodox self, especially as presented by Peter of les Vaux-de-Cernay, is a process based on love. Like the purification of the soul in Purgatory, holy warfare depended on the presence of a unifying love that was the fundamental basis of Christian community. The evil of heresy acted as a spur to the enlargement and deepening of this vital love, and the act of killing was something like an essential liturgical element in this drawing together of Christian community.

If, as Mark Gregory Pegg argues, the Albigensian Crusade "ushered genocide into the West" as an act of love, this entrance depended on centuries of recurrent portrayals of heretics and heresy as an instrument ultimately in the service of the faithful. This employment of heresy was itself an expression of a larger conviction regarding the nature of evil. Like the "rod of discipline" described by Bernard of Clairvaux, wicked creatures—angels or men—were employed by God to improve the good, and with this purpose fulfilled these evil beings were then discarded.[126]

Conclusion

The Uses of Exclusion and Fear
for a Community of Love

                                A number of themes, or recurrent conceptions, have surfaced in my close analyses of medieval sources associated with the immolation of living heretics. Many of these concepts build on medieval notions of community and its foundation in love. As the orthodox authors of these accounts reflected on the violent exclusion of the heretic, they returned again and again to interpretive negotiations between appearance and meaning, or the letter and its signification. As they portrayed it, the orthodox community was the group that read accurately, and its members alone could pierce the "outer shell of seeming" to access "the inner kernel of reality."[1] In contrast, the heretic (as well as the non-Christian more generally) was often portrayed as one who misinterpreted texts, a type of reader who fixated on the appearances of things to the detriment of inner meanings. The idea of heresy as an archetype of misinterpretation led on by an inner spiritual misalignment made the heretic a sign at the service of the orthodox observer; like many other medieval models of otherness, the heretic became a kind of text to be read. What this text said was both for the benefit of the orthodox and dictated by the ideological convictions and needs of the orthodox.

    Brian Stock, in his influential *The Implications of Literacy*, views the relationship between the eleventh-century rise of literacy and the formation of heretical or reformist groups through the lens of what he calls "textual communities." These communities were more than groups of people who valued the same texts; at the heart of Stock's textual community was an interpretation of a given text that acted as a guide to the reformation of a group's thought and action.[2] Medieval authors themselves often envisioned and described their textual communities through the idea of an emotive unity in God's illuminating love.[3] Orthodox interpretations, around which licit Christendom could cohere, were portrayed as arising from within this union in love, whereas non-Christian or heretical understandings of texts and signs came from outside it.

Of course, heresy, as is often said, arises in the eyes of the beholder, and as a concept it was useful in drawing the boundaries of the orthodox community.[4] The Apostle Paul said that "there must be also heresies: that they also, who are approved, may be made manifest among you" (1 Cor. 11:19). In the self-identification of orthodoxy, the heretic played an essential role, and this role was itself tied to larger religious and philosophical ideas regarding the usefulness of difference. Medieval authors insisted on this service provided by uncovered heretics, or by the category of evil more generally. Ralph Glaber was reminded of Paul's words on the necessity of heresy when he described the first medieval burning for heresy at Orleans. Hugh of St. Victor argued that evil exists because it allows the good to stand out more beautifully. Bernard, likewise, argued that the evil ultimately serves the good, while for the crusaders described by Peter of les Vaux-de-Cernay the confrontation with heresy in Languedoc was an opportunity to serve and grow in contact with God. In all these authors, there was a deep and abiding conviction that heresy, while still a threat to the individual members of the body of Christ on earth, helped to shape and confirm the community of the redeemed.

Tied to this conviction regarding the kind of work that evil was ultimately driven to do was the necessity of making a distinction between heresy and the reform of orthodoxy. In establishing that one's own call for change was reform rather than heresy, the identification and exclusion of the heretic was essential. The sources for the first burning of Christian heretics at Orleans in 1022 saw the confrontation with the revealed enemy of Christendom as part of the general renewal and sacralization of the world. Descriptions of the mid-twelfth-century executions in the Rhineland also situated and described heresy and orthodoxy as coconstitutive. It is just such a concern with differentiating reform and heresy that drove the remarkable treatise against Albero, the priest of Merke. Likewise, Ralph of Cogeshall's infamous account of the confrontation between Gervase of Tilbury and the maiden in a vineyard, through a remarkable narrative alchemy, transmuted the sinful clerk into a defender of the good through the uncovering and banishment of the heretic.

The study of medieval authorities' presentations of the heretics they and their brethren executed is an examination of the kinds of discourse still used in modern conflicts and persecutions. An enemy is useful in creating the self, and over time authorities' confrontations with even a spectral enemy can manage to create the very enemy that authority seeks to police. This process is not limited to the case of medieval heresies. It continues today in the form of the War on Terror, anti-Western Islamic extremism, and the so-called culture wars. Foucault described a similar process in his *History of Sexuality* as "the perverse implantation." The apparent multiplication of different types of perversity is a part of the extension of power. In the context of this extension, both those who persecute perversity and those who come to view themselves as embodiments of the perversity pursued create, in a sense, their social selves. In the dynamic of pursuit and avoidance, both archetypes find not only their purpose but also their pleasure.[5] As Julien Théry-Astruc suggests, it is in this way that, over time, the interrogatory power of the institutional Church attracted and then reified the theological peculiarities over which it kept watch, and, in fact, needed to find.[6] I hope this book will contribute to a useful genealogy of the ways in which we talk about our enemies and of what the portrayals of our confrontations with these enemies (as well as the cases made for the necessity of these confrontations) mean for our notions of ourselves.

My inquiry in *Burning Bodies* has frequently identified specific dynamics at work within its sources that remain relevant and all too familiar for scholars and policymakers concerned with the modern world. One dynamic of special importance is the participation of an imagined, or spectral, other in the construction and ongoing existence of the self. Sara Ahmed, for example, in *The Cultural Politics of Emotion*, approaches the creation of collective and individual identities in terms strikingly similar to those found in medieval descriptions of heretics' executions. In her examination of tensions within the modern nation-state, associated with racism, fascism, and the War on Terror, Ahmed argues that collective identities are formed through an "affective politics of fear" that creates a subject threatened by imagined others. These others threaten to take something away from the subject, or even replace the subject entirely. This politics of fear creates both the other, who threatens, and the threatened subject. In the creation of both sides of this duality, there is a shift between individual and collective bodies, based on likeness. Collective identities take shape as the result of the ways "others impress on us" as alike or as different. In this impression, the different seeks to consume the subject by incorporating him or her into its body. In the fear of this envelopment, "fear does not involve the defence of borders that already exist; rather fear makes those borders, by establishing objects from which the subject, in fearing, can stand apart, objects that become 'the not' from which the subject appears to flee."[7]

In particular, Ahmed stresses the intimate relationship between hatred and love in the creation of collective identities, suggesting that so-called negative emotions, such as fear or hatred, help to produce and to shape the experience of love.[8] Her argument is quite similar to what has been termed "motive attribution asymmetry" in political science.[9] Ahmed argues, "Love is crucial to how individuals become aligned with collectives through their identification with an ideal, an alignment that relies on the existence of others who have failed that ideal."[10] The presence of these failures "is imagined as a threat to the object of love," but the object of love is entangled with what threatens it.[11] The spectral existence of the object of hatred or fear, which is essential to the creation of the subject who hates or who fears, is required for the ongoing existence of the one who hates or who fears. Ahmed concludes that since the hated object has become part of the "life of the subject . . . hate then cannot be opposed to love."[12] We love what is like us, and we are threatened by the unlikeness on which we draw for our impressions of likeness. She finds this logic at work in the self-presentation of various modern hate groups, such as American white nationalists, which she summarizes as "Because we love, we hate, and this hate is what brings us together."[13] Ahmed appears to suggest that while a clearly defined and idealized community experientially is based on love, this love requires a process of repudiation built on fear and hate in order to come into being.

The medieval authors whose works I have examined would not agree that it is "hate that brings us together," but their theories of community made a great deal of room for fear as well as likeness and difference. In their minds, the issue of likeness or difference was fundamental. Although created in the likeness of God, humanity was, through sin, a distorted image. Trapped in the realm of unlikeness, human beings should be afraid and turn toward their God in the hopes that this deformation might be repaired. For Hugh of St. Victor, it was this fear that attracted charity to the soul. Hugh explained that when the soul considers Hell it seeks to flee from this potential fate. Once it finds Christ as the way of avoiding its immanent danger and embraces him in love, the foundational fear is alleviated by this love, and "so indeed charity is born from fear, but through charity fear is consumed."[14] In Hugh's opinion, Christian community, as the union of charity, does employ fear to spread love; it possesses a useful affective politics of fear, involved in the creation of the Christian subject. Hell, for theologians like Hugh, was the eternal continuation of the region of unlikeness. This unlikeness, and the terrestrial desires associated with it, had to be repudiated through a love invited into the human being by fear. Those human communities that were associated with the unredeemed postlapsarian human state logically shared this repudiation, and a consideration of their fate(s) could also attract charity to the soul.

In ways such as these, the history of love and the history of the "dark side"—hate, fear, or cruelty—are not different things; they travel together and create each other.[15] This study has followed the establishment of the medieval persecuting society through accounts of burning supposed heretics alive, the most notorious image of its supposed violence and intolerance. The pyre, however, and the fire that burned convicted heretics were symbolically linked to the most fundamental, optimistic, and aspirational symbols of unity that medieval culture possessed: the fiery love or charity of God. Aflame with the love of God, *Christianitas* became one burning body. Outside this body, the non-Christian was destined to burn in another way in Hell, and on the way to this destiny the damned could do terrible damage, by their very natures attempting to rip limbs off the body of Christ to go with them into damnation. In the face of such a perceived threat, medieval persecutors claimed that they acted in the defense of others, who through a union of love were a part of themselves. When medieval authors explained the necessity of killing, they did so through a discourse about love. They elaborated on this love rationally, appealing to the noblest of intentions and the most lucid logic. In the field of human conflict, these are appeals that remain familiar.

Finally, a book like this one has one essential danger that must be addressed directly. An analysis devoted to the persecutor's perspective can always take openness to the tone and point of view found in its sources too far, relating to the past with so much neutrality that it accepts all its errors.[16] In the recovery of the logic and imagery behind persecution there is a danger of perpetuating or even completing the erasure of the actual victims of persecution that persecutors attempted to perform in the past. My argument is particularly susceptible to this threat. In the reduction of the excluded into a sign to be read, a sign whose meaning serves the community that excludes, these banished heretics do seem to disappear. As Peter Biller has reminded us, we must not forget that these stories that I have told often reflect, albeit through a glass darkly, the real death of real people.[17] I have argued that these people, as they were themselves, are not readily recoverable through the sources I have examined. What we have encountered is the presence of various specters, but I believe that the erasure of the specter is never quite complete.

The type of difference embodied by the medieval heretic was a difference to be removed, banished, done away with. It had to exist and it had to be confronted, because in this confrontation it had work to do, and when this work was complete it had to disappear. The pyre or the scaffold was an ideal setting for the clear distillation of these essential elements. In the drama of the pyre, Catholic and heretic could take shape in the context of each other. Yet as Sarah Ahmed has argued, if the notion of orthodox community requires a threat against which it comes into being, this threat must, in some way, persist within it.

In fact, the erasure or the banishment of the heretic is never complete. At the beginning of this book I related the existence of the notion of heresy in medieval writers and medieval texts to spectrality. I suggested that images of the heretic existed within the authors I have examined as a kind of phantasmal presence, which these authors put to work. When this work was accomplished, these phantoms had to be abjured away, but this abjuration could never fully work, because the very being who attempted to banish relied on the phantom, or specter, for its sense of itself.[18] In this way, the excluded and the one who excludes were intimately bound together. In the same motion that drew a clear line between them, they were paradoxically made somehow the same.

I have frequently returned to an image from Bernard of Clairvaux, explaining the usefulness of the ill-willed creature to the larger good of creation. Bernard explained that God uses the evil as a rod of correction to help shape the good. With this shaping done, the rod is cast into the fire as a useless twig.[19] I have argued that narratives depicting heretics' executions attempt to employ their heretical protagonists in this way, but in this very image lies the implied persistence of the wicked. In the current life, the Christian community is never done being shaped; the disfigurement in the divine image inherent in man is never completely repaired.[20] So it is that the complete destruction of the useless twig is always as deferred as the final kingdom of God. In this infinite deference, there is endless time to listen to the voices of the specters and question if justice is still due to them.[21] Here, I think, we can find the seed of an ethical promise within my analysis of the spectral nature of orthodox portrayals of medieval heretics. The expulsion is not over; the erasure is never complete.

NOTES

Abbreviations

AA. SS.: Acta Sanctorum
CCCM: Corpus Christianorum Continuatio Medievalis
CCSL: Corpus Christanorum Series Latina
CSEL: Corpus Scriptorum Ecclesiasticorum Latinorum
LL: Leges (in folio)
MGH: Monumenta Germania Historica
PG: *Patrologia Graeca*
PL: *Patrologia Latina*, ed. J. P. Migne, 221 vols. Paris, 1844–1865.
SRG: Scriptores rerum Germanicarum in usum scholarum
SS: Scriptores (in folio)

Introduction

1. Caesarius of Heisterbach, *Dialogus miraculorum*, 5.19, ed. Nikolaus Nösges and Horst Schneider (Turnhout: Brepols, 2009), 3:1016, 1018; H. Von E. Scott and C. C. Swinton Bland, trans., *The Dialogue on Miracles* (London: George Routledge and Sons, 1929), 1:342. (Note that on subsequent citations of primary sources the page references in the modern edition cited are given in parentheses after the primary reference; page references in the translation cited are prefixed by "trans.").

2. The quote is drawn from the discussion of the legend of Saladin and the three rings in Dominique Iogna-Prat, *Order and Exclusion: Cluny and Christendom Face Heresy, Judaism, and Islam (1000–1150)*, trans. Graham Robert Edwards (Ithaca, NY: Cornell University Press, 2002), 360.

3. My phrasing is influenced by that of Steven F. Kruger in "The Spectral Jew," *New Medieval Literatures* 2 (1998): 21. On the relationship of his notions of spectrality and conjuration to medieval "categories of otherness" beyond Judaism, see his *The Spectral Jew: Conversion and Embodiment in Medieval Europe* (Minneapolis: University of Minnesota Press, 2006), 20.

4. Much like "thinking with demons" has served as a fruitful approach to the intellectual history of witchcraft in Europe, "thinking with heretics" allows scholars to approach the world of ideas and ideologies in which the medieval persecutors of heretics operated. See Stuart Clark, *Thinking with Demons: The Idea of Witchcraft in Early Modern Europe* (Oxford: Clarendon Press, 1997); R. I. Moore, review of *Heresy and Heretics in the Thirteenth Century: The Textual Representations*, by Lucy J. Sackville, *H-France Review* 12 (2012): 44. See discussion below.

5. See Antonio Sennis, ed., *Cathars in Question* (Woodbridge, UK: York Medieval Press, 2016). This edited collection represents the current state of the debate. Some of the essays in this collection illustrate an unfortunate tendency in the current scholarly conversation to employ ad hominem arguments in the context of heated debate and prolonged disagreement.

6. Different scholars give the opposing sides different names in different contexts. They are sometimes described as "traditionalists" and "skeptics." R. I. Moore, "Principles at Stake: The Debate of April 2013 in Retrospect," in Sennis, *Cathars in Question*, 258. Earlier, Lucy J. Sackville described the debate through a division between "functional" and "radical" skepticism in her *Heresy and Heretics in the Thirteenth Century: The Textual Representations* (Woodbridge, UK: York Medieval Press, 2011), 5.

7. Alessia Trivellone, *L'hérétique imaginé: Hétérodoxie et iconographie dans l'Occident medieval, de l'époque carolingienne à l'inquisition* (Turnhout: Brepols, 2009), 21–22.

8. James Given, "Chasing Phantoms: Philip IV and the Fantastic," in *Heresy and the Persecuting Society in the Middle Ages: Essays on the Work of R. I. Moore*, ed. Michael Frassetto (Leiden: Brill, 2006), 271. See also Given's review of Brunn's *Des contestataires aux "Cathares"* in which he concludes that Brunn's book provides much ammunition to those who argue that Catharism was "a mere spectre that haunted the minds of those troubled by the phenomenon of religious dissidence." James Given, review of *Des contestataires aux "Cathares" Discours de réforme et propagande antihérétique dans les pays du Rhin et de la Meuse avant l'Inquisition*, by Uwe Brunn, *Speculum* 83 (2008): 963.

9. Perhaps the most influential example of such assumptions lies in the work of Margaret Alice Murray, esp. *The Witch Cult in Western Europe: A Study in Anthropology* (Oxford: Clarendon Press, 1921). For the influence of Murray's thesis that the so-called cult was the survival of a pre-Christian religion, see Ronald Hutton, *The Triumph of the Moon: A History of Modern Pagan Witchcraft* (Oxford: Oxford University Press, 1999).

10. Norman Cohn, *Europe's Inner Demons: The Demonization of Christians in Medieval Christendom*, rev. ed. (London: Pimlico, 1993), 72–73. It was originally published as *Europe's Inner Demons: An Inquiry Inspired by the Great Witch-Hunt* (London: Sussex University Press, 1975). Cohn was far from the first to question Murray's thesis; see Keith Thomas, *Religion and the Decline of Magic: Studies in Popular Beliefs in Sixteenth and Seventeenth Century England* (Oxford: Oxford University Press, 1971), 514–16.

11. R. I. Moore, *The Formation of a Persecuting Society* (Malden, MA: Blackwell, 1987).

12. A process explored in more depth in R. I. Moore, *The First European Revolution, c. 970–1215* (Malden, MA: Blackwell, 2003).

13. Carol Lansing, epilogue to *The Albigensian Crusades*, by Joseph R. Strayer (Ann Arbor: University of Michigan Press, 1992), 179. Lansing questions whether Moore's argument can completely apply to Catharism because it is a different religion from Catholicism. As I will argue below, some scholarship has addressed this concern by doubting the existence of Catharism as another religion.

14. Mark Gregory Pegg, *The Corruption of Angels: The Great Inquisition of 1245–1246* (Princeton, NJ: Princeton University Press, 2001); *A Most Holy War: The Albigensian Crusade and the Battle for Christendom* (Oxford: Oxford University Press, 2008).

15. Mark Gregory Pegg, "The Paradigm of Catharism; or, the Historians' Illusion," in Sennis, *Cathars in Question*, 21.

16. R. I. Moore regards the identity of those called Cathars in medieval, or more often modern, scholarship as a serious problem; see his *The War on Heresy* (Cambridge, MA: Harvard University Press, 2012), 6n.

17. Mark Gregory Pegg, "Heresy, Good Men, and Nomenclature," in Frassetto, *Heresy and the Persecuting Society in the Middle Ages*, 238.

18. Moore, "Principles at Stake," 262.

19. Monique Zerner, ed., *Inventer l'hérésie? Discours polémiques et pouvoirs avant l'inquisition* (Nice: Centre d'Études Médiévales, 1998).

20. Uwe Brunn, *Des contestataires aux "Cathares" Discours de réforme et propagande antihérétique dans les pays du Rhin et de la Meuse avant l'Inquisition* (Paris: Institut d'Études Augustiniennes, 2006).

21. See the discussion in chapter 4 for more information on Eckbert's presentation of the Cathars. These are the *Sermones contra Catharos*, also called the *Liber contra hereses Katharorum*, PL 195:11–102. The first sermon, or section, of the work is translated in R. I. Moore, *Birth of Popular Heresy* (London: Edward Arnold, 1975), 88–94.

22. John H. Arnold, "The Cathar Middle Ages as a Methodological and Historical Problem," in *Cathars in Question*, 76.

23. Caterina Bruschi and Peter Biller use these words to describe the essential epistemology at work in Robert E. Lerner's *The Heresy of the Free Spirit in the Later Middle Ages* (Berkeley: University of California Press, 1972); see also their "Texts and the Repression of Heresy: Introduction," in *Texts and the Repression of Medieval Heresy*, ed. Caterina Bruschi and Peter Biller (Woodbridge, UK: York Medieval Press, 2003), 16–17.

24. Peter Biller, "Through a Glass Darkly: Seeing Medieval Heresy," in *The Medieval World*, ed. Peter Linehan and Janet L. Nelson (London: Routledge, 2001), 324.

25. Arnold, "Cathar Middle Ages as a Methodological and Historiographical Problem," 68.

26. Moore, "Principles at Stake," 272.

27. Jean-Louis Biget, *Hérésie et inquisition dans le Midi de la France* (Paris: Picard, 2007), 107–15.

28. Julien Théry-Astruc, "The Heretical Dissidence of the 'Good Men' in the Albigeois (1276–1329): Localism and Resistance to Roman Clericalism," in Sennis, *Cathars in Question*, 81.

29. Moore, "Principles at Stake," 271n31.

30. For example, Christine Caldwell Ames suggests that the success of Moore's thesis in his *Formation of a Persecuting Society* has counteracted his original goal of denaturalizing persecution, rendering persecution again into an inevitability as "what institutions do." She suggests that scholars take the sincerity of persecutors' religious convictions, and the importance of these convictions to their identities, into consideration. See Christine Caldwell Ames, *Righteous Persecution: Inquisition, Dominicans, and Christianity in the Middle Ages* (Philadelphia: University of Pennsylvania Press, 2009), 18–19.

31. I see the use of the heretic as an object to be interpreted as very similar to that of the "hermeneutic Jew" as the "living letters of the law"; see Jeremy Cohen, *Living Letters of the Law: Ideas of the Jew in Medieval Christianity* (Berkeley: University of California Press, 1999), 2. Cohen takes the phrasing "living letters" from Bernard of Clairvaux, "Letter 363," in *Sancti Bernardi Opera*, ed. J. Leclercq and H. Rochais (Rome: Editiones Cistercienses, 1977), vol. 8, 311–17.

32. For the kinds of justice that can be done with later sources to the convictions of those who chose to die for their religious views, see Brad S. Gregory, *Salvation at Stake: Christian Martyrdom in Early Modern Europe* (Cambridge, MA: Harvard University Press, 1999).

33. For influential explorations of this dynamic, see Kai T. Erikson, *Wayward Puritans: A Study in the Sociology of Deviance* (London: John Wiley and Sons, 1966); Judith Butler, *Bodies That Matter: On the Discursive Limits of "Sex"* (New York: Routledge, 1993), 3–8.

34. For similar points regarding the representation of Jews in medieval Christian literature and iconography, see Sara Lipton, *Dark Mirror: The Medieval Origins of Anti-Jewish Iconography* (New York: Metropolitan Books, 2014), 7; David Nirenberg, *Anti-Judaism: The History of a Way of Thinking* (New York: Head of Zeus, 2013), 12.

35. For example, Jacques Chiffoleau estimated that even though death sentences were a low percentage of the overall punishments inflicted by authorities, around fifteen to thirty individuals were condemned to death every year in the region of Avignon at the beginning of the fourteenth century; see *Les justices du pape: Délinquance et criminalité dans la region d'Avignon au quatorzième siècle* (Paris: Publications de la Sorbonne, 1984), 235. In fourteenth-century Paris, Bronislaw Geremek recorded seventy-three death sentences issued at the Châtelet alone in the years 1389–92, an average of about eighteen a year. For the entirety of Paris and the surrounding region, similar sentences at seigniorial courts would have increased that number; see Bronislaw Geremek, *Les marginaux parisiens aux XIVe et XVe siècles*, trans. Daniel Beauvois (Paris: Flammarion, 1976), 62. For comparison, since the reintroduction of the death penalty in the United States in 1976 until 2015 there have been an average of about thirty-six executions per year (with the actual numbers in any given year varying dramatically); see "Executions by Year," Death Penalty Information Center, accessed July 12, 2016, http://www.deathpenaltyinfo.org/executions-year.

36. On different modes of execution and their frequency, see Julius R. Ruff, *Violence in Early Modern Europe 1500–1800* (Cambridge: Cambridge University Press, 2001), 98–99.

37. Although from a later period, a good account of the skill involved in public decapitation, as well as the length of time required for the acquisition of that skill, can be found in Joel F. Harrington, *The Faithful Executioner: Life, Honor, and Shame in the Turbulent Sixteenth Century* (New York: Picador, 2013).

38. On the prohibition of hanging women, see J. Gessler, "Mulier suspensa: À délit égal peine différente?," *Revue Belge de philology et d'histoire* 18 (1939): 974–88.

39. Julien Havet, in his foundational study of punishment for heresy, argued that burning heretics alive became basically a customary punishment before it became a point of fixed, written law; see his "L'hérésie et le bras seculier au Moyen-Age jusqu'au treizième siècle," *Bibliothèque de l'Ecloe de Chartes* 41 (1880): 517.

40. James Given, *Inquisition and Medieval Society: Power, Discipline, and Resistance in Languedoc* (Ithaca, NY: Cornell University Press, 1997), 69.

41. Paul Friedland, *Seeing Justice Done: The Age of Spectacular Capital Punishment in France* (Oxford: Oxford University Press, 2012), 120–24.

1. Our God Is Like a Consuming Fire

1. Gregory the Great, *Homiliae in Hiezechihelem prophetam*, 1.8.28, ed. M. Adriaen, CCSL 142 (Turnhout: Brepols, 1971), 118: "Hinc de ipso omnium creatore scriptum

est: deus noster ignis consumens est. Ignis enim deus dicitur, quia flammis amoris sui incendit mentes quas replet. Et idcirco seraphim incendium dicuntur, quia potestates ei proximae in caelis inaestimabili amoris eius igne succensae sunt. Ex hoc igne succensa ardent in terra corda iustorum."

2. Augustine, *De civitate Dei*, 14.28, ed. Bernard Dombart and Alphonse Kalb, CCSL 47–48 (Turnhout: Brepols, 1955), 451: "Fecerunt itaque ciuitates duas amores duo, terrenam scilicet amor sui usque ad contemptum Dei, caelestem uero amor Dei usque ad contemptum sui."

3. Augustine, *De libero arbitrio*, 1.4.10, ed. W. M. Green, CCSL 29 (Turnhout: Brepols, 1970), 216–17.

4. On the root of the Earthly City in fratricide and its pursuit of peace through the conquest of others, see Augustine, *De civitate Dei*, 15.4–5, ed. Bernard Dombart and Alphonse Kalb, CCSL 48 (Turnhout: Brepols, 1955), 456–58, and 3.6 (CCSL 47, 68–69).

5. Nirenberg, *Anti-Judaism*, 508n121.

6. 1 Cor. 12:12–14: "Sicut enim corpus unum est, et membra habet multa, omnia autem membra corporis cum sint multa, unum tamen corpus sunt: ita et Christus. Etenim in uno Spiritu omnes nos in unum corpus baptizati sumus, sive Judaei, sive gentiles, sive servi, sive liberi: et omnes in uno Spiritu potati sumus. Nam et corpus non est unum membrum, sed multa." For the translations of biblical verses, I have used the Douay-Rheims 1899 American edition unless otherwise stated.

7. Gal. 3:28: "Non est Judaeus, neque Graecus: non est servus, neque liber: non est masculus, neque femina. Omnes enim vos unum estis in Christo Jesu." I have translated "servus" as slave rather than "bond."

8. The prominence to be given to any individual member of the Trinity as well as whether we might call charity the Holy Spirit itself were debated in the Middle Ages. See Geertjan Zuijdwegt, "'Utrum caritas sit aliquid creatum in anima': Aquinas on the Lombard's Identification of Charity with the Holy Spirit," *Recherches de Théologie et Philosophie Médiévales* 79 (2012): 39–74.

9. John 14:6–10.

10. Henri de Lubac, *Exégèse medieval: Les quatre sens de l'écriture* (Paris: Aubier, 1959–64), 41–42.

11. Gal. 4:26; Heb. 12:22.

12. See, for example, Augustine, *De civitate Dei*, 15.26 (p. 493): "Procul dubio figura est [archa Noe] peregrantis in hoc saeculo civitatis Dei, hoc est ecclesiae."

13. William S. Babcock, "Caritas and Signification in *De doctrina christiana* 1–3," in *De doctrina christiana: A Classic of Western Culture*, ed. Duane W. H. Arnold and Pamela Bright (Notre Dame, IN: University of Notre Dame Press, 1995), 157. See also Hannah Arendt, *Love and Saint Augustine*, ed. Joanna Vecchiarelli Scott and Judith Chelius Stark (Chicago: University of Chicago Press, 1996), 18.

14. Augustine, *De Genesi ad litteram libri duodecim*, 6.9, ed. Joseph Zycha, CSEL 28, section 3, pt. 2 (Prague: F. Tempsky, 1894), 181; John Hammond Taylor, trans., *The Literal Meaning of Genesis* (New York: Newman Press, 1982), 188: "Not in vain, however, does scripture say that even an infant is not free from sin if he has spent one day of life on earth. The Psalmist says, 'In iniquity I was conceived, and in sin my mother nourished me in her womb.' St. Paul says all die in Adam, 'in whom all have sinned.'"

15. Rom. 5:12: "Wherefore as by one man sin entered into this world, and by sin death; and so death passed on all men, in whom all have sinned." See also Ps. 50.7 and its common interpretation.

16. 1 John 4:8: "He that loveth not, knoweth not God: for God is charity"; John 4:16: "And we have known, and we have believed the charity, which God hath to us. God is charity: and he that abideth in charity, abideth in God, and God in him."

17. On the difficulty of translating "caritas," see Martha G. Newman, *The Boundaries of Charity: Cistercian Culture and Ecclesiastical Reform, 1098–1180* (Stanford, CA: Stanford University Press, 1996), 261–62n4. On the distinction between caritas and cupiditas, see also Barbara H. Rosenwein, *Generations of Feeling: A History of the Emotions, 600–1700* (Cambridge: Cambridge University Press, 2016), 96–97.

18. As Aelred of Rievaulx summarized: "Et manifestum quidem est quod caritas amor sit, quanquam non minus manifestum, quod non omnis amor caritas sit." *De speculum caritatis*, 3.7.20, ed. C. H. Talbot, CCCM 1 (Turnhout: Brepols, 1971), 114. The clear difference between loves is, of course, from the clerical viewpoint. William Reddy argues for the twelfth-century emergence of a secular and sexual concept of selfless love in opposition to the spiritual love outlined by churchmen; see his *The Making of Romantic Love: Longing and Sexuality in Europe, South Asia and Japan, 900–1200 CE* (Chicago: University of Chicago Press, 2012).

19. For the biblical foundation, see 1 Cor. 13. The formulation often cited by medieval authorities was the one offered by Augustine in his *De doctrina Christiana*, 3.16, ed. and trans. R. P. H. Green (Oxford: Oxford University Press, 1996), 148–49: "I call charity a movement of the soul toward loving God on account of Himself and toward loving oneself and one's neighbor on account of God." See also Thomas Aquinas's paraphrase of Augustine's description of charity from *De moribus ecclesiae catholicae et de moribus Manichaeorum*, 1.11: "Charity is a virtue which, when our affections are perfectly ordered, unites us to God, for by it we love Him," in *Summa Theologica*, 2–2.23.3, s. c., ed. J. de Rubeis and C.-R. Billuart (Turin: Marietti, 1938), 3:128.

20. Mark 12:31.

21. Deut. 4:24; Heb. 12:29.

22. This is a reference to 1 Cor. 3:11–15. The exegesis of this verse was particularly important to the development of the theology of purification after death, especially the fires of Purgatory; see Jacques Le Goff, *The Birth of Purgatory*, trans. Arthur Goldhammer (Chicago: University of Chicago Press, 1984), 43–44.

23. Jerome, *Tractatus de Psalmo 77*, ed. Germain Morin, CCSL 78 (Turnhout: Brepols, 1958), 72–73: "'Dominus noster ignis consumens est.' Ignis consumens. Non dixit, quid consumens: nobis intellegentiam dereliquit. Qui fundamentum Xpisti aedificauerunt lignum, faenum, stipulam, Dominus illis ignis consumens est. Ignis duplicem habet naturam: et lucet, et urit. Si peccatores sumus, incendit: si iusti, lucet nobis."

24. Ambrose of Milan, *De Isaac uel anima*, 8.77, ed. Karl Schenkl, CSEL 32, pt. 1 (Vienna: F. Tempsky, 1897), 695; Song of Sol. 8:6.

25. Ambrose, *De Isaac uel anima*, 8.78 (p. 696): "Sumamus igitur has alas, quae sicut flammae ad superiora dirigant."

26. Ambrose, *De Isaac uel anima*, 8.77 (p. 695): "Bona igitur caritas habens alas ignis ardentis, quae uolitat per pectora et corda sanctorum et exurit quicquid materiale atque terrenum est, quicquid uero sincerum est probat et quod contigerit suo igne meliorat."

27. Ambrose, *De Isaac uel anima*, 8.77 (p. 696): "Has alas habuit Seraphim, quando sumpsit carbonem ignis de altari et tetigit os prophetae et iniquitates eius abstulit et peccata purgauit . . . sicut testificatur Iohannes dicens de domino Iesu: ipse uos baptizabit in spiritu et igni."

28. Ambrose, *De Isaac uel anima*, 8.77 (p. 696): "Merito Hebraei pueri in furnace ardenti non sentiebant ignis incendia, quia caritatis eos flamma refrigerabat." See Dan. 3:50.

29. Ambrose, *De Isaac uel anima*, 8.78 (p. 698).

30. Gregory, *Homiliae in euangelia*, 3, Homilia 30.5, ed. Raymond Etaix, CCSL 141 (Turnhout: Brepols, 1999), 260: "Sed ignem Dominus in terram mittit [Luke 12:49] cum afflatu sancti Spiritus cor carnalium incendit. . . . Bene ergo in igne apparuit Spiritus, quia ab omni corde quod replet torporem frigoris excutit et hoc in desiderio suae aeternitatis accendit."

31. Gregory, *Homiliae in Hiezechihelem prophetam*, 1.8 (p. 118): "Et quia eius membra sunt electi angeli in coelo, eius membra sunt conversi homines in terra; unus homo est qui et super lumbos ardet intrinsecus, et sub lumbis inferius ignis sui splendorem in circuitu emittit, quia et angelos ad amorem suum per divinitatem tenuit, et homines ad sancti ardoris sui desiderium ex humanitate revocavit."

32. Gregory, *Homiliae in Hiezechihelem prophetam*, 1.8 (p. 118): "Unus itaque super thronum est, qui et super lumbos ignem intrinsecus habet in angelis, et sub lumbis ignem incircuitu habet in hominibus, quia in omne quod ab angelis amatur, per omne quod ab hominibus desideratur, unus est qui in cordibus ardet amantium." Gregory makes this commentary on the imagery of Ezek. 1:27.

33. Bernard of Clairvaux, "Sententia 97," *Sententiae Series 3*, in *Sancti Bernardi Opera*, ed. J. Leclercq and H. M. Rochais (Rome: Editiones Cistercienses, 1972), vol. 6, pt. 2, 155: "Spiritus autem Sanctus, a quo cuncta bona procedunt, quasi cum ferro et igne venit ad peccatorem, quando generat in eo contrationis amaritudinem. Contritio quasi palus acutus terram cordis nostril fodit, quasi ignis spinas et tribulos vitiorum exurit, quasi gladius acutus carnis illecebras exstirpat et recidit."

34. Bernard, "Sententia 97" (6:156): "Trahendum est igitur ferrum, voluntas relidendi tollenda. Quia huiusmodi effectus Spiritus, ignis dicitur."

35. As Bernard explains at the conclusion of the sententia: "Ecce modum, ecce ordinem texuimus, quomodo resurgens anima de abysso peccatorum promoveatur usque ad visionem Dei per gradus ascensionum" (6:159).

36. Bernard, "Sententia 97" (6:157): "Timor poenae est quasi umbra arboris in mane, quae multum protenditur, sed, sole ascendente, contrahitur, ita quod in meridie potest eam homo pertransire. Sol fervor est caritatis, quo ascendente, timor poenae contrahitur, ut leviter transiliatur." See also the argument of Hugh of St. Victor that fear attracts charity to the faithful and so is "born of fear" in his *De archa Noe*, 3.2, ed. Patrick Sicard, CCCM 176 (Turnhout: Brepols, 2001), 55.

37. Petrus Cantor, *Summa quae dicitur Verbum abbreuiatum (textus conflatus)*, 2.4, ed. M. Boutry, CCCM 196 (Turnhout: Brepols, 2004), 627: "Vnde cuidam querenti quid est Deus, responsum est: ignis est consumens, unde Moyses: Deus noster ignis consumens est; amor est, unde Iohannes: Deus caritas est et qui manet in caritate in Deo manet et Deus in eo." The biblical verses are Deut. 4:24 and John 4:16.

38. Petrus Cantor, *Summa quae dicitur Verbum abbreuiatum*: "Maior autem horum est caritas a qua surgit motus qui est quasi ignis a Deo in cordibus nostris accensus, quo ipsum ardenter diligimus."

39. Luke 12:49: "Ignem ueni mittere in terram et quid uolo nisi ut ardeat?" The modern vulgate has "accendatur" ("that it be kindled") in place of the common medieval "ardeat" that Peter uses, and I have modified the translation accordingly. For the source of this exegesis of the verse, see Gregory, *Homiliae in euangelia*, 2.30.5, 260.

40. Hildegard of Bingen, *Scivias*, 1.3.4, ed. A. Führkötter and A. Carlevaris, CCCM 43 (Turnhout: Brepols, 1978), 43.

41. Hildegard, "Letter 31r," ed. L. Van Acker, CCCM91 (Turnhout: Brepols, 1991), 86: "Spiritus Sanctus ignis est, et non exstinguibilis ignis, qui interdum per flagrantiam apparet et interdum exstinguitur . . . sicut faber duas uires eris cum igne in unum coniungit, unde est sicut uersatilis ensis, qui undique uibratur." All subsequent Hildegard letters cited are from this edition.

42. Hildegard, *Scivias*, "Protestificatio" (pp. 3–4).

43. Hildegard, "Letter 31r" (p. 88): "In omnibus prauis operibus inanitas est; fugiunt enim ignem Spiritus Sancti."

44. Hildegard, "Letter 28" (p. 79): "Caue etiam, ne tibi bona que tibi in animo uel in opera tuo sunt, quasi a te sint, sed Deo attribuas, a quo omnes uirtutes quemadmodum scintille ab igne procedunt, et esto memor quia cinis es et in cinerem reuerteris, et exhibe debitum honorem Deo de donis suis que in te cognoscis." See Sir. 10:9.

45. Hildegard, "Letter 24" (p. 66): "Causam intolerabilis doloris nostril in pura ueritate lacrimabiliter tibi aperimus, ea fiducia, quod ignea caritas, que Deus est, tibi inspire tut cum paterna pietate lamentabilem uocem, qua in tribulation nostra afflicte ad te clamamus misericorditer exaudire digneris." See also "Letter 16r" (p. 49).

46. Hildegard, "Letter 77r" (p. 168): "Sed planete, scilicet angeli iustitie qui flamma ignis sunt, cum Deo perstiterunt et inexstinguibili igni qui uita est, ministrabant. . . . Qui non timet, non amat, et qui non laudat, non operatur. Et timor ignis est, et caritas ut flamma se dilatat."

47. Discussed in the context of Hugh's mystical theology in Bernard McGinn, *The Growth of Mysticism: Gregory the Great through the Twelfth Century* (New York: Crossroad, 1994), 392–94.

48. Hugh of St. Victor, "De naturis ignis et speciebus," *Miscellanea*, 1.173, PL 177:567B–572B. Hereafter cited as "Hugh, 'De naturis.'"

49. Hugh, "De naturis," 570D–571A: "In omnibus autem quae videntur, et a quibus rerum invisibilium similitudo trahitur, solus ignis sicut loco supremus est."

50. Hugh, "De naturis," 571A: "In eo enim invenitur similitudo virtutis et vitii, ita ut acies mentis foris tacta per imaginem, intro redeat ad contemplandam veritatem."

51. Hugh, "De naturis," 571A: "Amor est enim ignis: et est amor bonus, ignis bonus, ignis videlicet charitatis; et est amor malus, ignis malus, ignis cupiditatis. Ignis bonus depascitur culpam; ignis malus demolitur naturam. Ignis bonus accenditur a Spiritu sancto; ignis malus inflammatur a diabolo. Ignis bonus charitas, fons virtutum; ignis malus cupiditas, radix vitiorum" (1 Tim. 6).

52. Hugh, "De naturis," 571B: "Sed videamus nunc quomodo in nobis operentur, hi ut ita dicam, duo opifices, Spiritus sanctus per ignem suum, et diabolus per ignem suum.

53. Hugh, "De naturis," 571B: "[Diabolus] inflando ignem in nobis excitat . . . excitat corruptionem quae sopita fuerat."

54. Hugh, "De naturis," 571B: "Nam Spiritus sanctus ipse ignis est, et affando ignem in nobis creat . . . creat virtutem quae non erat."

55. Hugh, "De naturis," 571B: "Diabolus autem non ignis, sed frigidus est."

56. Such was the meaning often found by exegetes in Song of Sol. 5:6–8. Hugh, *Expositio in hierarchiam coelestem S. Dionysii Areopagite*, 6, PL 175:1038B: "Anima mea liquefacta est, ut dilectus locutus est; quaesivi illum." Hereafter cited as "Hugh, *Expositio*." Aelred of Rievaulx, likewise, sees the soul liquefied by the fire of love: "Sermon 73," 9, *Sermones I–CLXXXII*, ed. G. Raciti, CCCM 2B (Turnhout: Brepols, 2012), 242.

57. Dante Alighieri, *La Commedia*, 1.34, ed. Giorgio Petrocchi (Milan: Mondadori, 1966), 2:583–98.

58. Hugh, *Expositio*, 1039B. Hugh, following the translation of the *Celestial Hierarchies* of John Scotus Eriugena, uses the word "superfervidum." For the original, see John Scotus Eriugena, *Expositiones in hierarchiam caelestem*, 7, ll. 90–101, ed. J. Barbet, CCCM 31 (Turnhout: Brepols, 1975), 94.

59. Hugh, *De sacramentis christiane fidei*, 2.16.5, ed. Rainer Berndt (Aschendorff: Monasterii Westfalorum, 2008); also in PL 176:587D–89B.

60. Hugh, "De naturis," 572A: "Et sicut massa liquefacta per fistulam in monetam funditur et formam accipit, ita mens, amoris igne solute per radium contemplationis usque in imaginem divinae similitudinis currit."

61. Hugh, *Expositio*, 1037D–38A: "Amor autem unum te facere vult cum ipso."

62. Augustine, *Enarrationes in Psalmos*, 80.14, ed. E. Dekkers and J. Fraipont, CCSL 39 (Turnhout: Brepols, 1956), 1128: "Ideo Samson caudas uulpium colligauit, uulpes insidiosos, maxime que haereticos significant."

63. Augustine, *Enarrationes in Psalmos*, 80.14 (p. 1128): "In terrenis cogitationibus consentiunt sibi; opinio diuersa est, uanitas una est. De illis in alio psalmo dicitur: ipsi de vanitate in unum; quamuis opinionum uarietate discordent, simili tamen uanitate colligantur."

64. Augustine, *Enarrationes in Psalmos*, 80.14 (p. 1129): "Colligauit [Samson noster], ut dicere coeperam, caudas uulpium, et ibi ignem alligauit; ignem ad incendendum, sed messes alienigenarum. Proinde tales consentientes in posterioribus, tamquam caudis colligati, trahunt ignem corrumpentem; sed non incendunt nostrorum segetes."

65. A. M. Dubarle, "Les renards de Samson," *Revue du Moyen Age latin* 7 (1951): 175–76. The bull is the famous *Vergentis in senium*, c. 10, X, 5, 7, ed. A. Friedberg, *Corpus juris canonici*, vol. 2 (Leipzig: Tauchnitz, 1881; repr., Union, NJ: Lawbook Exchange, 2000), 782.

66. I refer here to the traditional understanding of evil as a lack of good. For evil as a privation, or a form of nonbeing, see Gregory, *Moralia in Iob*, 14.18, ed. M. Adriaen, CCSL 143A (Turnhout: Brepols), 710–11; Isidore of Seville, *Sententiae*, 1.9, ed. P. Cazier, CCSL 111 (Turnhout: Brepols, 1998), 25–29; Jeffrey Burton Russell, *Lucifer: The Devil in the Middle Ages* (Ithaca, NY: Cornell University Press, 1984), 95–96.

67. John of Salisbury, *Policratici: Sive De nugis curialium et vestigiis philosophorum libri VIII*, 7.11, ed. C. C. I. Webb (Oxford: Clarendon Press, 1909; repr., New York: Arno Press, 1979), 661C: "Qui uero philosophando caritatem adquirit aut dilatat, suum philosophantis assecutus est finem. . . . Quicquid aliorsum uergit in artibus siue quibuscumque scripturis, non philosophiae dogmata sed inanes fabulae sunt et figmenta eorum super quorum impietatem ira Dei de celo reuelatur. Quicquid illi garriant, recte philosophanti ineptum uidetur insipidum et insulsum." Cary J. Nederman, trans.,

Policraticus: Of the Frivolities of Courtiers and the Footprints of Philosophers (Cambridge: Cambridge University Press, 1990), 161.

68. Stephen C. Ferruolo, *The Origins of the University: The Schools and Their Critics 1100–1215* (Stanford, CA: Stanford University Press, 1985), 137.

69. John Scotus Eriugena had used this same analogy to explain how the perfected human body after the resurrection would remain itself even though it appeared transformed into spirit. *Periphyseon*, 5, ed. E. A. Jeauneau, CCCM 165 (Turnhout: Brepols, 2003), 28.

70. Gerhoch of Reichersberg, *Commentarius aureus in Psalmos et cantica ferialia*, pt. 7, Ps. 72:19, 20, PL 194:349D–50A. Hereafter cited as "Gerhoch, *Commentarius aureus*."

71. Gerhoch, *Commentarius aureus*, pt. 7, Ps. 72:19, 20 (349D): "Qui cum sis ignis consumens rubiginem, consummans aurum . . ."

72. Gerhoch, *Commentarius aureus*, pt. 1, Ps. 6:1, PL 193:710A: "Quod ut perficiatur parum est corpus vitae, vitam sensui, sensum rationi adunari, nisi humana ratio angelorum sanctorum adjuvetur intellectu, ut sint sicut angeli Dei homines beati, nullumque sit ultra divortium inter angelicum et humanum de veritate intellectum."

73. 1 Cor. 13:3. Gerhoch, *Commentarius aureus*, pt. 1, Ps. 6:1 (710D).

74. Gerhoch, *Commentarius aureus*, pt. 1, Ps. 6:1 (711B–C): "Talis charitas est oleum illud evangelicum, per quod lampades ardent in praesenti vita, et multo magis in adventu sponsi, qui tum quinque virgines introducet in illud nuptial triclinium, ubi architriclinus est unus ac trinus Deus." Cassiodorus identified the wise virgins' oil as charity: *Expositio psalmorum*, Ps. 140.5, ed. M. Adriaen, CCSL 98 (Turnhout: Brepols, 1958), 1265.

75. Following this logic, Bernard called the Jews "living letters of the law" in "Letter 363," 8:311–17. See Jeremy Cohen, *Living Letters of the Law*, 234–36 (trans.), 221–45 (discussion in the context of Bernard's work and opinion of the Jews).

76. Gerhoch, *Commentarius aureus*, pt. 4, Ps. 40.14 (1486D): "Sunt enim Judaei capsarii nostril, qui nobis codices portant, quorum testimonio ipse et pagani et haeretici confutantur." I have translated rather loosely to convey the sense. A more literal rendering would be: "For the Jews are our *capsarii* (slaves who carry school boys' books), who carry our books . . ." For the original, see Augustine, *Enarrationes in Psalmos*, 40.14, ed. E. Dekkers and J. Fraipont, CCSL 38 (Turnhout: Brepols, 1956), 459. Gerhoch elaborated on the original in pointing out that these books convict the Jews, pagans, and heretics of error.

77. Jeremy Cohen, *Living Letters*, 233. "The Christian strives to unite, essentially, with Christ. The Jew, by contrast, is the letter of the law." As summarized by Nirenberg, the Jew becomes "the illiterate 'living letter' that exists only to be read by the Christian" (*Anti-Judaism*, 193).

78. Karl F. Morrison, *I Am You: The Hermeneutics of Empathy in Western Literature, Theology and Art* (Princeton, NJ: Princeton University Press, 1988), 198.

79. Augustine, *De magistro*, 10.31 and 10.33, ed. K. D. Daur CCSL 29 (Turnhout: Brepols, 1970), 189–90, 192. While this text would not have been available to many of the authors whose works are examined in this study, the recurrent "tautologies" and "hermeneutic circles" I find in their work illustrate that the essential dialectic of this Augustinian text is very much in play. Please see discussions in following chapters.

80. Louis Mackey, *Peregrinations of the Word: Essays in Medieval Philosophy* (Ann Arbor: University of Michigan Press, 1997), 65–66.

81. Michael D. Barbezat, "The Corporeal Orientation: A Medieval and Early Modern Framework for Understanding Deviance through the Object(s) of Love," in *The Routledge History Handbook to Emotions in Europe, 1100–1700* (New York: Routledge, forthcoming).

82. This formulation is very old, and often found in both orthodox and heterodox theologies. For example, Bernard McGinn argues that Hell for John Scotus Eriugena was really "the continuing existence in the minds of the wicked of the fantasies of the things that mislead them during their time on earth." *Periphyseon*, 5 [977AB], 689–90, in *The Growth of Mysticism* (New York: Crossroad, 1994), 112. While Eriugena's ultimate argument regarding the nature of the final Hell differs radically from the twelfth-century authors I discuss, he illustrates a theme in which they continued to participate.

83. Hugh, *De unione corporis et spiritus*, PL 177:288D. Aelred of Rievaulx, *Dialogus de anima*, 3.36, ed. C. H. Talbot, CCCM 1 (Turnhout: Brepols, 1971), 746.

84. As the late thirteenth-century supplement to the *Summa Theologica* summarizes: "In sinning the soul subjected itself to the body by sinful concupiscence. Therefore it is just that it should be punished by being made subject to a bodily thing by suffering therefrom" (Suppl. 70.3, s. c.).

85. Eudes of Châteauroux, "Sermon 1, 11," in *Crusade Propaganda and Ideology: Model Sermons for the Preaching of the Cross*, ed. Christoph T. Maier (Cambridge: Cambridge University Press, 2000), 133: "Qui noluerint ardere hoc igne in futuro ardeant igne gehenne."

86. Michael D. Barbezat, "In a Corporeal Flame: The Materiality of Hellfire before the Resurrection in Six Latin Authors," *Viator* 44 (2013): 1–20.

87. For example, the Parisian condemnations of 1270 and 1277 both included propositions which argued that a soul separated from its body could not suffer from a corporeal flame. See François-Xavier Putallaz, "L'âme et le feu: Notes franciscaines sur le feu de l'enfer après 1277," in *After the Condemnation of 1277. Philosophy and Theology at the University of Paris in the Last Quarter of the Thirteenth Century. Studies and Texts* (Berlin: De Gruyter, 2001), 889–901. For debates on how a soul can suffer in a material flame, see Donald Mowbray, *Pain and Suffering in Medieval Theology: Academic Debates at the University of Paris in the Thirteenth Century* (Woodbridge, UK: Boydell Press, 2009), esp. chap. 5, "*Anima Seperata*: Masters of Theology and the Controversy Surrounding the Suffering of the Separated Soul," and chap. 6, "Defining the Corporeal: Suffering in Hell according to the Masters of Theology at Paris, c.1230–c.1280." A small selection of the opinions of these authors on this subject can be found in Ioannis Pecham, "Quodlibet III," *Quodlibeta Quatuor*, q. 8, ed. Girard J. Etzkorn (Grottaferrata: Editiones Collegi S. Bonaventurae ad Claras Aquas, 1989), 148–151; Siger of Brabant, *Quaestiones in tertium de anima. De anima intellective. De aeternitate mundi*, q. 11, ed. Bernardo C. Bazàn (Leuven: Publications Universitaires, 1972), 31–32; Thomas Aquinas, *Quaestiones de anima: A Newly Established Edition of the Latin Text with an Introduction and Notes*, q. 21, ed. James H. Robb (Toronto: Pontifical Institute of Medieval Studies, 1968), 264–273; Matthew of Aquasparta, "Questiones de anima separata," *Questiones disputatae de anima seperata, de anima beata, de ieiunio, et de legibus*,

q. 6, ed. G. Gal, A. Emmen, I. Brady, and C. Piana (Florence: Collegii S. Bonaventurae, 1959), 93–119.

88. For example, early doctrinal conclusions regarding a purifying flame in the afterlife are clearly summarized in Julian of Toledo's seventh-century *Prognosticum futuri saeculi libri tres*, 2.19–20, ed. J. N. Hilgarth, CCSL 115 (Turnhout: Brepols, 1976), 55–56.

89. Le Goff, *Birth of Purgatory*, 3.

90. Le Goff placed the first use of the noun in the work of Peter Comestor in his *Birth of Purgatory*, 157. This identification is not accurate. See discussion below.

91. Graham Robert Edwards, "Purgatory: 'Birth' or Evolution?" *Journal of Ecclesiastical History* 36 (1985): 642.

92. Robert Easting, "Dialogue between a Clerk and the Spirit of a Girl *de purgatorio* (1153): A Medieval Ghost Story," *Mediaevistik* 20 (2007): 163–83.

93. R. W. Southern, *Scholastic Humanism and the Unification of Europe* (Oxford: Blackwell, 1997), 1:152–58.

94. For example, ghost stories proliferated in the twelfth century in what seemed almost an "invasion of ghosts." Most of these appeared in order to demand suffrages from the living. Jean-Claude Schmitt, *Ghosts in the Middle Ages*, trans. Teresa Lavender Fagan (Chicago: University of Chicago Press, 1998), 69.

95. Le Goff, *Birth of Purgatory*, 204–5.

96. Peter of Cornwall, *Liber revelationum*, 1.206, ed. and trans., Robert Easting and Richard Sharpe, *Peter of Cornwall's Book of Revelations* (Toronto: Pontifical Institute of Medieval Studies, 2013,), 264: "Querenti iterum ab eo ubi esset, respondit, 'Ego sum in inferno.'" A little later: "Tandem sacerdos resumpta audatia quesiuit iterum atque iterum si in ipso inferno esset sine spe saluationis. Cui respondit, se illic esse sine spe aliqua euasionis."

97. *Tractatus de Purgatorio sancti Patricii*, in *St. Patrick's Purgatory: Two Versions of Owayne Miles and the Vision of William of Stranton Together with the Long Text of the Tractatus de Purgatorio sancti Patricii*, ed. Robert Easting (Oxford: Oxford University Press, 1991), 122.

98. Aelred, *Dialogus de anima*, 3.36 (p. 746).

99. Augustine, *De civitate Dei*, 21.26 (pp. 796–99); R. W. Dyson, trans., *The City of God against the Pagans* (Cambridge: Cambridge University Press, 1998), 1094–98. The following translations are Dyson's unless otherwise noted.

100. For a very similar exegesis of this passage, see Augustine, *Enchiridion*, 68, ed. M. P. J. Van den Hout, CCSL 46 (Turnhout: Brepols, 1969), 86–87. For an overview of Augustine's ideas of postmortem purgation, see Le Goff, *Birth of Purgatory*, 61–85. For the foundation in love, see Augustine, *De civitate Dei*, 21.26 (p. 796): "Quisquis itaque sic habet in corde Christum, ut ei terrena et temporaria nec ea quae licita sunt atque concessa praeponat, fundamentum habet Christum."

101. Augustine, *De civitate Dei*, 21.26 (p. 797): "Delicias quippe huius modi amoresque terrenos, propter coniugalem quidem copulam non damnabiles, tribulationis ignis exuret."

102. Augustine, *De civitate Dei*, 21.26 (p. 797): "Et eorum amissione cruciabitur, quibus fruendo utique laetabatur."

103. For the categories, see Augustine, *Enchiridion*, 110, 108–9.

104. Augustine, *De civitate Dei*, 21.26 (p. 798): "Alios autem aliter, id est, ut quod superaedificauerunt ardeat damnumque inde patiantur, salui fiant autem, quoniam Christum in fundamento stabiliter positum praecellenti caritate tenuerunt." I have altered Dyson's translation of "with a surpassing love" to "with surpassing charity."

105. Augustine, *De civitate Dei* (p. 797): "Eandem tribulationem ignem uocat, sicut alibi legitur."

106. Augustine, *Enchiridion*, 68, 86–87: "Est quidam ignis temptation tribulationis . . . iste ignis in hac interim uita facit . . . quia urit eum dolor rerum quas dilexerat amissarum."

107. Le Goff, *Birth of Purgatory*, 70.

108. Augustine, *De civitate Dei*, 21.26 (p. 798): "Si hoc temporis interuallo spiritus defunctorum eius modi ignem dicuntur perpeti."

109. Augustine, *De civitate Dei*, 21.26 (p. 799): "Secundum cuiusque aedificium tempus quod eam sequitur ab unoquoque sentiatur."

110. Augustine, *De civitate Dei*, 20.16 (pp. 726–27).

111. Caroline Walker Bynum, *The Resurrection of the Body in Western Christianity, 200–1336* (New York: Columbia University Press, 1995), 101.

112. Dan. 3:19–29.

113. Augustine, *De civitate Dei*, 20.18 (p. 730).

114. On Julian's influence and the impact of the *Prognosticum futuri saeculi*, see J. N. Hillgarth, "St. Julian of Toledo in the Middle Ages," *Journal of the Warburg and Courtauld Institutes* 21 (1958): 14–15.

115. Julian, *Foreknowledge of the World to Come*, trans. Tommaso Stancati (New York: Newman Press, 2010), 256–57.

116. Julian, *Prognosticum futuri saeculi*, 2.20 (p. 56).

117. Barbezat, "In a Corporeal Flame," 10–11.

118. Whether Peter Lombard studied with Hugh has been the topic of some debate. It is certain that Bernard recommended him to Prior Gilduin of St. Victor as a promising student of theology worthy of support between 1134 and 1136. What actions followed this recommendation are uncertain. Marcia Colish regards Hugh's possible instruction of Peter "a lively possibility." For an overview of the arguments, see her *Peter Lombard* (New York: E. J. Brill, 1994), 1:17–20. For Bernard's recommendation, see "Letter 410," 8:391.

119. Southern, *Scholastic Humanism*, 2:143.

120. Peter Lombard, *Sententiae in IV libris distinctae*, 4.21.2 (Grottaferrata, Rome: Editiones Collegi S. Bonaventurae ad Claras Aquas, 1981), 2:380; Giulio Silano, trans., *The Sentences* (Toronto: Pontifical Institute of Medieval Studies, 2010), 4:127. Augustine, *De civitate Dei*, 21.26 (p. 799).

121. Peter Lombard, *Sententiae*, 4.21.5 (2:382–83; trans. 4:128); quoted in Augustine, *Enchiridion*, 68.

122. Peter Lombard, *Sententiae*, 4.21.3 (2:380); quoted in Augustine, *Enchiridion*, 69.

123. Peter Lombard, *Sententiae*, 4.21.4 (2:381; trans. 4:128); quoted in Augustine, *Enarrationes in Psalmos*, 37.2 (p. 383).

124. Peter Lombard, *Sententiae*, 4.21.5 (2:382; trans. 4:129): "Illa enim aedificatio perfectorum tantum est, qui non cogitant placer mundo, sed tantum Deo; qui etsi uenialiter aliquando peccant, feruore caritatis ita absumitur in eis peccatum, sicut

gutta aquae in camino ignis; et ideo nunquam secum portant cremabilia." In the period after the *Sententiae*, this image is widely found both in commentaries on the *Sententiae* and elsewhere. Many commentators, however, identified its origin with the Fathers rather than Peter Lombard. These identifications, at least as far I have been able to ascertain, are consistently erroneous; see discussion below. Hildegard does use a similar image in the *Scivias*, but I believe that its meaning is in fact quite different, if not oppositional. Hildegard, *Scivias*, 3. visio10.5, ed. A. Führkötter, CCCM 43A (Turnhout: Brepols, 1978), 550.

125. Peter Lombard, *Sententiae*, 4.21.6 (2:383; trans. 4:130): "Est enim aliquis bonus caritatem habens, sed adhuc quodam cupiditatis affectu amans haec secularia; talis existens subita morte opprimitur. In illo terreno affectu mortuus est, et tamen salvabitur, a quo non se hic absoluit; ergo post hanc uitam ab illo purgabitur."

126. Peter Lombard, *Sententiae*, 4.45.2 (2:524; trans. 4:245–46). Drawn from Augustine, "Sermon 172," *Sermones de scripturis*, PL 38:937: "Nam qui sine fide operante per dilectionem eius que sacramentis de corpore exierunt, frustra illis a suis huiusmodi pietatis officia impenduntur." The current Vulgate reads for this verse: "Nam in Christo Iesu neque circumcisio aliquid valet neque praeputium sed fides quae per caritatem operatur." All subsequent Augustine sermons cited are from this edition unless otherwise noted.

For Augustine's assertion that this *dilectio* is caritas, see "Letter 189," 2, *Epistulae*, ed. A. Goldbacher, CSEL 57 (Brepols: Turnhout, 1898), 132: "Ipsa est enim caritas, quae, sicut dicit apostolus, diffusa est in cordibus nostris per spiritum sanctum, qui datus est nobis; ipsa est, de qua item dicit: plenitudo legis caritas; ipsa est, per quam fides operatur, unde iterum dicit: neque circumcisio quicquam ualet neque praeputium sed fides, quae per dilectionem operatur."

127. Peter of Poitiers, *Sententiarum libri quinque*, 5.20, PL 211:1268A–B. My thanks to Alan Bernstein for drawing my attention to this reference. For Peter's career and the dating of his work, see Ferruolo, *Origins of the University*, 190–91.

128. Peter of Poitiers, *Sententiarum*, 5.20, 1269A.

129. Peter of Poitiers, *Sententiarum*, 3.5, 1054D.

130. Peter of Poitiers, *Sententiarum*, 3.5, 1055A: "Tantum enim habent fervorem charitatis, quod statim exstinguitur in eis veniale peccatum, sicut gutta aquae in camino."

131. Peter of Poitiers, *Sententiarum*, 3.25, 1119B–C.

132. William of Auxerre, *Summa Aurea*, 4.18.4.1.1, ed. J. Ribaillier (Rome: Editiones Collegii S. Bonaventurae ad Claras Aquas, 1985), 538: "Suffragia ecclesie naturaliter sunt satisfactoria et pene resolutoria, sed non in quocumque subiecto, sed solum in quo inveniunt fundamentum meriti et radicem, scilicet caritatem. Unde solum illis qui sunt in purgatorio prosunt suffragia, quia in illis inveniunt caritatem, et non in reprobis qui sunt in inferno." My thanks to Alan Bernstein for drawing my attention to this reference.

133. William of Auxerre, *Summa Aurea*, 4.18.4.1.4 (p. 548): "Illos enim in quibus invenit dyabolus expressam suam similitudinem, precipitat in infernum."

134. William of Auxerre, *Summa Aurea*, 4.18.4.1.2 (p. 541): "Ad secundo obiectum dicimus quod, antequam evolet ille qui est in purgatorio, oportet cremari omnia cremabilia sua; sed cum fiunt suffragia ecclesie pro eo, non cremantur igne purga-

torii, sed igne qui Deus est, quia, sicut dicitur in Deuteronomio, IIII: *Deus noster ignia consumens est.*"

135. Alan of Lille, *Theologiae regulae*, PL 210:665B; Garnerius Lingonensis, *Sermones*, 12, PL 205:650; Radulfus Ardens, *Homilia*, 30, PL 155:1772C; Innocent III (Incertus), PL 217:1008A; Jacobus de Voragine, *Legenda Aurea*, 159, ed. Giovanni Paolo Maggioni (Tavarnuzze: Sismel edizioni del Galluzzo, 1998), 2:1125; Thomas Aquinas, *In IV Sententiarum*, distinction 16, q. 2, art. 2.2.1, in *Opera Omnia* (Parma, 1858), vol. 7, 757; Chaucer, *Parson's Tale*, ll. 382–83, in *The Riverside Chaucer*, ed. Larry Dean Benson, 3rd ed. (Oxford: Oxford University Press, 2008). In all of these instances, so far as I am aware, the phrase and its sourcing is not remarked on by editors except to offer possible implicit origins in the cited sources, or remark on the erroneous derivation offered by the authors.

136. Aquinas, *In IV Sententiarum*, dist. 21, q. 1, art. 1, s. c. (7:850). See also *Summa Theologica*, Suppl., "Articuli duo de Purgatorio," art. 1. s. c., ed. De Rubeis and Billuart (Turin: Marietti, 1938), 5:807. The quotation is from Prov. 10:12: "Ergo post hanc vitam sunt aliqui a peccatis nondum absoluti, qui solvi possunt; et tales caritatem habent, sine qua non fit peccatorum remissio; quia 'universa delicta operit caritas.'"

137. Augustine, *Confessionum Libri XIII*, 7.10, ed. L. Verheijen, CCSL 27 (Turnhout: Brepols, 1981), 103–4: "Et inveni longe me esse a te in regione dissimilitudinis, tamquam audirem vocem tuam de excelso: 'cibus sum grandium: cresce et manducabis me. nec tu me in te mutabis sicut cibum carnis tuae, sed tu mutaberis in me.'" Discussed in the context of medieval specular imagery by Edward Peter Nolan, *Now through a Glass Darkly: Specular Images of Being and Knowing from Virgil to Chaucer* (Ann Arbor: University of Michigan Press, 1990), 57.

138. Bernard, "Sententia 91," 6:139: "Regio dissimilitudinis est praesens uita, quam quidam nimium amantes, long dissimiles Deo facti sunt et, iumentis comparati, descenderunt usque ad locum mortis."

2. Fields and Bodies

1. I have substituted "weeds" for the Douay-Rheims 1899 American Edition's "cockles."

2. See Alan Bernstein's argument that hell-belief provides premises that can be applied in secular contexts, "catalyz[ing] an interlocking sequence of stigmatization-persecution-eradication," in his "Named Others and Named Places: Stigmatization in the Early Medieval Afterlife," in *Hell and Its Afterlife: Historical and Contemporary Perspectives*, ed. Isabel Moreira and Margaret Merrill (Farnham, UK: Ashgate, 2010), 70–71.

3. In my discussion, rather than the more commonly found title "The Parable of the Wheat and the Tares," I refer to the parable through the clearer and more colloquial title "The Wheat and the Weeds."

4. Matt. 13: 27–30.

5. Matt. 13:37–42.

6. Roland H. Bainton, "The Parable of the Tares as the Proof Text for Religious Liberty to the End of the Sixteenth Century," *Church History* 1 (1932): 67–89.

7. On this influence, see Stephen L. Wailes, *Medieval Allegories of Jesus' Parables* (Berkeley: University of California Press, 1987), 103–8.

8. Jerome, *Commentariorum in Matheum libri IV* (*Commentaire sur S. Matthieu*), ed. Émile Bonnard (Paris: Les Éditions du Cerf, 1977), 1:286: "Homines qui dormiunt magistros ecclesiarum intellege . . . . Quamobrem non dormiat qui ecclesiae praeposis est, ne per illius neglentiam inimicus homo superseminet zizania, hoc est hereticorum dogmata." Hereafter cited as "Jerome, *Commentariorum.*"

9. Jerome, *Commentariorum*, 1:286: "Datur locus paenitentiae, et monemur ne cito amputemus fratrem."

10. Jerome, *Commentariorum*, 1:288: "Manifestum est hereticos quosque et hypocritas fidei gehennae ignibus concremandos."

11. Jerome, *Dialogus adversus Luciferianos*, 22, PL 23:186. W. H. Fremantle, trans., *Nicene and Post-Nicene Fathers*, 2nd ser., vol. 6 (Buffalo, NY: Christian Literature Publishing, 1890), 332. "Nemo potest Christi palmam sibi assumere, nemo ante diem judicii de hominibus judicare."

12. Chrysostom, *Commentarius in S. Matthaeum Evangelistam*, "Homilia 46," PG 58:477–78. Bainton, "Parable of the Tares," 72.

13. Augustine, *Quaestiones XVI in Matthaeum*, 11.1, ed. Almut Mutzenbecher, CCSL 44B (Turnhout: Brepols, 1980), 125. Hereafter cited as "Augustine, *Quaestiones.*"

14. Augustine, *Quaestiones*, 11.7 (p. 131).

15. Augustine, *Quaestiones*, 11.9 (p. 132): "Vtrum quia etiam boni, cum adhuc infirmi sunt, opus habent in quibusdam malorum permixtione, siue ut per eos exerceantur, siue ut eorum comparatione magna illis exhortation fiat ut nitantur ad melius, quibus sublatis altitudo caritatis quasi euulsa marcescat, quod est eradicari."

16. Augustine, "Sermon 73.1," 470: "Eradicare vultis malos: quiescite, non est tempus messis . . . Quid stomachamini? Quid aegere toleratis malos permixtos bonis? In agro vobiscum esse possunt, in horreo non erunt."

17. Augustine, "Sermon 73.4," 471–72.

18. Augustine, "Sermon 73.4," 472: "Boni tolerent malos."

19. Augustine, "Sermon 73.3," 471: "Hoc dico malis, et tamen christianis; hoc dico zizaniis. In agro enim sunt: et fieri potest ut qui hodie sunt zizania, cras sint frumentum. Ideo et triticum alloquor." Augustine, "Sermon 23 on the New Testament," trans. H Browne, *Nicene and Post-Nicene Fathers*, 1st ser. vol. 6 (Buffalo, NY: Christian Literature Publishing, 1888), 334.

20. For example, see Augustine, "Letter 153," *Epistulae*, ed. A. Goldbacher, CSEL 44 (Vienna: F. Tempsky, 1903), 250–62.

21. Augustine, *Contra epistolam Parmeniani*, 3.13, PL 43:92: "Quod si se non agnoverit, neque poenitendo correxit, ipse foras exiet, et per propriam voluntatem ab Ecclesiae communione dirimetur."

22. Augustine, *Contra epistolam Parmeniani*, 3.13, 92: "Ubi stais ostendit, cum metus iste non subest, sed omnino de frumentorum certa stabilitate certa securitas manet, id est, quando ita cujusque crimen notum est, et omnibus exsecrabile apparet, ut vel nullos prorsus vel non tales habeat defensores, per quos possit schisma contingere; non dormiat severitas disciplinae, in qua tanto est efficacior emendatio pravitatis, quanto diligentior consevatio charitatis."

23. "But now I have written to you, not to keep company, if any man that is named a brother, be a fornicator, or covetous, or a server of idols, or a railer, or a drunkard, or an extortioner: with such a one, not so much as to eat."

24. Augustine, *Contra epistolam Parmeniani*, 3.13, 92: "Tunc autem hoc sine labe pacis et unitatis, et sine laesione frumentorum fieri potest, cum congregationis Ecclesiae multitudo ab eo crimine quod anathematur, aliena est." For fraternal coercion: "ut nec cibum quisquam cum eo sumat, non rabie inimica, sed coercitione fraterna."

25. On his evolving ideas regarding religious coercion, see Peter Brown, "St. Augustine's Attitude to Religious Coercion," *Journal of Roman Studies* 54 (1964): 107–16.

26. Augustine, *Confessionum Libri XIII*, 3.11.19, 37–38.

27. Peter Brown, *Augustine of Hippo: A Biography*, rev. ed. (Berkeley: University of California Press, 2000), 237–38.

28. Peter Brown, *Augustine of Hippo*, 335.

29. Talal Asad, *Genealogies of Religion: Discipline and Reasons of Power in Christianity and Islam* (Baltimore: Johns Hopkins University Press, 1993), 34.

30. Augustine described preaching against heretics and schismatics as a spiritual war, waged in the image of the struggle of the spirit against the flesh that the faithful waged within themselves, "not in hatred but in love," because "the war of spiritual men is a rebuke in charity." *Contra litteras Petiliani*, 2.68.154, ed. M. Petschenig, CSEL 52 (Vienna: F. Tempsky, 1909), 100: "Quod autem spiritus facit aduersus carnem non odio, sed dilectione belligerans, hoc spiritales faciunt aduersus carnales, ut, quod agunt erga se, agant et erga illos, quia diligunt proximos tamquam se ipsos. Sed bellum spiritalium est illa in caritate correptio."

31. For the suicidal threat of immolating a basilica with its congregation inside, see W. H. C. Frend, *The Donatist Church: A Movement of Protest in Roman North Africa* (Oxford: Oxford University Press, 1985), 296. It appears the threat was never carried out.

32. Augustine, "Letter 204," 2, *Epistulae*, ed. A. Goldbacher, CSEL 57 (Vienna: F. Tempsky, 1911), 318: "Sed quoniam deus occulta satis dispositione sed tamen iusta nonnullos eorum poenis praedestinauit extremis, procul dubio melius incomparabili numerositate plurimis ab illa pestifera diuisione et dispersione redintegratis atque collectis quidam suis ignibus pereunt, quam pariter uniuersi sempiternis ignibus gehennarum merito sacrilegae dissensionis ardebunt." Augustine recognizes that this extreme reaction could have been influenced by the false belief that approaching imperial officials were going to execute them.

33. On the "common attitudes" between Augustine's doctrine of religious persecution and the just war, see Frederick H. Russell, *The Just War in the Middle Ages* (Cambridge: Cambridge University Press, 1975), 23.

34. Alexandra Walsham, *Charitable Hatred: Tolerance and Intolerance in England, 1500–1700* (Manchester: Manchester University Press, 2006), 2.

35. As emphasized and explored by Robert L. Holmes, "St. Augustine and the Just War Theory," in *The Augustinian Tradition*, ed. Gareth B. Matthews (Berkeley: University of California Press, 1999), 325.

36. Augustine, "Letter 93," 2.6, ed. Goldbacher, CSEL 34 (Vienna: F. Tempsky, 1895), 450. "Cum boni et mali eadem faciunt eadem patiuntur, non factis et poenis sed causis utique discernendi sunt."

37. Augustine, *In Iohannis epistulam ad Parthos tractatus*, 7.7, PL 35:2033; H. Browne, trans., *Nicene and Post-Nicene Fathers, First Series* (Buffalo, NY: Christian Literature Publishing, 1888), 7:866: "Diversa ergo intentio diversa facta fecit . . . Tantum valet charitas. Videte quia sola discernit, videte quia facta hominum sola distinguit."

38. For the Church as the victim of persecution by heresy, see "Letter 93," 2.6, 450: "Qui possunt, intellegant magis ecclesiam catholicam persecutionem pati superbia et impietate carnalium, quos temporalibus molestiis atque terroribus emendare conatur." For Augustine's exegesis of Luke 14:23 ("Whomsoever you shall find, compel them to come in") as referring to heretics, see "Letter 93," 2.5, 449; "Letter 173,"10, ed. A. Goldbacher, CSEL 44 (Vienna: F. Tempsky, 1904), 647.

39. Augustine, *Contra litteras Petiliani*, 2.82.182, ed. M. Petschenig, CSEL 52 (Vienna: F. Tempsky, 1909), 112: "Nec persequimur uos, nisi quemadmodum persequitur ueritas falsitatem."

40. Frederick H. Russell, *Just War*, 17.

41. Frederick H. Russell, *Just War*, 19.

42. Augustine, "Letter 93," 9.33–34 (pp. 478–80); 10.36 (p. 481).

43. Augustine, *Quaestionum in Heptateuchum libri VII*, 6.10, ed. J. Fraipont, CCSL 33 (Turnhout: Brepols, 1958), 319: "Iusta autem bella ea definirir solent quae ulciscuntur iniurias, si qua gens uel ciuitas, quae bello petenda est, uel uindicare neglecerit quod a suis inprobe factum est uel reddere quod per iniurias ablatum est."

44. Bede the Venerable, "In Matthaei Evangelium expositio," 2.13, PL 92:69A: "Sed inter triticum et zizaniam, quandiu herba est, aut nulla aut difficilis est distantia: et hic monemur a Domino, ne ubi quid ambiguum est, cito sententiam proferamus, sed Deo judici terminum reservemus." The influence of Jerome's *Commentariorum* is particularly apparent.

45. 1 Cor. 12:12.

46. 1 Cor. 6:15–16. "Know you not that your bodies are members of Christ? Shall I then take the members of Christ, and make them the members of a harlot? God forbid. Or know you not, that he who is joined to a harlot, is made one body?"

47. 1 Cor. 5: 6, Gal. 5:9.

48. R. I. Moore, "Heresy as a Disease," in *The Concept of Heresy in the Middle Ages (11th–13th Centuries)*, ed. W. Lourdaux and D. Verhelst (Leuven: Leuven University Press, 1976), 9.

49. Jerome, *Commentarius in epistolam ad Galatas*, 3.5, PL 26:430. Hereafter cited as "Jerome, *Commentarius*."

50. Matt. 16:6; 1 Cor. 5:7–5.

51. Jerome, *Commentarius*, 3.5, 430B: "Porro quae est ista alia doctria Pharisaeorum, nisi legis secundum carnem observatio?"

52. On Jerome's ideas of carnal reading under the umbrella of Judaism, as well as Judaism as a way to characterize "Christians whose sense of the balance between flesh and spirit, letter and figure, man and God was different from his own," see Nirenberg, *Anti-Judaism*, 121–23.

53. Jerome, *Commentarius*, 3.5, 430B–C: "Ita et doctrina perversa ab uno incipiens vix duos aut tres primum in exordio reperit auditores; sed paulatim ut cancer serpit in corpore et iuxta uulgare prouerbium, unius pecudis scabies, totum commaculat gregem." The reference to the scabrous animal is from Juvenal, *Satire II*.

54. Jerome, *Commentarius*, 3.5, 430B: "Scintilla res parva est . . . sed si fomitem comprehenderit, et nutrimenta sui quamvis parvus ignis invenerit, moenia, urbes, latissimos saltus, regionesque consumit."

55. Jerome, *Commentarius*, 3.5, 430C: "Igitur et scintilla statim ut apparuerit, extinguenda est, et fermentum a massae vicinia semovendum, secandae putridae carnes, et scabiosum animal a caulis ovium repellendum, ne tota domus, massa, corpus et pecora, ardeat, corrumpatur, putrescat, intereat."

56. Jerome, *Commentarius*, 3.5, 430C: "Arius in Alexandriae una scintilla fuit; sed quia non statim oppressa est, totum orbem ejus flamma populata est."

57. Gratian, *Decretum*, II, c. 24, q. 3, c. 16, in *Corpus iuris canonici*, ed. Friedberg (Leipzig: Tauchnitz, 1879–81. Reprint, Union, NJ: Lawbook Exchange, 2000), 1:995.

58. Peter Lombard, *Collectanea in omes Pauli apostolicas Epistulas*, PL 192:155.

59. Thomas Aquinas, *Summa Theologica*, 2–2.11.3, co., ed. Rubeis and Billuart, 3:74. The scriptural reference is to Tit. 3:10.

60. Iogna-Prat, *Order and Exclusion*, 360–62.

61. On the origin of this movement in the pontificate of Leo IX, see R. W. Southern, *Western Society and the Church in the Middle Ages* (London: Penguin, 1990), 100–101.

62. Moore, *Formation of a Persecuting Society*.

63. This argument arises from Glenn W. Olsen's reading of David Nirenberg, *Communities of Violence: Persecution of Minorities in the Middle Ages* (Princeton, NJ: Princeton University Press, 1996) in *Of Sodomites, Effeminates, Hermaphrodites, and Androgynes: Sodomy in the Age of Peter Damian* (Toronto: Pontifical Institute of Medieval Studies, 2011), 260.

64. Among the more famous manifestations of this impulse was the development of the Peace Movement in the late tenth and eleventh centuries, which led to the so-called Peace of God and the Truce of God; see Thomas Head, "The Development of the Peace of God in Aquitaine (970–1005)," *Speculum* 74, no. 3 (1999): 656–86. On the peace councils and the need to reform society, especially the use of violence, see Warren C. Brown, *Violence in Medieval Europe* (London: Longman, 2011), 116–28.

65. On the complex interactions between the Peace Movement, papal policies, and the crusades, in which "Western Christendom constituted itself as such by going jointly to war," see Ernst-Dieter Hehl, "War, Peace, and the Christian Order," in *The New Cambridge Medieval History*, vol. 4: *c. 1024–c. 1198, Part 1*, ed. David Luscombe and Jonathan Riley-Smith (Cambridge: Cambridge University Press, 2004), 185–228, quote at 185.

66. A dynamic first outlined by Herbert Grundmann, *Religious Movements in the Middle Ages: The Historical Links between Heresy, the Mendicant Orders, and the Women's Religious Movement in the Twelfth and Thirteen Century, with the Historical Foundations of German Mysticism*, trans. Steven Rowan (Notre Dame, IN: University of Notre Dame Press, 1995).

67. On simony as a heresy and its place in a context of more frequent accusations and counteraccusations of heresy, see Heinrich Fichtenau, *Heretics and Scholars in the Middle Ages: 1000–1200*, trans. Denise A. Kaiser (University Park: Pennsylvania State University Press, 1998), 48–49.

68. Moore, *War on Heresy*, 88.

69. For an account of the Patarene movement and its sources, see Stock, *The Implications of Literacy: Written Language and Models of Interpretation in the Eleventh and Twelfth Centuries* (Princeton: Princeton University Press, 1983), 151–240.

70. Malcolm Lambert, *Medieval Heresy: Popular Movements from the Gregorian Reform to the Reformation*, 3rd ed. (Oxford: Blackwell, 2002), 44–45 and 89. For the practical similarity between Publican, Paterene, and Cathar, see Moore, *War on Heresy*, 207.

71. Steven F. Kruger, *The Spectral Jew: Conversion and Embodiment in Medieval Europe* (Minneapolis: University of Minnesota Press, 2006), 25.

72. A discussion of these episodes, along with English translations of some of the source material, can be found in Moore, *Birth of Popular Heresy*, 8–21.

73. There are a number of sources for this event. See the discussion in chapter 3.

74. *Acta synodi Atrebatensis*, PL 142:1271–312. Steven Vanderputten and Diane J. Reilly, "Reconciliation and Record Keeping: Heresy, Secular Dissent and the Exercise of Episcopal Authority in Eleventh-Century Cambrai," *Journal of Medieval History* 37 (2011): 343–57.

75. Landulf Senior, *Historia Mediolanensis*, ed. L. C. Bethmann and W. Wattenbach, 2.27, MGH: SS 8:65–66. Hereafter cited as "Landulf, *Historia.*"

76. Vanderputten and Reilly, "Reconciliation and Record Keeping," 349.

77. Landulf, *Historia*, 2.27 (pp. 65–66): "Quos cum Mediolanum duxisset, et per multos dies et per suos sacerdotes in fide catholica eos reintregrari desiderans laborasset, timens, ne genus Italiae huius haeresi contaminaretur, perplurimum dolebat."

78. Landulf, *Historia*, 2.27 (p. 66): "Et factum est, ut aliqui ad crucem Domini venientes et ipsam confitentes fidem catholicam, salvi facti sunt; et multi manibus ante vultus missis inter flammas exilierunt, et misère morientes in miseros cineres redacti sunt."

79. Landulf, *Historia*, 3.19 (p. 87).

80. Landulf, *Historia*, 3.26 (p. 93). This last connection comes from Landulf's presentation of the priest Andrew's attempted refutation of the Patarene argument.

81. On the differences between the two accounts, see Stock, *Implications of Literacy*, 139–45. Landulf's version is the one usually detailed in source collections regarding medieval heresy; see Moore, *Birth of Popular Heresy*, 19–21.

82. Ralph Glaber, *Historiarum libri quinque*, 4.2.5, ed. and trans. John France (Oxford: Clarendon Press, 1989), 176–77. Hereafter cited as "Glaber, *Histories.*"

83. Glaber, *Histories*, 4.2.5 (p. 178): "Capientes ex eis nonnullos, quos, dum non quiuissent reuocare ab insania, igne cremauere."

84. Glaber, *Histories*, 4.2.5 (pp. 180–81): "Nulli denique dubium quoniam ista et sibi et nobis uidit."

85. Anselm of Liège, *Gesta episcoporum Leodiensis*, MGH SS 7:226–28. Hereafter cited as "Anselm, *Gesta.*"

86. Anselm, *Gesta*, 226: "Falsissime docmatizarent, incidentes in illam blasphemiam, quam iuxta Veritatis vocem et hic and in futuro impossibile est remitti." Compare to Matt. 12:31: "Ideo dico vobis omne peccatum et blasphemia remittitur hominibus Spiritus autem blasphemia non remittetur."

87. Anselm, *Gesta*, 226–27: "Quid de talibus praestet agendum, anxius praesul certum spaientiae consuluit secretarium, an terrenae potestatis gladio in eos sit animadvertendum, nec ne, modico fermento nisi exterminentur totam massam posse corrumpi."

88. Anselm, *Gesta*, 227: "Ut autem in promtu sit, quid de talibus velit fieri misericors et miserator Dominus, qui peccantes non statim iudicat, sed ad poenitentiam equanimiter expectat." Inspiration is likely Ezek. 33:11 and 1 Tim. 2:4.

89. Anselm, *Gesta*, 227: "Quid his verbis nisi pacientiam suam Dominus ostendit, quam praedicatores suos erga errantes proximos exibere desiderat, maxime cum hi qui hodie zizania sunt possibile sit cras converti et esse triticum?"

90. Acts 7:58–8:3.

91. Anselm, *Gesta*, 228: "Est tamen aliud quod sollicite communicantes catholica communione priventur, caeterisque omnibus publice denuntietur, ut secundum propheticam ammonitionem exeant de medio eorum et inmundissimam eorum sectam ne tetigerint, quoniam qui tetigerit picem, inquinabitur ab ea." Reference is to Isa. 52:11 and Sir. 13:1.

92. The source for this example is Sulpicius Severus, *Gallus (Dialogus tertius)*, 11–13, ed. Carolus Halm, CSEL 1 (Vienna, 1866), 208–11; F. R. Hoare, trans., *The Western Fathers* (New York: Sheed and Ward, 1954), 133–37. See also Sulpicius Severus, *Chronicles*, 2.46–51, ed. Halm, 99–105. Of interest is the lasting stain of guilt felt by Martin for even briefly entering into communion with the bishops set on the execution of Priscillian and his suspected followers. The saint felt he suffered "a diminution of his spiritual powers" for his implicit involvement: *Gallus*, 13 (p. 211).

93. Anselm, *Gesta*, 228: "Sicque per errorem simulque furorem eorum plerosque vere catholicorum fuisse aliquando interemptos."

94. Heriman of Reichinau, *Chronicon*, Ann. 1052, MGH SS 5:130: "Consensu cunctorum, ne heretica scabies latius serpens plures inficeret, in patibulo suspendi issit." The one specific detail offered for the heretics' Manichaeism is their refusal to eat the meat of animals.

95. Anselm, *Gesta*, 228: "Vere fatebor enim nec silebo, Wazonem nostrum, si heac tempora contigisset, huic sententiae assensum nequaquam praebiturum." My translation is loose.

96. *Chronicon S. Andreae*, 3.3. MGH SS 7:540. Moore, *Birth of Popular Heresy*, 24–25.

97. Gregory VII, *Register of Gregory VII*, MGH Epist. 2, 1, 328–29.

98. Gregory VII, *Register of Gregory VII*, 331–34.

99. This edition represents a later period of the development of the *Glossa* than the twelfth century, but it is the only edition widely available at present. The PL misattributes it to Walafrid Strabo. *Glossa ordinaria—Evangelium secundum Matthaeum*, PL 114:132A: "Et docet hic bonam voluntatem, et cautelam, et patientiam, et discretionem, et longanimitatem, et justitiam."

100. These borrowings are interwoven throughout the passage but they are particularly apparent at 132B (Augustine, *Quaestiones XVI in Matthaeum*, 11.7, ed. Mutzenbecher, CCSL 44B [Turnhout: Brepols, 1980], 131) and at 132C (Augustine, *Quaest.*, 11.9, 132).

101. *Glossa*, PL 114:132C: "Ibi patienter tolerandi sunt mali, ubi aliqui inveniuntur quibus adjuventur boni."

102. Gratian, *Decretum*, II, C. 23 (1:889).

103. Gratian, *Decretum*, II, C. 23 q. 1 (1:889–90).

104. Gratian, *Decretum*, II, C. 23 q. 1 c. 1 (1:890); Origen, *In Iesu Naue homiliae 15*.1, ed. W. A. Baehrens, *Origenes Werke* (Leipzig: J. C. Hinrichs, 1921), 7:381. Gratian attributes the passage to Gregory.

105. Gratian, *Decretum*, II, C. 23 q. 1 c. 2 (1:891–92); Augustine, "Letter 138," 12–15, ed. D. Daur, CCSL 31B (Turnhout: Brepols, 2009), 282–87.

106. As Gratian concludes, *Decretum*, II, C. 23 q. 1 c. 7 (1:894).

107. Pegg, *Most Holy War*, 57.

108. On the influence of this commentary through the work of Peter Comestor as well as the questions regarding its authorship, see Beryl Smalley, *The Gospels in the Schools c.1100–1280*. (London: Hambledon Press, 1985), 100.

109. *Enarrationes in Evangelium Matthaei*, PL 162:1374B: "Quaeritur ergo, cur quidam haeretici ab episcopis excommunicantur, et ab Ecclesia seperantur, quidam a potestatibus saecularibus interficiuntur?" Hereafter cited as *"Enarrationes."*

110. In this argument the author cites Luke 9:53–55.

111. *Enarrationes*, 1374C: "Et si quidam jam judicati et convicti et subversi occiduntur a saeculari potestate ad correctionem aliorum, tamen non est communis separatio malorum facienda, quia pauci boni remanerent, et hoc est temput immutationis, et qui hodie sunt mali, cras boni erunt."

112. *Enarrationes*, 1374D: *"Triticum congregate in horreum*, sic est intelligendum, ut punitis illis, qui diversitates et schismata secuti sunt, in coeleste horreum recipiantur et serventur, qui charitatis unitatem amaverunt."

113. On deterrence as a motive for spectacular punishments, see Friedland, *Seeing Justice Done*, 27–44.

114. I have drawn these summaries of the positions of Peter Comestor and Peter the Chanter from Smalley, *Gospels in the Schools*, 109–10.

115. This wording was borrowed from Pope Leo I in his discussion of the errors of the Priscillianists in *Epistolae*, 15, PL 54:680A.

116. *Concilium Lateranense III*, Canon 27, ed. Norman P. Tanner, *Decrees of the Ecumenical Councils* (Washington, DC: Georgetown University Press, 1990), 1:224.

117. *Ad abolendam diversarum haeresium pravitatem*, ed. Giovanni Gonnet, *Enchiridion fontium Valdensium* (Torre-Pellice: Claudiana, 1958), 1:50–53. Edward Peters, ed., *Heresy and Authority in Medieval Europe* (Philadelphia: University of Pennsylvania Press, 1980), 170–73.

118. Innocent III, *Innocentii III Regesta sive Epistolae*, 2.228 (December 1199), PL 214:788D.

119. A point stressed in the interpretation of Innocent's position by Lambert, *Medieval Heresy*, 95–96.

120. For an example of the deployment of this language, see Innocent III, 1199, decretal, X 5.7.10, *Vergentis in senium*, ed. Friedberg, *Corpus Iuris Canonici*, 2:782. See also the relevant canons of Lateran IV discussed below.

121. Innocent III, *Vergentis*, 2:782–83.

122. On the centrality of this logic, see Walter Ullmann, "The Significance of Innocent III's Decretal 'Vergentis,'" in *Études d'histoire du droit canonique dédiées à Gabriel Le Bras* (Paris: Sirey, 1965), 1:738.

123. Innocent III, *Vergentis*, 2:783: "Quum longe sit gravius aeternam quam temporalem laedere maiestatem?"

124. A point emphasized by Ullmann, "Significance of Innocent III's Decretal 'Vergentis,'" 737.

125. Emphasized by Clarence Gallagher, *Canon Law and the Christian Community: The Role of Law in the Church according to the Summa Aurea of Cardinal Hostiensis* (Rome: Università Gregoriana, 1978), 191.

126. Innocent III, 1207, decretal, *Cum ex officii nostri*. For text, see Peters, *Heresy and Authority in Medieval Europe*, 178.

127. Jeffrey Burton Russell finds the ambiguity in the wording "animadversione debita" to imply the death penalty at the hands of a secular authority; see his *Dissent and Order in the Middle Ages: The Search for Legitimate Authority* (New York: Twayne, 1992), 60.

128. For more on this crusade, its historical sources, and the presentation of the executions of heretics in these sources, see the discussion in chapter 7.

129. Judg. 15:4–5. A. M. Dubarle, "Les renards de Samson," *Revue du Moyen Age latin* 7 (1951): 175–76. See discussion in chapter 4.

130. *Concilium Lateranense IV*, Canon 3 (1:233): "Moneantur . . . saeculares potestates . . . quod de terris suae iurisdictioni subiectis universos haereticos ab ecclesia denotatos bona fide pro viribus exterminare studebunt." Tanner translates "exterminare" as "to expel." I have translated more literally to preserve what I believe is the original ambiguity.

131. The interpretation of this canon has been the topic of continued debate, some of it deeply colored by Protestant-Catholic polemics. See, for example, G. G. Coulton, *The Death Penalty for Heresy from 1184 to 1921 A.D.* (London: Simpkin, Marshall, Hamilton, Kent, 1924), 9–12. In the course of an openly polemical and sectarian argument, Coulton emphasizes the ambiguity in the verb "exterminare."

132. Cebrià Baraut, "Els incis de la Inquisició a Catalunya I les seves actuacions al Bisbat d'Urgell (segles XII–XIII)," *Urgellia* 13 (1997): 420–21. "Et si post tempus prefixum aliqui in tota terra nostra eos invenerint, duabus partibus rerum suarum confiscates, tertia sit inventoris, corpora eorum ignibus crementur." There is some question of the actual impact of Peter's decree in the Crown of Aragon. In 1226 King Jaime did not mention burning as the method of execution appropriate for heretics; see Edward Peters, *Inquisition* (New York: Free Press, 1988), 76.

133. For analysis of this development in the context for Frederick's legislative program, see David Abulafia, *Frederick II: A Medieval Emperor* (New York: Oxford University Press, 1988), 211–12.

134. Wolfgang Stürner, ed., "Die Konstitutionen Friedrichs II. für das Königreich Sizilien," const. I, 1, in *Constitutiones et acta publica imperatorum et regem* (Hanover: Hahnsche Buchhandlung, 1996), 2:151; James M. Powell, trans., *The Liber Augustalis or the Constitutions of Melfi Promulgated by the Emperor Frederick II for the Kingdom of Sicily in 1231* (Syracuse, NY: Syracuse University Press, 1971), 9: "Presentis nostre legis edicto dampnatos mortem pati Patarenos decernimus quam affectant, ut vivi in conspectus populi comburantur flammarum commissi iudicio."

135. William of Auvergne, *De fide et legibus*, in *Guilielmi Alverni episcopi Parisiensis, mathematici perfestissimi, eximii philosophi, ac theologi praestantissimi, Opera Omnia* (London: Robert Scott, 1674), 1:28b G–H: "Ad id autem, quod objicere nobis solent, quia praecepit veritas in Evangelio Matthaei 13 ut sinerent zizaniam crescere usque ad messem, ne forte simul eradicaretur et triticum."

136. William of Auvergne, *De legibus*, 1:28b G–H: "Non enim voluit parci zizaniis, sed tritico soli, quare noluit parci zizaniis in tritici detrimentum."

137. William of Auvergne, *De legibus*, 1:28b G–H: "Quare ubi non potest eis parci sine tritici detrimento, noluit eis parci."

138. William of Auvergne, *De legibus*, 1:28b H: "Ubi ergo impii in consumptionem populi Dei, vel diminutionem crescunt, ibi nullatenus crescere sinendi sunt, sed eradicandi, et hoc per corporalem mortem, quando alias eradicari non possunt."

139. William of Auvergne, *De legibus*, 1:28b H: "Alias autem eradicari non possunt incorrigibiles, et contemaces. Quare occidendi sunt ex necessitate."

140. William of Auvergne, *De legibus*, 1:28b H: "Quod si quis dixerit, quia ipsi qui modo sunt zizania possunt esse triticum, quia converti possunt ad vitam veritatis, verum utique dicunt, sed quod convertantur, et triticum fiant, hujusmodi videlicet contumaces, et in errore pertinaces, non est certum. Quod autem per ipsos illi qui triticum sunt, zizania fiant, hoc evidenter certum est. Simplices enim, et ineruditos astutia sua, credibili facilitate subvertunt Et insuper pauca zizania multam tritici segetem facile pervertit atque suffocat Difficile enim admodum, et raram videmus Haereticorum conversionem, facillimam autem et crebram fidelium subversionem. Quare bonum conversionis hujusmodi erroneorum, et parvum est, et rarum atque difficile, et eo usque incertum, ut propter quod prosperari merito possit, non appareat."

141. William of Auvergne, *De legibus*, 1:28b F–G: "Et propter hoc sicut per mortem corporum prosunt eis." Discussed in Alan E. Bernstein, "William of Auvergne and the Cathars," in *Autour de Guillaume d'Auvergne*, ed. Franco Morenzoni and Jean-Yves Tilliette (Turnhout: Brepols, 2005), 274.

142. In these comments, I make a comparison drawn from what has been termed "Motive Attribution Asymmetry" in modern political science; see Adam Waytz, Liane Young, and Jeremy Ginges, "Motive Attribution for Love vs. Hate Drives Intractable Conflict," *Proceedings of the National Academy of Sciences of the United States of America* 111, no. 44 (2014): 15687–92.

143. For an insightful exposition of this mode of reading in Augustine's confessions, see Mackey, *Peregrinations of the Word*, 22.

3. The Beginning at Orleans in 1022

1. Glaber, *Histories*, 3.31 (p. 150).

2. Thomas Head and Monica Blöcker have both noted the possible relationship between the fires at Orleans and the fires of Hell: Thomas Head, "Saints, Heretics, and Fire: Finding Meaning through the Ordeal," in *Monks and Nuns, Saints and Outcasts: Religion in Medieval Society*, ed. Sharon Farmer and Barbara H. Rosenwein (Ithaca, NY: Cornell University Press, 2000), 234; Monica Blöcker, "Volkszorn im frühen Mittelalter," *Francia* 13 (1985), 130–31.

3. A discussion of the major sources can be found in Michael Frassetto, "The Heresy at Orleans in 1022 in the Writings of Contemporary Churchmen," *Nottingham Medieval Studies* 49 (2005): 1–17.

4. For some of the more well-known treatments of the heresy at Orleans and its historical significance, see R. I. Moore, *The Origins of European Dissent* (Oxford: Basil Blackwell, 1985), 25–30; Stock, *Implications of Literacy*, 115–20.

5. The exact number of individuals executed varies by source. John of Ripoll gives the number as fourteen; Ralph Glaber states thirteen; finally, Ademar of Chabannes claims ten. See discussion below for details.

6. Havet, "L'hérésie et le bras seculier au Moyen-Age," 500–501.

7. Robert-Henri Bautier, "L'hérésie d'Orléans et le movement intellectual au début du XIe siècle: Documents et hypotheses," *Actes du 95e Congrès national des societies savantes (Reims 1970) Section de philologie et d'histoire jusqu'a 1610*, vol. 1: *Enseignement et vie intellectuelle (IXe–XVIe Siècle)* (Paris: Bibliothèque Nationale, 1975), 63–88. R. I. Moore added an appendix to his 1985 edition of *Origins of European Dissent* to take Bautier's work into account, as well as acknowledge the insights found in Stock's *Implications of Literacy*, 285–89. Bautier suggests that the king in fact burned men who had been members of his camp, perhaps as part of an attempted rapprochement with Odo inspired by his marital aspirations.

8. Thomas Head, *Hagiography and the Cult of the Saints: The Diocese of Orleans, 800–1200* (New York: Cambridge University Press, 1990), 267. Lambert, concludes that the heresy, in some form, was real: "The first burning in the West was a burning of true heretics." Lambert, *Medieval Heresy*, 21.

9. Moore, *Formation of a Persecuting Society*.

10. The existence of mass terror and hysteria around the millennium is rightfully debated, but scholars continue to argue for the presence of apocalyptic tensions in this period; see Sharon Roubach, "The Hidden Apocalypse: Richard of Saint-Vanne and the Otherworld," *Journal of Medieval History* 32 (2006): 302–14.

11. Cohn, *Europe's Inner Demons*, 39. Recent events in the United States, such as the so-called Pizzagate, illustrate the continued appeal of these kinds of accusations; see Amy Davidson, "The Age of Donald Trump and Pizzagate," *New Yorker*, December 5, 2016, accessed February 28, 2016, http://www.newyorker.com/news/amy-davidson/the-age-of-donald-trump-and-pizzagate.

12. A similar focus to that proposed in Sackville, *Heresy and Heretics in the Thirteenth Century*, 9.

13. John of Ripoll to Oliba, in Andreas of Fleury, *Vie de Gauzlin, abbé de Fleury (Vita Gauzlini abbatis Floriacensis monasterii)*, ed. Robert-Henri Bautier and Gillette Labory (Paris: Éditions du centre national de la recherché scientifique, 1969), 180: "Volo vos interea scire de heresia quę die sanctorum Innocentum fuit in Aurelianensi civitate. Nam verum fuit si aliquid audistis. Nam fecit rex Rotbertus vivos ardere de melioribus clericis sive de nobilioribus laicis prope XIIII ejusdem civitatis . . . ."

14. John of Ripoll to Oliba, 182: "Quam rem in vestro episcopatu sive abatias diligenter querite ne aliquis sub specie vane religionis in hoc crimine lateat, quod absit!"

15. Havet, "L'hérésie et le bras seculier au Moyen-Age," 500.

16. Theodor Mommsen and Paul Krueger, eds., *The Digest of Justinian*, trans. Alan Watson (Philadelphia: University of Pennsylvania Press, 1985), 4:851.

17. For enemies of the state and deserters, see *Digest*, 48.19.8.2 (4:847); for slaves, 48.19.28.11 (4:852); for arsonists, 48.19.28.12 (4:852).

18. *Digest*, 48.13.7 (4:832).

19. Karl August Eckhardt, ed., *Pactus legis Salicae*, MGH LL 2.1: vol. 4.1 (Hannover: Hahn, 1962), 19, 81. One prominent attribute of the charges raised against the heretics at Orleans is their creation of a powder from dead infants, filled with demonic power. This charge could be viewed as poisoning. Whether poisoning acted as a precedent for Robert the Pious matters little to the substance of my argument as none of the sources develop this connection. See discussion below.

20. On prohibitions against hanging women and the possible reasons for them, see Esther Cohen, *The Crossroads of Justice: Law and Culture in Late Medieval France* (Leiden: E. J. Brill, 1993), 97. Cohen suggests that burning men alive was actually a kind of feminization, by applying a form of punishment associated with women to men.

21. Ademar of Chabannes, *Chronicon*, 3.59, ed. P. Bourgain, R. Landes, and G. Pon, CCCM 129 (Turnhout: Brepols, 1999), 180. Ademar's *Chronicon* enjoyed the largest circulation of any of the main texts used in this study, and today survives in three recensions. For the manuscripts and their history, see *Chronicon*, xiii–lviii. This work is sometimes referred to as the *Historia*; see Richard Landes, *Relics, Apocalypse, and the Deceits of History: Ademar of Chabannes, 989–1034* (Cambridge, MA: Harvard University Press, 1995), 377; Ademar, *Chronicon*, xcix–c.

22. A biography of Ademar, as well as an introduction the context of his life and works, can be found in Landes, *Relics, Apocalypse, and the Deceits of History*. For the dating of the description of the heresy at Orleans, see 190.

23. Landes, *Relics, Apocalypse and the Deceits of History*, 18.

24. Landes, *Relics, Apocalypse and the Deceits of History*, 92.

25. The work of J. N. Hillgarth has established the importance of the *Prognosticum*, as well as its wide diffusion; see his "St. Julian of Toledo in the Middle Ages," 14–15.

26. Julian, *Foreknowledge of the World to Come*, 256–57.

27. Landes, *Relics, Apocalypse and the Deceits of History*, 93.

28. Barbezat, "In a Corporeal Flame," 9–11.

29. Julian, *Prognosticorum futuri saeculi*, 2.19–20 (pp. 55–58).

30. Ademar, *Chronicon*, 3.59 (p. 180): "Quos rex Rotbertus, cum nollent alicatenus ad fidem reverti, primo a gradu sacerdoti deponi, deinde ab ecclesia eliminari, et demum igne cremari jussit."

31. On liminality in the context of rituals of punishment, see Esther Cohen, *Crossroads of Justice*, 80–83.

32. Ademar, *Chronicon*, 3.59 (p. 180): "Cujus verbis obedientes [diabolus], penitus Christum latenter respuerant . . . et in aperto christianos veros se fallebant."

33. "For such false apostles are deceitful workmen, transforming themselves into the apostles of Christ. And no wonder: for Satan himself transforms himself into an angel of light. Therefore it is no great thing if his ministers be transformed as the ministers of justice, whose end shall be according to their works." Vulgate: "Nam eiusmodi pseudoapostoli operarii subdoli transfigurantes se in apostolos Christi. Et non mirum ipse enim Satanas transfigurat se in angelum lucis. Non est ergo magnum si ministri eius transfigurentut velut ministri iustitiae quorum finis erit secundum opera ipsorum."

34. With regard to the heretics' attempts to subvert others, Ademar briefly mentions another burning at Toulouse in the middle of his description of events at Orleans. He does not give a date, but they seem to be connected to the cell at Orleans. In the Alpha text of the *Chronicon*, Ademar specifies that the Manichaeans at Toulouse were burned (*cremati sunt*). In the Beta and Gamma texts he simply states that they were destroyed (*destructi*). Ademar, *Chronicon* (α), ed. P. Bourgain, R. Landes, and G. Pon (CCCM 129), 10. For the Beta and Gamma reading, see *Chronicon*, 3.59 (p. 180).

35. For the exclusion of heretics, lepers, and Jews from burial in consecrated ground as extension of their exclusion from the society of the living, see Paul Binski,

Medieval Death: Ritual and Representation (Ithaca, NY: Cornell University Press, 1996), 56–57.

36. Had the heretics survived, they would have successfully taken on the roles of Sidrach, Misach, and Abdenago, who were untouched by the fiery furnace in Dan. 3:17–29, or gold proved by flame in Wis. 3:5–6.

37. Ademar, *Chronicon*, 3.59 (p. 180): "Quasi secure nihil ignem timebant. Et a flammis se inlesos exire promittebant, et ridentes in medio ignis ligati sunt, et sine mora penitus in cinerem redacti sunt, ut nec de ossibus residuum inveniretur eorum."

38. Thomas Head has seen direct references to the ordeal in this episode, especially to the ordeal of doubtful relics by fire; see his *Hagiography and the Cult of the Saints*, 268–69. See the fuller discussion regarding Andreas of Fleury below. The ordeal could often be applied to heresy and questions of belief, which were hard to discern through observation, or to vindicate questionable beliefs. See Robert Bartlett, *Trial by Fire and Water* (Oxford: Clarendon Press, 1986), 20–22.

39. Ademar, *Chronicon*, 3.47 (p. 166).

40. Jeremy Cohen, *Living Letters of the Law*, 40.

41. Ademar, *Chronicon*, 3.47 (p. 167): "Lapidem monumenti cum nullatenus possent comminuere, ignem copiosum superadiciunt, sed quasi adamans immobilis mansit et solidus."

42. Ademar, *Chronicon*, 3.47 (p. 167): "Captus est ab eis rex Babilonius, qui se contra Deum erexerat in superbiam, et vivus, ventro dissecto visceribusque extractis, impiam animam ad baratrum projecit." See Acts 1:18.

43. Bynum, *Resurrection of the Body in Western Christianity*, 107.

44. Bautier, in particular, finds both Glaber's account and his personality lacking; see his "L'hérésie d'Orléans," 67.

45. Glaber, *Histories*, lxiv.

46. Richard Landes, "Rodolfus Glaber and the Dawn of the New Millennium: Eschatology, Historiography, and the Year 1000," *Revue Mabillon: Revue international d'histoire et de literature religieuses* ns 7 (1996): 57.

47. Landes, "Rodolfus Glaber and the Dawn of the New Millennium," 71–72n69.

48. Landes, "Rodolfus Glaber and the Dawn of the New Millennium," 72–73.

49. Glaber, *Histories*, 2.12.23 (p. 92). He reveals only that these unnamed followers were destroyed by "sword and by fire" ("qui et ipsi aut gladiis aut incendiis perierunt").

50. Glaber, *Histories*, 3.4.13 (pp. 114–17): "Ihitur infra supradictum millesimum tercio iam fere imminente anno, contigit in universe pene terrarium orbe, precipue tamen in Italia et in Galliis, innovari ecclesiarum basilicas . . . Erat enim instar ac si mundus ipse excutiendo semet, reiecta vetustate, passim candidam ecclesiarum vestem indueret."

51. Glaber, *Histories*, 3.6.19 (pp. 126–27): "Nam veluti quoddam resurrectionis decoramen."

52. Glaber, *Histories*, 3.6.19 (pp. 128–29): "Sed, ut sepissime contigit, quoniam unde humana utilitas sumit exordium, cupiditatis vicio impellente, exinde solet incurrere casum."

53. Glaber, *Histories*, 3.6.23 (pp. 132–33): "Partem etiam eius non modicum incendio cremavere."

54. Glaber, *Histories*, 3.7.25 (p. 136).

55. Philippa C. Maddern, *Violence and Social Order* (Oxford: University of Oxford Press, 1992), 84–87.

56. Geoffrey Koziol, *Begging Pardon and Favor: Ritual and Political Order in Early Medieval France* (Ithaca, NY: Cornell University Press, 1992), 128–31.

57. Jim Bradbury, *The Capetians: Kings of France, 987–1328* (New York: Continuum, 2007), 84–87.

58. The feminine element in the origin of the heresy would likely have reminded a medieval reader of 2 Tim. 3:5–7.

59. 1 Cor. 11:19: "For there must be also heresies: that they also, who are approved, may be made manifest among you."

60. Glaber, *Histories*, 3.8.28 (p. 144): "Si qua uero res procaciter ab eo deuiando in deterius cecidit, ceteris iure manentibus documentum prebuit."

61. Glaber, *Histories*, 3.29 (p. 144): "Quippe qui solus pre cunctis animantibus aeternitatis potuit consequi beatitudinem, nullum preter eum corporale animal proprii erroris uel flagitii aeternam sentient uindictam."

62. Glaber, *Histories*, 3.29 (p. 146): "Nam plures illius beneficiis per insipientiam ingrate ac misericordiae operibus illudentes atque increduli pecudibus deteriores effecti . . . ."

63. Glaber, *Histories*, 3.30 (p. 148): "Quibus scilicet omnibus, nisi conuersi sequantur Ihesum gesta penitudine, melius fuerat non fuisse."

64. Glaber, *Histories*, 3.31 (p. 150): "Quibus ad ultimum numero XIII igni traditis, cum iam cepissent acrius aduri, ceperunt uoce qua poterant ex eodem igne clamare se pessime deceptos arte diabolica, nuper de universorum Deo ac Domino male senisse, et ob hanc ab eisdem inlatam ei blasphemiam illos temporali atque aeterna ultione torqueri."

65. Glaber, *Histories*, 3.31 (p. 150): "Minime valuerunt, quoniam, vindice flamma consumente illos, continuo in pulverem sunt redacti."

66. Glaber, *Histories*, 4.2.5 (pp. 177–78).

67. Glaber, *Histories*, 4.4.10 (p. 188).

68. Glaber, *Histories*, 4.4.11 (pp. 188, 190).

69. Bautier, "L'Hérésie d'Orléans," 66.

70. Andreas states that he took up work on the *Miracles* eleven years after the death of Gauzlin, and presented the first three books of his additions in the twelfth year of King Robert's reign. *Les miracles de saint Benoît (Miracula Sancti Benedicti)*, 4.1, ed. E. de Certain (Paris: Jules Renouard, 1858), 173–74.

71. Andreas, *Les miracles de saint Benoît*, 6.20 (p. 247). See note 76 for the Latin.

72. Andreas, *Les miracles de saint Benoît*, 6.20 (p. 247): "Nec multo post unus fratrum nostrae congregationis in noctis vision vidit; et ecce praetaxati seductores, ac si a secessu emergentes latrinarum, habili suorum hospitio meritorum."

73. Andreas, *Les miracles de saint Benoît*, 6.20 (p. 247): "Domum quiescentium irrumpunt fratrum, postmodumque viritim lectisternia scrutantur singulorum. Nec mora, singularis omnium nostrum Benedictus pater, provisor et impiger procurator, a parte basilicae cum magni splendoris occurrit decore."

74. Andreas, *Les miracles de saint Benoît*, 6.20 (p. 248).

75. The order in which the versions were written down is unclear, and are in any case very close to one another; however, in the sole medieval manuscript, Vatican

Biblioteca Apostolica Vaticana, MS Reg. lat. 592, both texts are found, with the *Life of Gauzlin* being second. See Andreas, *Vie de Gauzlin*, 23. Bautier believes that the account found in the *Miracles* was written earlier.

76. Andreas, *Vie de Gauzlin*, 56 [b], 98: "Venerabilis autem presul hujus modi rem animadvertens, Aurelianis cum sapientioribus Floriacensis loci pervenit, cumvictisque adversariis divinorum librorum testimoniis, a prefato rege igni jussi sunt tradi, ignibus mancipandi perpetuis." Emphasis mine.

77. Andreas, *Vie de Gauzlin*, 56 [b], 100: "Et extra Aecclesiam catholicam nullum salvari Confiteor." This statement is an elaboration of the familiar ending of the Athanasian Creed: "Haec est fides catholica, quam nisi quisque fideliter firmiterque crediderit, salvus esse non poterit."

78. Head, "Saints, Heretics, and Fire," 234.

79. Thomas Head, "The Genesis of the Ordeal of Relics by Fire in Ottonian Germany: An Alternative Form of 'Canonization,'" in *Procès de canonisation au moyen âge: Aspects juridiques et religieux*, ed. Gábor Klaniczay (Rome: École française de Rome, 2004), 30–32.

80. Andreas, *Vie de Gauzlin*, 20 [b], 60.

81. For the appearance of the canons, see Ademar, *Chronicon*, 3.59 (p. 180), and the discussion above. For Gauzlin's test for the shroud, see Andreas, *Vie de Gauzlin*, 20 [b], 60, and discussion above. For the Holy Sepulcher's resistance to fire, see Ademar, *Chronicon*, 3.47 (p. 167).

82. Mitchell B. Merback, *The Thief, the Cross and the Wheel: Pain and the Spectacle of Punishment in Medieval and Renaissance Europe* (Chicago: University of Chicago Press, 1998), 155. The sources for events at Orleans in 1022 do not develop any overt connection between the fires of execution and purgatorial fires; rather, fire appears completely infernal.

83. For the world's rebirth in a "conflagration of fire," see Julian, *Prognosticum*, 3.46.

84. Bautier, "L'hérésie d'Orléans," 68.

85. Paul of St. Père de Chartres, *Gesta synodi Aurelianensis an. MXXII, adversos novos Manichaeos*, in *Recueil des historiens des Gaules et de la France*, vol. 10, ed. Martin Bouquet (Paris: Victor Palmé, 1874), 537C: "Qui sapienti usus consilio eum praedocuit, ut quotidie primo mane Omnipotentis opem quaesiturus, Ecclesiam devotus adiret, orationi incumberet, atque sacrosancta communion corporis et sanguinis Christi se muniret; deinde fidenter ad audiendum haereticam pravitatem signaculo sanctae cruces protectus pergeret, nihil horum quae ab eis audiret, contradiceret, sed simulato discipuli vultu, omnia tacitus in domicilio pectoris conferret." Hereafter cited as "Paul, *Gesta synodi Aurelianensis*."

86. See Jer. 7:31.

87. Paul, *Gesta synodi Aurelianensis*, 538C: "Cuius cinis tanta veneratione colligebatur, atque custodiebatur; ut Christiana religiositas corpus Christi custodire solet, aegris dandum de hoc saeculo exituris ad viaticum."

88. Paul, *Gesta synodi Aurelianensis*, 538C–D: "Inerat enim tanta vis diabolicae fraudis in ipso cinere, ut quicumque de praefata haeresi imbutus fuisset, et de eodem cinere quamvis sumendo parum praelibavisset, vix unquam postea de eadem haeresi gressum mentis ad viam veritatis dirigere valeret."

89. This function is one example of the ways in which the Eucharist held a "central signifying power" in the Middle Ages; see Miri Rubin, *Corpus Christi: The Eucharist in Late Medieval Culture* (Cambridge: Cambridge University Press, 1991), 5.

90. Paul, *Gesta synodi Aurelianensis*, 539B: "At illi Diabolo in inferno jam mansionem paratam habentes, vera esse memorata, et ita se sentire ac credere constanter asserunt."

91. This symbolism in no way precludes the simple utility of burning them in an existing, flammable structure. See note 92 for the quotation.

92. Paul, *Gesta synodi Aurelianensis*, 539E: "Deinde extra civitatis educti muros, in quodam tuguriolo copioso igne accenso, praeterquam unum Clericum, atque unam Monacham, cum nefario pulvere, de quo supra diximus, cremati sunt. Clericus enim et Monacha divino nutu resipuerunt."

93. Robert Mills, *Suspended Animation: Pain, Pleasure and Punishment in Medieval Culture* (London: Reaktion Books, 2005), 16.

94. Glaber, *Histories*, 3.8.28 (p. 144). See discussion above.

95. 1 Cor. 11:19. This verse is cited by Glaber as part of his argument. See discussion above.

96. Vanderputten and Reilly, "Reconciliation and Record Keeping," 349.

97. The cleric and nun in the account of Paul of St. Père de Chartres.

4. Likeness in Difference

1. Eckbert of Schönau, "Sermon 9," *Sermones contra Catharos*, 52–57. Eckbert's own title for this work was likely *Liber contra hereses Katharorum*. See analysis below. All sermons cited below are from this edition.

2. This dynamic is part of the "liminalization" process identified in Esther Cohen, *Crossroads of Justice*, 80.

3. My use of the hermeneutic circle is drawn most directly from Karl F. Morrison's use of it in his *Hermeneutics of Empathy Hermeneutics of Empathy in Western Literature, Theology, and Art* (Princeton, NJ: Princeton University Press, 1988), 40. My thanks to Anna Wilson, who first drew Morrison's work to my attention and suggested to me that empathy could be a hermeneutic. My use of empathy as a hermeneutic in this chapter develops its potential for violence beyond Morrison's treatment; see Nicholas Watson, "Desire for the Past," *Studies in the Age of Chaucer* 21 (1999): 76. For the origin of the hermeneutic circle, see Martin Heidegger, *Being and Time*, 1.5 §32, trans. John Macquarrie and Edward Robinson (New York: Harper and Row, 1962), 194–95.

4. Morrison, *I Am You*, 31.

5. For the larger European context of reform and the "simoniac heresy," see Moore, *War on Heresy*, 89. Perhaps the most famous appeal for the Church to separate itself from the world was the one proposed by Paschal II in 1111 to Henry V, offering to surrender all Church lands if the emperor refrained from meddling in ecclesiastical affairs forevermore. In 1145 Bernard of Clairvaux, in his articulation of the theory of the two swords of spiritual and temporal power, was less radical but still criticized the excessive interest of the recent ecclesiastical leadership in temporal affairs. Brian Tierney, *The Crisis of Church and State: 1050–1300* (Englewood Cliffs, NJ: Prentice-Hall, 1964), 85–88.

6. Rainald was also the mastermind behind the supposed transfer of the relics of the Three Magi to Cologne in the context of Frederick's struggles; see Patrick Geary, *Living with the Dead in the Middle Ages* (Ithaca, NY: Cornell University Press, 1994), 251.

7. This was particularly the case, for the period covered here, during the disputes between Frederick Barbarossa and Alexander III in 1157–77. Tierney, *Crisis of Church and State*, 110–11; Peter Munz, *Frederick Barbarossa: A Study in Medieval Politics* (London: Eyre and Spottiswoode, 1969), 205–332.

8. Malcolm Barber, "Northern Catharism," in Frassetto, *Heresy and the Persecuting Society in the Middle Ages*, 115–37. For the spread of reports of heresy, see 133. For the basic "dearth of Cathars" in the region, see 137.

9. Pilar Jiménez Sanchez, "Aux commencements du Catharisme: La communauté d''apôtres hérétiques' denoncée par Evervin de Steinfeld en Rhénanie," *Heresis 35* (2001): 43–44.

10. Grundmann, *Religious Movements in the Middle Ages*, 1.

11. Brunn, *Des contestataires aux "Cathares."* See analyses below for specific references.

12. Anne L. Clark, *Elisabeth of Schönau: A Twelfth-Century Visionary* (Philadelphia: University of Pennsylvania Press, 1992), 8.

13. Brunn, *Des contestataires aux "Cathares,"* 105.

14. Brunn, *Des contestataires aux "Cathares,"* 404.

15. Andrew P. Roach, *The Devil's World: Heresy and Society 1100–1300* (Harlow, UK: Pearson, 2005), 107. The origin of this expression is often attributed to Aristotle, *Politics*, 5.11 (1314a4), trans. Ernest Barker (Oxford: Clarendon Press, 1961), 246. It would have been familiar to a medieval reader through sources such as Jerome, "Letter 125," 14.1, *Epistolae*, ed. Hilberg, CSEL 56 (Turnhout: Brepols, 1918), 132. See Erasmus, *Adages*, 1.2.4, in *The Collected Works of Erasmus*, trans. Margaret Mann Phillips, annotated by R. A. B. Mynors (Toronto: University of Toronto Press, 1982), 31:148–49.

16. For two separate events and their dates, see Brunn, *Des contestataires aux "Cathares,"* 124 and 142–49. For both as the same incident, see Moore, *Birth of Popular Heresy*, 74.

17. This wording reflects the preinquisitorial nature of these proceedings. In order to charge an individual with a crime, a formal accusation was required. Henry Ansgar Kelly, "Inquisitorial Due Process and the Status of Secret Crimes," in *Proceedings of the Eighth International Congress of Medieval Canon Law (UCSD, 1988)*, ed. Stanley Chodorow, Monumenta iuris canonici, Series C: Subsidia, vol. 4 (Vatican City: Biblioteca Apostolica Vaticana, 1992), 407–9.

18. The Council of Reims in 1157 suggested that the ordeal be used to prove the innocence of suspected heretics. Purgation through ordeal especially lent itself to the resolution of accusations that depended on crimes whose existence was difficult to prove, such as heresy. Bartlett, *Trial by Fire and Water*, 20–22.

19. *Annales Brunwilarenses*, MGH SS 16:727: "Hic accusatio Colonie in ecclesia beati Petri presente Arnoldo archiepiscopo contra hereticos facta est; pluresque capti et vinculati, iudicio aquae se expurgaverunt, ceteri autem reatu suo confusi, fugam inierunt. Apud Veronam [Bonn] presidente Ottone comite igne consumpti sunt tres, malentes mori quam cedere sacrosancte catholice fidei."

20. Eberwin of Steinfeld, "Letter 472," PL 182:676–80; R. I. Moore, *Birth of Popular Heresy*, 74–78. Regarding the date of this letter, see Brunn, *Des contestataires aux "Cathares,"* 124–72; Monique Zerner, "L'hérétique Henri dans les sources de son temps (1135–1145)," *Revue Mabillon* 86 (2014): 114.

21. Brunn, *Des contestataires aux "Cathares,"* 87–94.

22. Moore, "Debate of April 2013 in Retrospect," 264–65.

23. William of Saint-Thierry, Arnold of Bonneval, and Geoffrey of Auxerre, *Vita Prima Sancti Bernardi*, 6, PL 185:387.

24. The little foxes had long been interpreted as heretics, originating with Origen, *Commentarium in Canticum Canticorum*, 4, PG 13:196. For example, see Cassiodorus, *Expositio in Cantica Canticorum*, 2, PL 70:1066D; Gregory, *Super Cantica Canticorum expositio*, 2. PL 79:500B; Isidore of Seville, *Codex Carolinus*, 1.26, PL 98:1060C. For a more thorough overview, see Trivellone, *L'hérétique imaginé*, 292–97; Karen Sullivan, *Truth and the Heretic: Crises of Knowledge in Medieval French Literature* (Chicago: University of Chicago Press, 2005), 65n62.

25. Eberwin, "Letter 472," 677C: "Cum per triduum essent admoniti, et resipiscere noluisset, rapti sunt a populis nimio zelo permotis, nobis tamen invitis, et in ignem positi, atque cremati."

26. Remigius of Auxerre had cited this same verse to establish that all "heretics and wicked doctors" were reserved for God's own judgment: "Homily 12," PL 131: 929D–30A. Bernard, in his possible reply to Eberwin, referred to the Titus passage as well; see *Sermones super Cantica Canticorum*, 65:8, in *Sancti Bernardi Opera*, ed. J. Leclercq, C. H. Talbot, and H. M. Rochais (Rome: Editiones Cistercienses, 1958), 2:177. See discussion below.

27. William of Newburgh, *Historia rerum anglicarum*, ed. R. Howlett, in *Chronicles of the Reigns of Stephen, Henry II, and Richard I*, Rolls Series 82 (London: Longman, 1884; repr. Wiesbaden: Kraus, 1964), 1:131–34. Henry's actions can be seen as a severe enactment of the penalty of branding and exile for heresy suggested at the Council of Reims in 1157. Paul Frédéricq, ed., *Corpus documentorum Inquisitionis haereticae pravitatis Neerlandicae* (Ghent: J. Vuylsteke, 1889), 1:35–36.

28. Eberwin, "Letter 472," 677C–D: "Et, quo magis mirabile est, ipsi tormentum ignis non solum cum patientia, sed et cum laetitia introierunt et sustinuerunt. Hic, sancte pater, vellem, si praesens essem, habere responsionem tuam, unde istis diaboli membris tanta fortitudo in sua haeresi, quanta vix etiam invenitur in valde religiosis in fide Christi."

29. These opinions are outlined in a sermon Bernard addressed to the clergy of Cologne during a visit to the city as well as in a letter composed by members of his entourage with Eberwin's help. William of Saint-Thierry et al., *Sancti Bernardi Vita Prima*, 6.7, 389–90; 6.2.6, 285–86.

30. Bernard, *Sermones super Cantica Canticorum*, 65, 66 (2:172–88); Kilian Walsh and Irene M. Edmonds, trans. *Bernard of Clairvaux: On the Song of Songs* (Kalamazoo, MI: Cistercian Publications, 1979), 3:179–206. Bernard had preached two earlier sermons on the verse (nos. 63 and 64), focusing on other meanings for the little foxes. Brunn, suggests that "Sermon 65" is not a response to Eberwin, and might in fact have been familiar to him when he wrote to Bernard. "Sermon 66" is a "partial" response to Eberwin but aimed at a wider audience; see *Des contestataires aux "Cathares,"* 169–70.

31. Bernard, "Sermon 65," 7 (2:176–77); Matt. 5:29.

32. Bernard, "Sermon 66," 1 (2:178–79). The cancer image draws on 2 Tim. 2:16.

33. Bernard, "Sermon 65," 8 (2:177).

34. Bernard, "Sermon 65," 2 (2:173): "Quid faciemus his malignissimis vulpibus, ut capi queant, quae nocere quam vincere malunt, et ne apparere quidem volunt, sed serpere?"

35. Bernard, "Sermon 66," 2 (2:179): "Quoniam non est ab homine illorum haeresis, neque per hominem illam acceperunt . . . absque dubio, uti Spiritus Sanctus praedixit, per immissionem et fraudem daemoniorum, in hypocrisi loquentium mendacium, prohibentium nubere."

36. Bernard, "Sermon 66," 7 (2:183): "Cum propterea vos corpus Christi, quod est Ecclesia, tamquam pollutes et immundos exspuerit."

37. Bernard, "Sermon 66," 12 (2:186; trans. 3:203–4): "Nam quantum ad istos, nec rationibus convincuntur, quia non intelligent, nec auctoritatibus corriguntur, quia non recipiunt, nec flectuntur suasionibus, quia subversi sunt. Probatum est: mori magis eligunt, quam converti." I have changed the translation of "quia subversi sunt" from "for they are utterly perverted."

38. Bernard, "Sermon 66," 12 (2:186; trans. 3:204): "Horum finis interitus, horum novissims incendium manet."

39. Judg. 15:4. This image appealed to Innocent III as well. See discussion in chapter 2.

40. Bernard, "Sermon 66," 12 (2:186–87; trans.: 204): "Itaque iruens in eos populus, novos haereticis suae ipsorum perfidiae martyres dedit. Approbamus zelum, sed factum non suademus, quia fides suadenda est, non imponenda."

41. Bernard, "Sermon 66," 12 (2:187): "Quamquam melius procul dubio gladio coercentur, illius videlicet qui 'non sine causa gladium portat,' quam in suum errorem multis traicere permittantur. 'Dei enim minister ille est, vindex in iram ei qui male agit.'" The scriptural quotation is Rom. 13:4.

42. Judas's suicide occurred under the Devil's influence; see Luke 22:3 and John 13:27. Bernard's reference draws on a long medieval tradition that linked Judas to damnation incurred through betrayal and suicide. Alexander Murray, *The Curse on Self-Murder*, vol. 2 of *Suicide in the Middle Ages* (Oxford: Oxford University Press, 2000), 323–34.

43. Bernard, "Sermon 66," 13 (2:187). The phrase "at the Devil's urging" (*diabolo instigante*) regularly accompanied descriptions of suicides, both literary and actual. The use of this clause acknowledged the belief that "it was the Devil who made people kill themselves, and the Devil, equally, who took their soul when they died." Alexander Murray, *Curse on Self-Murder*, 191.

44. Bernard, *De gratia et libero arbitrio*, 1.2, in *Sancti Bernardi Opera*, ed. J. Leclercq and H. M. Rochais (Rome: Editiones Cistercienses, 1963), 3:166–67: "Et ita gratiae operanti salutem cooperari dicitur liberum arbitrium dum consentit, hoc est dum salvatur. Constentire enim salvari est . . . Ubi consensus, ibi voluntas." At 9.36 (3:191): "Nemo quippe salvatur invitus."

45. Bernard, *De gratia et libero arbitrio*, 9.28–30 (3:185–87).

46. Bernard, *De gratia et libero arbitrio*, 9.31 (3:188). "Verumtamen si voluntas etiam in tormentis mala perdurat, quid ponderis habet operis abnegatio, ut ideo sapere quis putetur, quod iam in mediis flammis luxuriari non libeat?"

47. As Bernard appears to indicate: "Nam quamdiu corpus vivit in flamma, tamdiu constat in militia persistere voluntatem." *De gratia et libero arbitrio*, 9.31 (3:188).

48. Bernard, *De gratia et libero arbitrio*, 13.45 (3:198): "Utitur creatura rationali, sed malevola, quasi virga disciplinae, quam correpto filio, in ignem proiciet tamquam sarmentum inutile." Perhaps modeled on Prov. 3:12. On the wicked becoming tools of divine righteousness, see Augustine, *De gratia et libero arbitrio*, 21.42, PL 44:907–9.

49. Bernard, "Sermon 65," 4 (2:175): "Non est autem hominis scire quid sit in homine, nisi quis forte ad hoc ipsum fuerit vel illuminatus Spiritu Dei, vel angelica informatus industria. Quod signum dabitis, ut palam fiat pessima haeresis haec, docta mentiri non lingua tantum, sed vita?"

50. As Karen Sullivan observes, "Throughout his sermons on heretics, Bernard acknowledges and even amplifies the epistemological problems heretics are seen as posing by seeming not to be heretics, but he also shows himself able, through a mysterious interpretive power, to use these apparent obstacles to prosecution as evidence against them" (*Truth and the Heretic*, 64).

51. On the role Eckbert played in the recording and dissemination of his sister's visions, see Anne L. Clark, "Holy Woman or Unworthy Vessel? The Representations of Elisabeth of Schönau," in *Gendered Voices: Medieval Saints and Their Interpreters*, ed. Catherine M. Mooney (Philadelphia: University of Pennsylvania Press, 1999): 35–51; Clark, *Elisabeth of Shönau*, 50–67. F. W. E. Roth, ed., *Die Visionen der hl. Elisabeth und die Schiften der Aebte Ekbert und Emecho von Schönau* (Brno: Verlag der Studien aus dem Benedictiner-und Cistercienser-Orden, 1884).

52. Migne gives the title *Sermones contra Catharos*. For the title as *Liber contra hereses Katharorum*, see Brunn, *Des contestataires aux "Cathares,"* 193n1. The only widely available edition is PL 195:11–102. Only the first sermon has an English translation; see Moore, *Birth of Popular Heresy*, 88–94. The text has four nearly complete extant manuscript versions, of which two are medieval: Vatican, Pal. Lat. 482 and Leipzig, Ms. 1530. For a discussion of the manuscripts, see Brunn, *Des contestataires aux "Cathares,"* 276–85.

53. Lambert, *Medieval Heresy*, 63; Barber, "Northern Catharism," 119.

54. This identical short notice appears in the Annals of Erfurt, Aachen, and Altzelle, among others. *Annales Sancti Petri Erphesfurdenses*, MGH SS 16:22; *Annales Aquenses*, MGH SS 16: 686; *Annales Veterocellenses*, MGH SS 16:42: "Heretici combusti sunt Coloniae, e quibus una mulier se dedit precipitem in ignem nullo cogente." The presentation of the woman, in this and in the other sources that mention her, might be influenced by models such as Hasdrubal's wife; see Jerome, *Adversus Jovinianum*, 1.43, PL 23:286B.

55. Dietrich of Deutz, *Series achiepiscoporum coloniensis*, MGH SS 13:286–87: "Calafrigae sive Cathari, viri sex, mulieres duae cum suis heresiarchis, Arnoldo, Marsilio, Thioderico, in urbe Coloniensi deprehensi sunt. Qui a clero diiudicati et anathematizati, a iudicibus et populo civitatis, cum fidem catholicam recipere et suam profanam sectam nollent abicere, in colle qui Iudaicus appellatur iuxta Iudeorum sepulturas igni cremate sunt, tanta diaboli instinctu in suo proposito usi pertinatia, ut quidam ipsorum furentibus flammis se ipsos inicerent." The text originated from the *Codex Thioderici*, lost since 1947. M. Sinderhauf, *Die Abtei Deutz und ihre innere Erneuer-*

ung. Klostergeschichte im Spiegel des verschollenen Codex Thioderici (Vierow: SH-Verlag, 1996).

56. Quote is Phil. 3:13: "Brethren, I do not count myself to have apprehended. But one thing I do: forgetting those things that are behind, and stretching forth myself to those that are before, I press toward the mark, to the prize of the supernal vocation of God in Christ Jesus." Medieval exegetes often quoted this verse in contexts that demanded the ability to allegorically interpret signs through the divine illumination achieved (or perhaps only signified) through a pious life.

57. Eberwin, "Letter 472," 677C.

58. Bernard, "Sermon 66," 13 (2:187).

59. Eckbert himself recorded his sister's visions regarding Ursula and the martyrs. AA. SS. Oct IX (1869), 163. The most well-known version of the St. Ursula story arises from the thirteenth-century *Legenda Aurea*, 154, ed. Maggioni, 2:1206–11. Moore, *War on Heresy*, 167.

60. Moore, *War on Heresy*, 168.

61. Eckbert, "Sermon 11," 88B–C: "Fuit mihi concertatio de his rebus quadam vice in domo mea Bunnae, cum quodam viro qui suspectus erat nobis quod esset de secta Catharorum . . . ." Eckbert's vita repeats this assertion, suggesting that the heretics attempted his conversion. Emecho of Schönau, *Vita Eckeberti*, ed. S. Widmann, in *Neues Archiv der Gesellschaft für ältere deutsche Geschichtskunde* 2 (1886): 452–53.

62. Eckbert, "Sermon 11," 84C: "Memini vidisse aliquando in praesentia Coloniensis archiepiscopi Arnoldi, quemdam non parvi nominis virum, qui de schola Catharorum reversus fuerat ad suos, a quo dum inquireremus diligenter, quae essent haereses illorum." From this reference, it is not clear, however, if Eckbert refers to Arnold I (1138–51) or Arnold II (1152–56). Brunn believes the reference points to Arnold I. *Des contestataires aux "Cathares,"* 213.

63. Brunn, *Des contestataires aux "Cathares,"* 276, 357–64.

64. The latest possible date for the sermons is 1167, the year their addressee, Archbishop Rainhald of Cologne died. R. Manselli believed that the sermons were composed in 1163. Moore, *Birth of Popular Heresy*, 88.

65. Moore, *War on Heresy*, 169.

66. Hilbert Chiu suggests, "When we speak of the 'medieval Manichee,' it is more accurate to say that we speak of a phenomenon in the medieval intellectual history of the classroom and the textbook, and not of a phenomenon in the history of popular heresy"; see his "Alan of Lille's Academic Concept of the Manichee," *Journal of Religious History* 35 (2011): 494.

67. Eckbert's imagining of the Cathars is an example of how, as Alexander Patschovsky explains, "every deviant form of thinking was seen as the negative image of the world of God"; see his "Heresy and Society: On the Political Function of Heresy in the Medieval World," in Bruschi and Peter Biller, *Texts and the Repression of Medieval Heresy*, 39.

68. Eckbert, "Sermon 1," 18: "Unde autem Catharistae, ide est *purgatores*, primo vocati sint." Eighth Canon of the First Council of Nicaea, *Decrees of the Ecumenical Councils*, ed. and trans. Norman P. Tanner (London: Sheed and Ward, 1990), 9. Eckbert probably encountered this usage through Yves de Chartres, who himself drew from a quotation of this canon by Innocent I: Yves de Chartres, *Prologue*, ed. and

trans. J. Werckmeister (Paris: Les Éditions du Cerf, 1997), § 31, 95. Pegg, *Most Holy War*, 22–23.

69. Eckbert, "Excerptum de Manichaeis ex S. Augustino," 97–102. He draws particularly from Augustine, *De haeresibus*, 46, ed. Vander Plaetse and Beukers, CCSL 46 (Turnhout: Brepols, 1969), 312–20. The Augustinian appendix is not an excerpt from one treatise, but rather an "appendix of selections," which are abridged and edited, from Augustine's antiheretical works. For the description, see Moore, *War on Heresy*, 169.

70. Brunn, *Des contestataires aux "Cathares,"* 238.

71. Biget, *Hérésie et inquisition dans le Midi de la France*, 77.

72. The visions granted to his sister would constitute one aspect of this divine response to visible human failure. Clark, "Representations of Elisabeth of Schönau," 40–41; Roth, *Die Visionen*, 40.

73. Eckbert, "Sermon 3," 21.

74. Eckbert, "Sermon 1," 13: "Ut grande periculum patiatur Ecclesia Dei a veneno pessimo, quod undique adversus eam effundunt; nam sermo eorum serpit ut cancer, et quasi lepra volatilis longe lateque discurrit, pretiosa membra Christi contaminans."

75. For a similar discussion of origins and foundations for faith, see Augustine, *Contra litteras Petiliani*, 1.5.6 (pp. 6–7).

76. Eckbert, "Sermon 1," 16–17.

77. Eckbert, "Sermon 3," 24–25: "Doctrina Manichaei, qui non fuit Dei, sed diaboli; non Christi, sed antichristi."

78. Eckbert, "Sermon 11," 94C.

79. Elisabeth of Shönau also addressed similar objections to marriage, perhaps under Eckbert's influence. Roth, *Die Visionen*, 104.

80. Eckbert, "Sermon 5," 32D–33A: "Omnes enim angelicos spiritus creaverat simul, ita ut nullus angelus ex alio nasceretur. Humanum vero genus ita creare disponebat, ut sibi invicem succederent homines, et nascerentur alii ab aliis, quatenus causa consanguinitatis formior inter eos esset connexio charitatis. Omnes autem unum caput, et unam originem habere voluit primum hominem, ut videlicet ab ipso omne genus humanum propagaretur, essetque ei in hoc quaedam similitudo cum Deo, qui est caput et principium omnis creaturae."

81. Likely ultimately inspired by Augustine, *De civitate Dei*, 15.16 (pp. 476–79).

82. This is a recurrence of what has been termed "the hermeneutical Jew" and heretics as a cause of "epistemological instability." Jeremy Cohen, *Living Letters of the Law*, 2; Sullivan, *Truth and the Heretic*, 11. This linkage results from the perceived common allegiance of both groups to the Devil as the ultimate scrambler of language. See Augustine on demonic interference in linguistic and heuristic signs: *De doctrina Christiana*, 2.23.35–25.39 (pp. 96–102).

83. Dyan Elliott, *Fallen Bodies: Pollution, Sexuality, and Demonology in the Middle Ages* (Philadelphia: University of Pennsylvania Press, 1999), 135–37.

84. Anselm of Canterbury, *Cur Deus Homo*, 2.21, in *S. Anselmi opera Omnia*, ed. Francis Schmitt (Rome, 1940), 2:132.

85. For example, Gregory the Great, *Moralia in Iob*, 4.3.4 (p. 168); Isidore of Seville, *Sententiae*, 1.10–11 (pp. 32–41); Elliott, *Fallen Bodies*, 137.

86. See also, Augustine, *In Iohannis evangelium Tractatus*, 87:2–3, ed. R. Willems, CCSL 36 (Turnhout: Brepols, 1954), 544–45.

87. Eckbert, "Sermon 8," 52D.

88. Eckbert, "Sermon 11," 91D: "Manducatur hic cibus, sed non consumitur ut alius cibus: ad animam transit, animam confortat et illuminat, eamque conducit ad vitam aeternam."

89. For example, the Devil inspires their opposition to the baptism of infants so that he can claim more souls. Eckbert, "Sermon 7," 51A.

90. Eckbert, "Sermon 2," 20C.

91. This council allowed accused heretics to prove their innocence through the ordeal by fire. *Corpus Documentorum inquisitionis haereticae pravitatis Neerlandicae*, ed. Frédéricq, 1:35–36.

92. In the vulgate: "Ego quidem vos baptize in aqua in paenitentiam qui autem post me venturus est fortiori me est cuius non sum dingus calciamenta portare ipse vos baptizabit in Spiritu Sancto et igni."

93. Eckbert, "Sermon 8," 51D–52A: "Dicitur autem hic baptismus fieri in igne, propter ignem luminum, quae in circuitu ardent." The lamps are an important part of the imaginary world of nocturnal, secretive heresy. For example, the role of candles in Guibert of Nogent, *Autobiographie*, 3.17, ed. Edmond-René Labande (Paris: Les Belles Lettres, 1981), 430.

94. Eckbert, "Sermon 8," 51D: "Et faciunt filium gehennae, non regni Dei." In fact, shaping Eckbert's response is the next verse, holding the rest of John the Baptist's quotation (Matt. 3:12): "Whose fan is in his hand, and he will thoroughly cleanse his floor and gather his wheat into the barn; but the chaff he will burn with unquenchable fire."

95. Eckbert, "Sermon 8," 52A: "Melius ipsa verba attendite: 'Baptizabit,' inquit, 'in igne;' non juxta ignem, ut vos facitis."

96. Eckbert, "Sermon 8," 52A–B: "Struite ignem copiosum in medio synagogae vestrae, et tollite illum vestrum novitium, quem vultis catharizare, et in medio ignis eum locate, et tu archicathare, pone super verticem ejus manum tuam, ut soles, et sic benedicito illum. Et tunc si non adusseris tu ungulas tuas, et ille illaesus evaserit, fatebor certe, quia bene baptizatus est Catharus tuus."

97. The original is a play on words that does not survive translation: "Nonne mox ita calens ad coelum vadit?"

98. While one of the 1163 victims is named Theodric, this is more likely a reference to the earlier burnings at Bonn in 1143. If this supposition is true, this is the only reference to the name of the leader of that group.

99. Eckbert, "Sermon 8," 52A–B: "Imo ut verius dicatur, descenderunt in profundum inferni, ab igne temporali, ad ardorem ignis aeterni, et merito quidem. Ut enim exinanirent baptismum aquae, constitutum ab ipso Domino Salvatore, baptizandum esse in igne docuerunt. Ideoque justissimo Dei judicio factum est, ut sic in igne baptizarentur, ut ab eo irrevocabiliter devorarentur."

100. For example, Eckbert asked his sister what his own reward would be in Heaven and to inquire from the Virgin Mary if Origen of Alexandria had been damned for his heretical opinions. Roth, *Die Visionen*, 62–63; Clark, *Elisabeth of Shönau*, 57. Jean Leclercq discusses why Eckbert would have been eager to know that answer to this question in his *The Love of Learning and the Desire for God: A Study of Monastic Culture*, 2nd ed., trans. Catherine Misrahi (New York: Fordham University

Press, 1974), 118–22. For the question regarding his own reward, see Emecho, *Vita Eckeberti*, 451.

101. Eckbert, "Sermon 9," 69B–C.

102. Eckbert, "Sermon 9," 57C.

103. Eckbert, "Sermon 9," 62D–63A.

104. Eckbert, "Sermon 9," 57C.

105. Eckbert, "Sermon 9," 66A–B: "Nam in hac vita baptizat in Spiritu sancto, quando in baptism foris quidem per visibiles ministros baptizat nos in aqua, intus autem animas nostras propria operatione baptizat in Spiritu sancto, donans nobis remissionem omnium peccatorum. In igne autem nos baptizat, quando post hanc vitam in purgatoriis poenis animas nostras purificat a maculis peccatorum, quas in habitaculo corruptibilis corporis contraxerunt, quia nihil in illa sua purissima civitate recipere vult, quod non sit ab omni sorde defaecatum."

106. Eckbert, "Sermon 9," 64D. Eckbert's use of 1 Cor. 3: 10–15 illustrates the significance of this verse in the doctrine of Purgatory. See Le Goff, *Birth of Purgatory*, 43–44.

107. On the corporeality of purgatorial fire, see Hugh of St. Victor, *De sacramentis christiane fidei*, 2.16.3.

108. Georgius Waitz, ed., *Chronica regia Coloniensis*, Recensio I, codd. A., MGH SRG 18:114: "Quidam heretici de secta Catarorum de Flandriae partibus Coloniam venientes, ibi deprehensi sunt, et extra urbem igne concremati sunt Nonis Augusti quatuor mares et iuvencula, quae se igni invito etiam populo iniecit."

109. Waitz, *Chronica regia Coloniensis*, Recensio I, codd. A., MGH SRG 18:114: "Et cum hora combusionis eorum in civitate vehementissima nimis foret pluvia, ita ut clerus, qui in civitate totus remanserat, pluviam exhorreret, propter fidem debilis vulgi ne una quidam gutta tam vehementis pluviae ubi combusti sunt cecidit."

110. Waitz, *Chronica regia Coloniensis*, Recensio II, codd. B.C., MGH SRG 18:114: "Qui ecclesie catholice representati et satis diu de secta sua examinati, dum nullis probabilibus documentis corrigi possent, set in suo proposito pertinacissime persisterent, eiecti sunt ab aecclesia et in manus laicorum traditi. Qui eos extra urbem educentes, Non. Aug. ignibus tradiderunt, mares quatuor et iuvenculam unam."

111. Waitz, *Chronica regia Coloniensis*, Recensio II, codd. B.C., MGH SRG, 18:114. "Que dum miseratione populi prope servaretur, si forte interitu aliorum terreretur et saniori consilio acquiesceret, subito de minibus se tenentium elapse, ultro ignibus se iniecit et periit."

112. On Caesarius's version and how it conveys widely held "social and monastic attitudes," see Brian Patrick McGuire, "Written Sources and Cistercian Inspiration in Caesarius of Heisterbach," *Analecta Cisterciensia* 35 (1979): 274–76.

113. Caesarius of Heisterbach, *Dialogus miraculorum*, ed. Nikolas Nösges and Horst Schneider (Turnhout: Brepols, 2009), 5.19; *The Dialogue on Miracles*, trans. H. Von E. Scott and C. C. Swinton Bland (London: George Routledge and Sons, 1929), 1:342: "Qui cum fortiter arderent, multis videntibus et audientibus, Arnoldus semiustis discipulorum capitibus manum imponens, ait: 'Constantes estote in fide vestra, quia hodie eritis cum Laurentio.'; cum tamen nimis discordarent a fide Laurentii." An attempt to forestall possible comparisons of heretics' sufferings in fire to Laurence can also be found in the twelfth-century *Libellus adversus errores Alberonis sacerdotis merkensis*, in

E. Martene and U. Durand, eds., *Veterum scriptorium et monumentorum historicorum dogmaticorum moralium amplissima collectio*, vol. 9 (Paris, 1733; repr. New York: Burt Franklin, 1968), 1266. Hereafter cited as *Libellus adversus*. There is no modern critical edition.

114. See *De S. Laurentio archidiacono ac martyre*, AA. SS. Aug. II (1735), 485–532.

115. Caesarius, *Dialogus miraculorum*, 5.19: "Cum esset inter eos virgo quaedam speciosa, sed haeretica, et quorundam compassione ab igne subtracta, promittentium, quia vel eam viro traderent, vel si hoc magis placeret, in monasterio virginum locarent, cum verbo tenus consensisset, iam exstinctis haereticis, tenentibus se dixit: Dicite mihi, ubi iacet seductor ille? Cumque ei demonstrassent magistrum Arnoldum, ex manibus illorum elapsa, facie veste tecta, super exstincti corpus ruit, et cum illo in infernum perpetuo arsura descendit."

116. Friedland, *Seeing Justice Done*, 121.

117. P. Lemercier, "Une curiosité judiciaire au moyen âge: La grace par marriage subséquent," *Revue d'histoire du droit* 33 (1955): 464.

118. Lemercier, "Une curiosité judiciaire," 466.

119. Some later descriptions of this custom focus on the physical beauty of the person whom the proposer attempts to save. For example, in 1429 a crowd near Paris watched a group of looters be decapitated one by one, until the executioner removed the clothing of the eleventh criminal, "a very good looking young man around twenty-three years of age," at which point a young woman asked for him in marriage. See Lemercier, "Une curiosité judiciaire," 467.

120. Esther Cohen, *Crossroads of Justice*, 194–95. Lemercier sees proposals of marriage as the kind of happy occasion that provided an opportunity for higher authorities to exercise and emphasize their power to pardon; see "Une curiosité judiciaire," 474.

121. Innocent III, Decretal X, 4.1.20 (p. 667). For its context in contemporary efforts to reform prostitutes, see James A. Brundage, *Law, Sex, and Christian Society in Medieval Europe* (Chicago: University of Chicago Press, 1987), 395–96. This decretal builds on the observations of Alexander III; see Brundage, "Prostitution in the Medieval Canon Law," *Signs* 4 (1976): 843. For its logical relationship to the custom of pardon through marriage, see Lemercier, "Une curiosité judiciaire," 469. For its contrast in tone to Gratian, see Brundage, *Law, Sex, and Christian Society*, 248–49.

122. Innocent III, Decretal X, 4.1.20 (p. 667): "Inter opera caritatis . . . non minimum est, errantem ab erroris sui semita revocare."

123. Brundage, "Prostitution in the Medieval Canon Law," 842. An order of ex-prostitutes, the Order of Mary Magdalene, was established by Gregory IX in 1227, and similar convents were established by Louis IX of France.

124. Ezek. 18:23: "Is it my will that a sinner should die, saith the Lord God, and not that he should be converted from his ways, and live?" My thanks to Andrew Lynch who suggested this comparison.

125. Hildegard of Bingen, "Letter 15" and "Letter 15r" (pp. 32–47); Joseph L. Baird and Radd K. Ehrman, trans., *The Letters of Hildegard of Bingen* (Oxford: Oxford University Press, 1994), 1:53–65. On Philip's involvement, see Brunn, *Des contestataires aux "Cathares,"* 206.

126. On this sermon, see Sabina Flanagan, *Hildegard of Bingen: A Visionary Life*, 2nd ed. (London: Routledge, 1998), 167–68.

127. On "Letter 169r," CCCM 91A (pp. 378–82), see Kathryn Kerby-Fulton, "Prophet and Reformer: 'Smoke in the Vineyard,'" in *Voice of Living Light: Hildegard of Bingen and Her World*, ed. Barbara Newman (Berkeley: University of California Press, 1998), 74–76.

128. Hildegard, "Letter 15r" (p. 37; trans. 1:56): "Oculos non habetis, cum opera uestra in igne Spiritus Sancti hominibus non lucent et cum bona exempla eis non ruminatis."

129. Hildegard, "Letter 15r" (p. 37; trans. 1:57): "Per doctrinam quoque Scripturam, que de igne Spiritus Sancti composite sunt, anguli fortitudinis Ecclesie esse deberetis."

130. Hildegard, "Letter 15r" (pp. 40–41 trans. 1:59): "Nam diabolus per aerios spiritus hec operatur . . . Ipse enim homines istos hoc modo infundit, quod castitatem eis non aufert et quod eos castos esse permittit, cum castitatem habere uoluerint."

131. Hildegard, "Letter 15r" (p. 42; trans. 1:59): "Sed *qui sum*, dico: Sic iniquitas que iniquitatem purgabit, super uos ducetur."

132. Most occurrences of this proverb suggest the replacement of one equivalent thing or emotion with the other, not a transformative expulsion of both. See Aristotle, *Politics*, 5.11 (1314a4) (trans. p. 220); Jerome, "Letter 125," 14.1 (p. 132); Erasmus, *Adages*, 1.2.4 (trans. 31:148–49).

133. Gregory of Nazianzus, "Excerptum 35," ed. P.I. Fransen, B. Coppieters 'T Wallant, and R. Demeulenaere, CCCM 193B (Turnhout: Brepols, 2007), 74: "Hic ad imaginem suam, quam prius ipse condiderat, uenit et carnem suscepit propter carnem et animae rationabili propter animam admiscetur, similia similibus purificans et expurgans."

134. On Hildegard and Sigewize, see Flanagan, *Hildegard*, 160–64. In the vita the Sigewize episode occurs in 3.20–23; see *Vita sanctae Hildegardis*, ed. Monica Klaes, CCCM 126 (Turnhout: Brepols, 1993), 55–66.

135. Hildegard, "Letter 68," in *Vita sanctae Hildegardis*, 3.21 (pp. 58–59; trans. 1:147–48).

136. Hildegard, "Letter 68r," *Vita sanctae Hildegardis*, 3.21 (pp. 60–62; trans. 1:148–50).

137. Hildegard, "Letter 69," *Vita sanctae Hildegardis*, 3.21 (pp. 62–63; trans. 1:151–52).

138. *Vita sanctae Hildegardis*, 3.22 (p. 64); Peter Dronke, *Women Writers of the Middle Ages: A Critical Study of Texts from Perpetua (203) to Marguerite Porete (1310)* (Cambridge: Cambridge University Press, 1984), 238.

139. *Vita sanctae Hildegardis*, 3.22 (p. 64); Dronke, *Women Writers*, 238. "Interim, per dei potentiam coactus, inmundus spiritus multa de salute baptismi, de sacramento corporis Christi, de periculo excommunicatorum, de perditione Catharorum et his similium, ad confusionem sui . . . protulit."

140. Barbara Newman, "'Sibyl of the Rhine:' Hildegard's Life and Times," in Newman, *Voice of Living Light*, 23.

141. A point made by Barbara Newman, who argues that this occurrence of a female "demon preacher" is the first medieval example of its kind, in "Possessed by the Spirit: Devout Women, Demoniacs, and the Apostolic Life in the Thirteenth Century," *Speculum* 73 (1998): 753–55.

142. Emecho, *Vita Eckeberti*, 452: "Demon non sua, sed Domini voluntate ductus Kataros quosdam numero circiter quadraginta Magoncie habitants pro-

didit, et ubi habitarent et ubi mortuos suos sepelissent, occulte edixit." On this episode in the context of the life of Elisabeth and her brother, see Clark, *Elisabeth of Schönau*, 24.

143. Emecho, *Vita Eckeberti*, 453: "Manifestati itaque et convicti per ipsum et deprehensi in erroribus suis, qui erant Magoncie, eiecti sunt de civitate universi, uno excepto qui heresiarcha inter eos fuerat et magister annis pluribus, qui errorem suum detestatus ad fidem catholicam rediit, Deo gracias agens de anime sue a morte liberacione."

144. The timing of the spirit's flight, as the priest recited Genesis 1:2, fulfills one of Hildegard's predictions regarding the exorcism ritual required to defeat the demon, that "the Spirit of God, which at the beginning 'moved over the waters' (Gen. 1:2) and 'breathed into his face the breath of life' (Gen. 2:7) may blow away the unclean spirit." See "Letter 68r," *Vita sanctae Hildegardis*, 3.21 (61; 1:149).

145. *Vita sanctae Hildegardis*, 3.22 (p. 65); Dronke, *Women Writers*, 239. "Mox in uera uisione uidi et audiui quod vis altissimi . . . dixit: 'Vade, Sathanas, de tabernaculo corporis mulieris huius, et da in eo locum spiritui sancto! Tunc inmundus spiritus per uerecunda loca femine cum egestione horribiliter egressus est."

146. Word of this feat traveled widely, reaching Arnold, the archbishop of Trier; see Hildegard, "Letter 27" (pp. 76–77).

147. Bernard, for example, suffused his exegesis with concerns regarding the extension of the self; see Denis Farkasfalvy, "The Use of Paul by Saint Bernard as Illustrated by Saint Bernard's Interpretation of Philippians 3:13," in *Bernardus Magister: Papers Presented at the Nonacentenary Celebration of the Birth of Saint Bernard of Clairvaux*, ed. John R. Sommerfeldt (Spencer, MA: Cistercian Publications, 1992), 166. On the fashioning of the self in the context of group and role identity in the twelfth century, see Caroline Walker Bynum, "Did the Twelfth Century Discover the Individual?," in *Jesus as Mother: Studies in the Spirituality of the High Middle Ages* (Berkeley: University of California Press, 1984), 87–90.

5. Like Rejoices in Like

1. Augustine, *De doctrina Christiana*, 14.13.30 (p. 25): "Vel a contrariis vel a similibus medicinae christianae apparet instructio." Gregory the Great offered a similar comparison also suffused with medical imagery in *Moralia in Iob*, 24.2: "Mos medicinae est ut aliquando similia similibus, aliquando contraria contrariis curet."

2. Brunn, *Des contestataires aux "Cathares,"* 365. For its relative neglect in histories of heresy, see 372.

3. A twelfth-century manuscript version is among the manuscripts at the University of Düsseldorf, Ms. B 49 (146va–152rb). The manuscript is a Third Party Property (permanent loan by the City of Düsseldorf to the Universitäts-und Landesbibliothek Düsseldorf). The catalogue states that the manuscript originating at the abbey is very likely but not certain. Irmgard Siebert, ed., *Universitäts-und Landesbibliothek Düsseldorf, Katalogue der Handschriftenateilung*, vol. 1, 1 (Wiesbaden: Otto Harrassowitz, 2005), 175.

4. Brunn, *Des contestataires aux "Cathares,"* 378. The document can be dated by internal references to the Alexandrine Schism. For another argument regarding the

method of dating (that essentially arrives at the same conclusion), see Albert Hauck, *Kirchengeschichte Deutschlands* (Leipzig, 1887–1906), 4:860.

5. The tone of the document is so remarkable that scholars who believed in the existence of a continent-spanning Cathar sect still regarded Albero as a reformer rather than a Cathar; see Jeffrey Burton Russell, *Dissent and Reform in the Early Middle Ages* (Berkeley: University of California Press, 1965), 87.

6. *Libellus adversus*, 1, 1253A–C.

7. *Libellus adversus*, 16, 1264E.

8. *Libellus adversus*, 1, 1253C.

9. For the knowledge of the living, see *Libellus adversus*, 8, 1259E–1260A. For the dead, see 14, 1263E.

10. Düsseldorf Ms. B 49 (148va); *Libellus adversus*, 6, 1259A. I have followed the reading in the manuscript: "Sed quia plerique dum vicia fugiunt, contraria incident. Nam in vicium culpe ducit fuga, si caret arte. Perscrutandum est quomodo verum sit quod dicimus." Horace, *Ars Poetica*, ed. C. O. Brink (Cambridge: Cambridge University Press, 1971), 31: "in vitium ducit culpae fuga, si caret arte." The direct source for this passage is likely Hildebert of Lavardin, *Moralis philosophia de honesto et utili*, 8, PL 171:1012–13: "HORATIUS: In vitium culpae ducit fuga, si caret arte, Dum stulti vitant vitia, in contraria currunt." The printed edition substitutes "culpa" for "fuga." I have translated according to Hildebert and the Ms.

11. *Libellus adversus*, 20, 1265E: "Quia scriptum est similia similibus gaudere, sicut intus male inflammatus fuit, sic foris flammas petit, per ignem examinari deposcens, ut hoc visibili argumento veritas assertionis suae omnibus innotesceret, si per ignem sine incendio pertransiret, tamquam si elementum per quodcumque maleficium vim suam omitteret." For the origin of the phrase, see the discussion below.

12. See Latin text in note 11.

13. The author cites Matt. 4:7 and makes a comparison with the martyrdom of St. Laurence (see discussion below).

14. For the general clerical tendency toward the diminution of the ordeal, see Bartlett, *Trial by Fire and Water*, 90–102. For the ordeal as something between sacrament and miracle, see 88.

15. *Decretum*, II, C. 2, q. 5, c. 7, ed. E. Friedberg, *Corpus iuris canonici* (Leipzig, 1879–82; repr. Union, NJ: Lawbook Exchange, 2000), 1:456–57. For the history of this letter and its unaltered form, see Bartlett, *Trial by Fire and Water*, 50n48.

16. *Libellus adversus*, 20, 1266A–B: "Laurentius flammas non petit, sed admotus patienter sustinuit."

17. *Libellus adversus*, 21, 1266B–C: "Illud denique quomodo ferendum est, quod deficientibus scripturis ad revelationes venit, tamquam per visiones et somnia instructus sit, vel angelos de coelo novum evangelium ei locutus sit. . . . Non prophetica, sed fantastica esse visio, vel magis phrenetica illusio, ex ore suo judicatur, qui semper daemones, raro bonos angelos sibi apparere confitetur."

18. *Libellus adversus*, 22, 1267B: "Fides tua non solum nova, sed solitaria est: ideoque fides catholica non est. Si Catholicus esses, id est universalis, in fide communis, in vita singularis fieri studeres. Vox tua ab universali harmonia dissonant, ideoque in tanta fidei nostrae consonantia vox solius, vox nullius est."

19. *Libellus adversus*, 22, 1267D: "Qui enim non est Christi, est antichristi."

20. *Libellus adversus*, 24, 1268B: "Pertimescant ipsi, qui sub officio sanctitatis operarii sunt iniquitatis, sub figura lucis principes tenebrarum, sub stipendio Chisti satellites antichristi . . ."

21. Jeffrey Burton Russell found this about-face "an admission unusual for the time" (*Dissent and Reform*, 89). For similar sentiments about the overall results of clerical corruption (although more contained in their implications), see *Une somme anticathare: Le Liber contra manicheos de Durand de Huesca*, Prologus, ed. Christine Thouzellier (Leuven: Spicilegium sacrum Lovaniense Administration, 1964), 76, 78. For criticism of Thouzellier's characterization of the work and its author, see Biget, *Hérésie et inquisition dans le Midi de la France*, 49.

22. *Libellus adversus*, 24, 1268C: "Zelatores virtutis haereticos se fecerunt, dum sacramentis sanctitatem et contractantium perversitatem compararent, reputantes tam opposita in eodem simul non debere esse nec posse."

23. In this sense the treatise is a notable departure from what Bruschi and Biller describe as the usual "model for describing and pigeonholing a 'heresy' with its name, a terse account of origin and the crisp formulation of one wrong doctrine or practice" ("Texts and the Repression of Heresy," 4).

24. For a similar attempt at demonization using the phrase in the *Chronica* of Salimbene de Adam, see Martha Bayless, *Sin and Filth in Medieval Culture: the Devil in the Latrine* (New York: Routledge, 2012), 2.

25. This saying or adage was widely quoted in the twelfth century. For example, *Liber de spiritu et anima*, 14, PL 40:789; Hugh of St. Victor: *Sententiae de diuinitate*, pt. 2, ed. A. M. Piazzoni, in *Studi Medievali* 23 (1982): 945; Alexander Neckam, *De naturis rerum*, 2.4, ed. Thomas Wright (London: Longman, 1863). I will argue below that some of these occurrences are directly linked.

26. "Every beast loveth its like: so also every man him that is nearest to himself."

27. Erasmus, *Adages*, 1.2.21 (31:167–68). Aristotle, *Ethica Nicomachea*, 8.1.2 (1155b7) and 9.3.3 (1165b17).

28. René-Antoine Gauthier believes that a translation of books 2 and 3 of the *Ethica* was completed in the late twelfth century (*Ethica vetus*), and that an entire translation (*Ethica nova*) did not exist until around 1200. René-Antoine Gauthier, *Ethica Nicomachea, Praefatio* (Leiden: E. J. Brill, 1974), 26, fasc. 1, xv–xvi.

29. For the argument that Bernardo translated the entire *Ethica*, see F. Bossier, "L'élaboration du vocabulaire philosophique chez Burgundio de Pise," in *Aux origins du lexique philosophique européen: L'influence de la Latinitas*, ed. J. Hamesse (Louvain-la-Neuve: Brepols, 1997), 81–116.

30. The critical edition is Caterina Tarlazzi, "L'*Epistola de anima* di Isacco di Stella: studio della tradizione ed edizione del testo," *Medioevo* 36 (2011): 167–278. The text can also be found in PL 194:1875–90. I cite here the edition by Tarlazzi as "Isaac, *Epistola*."

31. For an overview on the current state of research into Isaac's life and what of its details scholars can learn from his works, see Elias Dietz, "When Exile Is Home: The Biography of Isaac of Stella," *Cistercian Studies Quarterly* 41 (2006): 141–65. For an exposition of Isaac's theology, his life, and his context, see Bernard McGinn, *The Golden Chain: A Study in the Theological Anthropology of Isaac of Stella* (Washington, DC: Cistercian Publications, 1972).

32. For a discussion of Cistercian anthropologies and translations of the *Epistola de anima* and the *Liber de spiritu et anima*, see Bernard McGinn, *Three Treatises on Man: A Cistercian Anthropology* (Kalamazoo, MI: Cistercian Publications, 1977).

33. For an explanation of the date and a brief overview of dissenting opinions, see Isaac, *Epistola*, 174–75.

34. *Liber de spiritu et anima*, 14, 789–90. Roughly drawn from Isaac, *Epistola*, 265–67, ll. 245–91.

35. Isaac, *Epistola*, 265–66, ll. 245–52: "Sunt tamen utriusque quedam similia, corporis uidelicet supremum et spiritus infimum, in quibus sine naturarum confusion personali tamen unione facile necti possunt. Similia enim gaudent similibus et facile coherent annexione que non resiliunt dissimilitudine. Itaque anima, que uere spiritus est et non corpus, et caro que uere corpus est et non spiritus, facile et conuenienter in suis extremitatibus uniuntur, idest in phantastico anime, quod fere corpus est, et sensualitate carnis, que fere spiritus est." For the origin of the principle of mediation or concatenation that lies at the heart of the argument here, see Plato, *Timaeus*, 31 B.C., trans. Francis M. Cornford (New York: Bobbs–Merrill, 1959), 21.

36. Isaac, *Epistola*, 267, ll. 287–91: "Conuenientisima autem media sunt anime et carnis, iuxta quod dictum est et multiplicius assignari posset, sensualitas carnis, que maxime ignis est, et phantasticum spiritus, quod igneus uigor dicitur. 'Igneus est,' ait quidam de animabut loquens, 'illis uigor et celestis origo.'" Virgil, *Aeneid*, 6.730, ed. Frank Fletcher (Oxford: Clarendon Press, 1941), 21. For discussion of this passage in the context of an *involucrum*, see McGinn, *Golden Chain*, 165.

37. Fire as the meeting-point between the corporeal and the spiritual natures of humanity also appears in Hugh of St. Victor's "De unione corporis et animae" (PL 177:285–89), which is an important influence on Isaac's account of cognition and the mediation between the human body and the human soul. Portions of this work were also included in the *Liber de spiritu et anima*.

38. The poet is Homer, likely drawn here from Macrobius, *In somnium Scipionis*, 1.14.15, ed. Mireille Armisen–Marchetti, *Commentaire au Songe de Scipion* (Paris: Les belles lettres, 2011), 1:80.. Isaac, *Epistola*, 271–72, ll. 420–23; *Letter on the Soul*, 171: "Ipsi quoque supremum corpus, idest ignis, quadam similitudine iungitur, et igni aer, aeri aqua, aque terra. Hac igitur quasi aurea cathena poete uel ima dependent a summis uel erecta scala prophete ascenditur ad summa de imis." Note the reference to Jacob's ladder, a more central reference for Hugh of St. Victor than the golden chain. McGinn sees the image of the golden chain as "the symbolic key to [Isaac's] theology of man" (*Golden Chain*, 62); for a history of the golden chain, see 63–102.

39. Isaac, *Epistola*, 264, l. 195. I have translated "rogum caritatis," literally "funeral pyre," as "the consuming pyre of charity." The progression is *sensus, imaginatio, ratio, intellectus, intelligentia*. For the background of this scheme, see McGinn, *Golden Chain*, 214–19. The mirroring only works if one adds the empyrean to the standard elements.

40. Hugh, "De naturis," 571A.

41. The *Sententiae de diuinitate* is a complex source. Generally treated by scholars as a work by Hugh, it is in fact a *reportatio*, likely made by Laurence of Westminster, of Hugh's lectures, which underlay the later composition of the *De sacramentis christiane fidei*. Laurence addressed the report to Maurice of Rievaulx. As Laurence com-

piled his report, Hugh personally edited it to such an extent that Laurence regarded himself as more its craftsman than its author ("Non enim me huius operis auctorem, sed quodammodo artificem profiteer"). The correspondence between the *Sententiae* and the *De sacramentis* leads experts to take Laurence at his word. For the letter of Laurence, detailing the composition of the work and the current critical edition, see Hugh, *Sententiae de diuinitate*. On the identity of Laurence and Maurice, see F. E. Croydon, "Abbot Laurence of Westminster and Hugh of St. Victor," *Medieval and Renaissance Studies* 2 (1950): 169–71. For a summary of its relationship to the *De sacramentis*, see Paul Rorem, *Hugh of St. Victor* (Oxford: Oxford University Press, 2009), 62. See also Beryl Smalley, *The Study of the Bible in the Middle Ages* (Oxford: Blackwell, 1983), 202.

42. McGinn, *Golden Chain*, 8–10; McGinn, *Three Treatises*, 47. McGinn also notes Isaac's familiarity with the "School of Chartres," Abelard and Gilbert of Poitiers. He concludes, however, that all one can say with certainty is that Isaac "studied in France in the late 1120s and 1130s."

43. The critical edition of the *Epistola de anima* notes some of these instances. For examples of others, see Caterina Tarlazzi, "Alan of Lille and the *Periesichen Augustini*," *Bulletin de Philosophie Médiévale* 51 (2009): 48–49. On the similarities between Cistercian and Victorine speculation on the soul, see McGinn, *Three Treatises*, 21–22.

44. Hugh, *Sententiae de diuinitate*, 945: "Deus uult omne bonum; omne bonum placet Deo, quia talis nature est Deus quod omne bonum concordat eius uoluntari, que summe bona est, quia similis similibus gaudent et sicut omne bonum nature Dei concordat, ita omne malum eidem nature discordat, quia dissimulatio odiosa atque contraria."

45. Hugh, *Sententiae de diuinitate*, 945: "Et sicut aliud est 'uolo ignem' et 'uolo esse ignem,' quia 'uolo ignem' nihil aliud est quam 'diligo ignem' uel 'uolo calefieri.' Sed 'uolo esse ignem' est 'uolo quod ignis sit' in domo unde in aliis calor perueniat, licet tamen ego ignem non curem. Sicut hec, inquam, diuersa sunt, sic aliud est 'Deus uult bonum' et 'Deus uultesse bonum,' 'Deus non uult malum' et 'Deus non uult esse malum.'" See also Anselm of Canterbury, *De casu Diaboli*, 3, in *S. Anselmi Cantuariensis archiepiscopi opera omnia*, ed. Francis Schmitt (Edinburgh: Thomas Nelson and Sons, 1946), 1:236–40.

46. Hugh, *Sententiae de diuinitate*, 945: "Itaque dicimus quod Deus omne bonum uult et nullum malum uult: malum enim nihil aliud est nisi defectus boni."

47. Hugh, *Sententiae de diuinitate*, 945: "Si in creaturis alicuius boni decet defectus, per hoc enim uniuersitas speciosior eminet quod in aliqua parte alicuius boni defectus apparet." See *De sacramentis christiane fidei*, 1.4.6; *In Salomonis Ecclesiasten homiliae*, 11, PL 175:183B. For similar arguments of this kind, see Augustine, *De ciuitate Dei*, 11.18 (p. 337); Aquinas, *Summa Theologica*, Suppl. 3ae.94.1, co. (ed. Rubeis and Billuart, p. 5:746).

48. Hugh, *Sententiae de diuinitate*, 946: "Vult esse malum quia eius euentus uniuersitati utilis est."

49. *Maleficium* (plural *maleficia*), translated as "sorcery," "magic," or "witchcraft," refers to a specifically harmful type of magic enabled through human interaction with demons. It literally means "evil-doing." On demonic magic and causation, see Richard Kieckhefer, "The Specific Rationality of Medieval Magic," *American Historical Review* 99 (1994): 817–18.

50. For this story in context of the larger history of the pact with the Devil, see Jeffrey Burton Russell, *Lucifer*, 82–83.

51. Caesarius links the two stories in the beginning of his version of the 1163 Cologne burnings (*Dialogus miraculorum*, 5.19, ed. Schneider, 3:1014). For the composition date, see Brian Patrick McGuire, "Friends and Tales in the Cloister: Oral Sources in Caesarius of Heisterbach's *Dialogus Miraculorum*," *Analecta Cisterciensia* 36 (1981): 199.

52. Caesarius, *Dialogus miraculorum*, 5.18 (ed. Schneider, 3:1010): "Rogo te ut investiges a diabolo per artem tuam, qui sint, unde veniant, vel qua virtute tanta ac tam stupenda operentur miracula."

53. Caesarius, *Dialogus miraculorum*: 5.18 (ed. Schneider, 3:1012): "Respondit diabolus: 'Mei sunt, et a me missi, et quae in ore illorum posui, illa praedicant.' Respondit clericus: 'Quid est quod laedi non possunt, nec in aquis mergi, neque igne comburi?' Respondit iterum daemon: 'Cyrographa mea, in quibus hominia mihi ab eis facta, sunt conscripta, sub ascellis suis inter pellem et carnem consuta conservant, quorum beneficio talia operantur, nec ab aliquo laedi poterunt.' Tunc clericus: 'Quid si ab eis tollerentur?' Respondit diabolus: 'Tunc infirmi essent sicut ceteri homines.'"

54. Moshe Lazar, "Theophilus: Servant of Two Masters. The Pre-Faustian Theme of Despair and Revolt," *Modern Language Notes* 87 (1972): 31–50. See also Alan Boureau, *Satan the Heretic: The Birth of Demonology in the Medieval West*, trans. Teresa Lavender Fagan (Chicago: University of Chicago Press, 2006), 69–74.

55. Jeffrey Burton Russell, *Witchcraft in the Middle Ages* (Ithaca, NY: Cornell University Press, 1972), 19. For the legends surrounding Gerbert, see R. Allen, "Gerbert, Pope Silvester II," *English Historical Review* 7 (1892): 663–68; For the story regarding Gerbert as a response to learning and Christian engagement with Islamic scholarship, see Richard Kieckhefer, *Magic in the Middle Ages* (Cambridge: Cambridge University Press, 1989; repr. Canto Classics, 2000), 143–44.

56. A chirograph would most often be split into two or three parts. For more information regarding the origin of this type of contract and surviving exemplars, see Kathryn A. Lowe, "Lay Literacy in Anglo-Saxon England and the Development of the Chirograph," in *Anglo-Saxon Manuscripts and Their Heritage*, ed. Phillip Pulsiano and Elaine M. Treharne (Brookfield, VT: Ashgate, 1998), 161–204; M. T. Clanchy, *From Memory to Written Record: England 1066–1307* (Oxford: Blackwell, 1993), 87–88.

57. On miracle and demonic magic (often worked by/through heretics) as the "two extremes" of dealing with the supernatural, see Benedicta Ward, *Miracles and the Medieval Mind: Theory, Record and Event 1000–1215* (London: Scolar Press, 1982), 12–13.

58. Brian Stock, *Myth and Science in the Twelfth Century: A Study of Bernard Silvester* (Princeton, NJ: Princeton University Press, 1972), 48–54; De Lubac, *Exégèse médiévale*, 4:189–90.

59. Rita Copeland and Stephen Melville, "Allegory and Allegoresis, Rhetoric and Hermeneutics," *Exemplaria* 3 (1991): 170–71.

60. Caesaris, *Dialogus miraculorum*, 5.18 (ed. Schneider, 3:1014): "Volo videre si aliqua circa vos habeatis maleficia."

61. The word used at this point to refer to these chirographs/contracts is *chartulas*.

62. Caesarius, *Dialogus miraculorum*, 5.18 (ed. Schneider, 3:1014): "Tunc universi furentes, diaboli ministros, cum diabolo in ignibus aeternis cruciandos, in ignem praeparatum proiecerunt."

63. Paul de Man, *Blindness and Insight: Essays in the Rhetoric of Contemporary Criticism*, 2nd ed. (Minneapolis: University of Minnesota Press, 1983), 31. De Man originally referred to "literary form" as "the result of the dialectic interplay between the prefigurative structure of the foreknowledge and the intent at totality of the interpretive process." I suggest that the heretic as a type, as presented by Caesarius, is essentially a literary form.

64. I situate the following questions regarding signification and interpretation within the framework of a rhetorical battle following Augustine's suggestion that the manipulation of words rhetorically can commend "both truth and falsehood." *De doctrina Christiana*, 4.2.3 (p. 196): "Nam cum per artem rhetoricam et vera suadeantur et falsa, quis audeat dicere adversus mendacium in defensoribus suis inermem debere consistere veritatem."

65. Augustine, *De doctrina Christiana*, 1.2 (p. 12): "Omnis doctrina vel rerum est vel signorum, sed res per signa discuntur."

66. Augustine, *De doctrina Christiana*, 2.1.1 (p. 56): "Signum est enim res praeter speciem quam ingerit sensibus aliud aliquid ex se faciens in cogitationem venire."

67. Augustine, *De doctrina Christiana*, 2.2.3 (p. 56).

68. Augustine, *De doctrina Christiana*, 2.10.15 (p. 70): "Duabus autem causis non intelleguntur quae scripta sunt, si aut ignotis aut ambiguis signis obteguntur."

69. Augustine, *De doctrina Christiana*, 1.22.20 (pp. 28, 30).

70. In this fashion, medieval authors could describe the sensible world as a text, written by the finger of God. See Hugh of St. Victor, *De tribus diebus*, ed. Dominic Poirel, CCCM 177 (Turnhout: Brepols, 2002), 9: "Vniuersus enim mundus iste sensilis quasi quidam liber est scriptus digito Dei." Alexander Neckham, *De naturis rerum*, 2. For more references, see Henri de Lubac, *Medieval Exegesis: The Four Senses of Scripture*, trans. Mark Sebanc (Grand Rapids, MI: Eerdmans, 1998), 1:78n51.

71. Augustine, *De doctrina Christiana*, 1.33.36 (p. 44).

72. Augustine, *De doctrina Christiana*, 2.7.10 (p. 64): "Necesse est ergo, ut primo se quisque in scripturis inveniat amore huius saeculi, hoc est temporalium rerum, implicatum, longe seiunctum esse a tanto amore dei et tanto amore proximi quantum scriptura ipsa praescribit."

73. Augustine, *De doctrina Christiana*, 2.24.37 (p. 100): "Et ideo diversis diverse proveniunt secundum cogitationes et praesumptiones suas. Illi enim spiritus qui decipere volunt talia procurant cuique qualibus eum irretitum per suspiciones et consensiones eius vident."

74. Augustine, *De doctrina Christiana*, 2.23.36 (p. 98).

75. Augustine, *De doctrina Christiana*, 2.20.30 (p. 90): "Superstitiosum est quidquid institutum est ab hominibus ad facienda et colenda idola pertinens vel ad colendam sicut deum creaturam partemve ullam creaturae vel ad consultationes et pacta quaedam significationum cum daemonibus placita atque foederata, qualia sunt molimina magicarum artium, quae quidem commemorare potius quam docere assolent poetae."

76. On the Augustinian pact and its reception in canon law collections, see Claire Fanger, *Rewriting Magic: An Exegesis of the Visionary Autobiography of a Fourteenth-Century French Monk* (University Park: Pennsylvania State University Press, 2012), 113–14.

77. Innocent III applied the concept to heresy as a crime against the Divine Majesty in the bull *Vergentis in senium* (1199); see Ullmann, "Significance of Innocent III's Decretal 'Vergentis,'" 1:729–41. In the development of the late medieval or early modern idea of witchcraft, this notion became synonymous with a pact of apostasy and the practice of harmful sorcery; see Kieckhefer, *Magic in the Middle Ages*, 197; Thomas, *Religion and the Decline of Magic*, 455–56.

78. Augustine, *De doctrina Christiana*, 2.23.35 (p. 96): "Hinc enim fiet ut occulto quodam iudicio divino cupidi malarum rerum homines tradantur illudendi et decipiendi pro meritis voluntatum suarum, illudentibus eos atque decipientibus praevaricatoribus angelis, quibus ista mundi pars infima secundum pulcherrimum ordinem rerum divinae providentiae lege subiecta est."

79. Augustine, *De doctrina Christiana*, 1.40.44 (p. 52).

80. In fact, this decisive divine assistance is strengthened by the very acknowledgment of misplaced love: Augustine, *De doctrina Christiana*, 2.7.10 (p. 64).

81. Augustine, *De doctrina Christiana*, 3.8.12 (p. 144): "Quam ob rem christiana libertas eos quos invenit sub signis utilibus tamquam prope inventos, interpretatis signis quibus subditi erant, elevatos ad eas res quarum illa signa sunt liberavit. Ex his factae sunt ecclesiae sanctorum Israhelitarum. Quos autem invenit sub signis inutilibus, non solum servilem operationem sub talibus signis sed etiam ipsa signa frustravit removitque omnia, ut a corruptione multitudinis simulatorum deorum, quam saepe ac proprie scriptura fornicationem vocat, ad unius dei cultum gentes converterentur, nec sub ipsis iam signis utilibus serviturae, sed exercitaturae potius animum in eorum intellegentia spiritali."

82. On Augustine's ideas of similarity and knowledge, see Gerhart B. Ladner, *The Idea of Reform* (Cambridge, MA: Harvard University Press, 1959), 191–94.

83. Augustine, *Enarationes in Psalmos*, 144.17 (p. 2100): "Et sic transcurrunt ista saecula cedentibus succedentibusque mortalibus; scriptura Dei manere debuit, et quoddam chirographum Dei, quod omnes transeuntes legerent, et uiam promissionis eius tenerent."

84. For Augustine's probable definition, see Emily Steiner, *Documentary Culture and the Making of Medieval English Literature* (Cambridge: Cambridge University Press, 2003), 140. For an analysis of Augustine's "Chirographum Dei," see 123–39.

85. Augustine, *Enarationes in Psalmos*, 144.19 (p. 2102).

86. Augustine, *Enarationes in Psalmos*, 144.17 (p. 2100): "Ibi in chirographo meo lege omnia quae promisi." For the reference to eternal fire, see 144.24 (p. 2105).

87. Slavoj Žižek, *How to Read Lacan* (New York: W. W. Norton, 2006), 12.

88. Kruger, "Spectral Jew," 21.

6. Witches and Orgiastic Rituals

1. Ralph of Coggeshall, *Chronicon Anglicanum*, ed. Joseph Stevenson, Rolls Series 66 (London: H. M. Stationery Office, 1875; repr. Wiesbaden: Kraus, 1965), 117–28.

2. Peter the Cantor, *Summa quae dicitur Verbum Abbreviatum (textus conflatus)*, 1.76 (pp. 503–4). See also Grundmann, *Religious Movements in the Middle Ages*, 80; Moore, *War on Heresy*, 5.

3. Following the well-known concept that a reader can become lost in the material letter while missing its immaterial meaning as suggested in the tradition regarding 2 Corinthians 3:6.

4. The title given by A. C. Kors and Edward Peters in the 1973 edition of *Witchcraft in Europe 1100–1700* (Philadelphia: University of Pennsylvania Press, 1973) has left a large imprint on the secondary scholarship. The 2001 edition of this work changes the title to be more factually accurate: "The Heretics of Rheims (1176–80)" (78).

5. For example, Walter L. Wakefield and Austin P. Evans use it as a proof text in a section entitled "From Heresy to Witchcraft"; see their *Heresies of the High Middle Ages* (New York: Columbia University Press, 1991), 249–54.

6. David Knowles, C. N. L. Brooke, and Vera C. M. London, *The Heads of Religious Houses, Volume 1 England and Wales, 940–1216* (Cambridge: Cambridge University Press, 2001), 130.

7. David Corner, "Coggeshall, Ralph of (*fl.* 1207–1226)," *Oxford Dictionary of National Biography*, Oxford University Press, 2004, accessed March 9, 2017, http://www.oxforddnb.com/view/article/5816.

8. Antonia Gransden, *Historical Writing in England, c. 550–1307* (London: Routledge and Kegan Paul, 1974), 1:324–28.

9. In addition to the tales in his *Chronicon Anglicanum*, Ralph has been regarded as the most likely author of the Vision of Thurkill, the last of the great panoramic Latin-language visions of the world after death; see H. L. D. Ward, ed., "The Vision of Thurkill, Probably by Ralph of Coggeshall, Printed from a MS in the British Museum," *Journal of the British Archeological Association* 31 (1875): 420–59. For Ralph's reputation as a collector of visions, see Easting and Sharpe, *Peter of Cornwall's Book of Revelations*, 60–61.

10. Ralph, *Chronicon Anglicanum*, 117–28. There are numerous translations of the Rheims story into English; see Moore, *Birth of Popular Heresy*, 86–88; Kors and Peters, *Witchcraft in Europe*, 2nd ed., 78–81; Peters, *The Magician, the Witch, and the Law* (Philadelphia: University of Pennsylvania Press, 1978), 35–37. See also Wakefield and Evans, *Heresies of the High Middle Ages*.

11. A recent study of the possible order of composition for the *Chronicon Anglicanum* suggests the period 1201–05 and can be found in David A. Carpenter, "Abbot Ralph of Coggeshall's Account of the Last Years of King Richard and the First Years of King John," *English Historical Review* 113 (1998): 1210–30. The wonder stories may have been written much later in the second decade of the thirteenth century. This later date would correspond with Gervase of Tilbury's retirement from secular employment after 1222; see notes below.

12. Elizabeth Freeman, "Wonders, Prodigies and Marvels: Unusual Bodies and the Fear of Heresy in Ralph of Coggeshall's *Chronicon Anglicanum*," *Journal of Medieval History* 26 (2000): 128.

13. Freeman, "Wonders, Prodigies and Marvels," 143.

14. Christine M. Neufeld, "Hermeneutical Perversions: Ralph of Coggeshall's 'Witch of Rheims,'" *Philological Quarterly* 85 (2006): 1–2.

15. There is an edition of this text with an English facing-page translation: S. E. Banks and J. W. Binns, *Otia Imperialia: Recreation for an Emperor* (Oxford: Clarendon Press, 2002).

16. Ralph says that Gervase told him the Rheims story "when he was a canon." *Chronicon Anglicanum*, 122. Other evidence points to Gervase's possible entrance into the Premonstratensian Order; see Banks and Binns, *Otia*, xxxvii–xxxviii. For most of his life, Gervase was not in major orders that required celibacy, and he married a relative of the archbishop of Arles after the period of the Rheims story.

17. For background on Gervase, see S. E. Banks, "Tilbury, Gervase of," *Oxford Dictionary of National Biography*, ed. H. C. G. Matthew and Brian Harrison (Oxford: Oxford University Press, 2004), accessed April 21, 2016, http://www.oxforddnb.com /view/article/10572.

18. William had a long and storied career. He was elected as the bishop of Chartres in 1165, became the archbishop of Sens (1168–76), then the archbishop of Rheims (1176–1202), a cardinal priest (1179) and papal legate thereafter. Ralph stresses the familial relation between William and the kings of France, repeating that he was brother to Louis VII and uncle to Philip II. This relation was through the marriage of Louis VII to William's sister, Adela of Champagne. For William's life, see Ludwig Falkenstein, "Guillaume aux Blanches Mains, archevêque de Reims et légat du siège apostolique (1176–1202)," *Revue d'histoire de l'église de France* 91 (2005): 5–25. For his role in the publication of the details regarding the murder of Thomas Becket, see Anne J. Duggan, "Becket Is Dead! Long Live St Thomas," in *The Cult of St Thomas Becket in the Plantagenet World, c.1170–c.1220*, ed. Paul Webster and Marie-Pierre Gelin (Woodbridge, UK: Boydell Press, 2016), 25–26.

19. Ralph, *Chronicon Anglicanum*, 122: "Lubricae juventutis curiositate ductus, divertit ad eam."

20. The similarity to the pastourelle is noted by Peters in *Magician, the Witch, and the Law*, 37. Neufeld recognizes the potential of the vineyard location in "Hermeneutical Perversions," 19–20n6.

21. Kathleen M. Llewellyn, "At Play in the Fields and Playing the Field: The *débat amoureux* in the *Pastourelle* and the *Heptaméron*," *Parergon* 27 (2010): 105–6.

22. For example, Isa. 5:1–7; Ps. 79:9–16; Matt. 20:1–16, 21:28–43; Mark 12:1–12; Luke 20:9–19.

23. Augustine, *Enarrationes in Psalmos*, 66.1 (p. 857).

24. Augustine, *Enarrationes in Psalmos*, 80.14 (p. 1128). The reference is to Song of Sol. 2:15. See notes below and discussion in chapter 4.

25. I borrow the phrase "domain of effort" from William Reddy, *The Navigation of Feeling: A Framework for the History of Emotions* (Cambridge: Cambridge University Press, 2004), 57.

26. Bernard, "Sermon 63," 2.5 (2:164; trans. 3:165).

27. Bernard, "Sermon 65," 1.1 (2:172; trans. 3:179). Beverly Mayne Kienzle argues that this image is essential for understanding Cistercian efforts against heresy in the twelfth century; see her *Cistercians, Heresy and Crusade in Occitania, 1145–1229* (Woodbridge, UK: York University Press, 2001), 8–9 and 85–90.

28. For Bernard's exegesis of the verse in his sermons on the Song of Songs, see Bernard, "Sermons 63–66" (2:172–88). Also see the discussion in chapter 4. For another example of a contemporary references to heretics as "little foxes," see William of Newburgh, *Historia rerum anglicarum*, 2.13 (1:132).

29. Ralph, *Chronicon Anglicanum*, 122: "Cum ejus pulchritudinem diutius attendisset, hanc tandem de amore lascivo curialiter affatur."

30. Ralph, *Chronicon Anglicanum*, 122: "Numquam velit Deus, O bone adolescens, ut tua amica, sive alicujus umquam hominis existam, quia si virginitatem amisissem et caro mea semel corrupta esset, aeternae damnationi proculdubio absque omni remedio subjacerem." I have based the beginning of my translation of this passage on that of R. I. Moore, but I have altered the parts that reflect the maiden's possible heresy to more literally render the theological implications in her wording; see Moore, *Birth of Popular Heresy*, 86.

31. Kors and Peters comment that "the vow of virginity in itself, of course, was not at all heretical" (*Witchcraft in Europe*, 2nd ed., 78). Neufeld focuses on the young woman's seemingly impossible position, occluding somewhat the doctrinal content of her words ("Hermeneutical Perversions," 4–6). I do, however, grant that the maiden in this story is in an effective rather than theologically literal "damned if she does, damned if she doesn't" situation. Furthermore, she is indeed tasked with avoiding sexual encounters while simultaneously being required to uphold the rights of men to sexually abuse her. According to this theological double bind, the orthodox implication might be that she should insist on her ability to perform the penance this abuse would further demand of her.

32. Ralph knows of Henry's encounter around 1163 with heretics at Oxford, but does not mention their exile into the snow. I provide that detail from the account of William of Newburgh, *Historia rerum anglicarum*, 2.13 (1:134).

33. Ralph, *Chronicon Anglicanum*, 123. I have translated "illa malefici erroris magistra" as "this instructrix of wicked error." This translation cannot accurately reflect the possible meanings here, as "malefici" also implies demonic sorcery.

34. Ralph, *Chronicon Anglicanum*, 123: "Veris falsa commiscens, et veram fidei nostrae explanationem quodam pernicioso intellectu deludens." I have followed Peters's translation in his *Magician, the Witch, and the Law*, 35.

35. Ralph, *Chronicon Anglicanum*, 123: "Ita omnes auctoritates prolatas quadam sinistra interpretatione pervertebat ut satis patenter cunctis innotuerit spiritum totius erroris per os ejus fuisse locutum." It is noteworthy that in the Latin the spirit who speaks through her is male.

36. Following this logic, Neufeld perceptively argues that "the two women in this story effectively become one" ("Hermeneutical Perversions," 10).

37. Barbara Spackman, "*Inter musam et ursam moritur*: Folengo and the Gaping 'Other' Mouth," in *Refiguring Woman: Perspectives on Gender and the Italian Renaissance*, ed. Marilyn Migiel and Juliana Schiesari (Ithaca, NY: Cornell University Press, 1991), 22. In a modern employment of this topos, the beautiful priestess Melisandre in the television adaptation of *Game of Thrones* is revealed truly to be an impossibly old woman in disguise. "The Red Woman," *Game of Thrones*, HBO (April 24, 2016).

38. Carolyn Dinshaw, *Chaucer's Sexual Poetics* (Madison: University of Wisconsin Press, 1989), 9.

39. Dinshaw, *Chaucer's Sexual Poetics*, 24. On the linkage between pleasure and the type of cognition involved in spiritual interpretation, see Giacinta Spinosa, "Plaisir de la connaissance comme émotion intellectuelle chez Hugues de Saint-Victor," *Quaestio* 15 (2015): 373–82.

40. Ralph, *Chronicon Anglicanum*, 123: "Communi consilio decretum est flammis concremarentur."

41. Ralph, *Chronicon Anglicanum*, 123: "O insensati et judices injusti! Putatisne quod me ignibus vestris nunc concremabitis? Judicium vestrum non formido, et ignem praeparatum non perhorresco."

42. Ralph, *Chronicon Anglicanum*, 124: "Malignorum spiritum ministerio, ut credimus, subvecta, qui quondam Simonem Magnum in aere sustulerunt."

43. Ralph, *Chronicon Anglicanum*, 124: Ralph calls her "illa malefica." "Malefica" is the Latin word for witch, literally meaning a woman who does evil. Its use here, in the context of demonic sorcery, predates what many scholars see as the full maturation of the concept of witchcraft in Europe.

44. For the role of Simon Magus in Christian conceptions of magic, see Kieckhefer, *Magic in the Middle Ages*, 34 and 40.

45. On simony as a heresy, see Moore, *War on Heresy*, 71–92.

46. M. R. James, *The Apocryphal New Testament: Being the Apocryphal Gospels, Acts, Epistles, and Apocalypses, with Other Narratives and Fragments* (Oxford: Clarendon Press, 1975), 331–32.

47. This version of the story found its way into the *Golden Legend*. Jocobus de Voragine, *Legenda aurea*, 84, ed. Maggioni, 566–67.

48. Jeffrey Burton Russell, *Dissent and Order in the Middle Ages*, 4.

49. Ralph, *Chronicon Anglicanum*, 124: "Nec rationum persuasione, nec divitiarum sponsione, ab incepta obstatione revocari potuisset, igne consumpta est, non sine admiratione multorum, cum nulla suspira, nullos fletus, nullum planctum emitteret, sed omne conflagrantis incendii tormentum constanter et alacriter perferret, instar martyrum Christi, (sed disparili causa,) qui olim pro Christiana religione a paganis trucidabantur." For an analysis of this statement in the context of the "rhetoric of martyrdom" and women's bodies as objects of male interpretation, see Dyan Elliott, *Proving Woman: Female Spirituality and Inquisitorial Culture in the Later Middle Ages* (Princeton, NJ: Princeton University Press, 2004), 60.

50. Bernard, "Sermon 66," 13 (2:187).

51. Nancy Caciola, *Discerning Spirits: Divine and Demonic Possession in the Middle Ages* (Ithaca, NY: Cornell University Press, 2003), 125.

52. Bernard, *De gratia et libero arbitrio*, 13.45 (p. 198): "Utitur creatura rationali, sed malevola, quasi virga disciplinae, quam correpto filio, in ignem proiciet tamquam sarmentum inutile." Perhaps modeled on Prov. 3:12. On the wicked becoming tools of divine righteousness, see Augustine, *De gratia et libero arbitrio*, 21.42 PL 44: 907–9.

53. Some of these anxieties, termed the "clerical dilemma," as experienced by men outside holy orders, like Gervase for the majority of his career, are explored by John D. Cotts, *The Clerical Dilemma* (Washington, DC: Catholic University of America, 2009).

54. See, for example, Jo Ann McNamara, "The Herrenfrage: The Restructuring of the Gender System, 1050–1150," in *Medieval Masculinities: Regarding Men in the Middle Ages*, ed. Jo Ann McNamara, Thelma S. Fenster, and Clare A. Lees (Minneapolis: University of Minnesota Press, 1994), 19–23.

55. Ralph, *Chronicon Anglicanum*, 124: "Nuptias damnant, virginitatem praedicant in operimentum suae turpitudinis."

56. Ralph, *Chronicon Anglicanum*, 124: "Aiunt etiam alii qui de secretis eorum investigaverunt . . . ."

57. Ralph, *Chronicon Anglicanum*, 125: "Corpus a diabolo dicunt formari, animam vero a Deo creari et corporibus infundi; unde fit ut semper quaedam pertinax pugna inter corpus et animam geratur."

58. Ralph, *Chronicon Anglicanum*, 124: "Rusticani homines sunt, et ideo nec rationibus convicuntur, nec auctoritatibus corriguntur, nec persuasionibus flectuntur."

59. I have based this formulation on Butler, *Bodies That Matter*, 3.

60. I have borrowed this phrasing about the usefulness of evil from Hugh of St. Victor, "Sententiae de diuinitate," 945: "Si in creaturis alicuius boni decet defectus, per hoc enim uniuersitas speciosior eminet quod in aliqua parte alicuius boni defectus apparet." See discussion in chapter 5.

61. On what such claims could entail (i.e., not eating normally rather than total abstention from all food), see Caroline Walker Bynum, *Holy Feast and Holy Fast: The Religious Significance of Food to Religious Women* (Berkeley: University of California Press, 1987), 82–83.

62. The dates for her life are often given as c. 1150/1155–1211. For biographical details, see Renate Blumenfeld-Kosinski, "Holy Women in France: A Survey," in *Medieval Holy Women in the Christian Tradition c. 1100–c. 1500*, ed. Alastair Minnis and Rosalynn Voaden (Turnhout: Brepols, 2010), 242–44.

63. *Chronicon*, ed. Stevenson, 125, n. 1. A later hand adds: "jam plus quam xxx."

64. For a list of references, see AA. SS., November, vol. 2, pt. 1 (Brussels, 1894), 167–209. Alpais is one of the women discussed in Bynum, *Holy Feast and Holy Fast*, esp. 336, n77.

65. Freeman, "Wonders, Prodigies and Marvels," 137.

66. Freeman, "Wonders, Prodigies and Marvels," 138–39.

67. William, evidently, encountered Alpais when he was archbishop of Sens (1169–76), before he became archbishop of Rheims (1175–1202).

68. Blumenfeld-Kosinski, "Holy Women in France," 242. Ulcers (*ulcera*) could certainly denote leprosy as well.

69. Ralph, *Chronicon Anglicanum*, 127. Speaking sweetly (*suaviter*) is a notable contrast to the courtly (*curialiter*) speech Gervase employed with the maiden outside Rheims.

70. Ralph, *Chronicon Anglicanum*, 125: "Dicunt etiam nonulli quod in subterraneis suis quaedam nefanda sacrificia Lucifero suo temporibus agant constitutis, et quasdam sacrelegas turpitudines ibidem operentur."

71. Cohn, *Europe's Inner Demons*, 72–73.

72. Augustine, *De haeresibus*, 46.9–10 (pp. 314–16).

73. Jason BeDuhn, "The Metabolism of Salvation: Manichaean Concepts of Human Physiology," in *The Light and the Darkness: Studies in Manichaeism and its World*, ed. Paul Mirecki and Jason BeDuhn (Boston: Brill, 2001): 5–37. Augustine's accusation may be a polemical elaboration on the Manichaeans' ideas to what he regarded as their logical outcome. For an analysis that attempts to suggest that Augustine's "human semen eucharist" was based in fact, see Johannes van Oort, "Human Semen Eucharist among the Manichaeans? The Testimony of Augustine Reconsidered in Context," *Vigiliae Christianae* 70 (2016): 193–216.

74. In PL 195 the title is given as the *Sermones contra Catharos*; see "Excerptum de Manichaeis," 7, PL 195:100D–101C.

75. Michael D. Barbezat, "Bodies of Spirit and Bodies of Flesh: The Significance of the Sexual Activities Attributed to Heretics from the Eleventh to the Fourteenth Century," *Journal of the History of Sexuality* 25, no. 3 (2016): 387–419.

76. Paul, *Gesta synodi Aurelianensis*, 538: "Congregabantur siquidem certis noctibus in domo denominate, singuli lucernas tenentes in manibus, ad instar letaniae daemonum nomina declamabant, donec subito Daemonem in similitudine cujuslibet bestiolae inter eos viderent descendere. Qui statim, ut visibilis illa videbatur visio, omnibus extinctis luminaribus, quamprimum quisque poterat, mulierem quae ad manum sibi veniebat, ad abutendum arripiebat; sine peccati respectu, et utrum mater, aut soror, aut monacha haberetur. Pro sanctitate et religione ejus concubitus ab illis aestimabatur." The translation is mine.

77. Paul, *Gesta synodi Aurelianensis*: "Cuius cinis tanta veneratione colligebatur, atque custodiebatur; ut Christiana religiositas corpus Christi custodire solet, aegris dandum de hoc saeculo exituris ad viaticum."

78. Paul, *Gesta synodi Aurelianensis*: "Inerat enim tanta vis diabolicae fraudis in ipso cinere, ut quicumque de praefata haeresi imbutus fuisset, et de eodem cinere quamvis sumendo parum praelibavisset, vix unquam postea de eadem haeresi gressum mentis ad viam veritatis dirigere valeret."

79. For an analysis of these examples, see Barbezat, "Bodies of Spirit and Bodies of Flesh," 403–15. For a study of other examples and the occurrence of the trope in the work of the inquisitor Bernard Gui, see Peter Biller, "Bernard Gui, Sex and Luciferanism," in *Praedicatores, inquisitores I: The Dominicans and the Medieval Inquisition*, ed. Wolfram Hoyer (Rome: Institute of Dominican Studies, 2004), 455–70.

80. On Walter Map's career and identification as a satirist, see Antonia Gransden, *Historical Writing in England, c. 550 to c. 1307* (London: Routledge and Kegan Paul, 1974), 242–44.

81. The *De nugis curialium* is known today through a single fourteenth-century manuscript, although a part of it, known as the *Dissuasio Valerii*, traveled independently. On the state of the text and the date(s) of its composition, see *De nugis curialium or Courtiers' Trifles*, ed. M. R. James; rev. C. N. L. Brooke and R. A. B. Mynors (Oxford: Clarendon Press, 1983), xxiv–xxxii. For convincing reappraisals of Walter's background, ethnicity, and his surviving work, see Joshua Byron Smith, *Walter Map and the Matter of Britain* (Philadelphia: University of Pennsylvania Press, 2017). On the difficulty of reading the *De nugis curialium* as something between a satire and a jeremiad, particularly in its treatment of sexuality and the society of its time, see Robert Levine, "How to Read Walter Map," *Mittellateinisches Jahrbuch* 23 (1988): 91–105.

82. Christopher Brooke, *The Twelfth Century Renaissance* (London: Thames and Hudson, 1969), 172. On the unsteady temperature of Map's work as a thermometer of his age, and how it reflects the instabilities of its author's social position, see Tony Davenport, "Sex, Ghosts, and Dreams: Walter Map (1135?–1210?) and Gerald of Wales (1146–1223)," in *Writers of the Reign of Henry II: Twelve Essays*, ed. Ruth Kennedy and Simon Meecham-Jones (New York: Palgrave Macmillan, 2006), 133–50.

83. On Map's reputation among contemporary and later audiences, see A. G. Rigg, *A History of Anglo-Latin Literature* (New York: Cambridge University Press, 1992), 88.

84. Map, *De nugis curialium*, 1.30 (p. 120): "Quisque sibi proximum aut proximam arripit, commiscenturque quantum quisque ludibrium extendere preualet. Dicunt

eciam magistri docentque nouicios caritatem esse perfectam agere uel pati quod desiderauerit et pecierit frater aut soror, extinguere scilicet inuicem ardentes, et a paciendo Paterini dicuntur."

85. The verb *patior*, "to suffer" or "to endure," was the technical term for the passive role (the one penetrated) in intercourse. J. N. Adams, ed., *The Latin Sexual Vocabulary* (Baltimore: Johns Hopkins University Press, 1982), 189–90.

86. Helped by ready associations with Donatism, "Paterene" became a technical term applied to Italian heretics by the time of the Third Lateran Council (1179) and the bull *Ad abolendam* (1184). Lambert, *Medieval Heresy*, 44–45 and 89. In practice, Publican, Paterene, and Cathar became synonymous; see Moore, *War on Heresy*, 207.

87. Gal. 3:28: "There is neither Jew nor Greek: there is neither slave or free: there is nether male nor female. For you are all one in Christ Jesus." I have altered the translation of "servus" from "bond" to "slave."

88. Map, *De nugis curialium*, 1.30 (pp. 120–22).

89. Map, *De nugis curialium*, 1.31 (pp. 124–29).

90. Walter's exposition makes clear that by "illiterate" he means untrained in the Latin language rather than unable to read or write at all. The Waldensians bring with them a French version of the Psalter and many of the other books of the Bible, which one assumes they could read. On the common assumption that a truly literate man could "read, understand, compose by dictation, make verse, and express oneself in the Latin language," see Clanchy, *From Memory to Written Record*, 230.

91. Peter Biller cites this exchange as the "classic example" of the orthodox topos of the heretic as stupid or illiterate in his *The Waldenses, 1170–1530* (Aldershot, UK: Ashgate, 2001), 170.

92. Sebastian Coxon, "Wit, Laughter, and Authority in Walter Map's *De nugis curialum* (Courtier's Trifles)," in *Author, Reader, Book: Medieval Authorship in Theory and Practice*, ed. Stephen Partridge and Erik Kwakkel (Toronto: University of Toronto Press, 2012), 42.

93. Pegg, *Most Holy War*, 21.

94. An excellent study of the complex regional politics that lay underneath this episode can be found in Elaine Graham-Leigh, *The Southern French Nobility and the Albigensian Crusade* (Woodbridge, UK: Boydell Press, 2005), 94–102.

95. Moore, *War on Heresy*, 216.

96. An account of the 1178 mission can be found in Roger of Hoveden, *Chronica*, ed. William Stubbs, Rolls Series 51 (London: H. M. Stationery Office, 1869; repr. Wiesbaden: Kraus, 1964), 2:150–66. For the quote, see 2:166.

97. Pegg, *Most Holy War*, 20–21.

98. For the actions of Henry of Marcy in context, see Kienzle, *Cistercians, Heresy and Crusade in Occitania*, 121–35.

99. Biget, *Hérésie et inquisition dans le Midi de la France*, 161.

100. Moore, *War on Heresy*, 217.

101. Geoffrey Vigeois, *Chronicon Gaufredi Vosiensis*, in *Receuil des historiens des Gaules*, ed. Léopold Delisle (Paris: Victor Palmé, 1877), 12:448E–49B.

102. Geoffrey, *Chronicon Gaufredi Vosiensis*, 449B: "In carnali consuetudine cujuslibet maris et foeminae, sive parentes, sive fratres, sive communes matres, aut cujuslibet consanguinitatis vel affinitatis mulieres existant, par dicunt esse delictum. Mulieres

quae inter ipsos concipiunt, foetus interimunt; tamen dicebatur a peritioribus eorum id evitari: cum manifeste inter illas multae conceperint, proles non comparent."

103. Geoffrey, *Chronicon Gaufredi Vosiensis*, 449C: "Guarino olim Archiepiscopo Bituricensi illic praedicanti, Vienna conjux Sicardi de Bossa et de Granouillet palam confessa est a quinquaginta religioribus ejusdem sectae nocte quadam fuisse stupratam, cum ipsa eisdem, vitae causa sanctioris, thoro viri spreto, se conjuxisset."

104. Elizabeth Archibald, *Incest and the Medieval Imagination* (Oxford: Oxford University Press, 2001), xv.

105. See the discussion in Nirenberg, *Communities of Violence*, 155.

7. Leaping from the Flames

1. The Albigensian Crusade(s) was not the first holy war launched against Christians. On the development of internal crusades, see Norman Housley, "Crusades against Christians: Their Origins and Early Development, c. 1000–1216," in *Crusade and Settlement*, ed. Peter W. Edbury (Bristol: University College Cardiff Press, 1985), 17–36.

2. Joseph R. Strayer, preface to *The Albigensian Crusades* (New York: Dial Press, 1971; repr. Ann Arbor: University of Michigan Press, 1992), 1.

3. Kienzle, *Cistercians, Heresy and Crusade in Occitania, 1145–1229*, 1.

4. Lambert, *Medieval Heresy*, 106.

5. Pegg, *Most Holy War*; for the "homicidal ethic," see 77; for genocide, see 188.

6. Pegg, *Most Holy War*, 188.

7. Moore, *War on Heresy*, 253.

8. Peter of les Vaux-de-Cernay, *Hystoria Albigensis*, § 156, ed. Pascal Guébin and Ernest Lyon (Paris: Champion, 1926–39), 1:160–61. Hereafter cited as "Peter, *Historia*."

9. Peter, *Historia*, § 227 (1:227–28). Peter claims the heretics burned were "innumerable." The number three hundred comes from William of Puylaurens, *Chronica magistri Guillelmi de Podio Laurentii*, 16, ed. Jean Duvernoy (Paris: Centre national de la recherché scientifique, 1976), 70. Hereafter cited as "William, *Chronica*." William of Tudela gives four hundred; see Eugène Martin-Chabot, ed. *La chanson de la croisade albigeoise*, 68 (Paris: Les Belles Lettres, 1960–61), 1:164. Hereafter cited as *Chanson*.

10. Peter, *Historia*, §233 (1:233). William of Puylaurens gives the same figure. William of Tudela claims 94 in *Chanson*, 84 (1:200).

11. William, *Chronica*, 44 (pp. 174, 176).

12. For the untranslated critical editions of these three main sources, see notes above. English translations of all three now exist: Peter of Les Vaux-de-Cernay, *The History of the Albigensian Crusade*, trans. W. A. Sibly and M. D. Sibly (Woodbridge, UK: Boydell Press, 1998); *The Chronicle of William of Puylaurens: The Albigensian Crusade and Its Aftermath*, trans. W. A. Sibly and M. D. Sibly (Woodbridge, UK: Boydell Press, 2003); Janet Shirley, trans. *The Song of the Cathar Wars: A History of the Albigensian Crusades* (Aldershot, UK: Ashgate, 1996). Other narrative sources, such as the *Chronique* of William of Pelhisson cover a later period (1229–44) after the large-scale hostilities had concluded. William Pelhisson, *Chronique, 1229–1244; suivie du, Récit des troubles d'Albi, 1234*, ed. Jean Duvernoy (Paris: CNRS Editions, 1994). For a preliminary study of non-

narrative sources for the crusade, particularly the evidence from charters, see Daniel Power, "Who Went on the Albigensian Crusade?," *English Historical Review* 128 (2013): 1047–85.

13. *Chanson*, 208, ll. 3–16 (3:228; trans. 176): "E ditz e l'epictafi, cel quil sab ben legir, / Qu'el es sans ez es martirs e que deu resperir / E dins el gaug mirable heretar e florir / E portar la corona e e l regne sezir. / Ez ieu ai auzit dire c'aisis deu avenir / Si, per homes aucirre ni per sanc espandir / Ni per espertiz perdre ni per mortz cosentir / E per mals cosselhs creire e per focs abrandir / E per baros destruire e per Paratge aunir / E per las terras toldre e per Orgolh suffrir / E per los mals escendre e pels bes escantir / E per donas aucirre e per efans delir, / Pot hom en aquest segle Jhesu Crist comquerir, / El deu portar corona e el cel resplandir." On the meaning of "paratge" in the *Chanson*, especially "as the right to one's inheritance: the right not only of a noble lineage but also of a whole society," see Linda M. Paterson, *The World of the Troubadours: Medieval Occitan Society, c. 1100–c. 1300* (Cambridge: Cambridge University Press, 1993), 70.

14. Moore, *War on Heresy*, 254.

15. Among these differences is the notion of *paratge*. See C. P. Bagley, "*Paratge* in the Anonymous *Chanson de la Croisade albigeoise*," *French Studies* 21, no. 3 (1967): 195–204. It is discussed within the context of the counts of Toulouse and their social bonds with the southern nobility in Rosenwein, *Generations of Feeling*, 114–16.

16. This was particularly true regarding the counts of Toulouse and their supposed vassals; see Malcolm Barber, *The Cathars: Dualist Heretics in Languedoc in the High Middle Ages* (New York: Pearson, 2000), 46–49.

17. The Crown of Aragon had recently expanded its influence in the region, and Elaine Graham-Leigh argues that the kings of Aragon had become the effective overlords of the Trencavel, the first targets of the crusade; see her *Southern French Nobility and the Albigensian Crusade*, 112.

18. Housley, "Crusades against Christians," 25–27.

19. For an account of these efforts, see Kienzle, *Cistercians, Heresy and Crusade in Occitania*, esp. 81–135.

20. Zerner, "L'hérétique Henri dans les sources de son temps (1135–1145)," 127–29; for Bernard's mission, see 112–25.

21. Moore, *War on Heresy*, 191–92.

22. Henry was the cardinal bishop of Albano at the time of the assault. Geoffredus Vosiensis, *Chronicon*, ed. Martin Bouquet, *Receuil des historiens des Gaules* (Paris: V. Palmé, 1877), 12:448–49. Geoffroi's account also features a lurid description of the heretics' sexual activities. For the small summer war, see Pegg, *Most Holy War*, 21.

23. Biget, *Hérésie et inquisition dans le Midi de la France*, 168.

24. These reasons are some of the major conclusions reached by Graham-Leigh, *Southern French Nobility and the Albigensian Crusade*, 166–67.

25. On the frequent misconception that inquisitorial procedure was uniquely applied to heresy investigations or that medieval inquisitorial procedures were part of one unified, pan-European entity, see Henry Ansgar Kelly, "Inquisition and the Prosecution of Heresy: Misconceptions and Abuses," *Church History* 58 (1989): 439–51.

26. The landmark study of this inquisition is Pegg, *Corruption of Angels*.

27. The period 1275–1325 is the focus of Given, *Inquisition and Medieval Society*.

28. Peter, *Historia*, § 3 (1:2).

29. Peter, *Historia*, § 5 (1:5; trans. 7).

30. Peter, *Historia*, § 9 (1:8). Jerome, *Commentarius*, 3.5, 430B–C. This passage was perhaps available to Peter through Peter Lombard, *Collectanea in omnes Pauli apostolicas Epistulas*, 5,,155B. See discussion in chapter 2.

31. Peter, *Historia*, § 12 (1:12; trans. 11–12).

32. William, *Chronica*, Prologue, 22–26 (trans. 26): "Diabolus . . . terram in pace sua velut suum atrium possidebat."

33. William, *Chronica*, Prologue, 22 (trans. 27).

34. Peter, *Historia*, § 25 (1:27–28).

35. Christopher M. Kurpiewski argues for a similar reading in "Writing beneath the Shadow of Heresy: The *Historia Albigensis* of Brother Pierre des Vaux-de-Cernay," *Journal of Medieval History* 31 (2004): 13. Megan Cassidy-Welch offers a different interpretation based on Eucharistic symbolism in "Images of Blood in the *Historia Albigensis* of Pierre des Vaux-de-Cernay," *Journal of Medieval History* 35 (2011): 484–86.

36. The equivalence of heresy to treason against one's lord, or lèse-majesté (*laesa majestatis*) in Roman law, is often presented as a legal development made by Innocent III in the decretal *Vergentis in senium* (1199); see Peters, *Inquisition*, 48. Peter makes no such legalistic argument, but his presentation of characters and events makes the logical and emotional equivalence between heresy and treason clear. See also Graham-Leigh, *Southern French Nobility and the Albigensian Crusade*, 27.

37. William, *Chronica*, 20 (p. 80; trans. 47): "Considerans quod causam Dei et fidei prosequebatur, ceteris in contrarium currentibus vincula excommunicationis astrictis satius duxit una dei periculum experiri."

38. See also the comments made by Peter of les Vaux-de-Cernay, *Historia*, §§ 438–63 (2:128–55). On Peter's burning of heretics, see Cebrià Baraut, "Els incis de la Inquisició a Catalunya I les seves actuacions al Bisbat d'Urgell (segles XII–XIII)," *Urgellia* 13 (1997): 420–21.

39. Peter, *Historia*, § 10–19 (1:9–20); William of Puylaurens, *Chronica*, Prologue, 24 (trans. 26).

40. Pegg, *Most Holy War*, 22. Likewise, none of the almost six thousand witnesses at the inquisition of 1245–46 used the term Cathar. Pegg, "Heresy, Good Men, and Nomenclature," 228.

41. Peter, *Historia*, §§ 3–4 (1:2–4). Contemporary charters also often used "Albigensian" to refer to the heretics, even before 1209. See Power, "Who Went on the Albigensian Crusade?," 1071.

42. Peter, *Historia*, § 18 (1:18–19). The Siblys, and presumably many earlier readers, use the inclusion of Waldensians to explain why Peter claims the heretics belong to multiple sects, namely Cathars and Waldensians (*History of the Albigensian Crusade*, 10n27).

43. William, *Chronica*, Prologue, 24 (trans. 8): "Qui, licet inter se essent dissides, omnes tamen in animarum perniciem contra fidem catholicam conspirabant."

44. The image originates in Judg. 15:4. For its utilization in conceptions of heresy, see discussions in chapters 2 and 4. See also Dubarle, "Les renards de Samson," 175–76.

45. John 15:13: "Greater love than this no man hath, that a man lay down his life for his friends."

46. Jonathan Riley Smith, "Crusading as an Act of Love," *History* 65 (1980): 177–92.

47. *Innocentii III Regesta sive Epistolae*, 11.26 (March 10, 1208), PL 215:1354–58. Hereafter noted as Reg. Inn. III. Peter, *Historia*, § 55–65 (1:51–65; trans. 31–38).

48. Reg. Inn. III, 10.149 (November 17, 1207), PL 215:1247. Christian Chenu, "Innocent III and the Case for War in Southern France in 1207," *Journal of Religious History* 35 (2011), 513. Reg. Inn. III, 10.149 (November 17, 1207). This was not the first time that Innocent III offered a crusade indulgence for a holy war against a Christian target; see Housley, "Crusades against Christians," 27–28.

49. Power, "Who Went on the Albigensian Crusade?," 1078.

50. Peter, *Historia*, § 64 (1:64–65).

51. Matt. 10:28. Reg. Inn. III, 11.26, PL 215:1357C. Peter, *Historia*, § 63 (1:62–63): "Non solum timorem non incutiet, sed accendet amorem."

52. Innocent describes the crusade as an opportunity to serve God "in a way that is acceptable to Him." Peter, *Historia*, § 64 (1:64; trans. 37): "Occasionem tamen in hoc articulo vobis tribuit Sibi acceptibiliter serviendi."

53. Jacques de Vity, "Sermon 2: Item sermo ad crucesignatos vel—signandos," in *Crusade Propaganda and Ideology: Model Sermons for the Preaching of the Cross*, ed. Christoph T. Maier (Cambridge: Cambridge University Press, 2000), 117–25.

54. The image is from Peter Lombard, *Sententiae in IV libris distinctae*, 4.21.5 (2:382). See discussion in chapter 1.

55. For Peter's naiveté, see Sibly and Sibly, *History of the Albigensian Crusade*, xvi; for the defense of the indefensible, see Andrew P. Roach, "(Review) The History of the Albigensian Crusade: Peter of Les Vaux-de-Cernay's *Historia Albigensis*," *History* 85 (2000): 316.

56. H. Martin, "Inventaires des biens et des livres de l'Abbaye des Vaux-de-Cernay aux XIIe siècle," *Bulletin de la societé de l'histoire de Paris et de L'Ile-de-France* (1886): 36–42.

57. A point stressed by Kurpiewski, "Writing beneath the Shadow of Heresy," 7.

58. Peter, *Historia*, § 106 (1:106–11).

59. Sibly and Sibly, *History of the Albigensian Crusade*, xxiv.

60. These divisions were introduced by the current critical edition of Guébin and Lyon. The English translation by the Siblys introduces another set of eighteen divisions.

61. "De hereticis" §§ 5–19; "De predicatoribus" §§ 20–54; "De crucesignatis" §§ 55–620.

62. Peter, *Historia*, § 2 (1:1–2).

63. Guébin and Lyon argue for this explanation, citing the less completed state of the later portions of the text as evidence that Peter was unable to revise it. The Siblys concur with their argument (*History of the Albigensian Crusade*, xxv–xxvi).

64. Kurpiewski, "Writing beneath the Shadow of Heresy," 24.

65. Simon's election happened before the end of August 1209. The trip to Castres is explained in *Historia* § 112 (1:116–17). For the association of Castres with heresy by Henry of Marcy, see "Letter 29," PL 204:240A–B.

66. The duke of Burgundy, in particular, emphasized the strategic significance of the site to Simon. The townsmen later repudiated their allegiance to Simon when the tide of war turned against him; see Peter, *Historia*, § 132 (1:136–37).

67. Peter, *Historia*, § 117 (1:122). Simon would have arrived in Lombers after his time at Pamiers in September and his subsequent visit to Saverdun; see Sibly and Sibly, *History of the Albigensian Crusade*, 65n109.

68. Peter, *Historia*, § 113 (1:117–18; trans. 62–63).

69. The *Chanson* mentions a crusading expedition in the Agenais around or before the end of June 1209 that would predate the burning at Castres. William records only that "this host condemned many heretics to be burned and had many fair women thrown into the flames, for they refused to recant however much they were begged to do so." *Chanson*, 2.14 (1:42; trans. 18).

70. Peter, *Historia*, § 113 (1:117–18): "Tractus dolore cordis intrinsecus, cepit conteri promisitque quod libenter abjuraret heresim."

71. Peter, *Historia*, § 113 (1:118; trans. 63): "Ex quo ille paratus erat ea que diximus adimplere, non debebat morte condempnari."

72. Peter, *Historia*, § 113 (1:118): "Quod ea que dicebat potius timore imminentis mortis promitteret quam amore christiane religionis observande."

73. Peter calls the discussion between the crusaders a "grandis altercatio" (Peter, *Historia*, § 113, p. 1:118).

74. Peter, *Historia* § 113 (1:118; trans. 63): "Acquievit comes quod combureretur, hac intentione quod, si vere conterebatur, ignis esset ei pro expiation peccatorum; si vero ficte loqueretur, reciperet pro perfidia talionem."

75. Peter, *Historia*, § 113 (1:118; trans. 63): "Inquiritur ab illo qui conteri videbatur in qua fide vellet mori; qui ait: 'Abjuro pravitatem hereticam. In fide sancte Romane ecclesie volo mori, orans ut michi sit pro purgatorio ignis iste.'"

76. This point originates with Augustine, *Enarrationes in Psalmos*, 37.3 (pp. 383–84); Peter Lombard, *Sententiae in IV libris distinctae*, 4.21.2 (2:380). For its citation in later commentaries, see Thomas Aquinas, *In IV Sententiarum*, dist. 21, q. 1, art. 1.1.

77. Peter, *Historia*, § 461 (2:152; trans. 209): "Ite in nomine Jhesu Christi! Et ego vobis testis sum et in die Judicii fidejussor existo quod quicumque in isto glorioso occubuerit bello absque ulla purgatorii pena statim eterna premia et martyrii gloriam consequetur, dummodo contritus sit et confessus vel saltem firmum habeat propositum quod statim peracto bello, super peccatis de quibus nondum fecit confessionem ostendet se sacerdoti."

78. The way this story allows the crusaders to know the truth of the penitent heretic is an example of what Karl F. Morrison termed "the hermeneutics of empathy" in his *I Am You.*

79. 1 Cor. 3:13–15. For the centrality of these verses to ideas of postmortem purgation, see Le Goff, *Birth of Purgatory*, 43.

80. Mitchell B. Merback, working with later sources, has also identified public executions as an opportunity for audience members to reflect on their own future encounters with fire; see his *Thief, the Cross and the Wheel*, 155.

81. Peter, *Historia*, § 113 (1:118; trans. 63): "Illo autem qui 'perfectus' erat in heresi in momento combusto, alter, statim confractis vinculis fortissimis, ita sanus exivit ab igne quod nulla apparuit in eo combustionis nota, nisi quod summitates digitorum aliquantulum sunt aduste."

82. Asad, *Genealogies of Religion*, 103.

83. Pegg identifies this exemplum from Caesarius as an encapsulation of the "homicidal ethic." Pegg, *Most Holy War*, 77.

84. Laurence W. Martin argues that the killing of a large portion of the population of a city taken by storm was not particularly unusual, and that what was remarkable

about the fall of Béziers was its rapidity and the suggestion made by such an easy capture that God clearly favored the crusaders' cause; see his "The Massacre at Béziers July 22, 1209: A Revisionist Look," in Frassetto, *Heresy and the Persecuting Society in the Middle Ages*, 220–25.

85. Peter, *Historia*, § 84–91; Elaine Graham-Leigh, "Justifying Deaths: The Chronicler Pierre des Vaux-de-Cernay and the Massacre of Béziers," *Mediaeval Studies* (2001): 299–301. The Siblys argue that Peter got the church wrong since La Madeleine could not hold that many people, suggesting that the cathedral church of St. Nazaire would be more probable (*History of the Albigensian Crusade*, 51n35). The legates reported to Innocent III that the number of those killed was 20,000: Reg. Inn. III, 12.108 (1209), PL 216:139C. The purported number of those killed has come under scrutiny. Martin suggests that the actual numbers of those killed might be around 10 percent of the reported figures ("Massacre at Béziers," 219).

86. Caesarius, *Dialogus miraculorum*, 5.21: "Dixerunt Abbati: 'Quid faciemus, domine? Non possumus discernere inter bonos et malos.' Timens tam Abbas quam reliqui, ne tantum timore mortis se catholicos simularent, et post ipsorum abcessum iterum ad perfidiam redirent, fertur dixisse: 'Caedite eos. Novit enim Dominus qui sunt eius.'" For the origin of the expression, see 2 Tim. 2:19. I have translated the Latin literally, but it is most often translated as "Kill them all; God will know his own."

87. The most thorough recent investigation of the question by Jacques Berlioz concludes that Caesarius's story cannot be verified but that it is certainly plausible. Jacques Berlioz, *"Tues-les tous, Dieu reconnaîtra les siens:" Le massacre de Béziers (22 juillet 1209) et la croisade contre les Albigeois vus par Césaire de Heisterbach* (Portet-sur-Garonne: Éditions Loubatières, 1994), 99. In another example, Strayer in the 1970s regarded the story as false, but still indicative of the actual "mood" of the crusaders (*Albigensian Crusades*, 62). Graham-Leigh suggests that Caesarius's source for this anecdote might have been the legate himself in 1209 or the general perceptions of the assembled abbots at the annual meeting of the Cistercian General Chapter. Such an origin might account for the thematic similarity between Caesarius's unique anecdote and the spin given to other events of the crusade ("Justifying Deaths," 301).

88. For overviews of this episode in the context of the history of the crusade, see Moore, *War on Heresy*, 252–53; Mark Gregory Pegg, *Most Holy War*, 103–5; Michael Costen, *The Cathars and the Albigensian Crusade* (Manchester: Manchester University Press, 1997), 131; Strayer, *Albigensian Crusades*, 71.

89. Peter, *Historia*, § 151 (1:154–55).

90. Peter, *Historia*, § 154 (1:157–58).

91. Peter, *Historia*, § 154 (1:158; trans. 84): "Utpote inimicos Christi mori desiderans et tamen ad mortem judicare non audens, cum esset monachus et sacerdos; cogitans ergo quomodo comitem vel dictum Guillelmum . . . posset a compromissione quam in se fecerant revocare."

92. The manipulation of a debate through written exchanges in the way I describe appears clearly in Kruger's analysis of the Tortosa disputation of 1414 in his *Spectral Jew*, 199–200.

93. Iogna-Prat, *Order and Exclusion*, 360–62.

94. William, *Chronica*, 9 (pp. 50, 52; trans. 26).

95. Peter, *Historia*, § 74 (1:75; trans. 42): "Convocavit [Milo] archiepiscopos et epis-copos quamplures; qui cum ad eum venissent, quesivit ad eis diligenter qualiter pro-cedendum esset in negotio pacis et fidei et precipue in facto comitis Tholosani."

96. Peter, *Historia*, § 74 (1:75; trans. 42): "Sua ei traderent consilia scripta et sigil-lata; factum est ut precepit et (quod auditu est mirabile) omnia tam abbatis Cister-ciensis quam prelatorum consilia sine dissensione aliqua convenerunt. A Domino factum est istud!"

97. Peter, *Historia*, § 154 (1:158–59; trans. 84): "Ordinavit igitur abbas ut dominus castri et omnes qui in castro erant, credentes etiam hereticorum, si vellent reconciliari et stare mandato ecclesie, vivi evaderent, castro comiti remanente."

98. Robert was a longtime friend and companion of Simon de Montfort. He is also mentioned in *Historia*, §§ 129, 154, 286, and 336. Mauvoisin means "bad neighbor" and is essentially the same name given to the largest siege engine deployed against Mi-nerve; see *Chanson*, 48 (1:114; trans. 32–33). Moore, *War on Heresy*, 253. Peter calls him a "vir nobilis et totus in fide catholicus" at *Historia*, § 155 (1:159; trans. 84).

99. Peter, *Historia*, § 154 (1:159): "Ne timeatis, quia credo quod paucissimi conver-tentur." The translation is mine.

100. Peter, *Historia*, § 155 (1:160; trans. 85): "A secta quam tenemus neque mors neque vita nos poterit revocare."

101. Peter, *Historia*, § 156 (1:161; trans. 85). Rather than a precise number, William of Tudela records that "they burned many heretics, frantic men of an evil kind and crazy women who shrieked among the flames." *Chanson*, 49 (1:116; trans. 33).

102. Peter, *Historia*, § 156 (1:161; trans. 85): "Preparato igitur igne copioso, omnes in ipso proiciuntur; nec tamen opus fuit quod nostril eos proicerent, quia, obstinati in sua nequicia, omnes se in ignem ultro precipitabant."

103. Kienzle is especially strong in her denunciation of the massacre, particularly Arnold's role in it, writing "it is difficult not to ascribe partial responsibility for their deaths to Arnaud Amaury [Arnold Almaric]: the chronicler's distinction ordering them put to death, on the one hand—and offering an alternative that assuredly would lead to their deaths, on the other—does little to convince this writer of his integrity as a monk and priest" (*Cistercians, Heresy and Crusade in Occitania*, 157). I share Kienzle's disapproval. I would suggest, however, that in the presentation of the *Historia* the re-sponsibility is rhetorically placed entirely on the heretics and their wickedness to underline the integrity of the legate as a monk and a priest.

104. Peter, *Historia*, § 156 (1:161; trans. 85): "Tres tantum mulieres evaserunt, quas nobilis domina mater Buchardi de Marliaco ab igne eripuit et sancte ecclesie recon-ciliari fecit."

105. At Minerve itself, during and immediately after the siege, there are two mira-cles: *Historia*, § 158 and 159 (1:161–63). Below I examine one of these (§159) and pair it with another that happened at Toulouse during the siege of Minerve.

106. Peter, *Historia*, § 159 (1:162; trans. 86): "In altum per totam vallem flamma erupit ac si aliqua civitas maxima combureretur."

107. Regarding the conflagration of fire that will consume the corruption of the temporal world, see Augustine, *De civitate Dei*, 20.16 (pp. 726–27).

108. In Peter's *Historia* this is the term most often translated into modern English as crusader(s). For a discussion of the significance of the term for the crusaders' self-conception, see Pegg, *Most Holy War*, 67.

109. The status of Lavaur itself at this time was ambiguous. It was most certainly part of the historical Trencavel territory, but Raymond might have been attempting to absorb it or at least covertly defend it from the crusaders due to its strategic location. See Sibly and Sibly, *History of the Albigensian Crusade*, 111n 9.

110. Simon might have regarded these knights as traitors; see Barber, *Cathars*, 41–42.

111. Peter, *Historia*, § 227 (1:228): "Innumerabiles etiam hereticos peregrini nostri cum ingenti gaudio combusserunt." For the disapproval of the cruel murder of Lady Girauda, see *Chanson*, 68 (1:164, 166; trans. 41).

112. Moore, *War on Heresy*, 251–52.

113. William, *Chronica*, 16 (p. 70); *Chanson*, 68 (1:164; trans. 41).

114. Peter, *Historia*, § 229 (1:229; trans. 117–18).

115. Peter, *Historia*, § 220 (1:219; trans. 113). The identification of Lavaur with long-standing heresy recalls the siege of 1181 under the direction of Abbot Henry of Clairvaux.

116. Peter, *Historia*, § 219 (1:218–19).

117. Peter, *Historia*, § 221 (1:220–22).

118. Peter, *Historia*, § 223 (1:223).

119. William, *Chronica*, 16 (p. 70; trans. 40): "Hereticos vero circiter trecentos flammis exustos materialibus igni concemandos perpetuo [Symon] assignavit."

120. Peter, *Historia*, § 54 (1:47–49).

121. In Peter's account of this episode, Dominic's authorities sound like a simple list of where to find authoritative passages, perhaps written on one leaf of paper (*cedula*). It would conform with the model of early antiheretical *Summae auctoritatum*, represented by examples such as those published by C. Douais, *La Somme des autorités, à l'usage des prédicateurs méridionaux au XIIIe siècle* (Paris: Picard, 1896), 34–66. For an analysis of the genre, see Sackville, *Heresy and Heretics in the Thirteenth Century*, 42–53.

122. This miraculous sign would follow the model of visions or signs shown to individuals for others' benefit rather than their own; see Gregory the Great, *Dialogues*, 4.40.6–9, ed. Adalbert de Vogüé (Paris: Éditions du cerf, 1980) (pp. 3:142, 144).

123. For an overview of medieval accounts of Jewish host desecration and its contexts, see Miri Rubin, *Gentile Tales: the Narrative Assault on Late Medieval Jews* (Philadelphia: University of Pennsylvania Press, 1999).

124. Such was the argument advanced by Aquinas that the Jews killed Christ not out of ignorance but because they understood who he was. For a discussion of this point in connection to medieval accusations of host desecration, see Jeremy Cohen, *Christ Killers: The Jews and the Passion from the Bible to the Big Screen* (Oxford: Oxford University Press, 2007), 108–9.

125. Jordan of Saxony, *Libellus de principiis ordinis Praedicatorum*, 24–25, ed. H. C. Scheeben, (Rome: Institutum Historicum Ordinis Fratrum Praedicatorum), 38. Jordan places the contest in Fanjeaux.

126. Bernard, *De gratia et libero arbitrio*, 13.45 (p. 198). See discussion in chapter 4.

Conclusion

1. Mackey, *Peregrinations of the Word*, 22. See discussion in chapter 2.

2. Stock, *Implications of Literacy*, 90.

3. From the point of view of these authors, the body of Christ was also something like an "emotional community," which tautologically allowed the unifying interpretations of foundational texts within a state of unity. For the term emotional community, see Barbara H. Rosenwein, *Emotional Communities in the Early Middle Ages* (Ithaca, NY: Cornell University Press, 2006), 2.

4. Moore, *Formation of a Persecuting Society*, 67–68. For one repetition out of many of this point, see Carol Lansing, *Power and Purity: Cathar Heresy in Medieval Italy* (Oxford: Oxford University Press, 1998), 12. For a critique of the adage "that heresy *was* in the eye of the beholder" (emphasis mine), see Andrew P. Roach and James R. Simpson, eds., *Heresy and the Making of European Culture: Medieval and Modern Perspectives* (Farnham, UK: Ashgate, 2013), 12–15.

5. Michel Foucault, *The History of Sexuality*, vol. 1: *An Introduction*, trans. Robert Hurley (New York: Random House, 1978; repr. New York: Vintage, 1990), 45–48.

6. Julien Théry-Astruc, "L'hérésie des bons homes. Comment nommer la dissidence religieuse non vaudoise ni beguine en Languedoc?," *Heresis* 36–37 (2002): 99–112; "Heretical Dissidence of the 'Good Men' in the Albigeois (1276–1329," 81. Andrew Roach and James Simpson argue that "'heresy' could become a label consciously embraced as part of a defiance of or tactical negotiation with authority, a medieval religious analogue of the gay rights rallying call, 'We're queer; we're here. Get used to it.'" Of course, what is at issue here is the origin and dissemination of the concept of queer to which the "we" can proclaim to belong (*Heresy and the Making of European Culture*, 7).

7. Sara Ahmed, *The Cultural Politics of Emotion*, 2nd ed. (Edinburgh: Edinburgh University Press, 2014), 67. François Soyer, in work on premodern Spain that he shared in a seminar at the University of Western Australia, first drew my attention to the ways in which Ahmed's arguments could be applied to contexts outside the modern.

8. Ahmed, *Cultural Politics of Emotion*, 68–73.

9. Waytz, Young, and Ginges, "Motive Attribution for Love vs. Hate Drives Intractable Conflict," 15687–92. See discussion in chapter 2.

10. Ahmed, *Cultural Politics of Emotion*, 124.

11. Ahmed, *Cultural Politics of Emotion*, 43.

12. Ahmed, *Cultural Politics of Emotion*, 50.

13. Ahmed, *Cultural Politics of Emotion*, 43.

14. Hugh of St. Victor, *De archa Noe*, 3.2 (p. 55): "Et sic de timore quidem caritas nascitur, sed per caritatem timor consumitur." Hugh's discussion of the role of fear occurs in the context of a consideration of how wisdom is sown in the human soul, because "charity is wisdom itself." For the biblical basis, see Prov. 1:7. For fear and love as the "two movements of the heart by which the rational soul is impelled to do everything which it does," see *De sacramentis christianae fidei*, 2.13.3, PL 176:527C; *On the Sacraments of the Christian Faith*, trans. Roy J. Deferrari (Cambridge, MA: Mediaeval Academy of America Press, 1951), 377. For love and fear in Hugh's larger thought regarding human emotions, see Ineke Van 't Spijker, "'Ad commovendos affectus': Exegesis and the Affects in Hugh of Saint-Victor," in *Bibel und Exegese in der Abtei Saint-Victor zu Paris: Form und Funktion eines Grundtextes im europäischen Rahmen*, ed. Rainer Berndt (Munster: Aschendorff Verlag, 2009), 229.

15. Barbara Rosenwein influentially characterized the early historical investigations of emotions undertaken by Lucien Febvre as histories of what we would call the

"dark side" undertaken in order to "stave off fascist nightmares." As Rosenwein suggested, Febvre's assumption relies on the problematic premise that what one calls emotion generates but not is not part of civilized life, and that it is better restrained in some periods than in others. Civilized life, in contrast, may need its nightmares. Barbara Rosenwein, "Worrying about Emotions in History," *American Historical Review* 107, no. 3 (2002): 822–23.

16. Alan Bernstein proposed these possibilities to me while discussing a draft portion of this book.

17. Biller, "Through a Glass Darkly," 324.

18. For the haunting of an hegemony in this fashion, see Jacques Derrida, *Spectres of Marx: The State of the Debt, the Work of Mourning, and the New International*, trans. Peggy Kamuf (New York: Routledge, 1994), 37.

19. Bernard, *De gratia et libero arbitrio*, 13.45 (p. 198).

20. On this point, see the influential distinction drawn by Origen in *De principiis libri IV Rufino interprete*, 3.6, in *Origenes Werke*, ed. Paul Koetschau (Leipzig: J. C. Hinrichs, 1913), 5:279–91, between image (in which man is made) and likeness (the perfection of the image). The likeness is only attained at the consummation, not the present life. See discussion in Ladner, *Idea of Reform*, 87–88.

21. On living with specters as "a way of thinking and responding ethically within history," see Carla Freccero, *Queer/Early/Modern* (Durham, NC: Duke University Press, 2006), 70.

WORKS CITED

Primary Sources

Manuscripts

University of Düsseldorf

Ms. B 49 Expositio in Psalmos. Eucherius Lugdunensis. Isidorus Hispalensis. Hugo de Sancto Victore. Ps.-Seneca, Lucius Annaeus. Bernardus Claraevallensis (?). Odo Cluniacensis. Vitae et miracula s. Mariae Magdalenae. Beda Venerabilis. Heito. Computus ecclesiasticus. Petrus Pictor. Libellus adversus errores Alberonis sacerdotis Merkensis. Grammatica latina.

The manuscript is a Third Party Property (permanent loan by the City of Düsseldorf to the Universitäts-und Landesbibliothek Düsseldorf).

Printed Sources

Acta synodi Atrebatensis. PL 142:1271–312.

Ad abolendam diversarum haeresium pravitatem. Edited by Giovanni Gonnet, 1:50–53. *Enchiridion fontium Valdensium,* Torre-Pellice: Claudiana, 1958.

Ademar of Chabannes. *Chronicon.* Edited by P. Bourgain, R. Landes, and G. Pon. CCCM 129 Turnhout: Brepols, 1999. Also titled *Historia.*

Aelred of Rievaulx. *De speculo caritatis.* Edited by C. H. Talbot. CCCM 1:3–161. Turnhout: Brepols, 1971.

——. *Dialogus de anima.* Edited by C. H. Talbot. CCCM 1:685–754. Turnhout: Brepols, 1971.

——. *Sermones I–CLXXXII.* Edited by G. Raciti. CCCM 2–2C. Turnhout: Brepols, 1989–2012.

Alan of Lille. *Theologiae regulae.* PL 210:617–684.

Alexander Neckam. *De naturis rerum, libro duo: With the Poem of the Same Author, De laudibus divinae.* Edited by Thomas Wright. London: Longman, 1863.

Ambrose of Milan. *De Isaac uel anima.* Edited by Karl Schenkl. CSEL 32.1:641–700. Vienna: F. Tempsky, 1897.

Andreas of Fleury. *Les miracles de saint Benoît.* Edited by E. de Certain. Paris: Jules Renouard, 1858.

——. *Vie de Gauzlin, abbé de Fleury (Vita Gauzlini abbatis Floriacensis monasterii).* Edited by Robert-Henri Bautier and Gillette Labory. Paris: Éditions du centre national de la recherché scientifique, 1969.

Annales Aquenses, MGH SS 16:684–687.

Annales Brunwilarenses, 1000–1179. MGH SS 16:724–728.

Annales Sancti Petri Erphesfurdenses, MGH SS 16:15–25.

Annales Veterocellenses, MGH SS 16:41–47.

Anselm of Canterbury. *Cur Deus Homo*. Edited by Francis Schmitt. In *S. Anselmi opera omnia*. Vol. 2. Rome, 1940.

——. *De casu Diaboli*. Edited by Francis Schmitt. In *S. Anselmi Cantuariensis archiepiscopi opera omnia*. Vol. 1. Edinburgh: Thomas Nelson and Sons, 1946.

Anselm of Liège. *Gesta episcoporum Leodiensis*. MGH SS 7:189–234.

Aristotle. *The Nicomachean Ethics*. Translated by H. Rackham. Rev. ed. Cambridge, MA: Harvard University Press, 1934.

——. *Politics*. Translated by Ernest Barker. Oxford: Clarendon Press, 1961.

Augustine of Hippo. *Confessionum Libri XIII*. Edited by Lucas Verheijen. CCSL 27. Turnhout: Brepols, 1981. Trans. R. S. Pine-Coffin. *Confessions*. Harmondsworth, UK: Penguin, 1961.

——. *Contra epistolam Parmeniani*. PL 43:33–108.

——. *Contra litteras Petiliani*. Edited by M. Petschenig. CSEL 52:3–227. Vienna: F. Tempsky, 1909.

——. *De civitate Dei*. Edited by Bernard Dombart and Alphonse Kalb. CCSL 47–48. Turnhout: Brepols, 1955. Trans. R. W. Dyson. *The City of God against the Pagans*. Cambridge: Cambridge University Press, 1998.

——. *De doctrina Christiana*. Edited and translated by R. P. H. Green. Oxford: Oxford University Press, 1996.

——. *De Genesi ad litteram libri duodecim*. Edited by Joseph Zycha. CSEL 28.1:1–435. Prague: F. Tempsky, 1894. Trans. John Hammond Taylor. *The Literal Meaning of Genesis*. New York: Newman Press, 1982.

——. *De gratia et libero arbitrio*. PL 44:881–912.

——. *De haeresibus*. Edited by Vander Plaetse and Beukers. CCSL 46:290–342. Turnhout: Brepols, 1969.

——. *De libero arbitrio*. Edited by W. M. Green. CCSL 29:211–321. Turnhout: Brepols, 1970.

——. *De magistro*. Edited by K. D. Daur. CCSL 29. Turnhout: Brepols, 1970.

——. *Enarrationes in Psalmos*. Edited by E. Dekkers and J. Fraipont. CCSL 38–40. Turnhout: Brepols, 1956.

——. *Enchiridion de fide, spe et caritate*. Edited by M. P. J. Van den Hout. CCSL 46:49–114. Turnhout: Brepols, 1969.

——. *Epistulae*. Edited by D. Daur. CCSL 31, 31 A, 31 B. Turnhout: Brepols, 2004–2009.

——. *In Iohannis epistulam ad Parthos tractatus*. PL 35:1977–2062.

——. *In Iohannis evangelium Tractatus*. Edited by D. Radbodus Willems. CCSL 36. Turnhout: Brepols, 1954.

——. *Quaestiones XVI in Matthaeum*. Edited by Almut Mutzenbecher. CCSL 44B:119–40. Turnhout: Brepols, 1980.

——. *Quaestionum in Heptateuchum libri VII*. Edited by J. Fraipont. CCSL 33:1–377. Turnhout: Brepols, 1958.

——. *Sermones de scripturis*. PL 38.

Bede the Venerable. *In Matthaei Evangelium expositio*. PL 92:9–132.

Bernard of Clairvaux. *De gratia et libero arbitrio*. In *Sancti Bernardi Opera*, edited by J. Leclercq and H. M. Rochais. Vol. 3:165–203. Rome: Editiones Cistercienses, 1963.

——. *Epistolae*. In *Sancti Bernardi Opera*, edited by J. Leclercq and H. M. Rochais. Vols. 7–8. Rome: Editiones Cistercienses, 1974–77.

——. *Sententiae Series 3*. In *Sancti Bernardi Opera*, edited by J. Leclercq and H. M. Rochais. Vol. 6.2:59–255. Rome: Editiones Cistercienses, 1972.

——. *Sermones super Cantica Canticorum*. In *Sancti Bernardi Opera*, edited by J. Leclercq, C. H. Talbot, and H. M. Rochais. Vols. 1–2. Rome: Editiones Cistercienses, 1958. Trans. Kilian Walsh and Irene M. Edmonds. *Bernard of Clairvaux: On the Song of Songs*. 4 vols. Kalamazoo, MI: Cistercian Publications, 1979.

Caesarius of Heisterbach. *Dialogus miraculorum*. Edited by Nikolaus Nösges and Horst Scheider. 5 vols. Turnhout: Brepols, 2009. Trans. H. Von E. Scott and C. C. Swinton Bland. *The Dialogue on Miracles*. 2 vols. London: George Routledge and Sons, 1929.

Cassiodorus. *Expositio in Cantica Canticorum*. PL 70:1055–1106.

——. *Expositio Psalmorum*. Edited by M. Adriaen. CCSL 97, 98. Turnhout: Brepols, 1958.

La chanson de la croisade albigeoise. Edited by Eugène Matin-Chabot. 3 vols. Paris: Les Belles Lettres, 1960–61. Trans. Janet Shirley. *The Song of the Cathar Wars: A History of the Albigensian Crusades*. Aldershot, UK: Ashgate, 1996.

Chaucer, Geoffrey. *The Riverside Chaucer*. Edited by Larry Dean Benson. 3rd ed. Oxford: Oxford University Press, 2008.

Chronica regia Coloniensis. Edited by Georgius Waitz. MGH SRG, 18.

Chronicon S. Andreae. MGH SS 7:481–568.

Corpus documentorum inquisitionis haereticae pravitatis Neerlandicae. 3 vols. Edited by Paul Frédéricq. *Werken van den practischen leergang van vaderlandsche geschiedenis*, 1, 5, 8. Ghent: J. Vuylsteke, 1889.

Corpus iuris canonici. Edited by Aemilius Friedberg. 2 vols. Leipzig: Tauchnitz, 187–81. Reprint, Union, NJ: Lawbook Exchange, 2000.

Dante Alighieri. *La Commedia: secondo l'antica vulgata*. 4 vols. Edited by Giorgio Petrocchi. Milan: Mondadori, 1966–1967.

De S. Laurentio archidiacono ac martyre. AA. SS. Aug. II (1735), 485–532.

De S. Ursula et undecim millibus sociarum virginum et martyrum Coloniae Agrippinae. AA. SS. Oct IX (1869): 73–303.

Dietrich of Deutz. *Series achiepiscoporum coloniensis*. Edited by O. Holder-Egger. MGH SS 13:282–87.

Douais, C. *La Somme des autorités, à l'usage des prédicateurs méridionaux au XIIIe siècle*. Paris: Picard, 1896.

Eberwin of Steinfeld. "Letter 472." PL 182:676–80.

Les Ecclesiastica officia cisterciens du XIIème siècle. Edited by Danièle Choisselet and Placide Vernet. Reiningue: Abbaye d'Oelenberg, 1989. Trans. *The Ancient Uses of the Cistercian Order (Ecclesiastica Officia)*. Lafayette, OR: Guadalupe Translations, 1998.

Eckbert of Schönau. *Sermones contra Catharos*. PL 195:11–102. Also known as *Liber contra hereses Katharorum*. Trans. (Sermon 1). R. I. Moore. *The Birth of Popular Heresy*, 88–94. London: Edward Arnold, 1975.

Elizabeth of Schönau. *Die Visionen der hl. Elisabeth und die Schiften der Aebte Ekbert und Emecho von Schönau*. Edited by F. W. E. Roth. Brno: Verlag der Studien aus dem Benedictiner-und Cistercienser-Orden, 1884.

Emecho of Schönau. *Vita Eckeberti*. Edited by S. Widmann. *Neues Archiv der Gesellschaft für ältere deutsche Geschichtskunde* 2 (1886): 447–54.

Enarrationes in Evangelium Matthaei. PL 162:1227–500. Falsely attributed to Anselm of Laon.

Erasmus, Desiderius. *Adages*. Translated by Margaret Mann Phillips and annotated by R. A. B. Mynors. *Collected Works of Erasmus*, vol. 31. Toronto: University of Toronto Press, 1982.

Eudes of Châteauroux. "Sermon 1." In *Crusade Propaganda and Ideology: Model Sermons for the Preaching of the Cross*, edited by Christoph T. Maier, 128–43. Cambridge: Cambridge University Press, 2000.

Frederick II. "Die Konstitutionen Friedrichs II. für das Königreich Sizilien." Edited by Wolfgang Stürner. In *Constitutiones et acta publica imperatorum et regem*. Vol. 2. Hanover: Hahnsche Buchhandlung, 1996. Trans. James M. Powell. *The Liber Augustalis or the Constitutions of Melfi Promulgated by the Emperor Frederick II for the Kingdom of Sicily in 1231*. Syracuse, NY: Syracuse University Press, 1971.

Garnerius Lingonensis. *Sermones*. PL 205:559–828.

Geoffrey Vigeois. *Chronicon Gaufredi Vosiensis*. In *Receuil des historiens des Gaules*, edited by Martin Bouquet. Vol. 12:421–51. Paris: Victor Palmé, 1877.

Gerhoch of Reichersberg. *Commentarius aureus in Psalmos et cantica ferialia*. PL 193–94.

Gervase of Tilbury. *Otia Imperialia: Recreation for an Emperor*. Edited by S. E. Banks and J. W. Binns. Oxford: Clarendon Press, 2002.

Glossa ordinaria—Evangelium secundum Matthaeum. PL 114:63–178.

Gregory VII. *Das Register Gregors VII*. Edited by Erich Caspar. MGH Epist. 2:1–2.

Gregory of Nazianzus. "Excerpta." Edited by P. I. Fransen, B. Coppieters 't Wallant, and R. Demeulenaere. CCCM 193B:45–77. Turnhout: Brepols, 2007.

Gregory the Great. *Dialogues*. Edited by Adalbert de Vogüé. Paris: Éditions du cerf, 1980. Trans. Odo John Zimmerman. New York: Fathers of the Church, 1959.

——. *Homiliae in euangelia*. Edited by Raymond Etaix. CCSL 141. Turnhout: Brepols, 1999.

——. *Homiliae in Hiezechihelem prophetam*. Edited by M. Adriaen. CCSL 142. Turnhout: Brepols, 1971.

——. *Moralia in Iob*. Edited by M. Adriaen. CCSL 143–143B. Turnhout: Brepols, 1979–85.

——. *Super Cantica Canticorum expositio*. PL 79:471–548.

Guibert of Nogent. *Autobiographie*. Edited by Edmond-René Labande. Paris: Les Belles Lettres, 1981.

Henry of Marcy. *Epistolae*. PL 204:215–52.

Heriman of Reichinau. *Chronicon*. MGH SS 5:67–133.

Hildebert of Lavardin. *Moralis philosophia de honesto et utili*. PL 171:1003–56.

Hildegard of Bingen. *Epistulae Hildegardis Bingensis.* Edited by L. Van Acker. CCCM 91–91A. Turnhout: Brepols, 1991. Trans. Joseph L. Baird and Radd K. Ehrman. *The Letters of Hildegard of Bingen.* 3 vols. Oxford: Oxford University Press, 1994.

———. *Scivias.* Edited by Adelgund Führkötter and Angela Carlevaris. CCCM 43. Turnhout: Brepols, 1978.

Holdsworth, C. J., ed. "Eleven Visions Connected with the Cistercian Monastery of Stratford Langthorne." *Cîteaux: Commentarii Cistercienses* 13 (1962): 185–204.

Horace. *Ars Poetica.* Edited by C. O. Brink. Cambridge: Cambridge University Press, 1971.

Hugh of St. Victor. *De archa Noe.* Edited by Patrick Sicard. CCCM 176:1–117. Turnhout: Brepols, 2001.

———. *De sacramentis christiane fidei.* Edited by Rainer Berndt. Aschendorff: Monasterii Westfalorum, 2008. Also in PL 176:173–618. Trans. Roy J. Deferrari. *On the Sacraments of the Christian Faith.* Cambridge, MA: Medieval Academy of America, 1951.

———. "De unione corporis et anima." PL 177:285–94.

———. *Didascalicon de studio legendi.* Edited by H. Buttimer. Washington, DC: Catholic University Press, 1939. Also in PL 176:739–838.

———. *Expositio in hierarchiam coelestem S. Dionysii Areopagite.* PL 175:923–1154.

———. *In Salomonis Ecclesiasten homiliae XIX.* PL 175:113–256.

———. *Miscellanea.* PL 177:470–900.

———. *Sententiae de diuinitate.* Edited by A. M. Piazzoni. *Studi Medievali* 23 (1982): 912–55.

Innocent III. *Commentarium in septem Psalmos poenitentiales.* PL 217:967–1130.

Innocent III. *Innocentii III Regesta sive Epistolae.* PL 214–16.

Isaac of Stella. *"L'Epistola de anima di Isacco di Stella: studio della tradizione ed edizione del testo."* Edited by Caterina Tarlazzi. *Medioevo* 36 (2011): 167–278. Also in PL 194:1875–90. Trans. Bernard McGinn. *Three Treatises on Man: A Cistercian Anthropology.* Kalamazoo, MI: Cistercian Publications, 1977.

Isidore of Seville. *Codex Carolinus,* 1.26. PL 98:941–1350.

———. *Etymologies.* Edited and translated by Jacques André. Paris: Les Belles Lettres, 1981–2007.

———. *Sententiae.* Edited by P. Cazier. CCSL 111. Turnhout: Brepols, 1998.

Jacobus de Voriagine. *Legenda Aurea.* Edited by Giovanni Paolo Maggioni. 2 vols. Tavarnuzze: SISMEL edizioni del Galluzzo, 1998.

Jacques de Vitry. "Sermon 2: Item sermo ad crucesignatos vel–signandos." In *Crusade Propaganda and Ideology: Model Sermons for the Preaching of the Cross,* edited by Christoph T. Maier, 100–127. Cambridge: Cambridge University Press, 2000.

James, Montague Rhodes, ed. *The Apocryphal New Testament: Being the Apocryphal Gospels, Acts, Epistles, and Apocalypses, with Other Narratives and Fragments.* Oxford: Clarendon Press, 1975.

Jerome. *Adversus Jovinianum.* PL 23:221–354.

———. *Commentariorum in Matheum libri IV (Commentaire sur S. Matthieu).* Edited by Émile Bonnard. 2 vols. Paris: Les Éditions du Cerf, 1977.

———. *Commentarius in epistolam ad Galatas.* PL 26:331–468.

———. *Dialogus adversus Luciferianos*. PL 23:163–92.

———. *Epistolae*. Edited by I. Hilberg. CSEL 54–56. Turnhout: Brepols, 1910–18.

———. *Tractatus de Psalmo 77*. Edited by Germain Morin. CCSL 78:64–73. Turnhout: Brepols, 1958.

John Chrysostom. *Commentarius in S. Matthaeum*. PG 57:13–472; 58:471–794.

John of Salisbury. *Policratici: sive De nugis curialium et vestigiis philosophorum libri VIII*. Edited by C. C. I. Webb. Oxford: Clarendon Press, 1909. Reprint, New York: Arno Press, 1979. Trans. Cary J. Nederman. *Policraticus: Of the Frivolities of Courtiers and the Footprints of Philosophers*. Cambridge: Cambridge University Press, 1990.

John Pecham (Ioannis Pecham). *Quodlibeta Quatuor*. Edited by Girard J. Etzkorn. Grottaferrata, Rome: Editiones Collegi S. Bonaventurae ad Claras Aquas, 1989.

John Scotus Eriugena. *Expositiones in hierarchiam caelestem*. Edited by J. Barbet. CCCM 31. Turnhout: Brepols, 1975.

———. *Periphyseon*. Edited by E. A. Jeauneau. CCCM 161–65. Turnhout: Brepols, 1996–2003.

Jordan of Saxony. *Libellus de principiis ordinis Praedicatorum*. Edited by H. C. Scheeben. Rome: Institutum Historicum Ordinis Fratrum Praedicatorum, 1935.

Julian of Toledo. *Prognosticorum futuri saeculi libri tres*. Edited by J. N. Hilgarth. CCSL 115. Turnhout: Brepols, 1976. Also titled *Progosticum futuri saeculi*. Trans. Tommaso Stancati. *Foreknowledge of the World to Come*. New York: Newman Press, 2010.

Landulf Senior. *Historia Mediolanensis*. Edited by L. C. Bethmann and W. Wattenbach. MGH: SS 8:32–100.

Leo I. *Epistolae*. PL 54:593–1218.

Libellus adversus errores Alberonis sacerdotis merkensis. In *Veterum scriptorium et monumentorum historicorum dogmaticorum moralium amplissima*, edited by E. Martene and U. Durand, Vol. 9:1251–70. Paris, 1733. Reprint, New York: Burt Franklin, 1968.

Liber de spiritu et anima. PL 40:779–832.

Macrobius. *Commentaire au Songe de Scipion*. Edited and translated by Mireille Armisen–Marchetti. 2 vols. Paris: les belles lettres, 2011.

Matthew of Aquasparta. *Questiones disputatae de anima seperata, de anima beata, de ieiunio, et de legibus*. Edited by G. Gal, A. Emmen, I. Brady, and C. Piana. Florence: Collegii S. Bonaventurae, 1959.

Mommsen, Theodor, and Paul Krueger, eds. *The Digest of Justinian*. Translated by Alan Watson. Philadelphia: University of Pennsylvania Press, 1985.

Moore, R. I. *The Birth of Popular Heresy*. London: Edward Arnold, 1975.

Origen of Alexandria. *Commentarium in Canticum Canticorum*. PG 13:61–198.

———. *De principiis libri IV Rufino interprete*. In *Origenes Werke*, edited by Paul Koetschau, 5:7–364. Leipzig: J. C. Hinrichs, 1913.

———. *In Iesu Nave homiliae*. In *Origenes Werke*, edited by W. A. Baehrens, 7:286–463. Leipzig: J. C. Hinrichs, 1921.

Pactus legis Salicae. Edited by Karl August Eckhardt. MGH LL 2.1: vol. 4.1. Hannover: Hahn, 1962.

Paul of St. Père de Chartres. *Gesta synodi Aurelianensis an. MXXII, adversos novos Manichaeos*. In *Recueil des historiens des Gaules et de la France*. Vol. 10. Edited by Martin Bouquet. Paris: Victor Palmé, 1874.

Peter Lombard. *Collectanea in omnes Pauli apostolicas Epistulas*. PL 192:9–520.

———. *Sententiae in IV libris distinctae*. Grottaferrata, Rome: Editiones Collegi S. Bonaventurae ad Claras Aquas, 1981. Trans. Giulio Silano. *The Sentences*. 4 vols. Toronto: Pontifical Institute of Medieval Studies, 2010.

Peter of Cornwall. *Peter of Cornwall's Book of Revelations*. Edited by Robert Easting and Richard Sharpe. Toronto: Pontifical Institute of Medieval Studies, 2013.

Peter of les Vaux-de-Cernay. *Hystoria Albigensis*. Edited by Pascal Guébin and Ernest Lyon. 3 vols. Paris: Champion, 1926–39. Trans. W. A. Sibly and M. D. Sibly. *The History of the Albigensian Crusade*. Woodbridge, UK: Boydell Press, 1998.

Peter of Poitiers. *Sententiarum libri quinque*. PL 211:783–1280.

Peter the Cantor. *Summa quae dicitur Verbum adbreuiatum (textus conflatus)*. Edited by M. Boutry. CCCM 196. Turnhout: Brepols, 2004.

Peters, Edward, ed. *Heresy and Authority in Medieval Europe: Documents in Translation*. Philadelphia: University of Pennsylvania Press, 1980.

Peters, Edward, and A. C. Kors, eds. *Witchcraft in Europe, 1100–1700: A Documentary History*. Philadelphia: University of Pennsylvania Press, 1973.

———. *Witchcraft in Europe, 1100–1700: A Documentary History*. 2nd ed. Philadelphia: University of Pennsylvania Press, 2001.

Plato. *Timaeus*. Translated by Francis M. Cornford. New York: Bobbs–Merrill, 1959.

Radulf Ardens. *Homilia*. PL 155:1667–2118.

Ralph Glaber. *Historiarum libri quinque*. Edited and translated by John France. Oxford: Clarendon Press, 1989.

Ralph of Coggeshall. *Chronicon Anglicanum*. Edited by Joseph Stevenson. Rolls Series 66:1–208. London: H. M. Stationery Office, 1875. Reprint, Wiesbaden: Kraus, 1965.

Reginald of Durham. *Libellus de vita et miraculis S. Godrici, heremitae de Finchale*. Edited by J. Stevenson. *Surtees Society* 20 (1847).

Remy of Auxerre. *Homiliae duodecim*. PL 131:865–932.

Roger of Hoveden. *Chronica*. Edited by William Stubbs. Rolls Series 51. 4 vols. London: H. M. Stationery Office, 1869. Reprint, Wiesbaden: Kraus, 1964.

Shakespeare, William. *Titus Andronicus*. In *The Complete Works of Shakespeare*, edited by David Bevington. 4th ed., 938–76. New York: HarperCollins, 1992.

Siger of Brabant. *Quaestiones in tertium de anima. De anima intellective. De aeternitate mundi*. Edited by Bernardo C. Bazàn. Leuven: Publications Universitaires, 1972.

Une somme anti-cathare: Le Liber contra manicheos de Durand de Huesca. Edited by Christine Thouzellier. Leuven: Spicilegium sacrum Lovaniense Administration, 1964.

St. Patrick's Purgatory: Two Versions of Owayne Miles and the Vision of William of Stranton Together with the Long Text of the Tractatus de Purgatorio sancti Patricii. Edited by Robert Easting. Oxford: Oxford University Press, 1991.

Sulpicius Severus. *Chronica*. Edited by Carolus Halm. CSEL 1:3–105. Vienna, 1866.

———. *Dialogi*. Edited by Carolus Halm. CSEL 1:152–216. Vienna, 1866. Translated by F. R. Hoare. *The Western Fathers*. New York: Sheed and Ward, 1954, 68–144.

Tanner, Norman P., trans. *Decrees of the Ecumenical Councils.* 2 vols. London: Sheed and Ward, 1990.

Thomas Aquinas. *In IV Sententiarum.* In *Opera Omnia.* Vol. 7. Parma, 1858.

——. *Quaestiones de anima: A Newly Established Edition of the Latin Text with an Introduction and Notes.* Edited by James H. Robb. Toronto: Pontifical Institute of Medieval Studies, 1968.

——. *Summa Theologica.* Edited by J. de Rubeis and C.-R. Billuart. 5 vols. Turin: Marietti, 1938.

Virgil. *Aeneid VI.* Edited by Frank Fletcher. Oxford: Clarendon Press, 1941.

Vita sanctae Hildegardis. Edited by Monica Klaes. CCCM 126. Turnhout: Brepols, 1993.

Wakefield, Walter L., and Austin P. Evans, eds. *Heresies of the High Middle Ages.* New York: Columbia University Press, 1991.

Walter Map. *De nugis curialium or Courtiers Trifles.* Edited and translated by M. R. James; revised by C. N. L. Brooke and R. A. B. Mynors. Oxford: Clarendon Press, 1983.

Ward, H. L. D., ed. "The Vision of Thurkill, Probably by Ralph of Coggeshall, Printed from a MS in the British Museum." *Journal of the British Archeological Association* 31 (1875): 420–59.

William of Auvergne. *De legibus.* In *Guilielmi Alverni episcopi Parisiensis, mathematici perfestissimi, eximii philosophi, ac theologi praestantissimi, Opera Omnia.* 2 vols. London: Robert Scott, 1674.

William of Auxerre. *Summa Aurea.* Edited by Jean Ribaillier. Rome: Editiones Collegii S. Bonaventurae ad Claras Aquas, 1985.

William of Newburgh. *Historia rerum anglicarum.* Edited by R. Howlett. In *Chronicles of the Reigns of Stephen, Henry II, and Richard I.* Rolls Series 82. 4 vols. London: Longman, 1884. Reprint, Wiesbaden: Kraus, 1964.

William of Puylaurens. *Chronica magistri Guillelmi de Podio Laurentii.* Edited by Jean Duvernoy. Paris: Centre national de la recherché scientifique, 1976. Trans. W. A. Sibly and M. D. Sibly. *The Chronicle of William of Puylaurens: The Albigensian Crusade and Its Aftermath.* Woodbridge, UK: Boydell Press, 2003.

William of Saint-Thierry, Arnold of Bonneval, and Geoffrey of Auxerre. *Vita Prima Sancti Bernardi.* PL 185:225–466.

William Pelhisson. *Chronique, 1229–1244; suivie du, Récit des troubles d'Albi, 1234.* Edited by Jean Duvernoy. Paris: CNRS Editions, 1994.

Yves de Chartres. *Prologue.* Edited and translated by Jean Werckmeister. Paris: Les Éditions du Cerf, 1997.

Secondary Sources

Abulafia, David. *Frederick II: A Medieval Emperor.* New York: Oxford University Press, 1988.

Adams, J. N. ed. *The Latin Sexual Vocabulary.* Baltimore: Johns Hopkins University Press, 1982.

Adler, Shelly. *Sleep Paralysis Night-Mares, Nocebos and the Mind-Body Connection.* New Brunswick, NJ: Rutgers University Press, 2011.

Ahmed, Sara. *The Cultural Politics of Emotion.* 2nd ed. Edinburgh: Edinburgh University Press, 2014.

Allen, R. "Gerbert, Pope Silvester II." *English Historical Review* 7 (1892): 663–68.

Ames, Christine Caldwell. *Righteous Persecution: Inquisition, Dominicans, and Christianity in the Middle Ages.* Philadelphia: University of Pennsylvania Press, 2009.

Archibald, Elizabeth. *Incest and the Medieval Imagination.* Oxford: Oxford University Press, 2001.

Arendt, Hannah. *Love and Saint Augustine.* Edited by Joanna Vecchiarelli Scott and Judith Chelius Stark. Chicago: University of Chicago Press, 1996.

Arnold, John H. "The Cathar Middle Ages as a Methodological and Historical Problem." In *Cathars in Question,* edited by Antonio Sennis, 53–78. Woodbridge, UK: York Medieval Press, 2016.

Asad, Talal. *Genealogies of Religion: Discipline and Reasons of Power in Christianity and Islam.* Baltimore: Johns Hopkins University Press, 1993.

Babcock, William S. "Caritas and Signification in *De doctrina christiana* 1–3." In *De doctrina christiana: A Classic of Western Culture,* edited by Duane W. H. Arnold and Pamela Bright, 145–63. Notre Dame, IN: University of Notre Dame Press, 1995.

Bagley, C. P. "*Paratge* in the Anonymous *Chanson de la Croisade albigeoise.*" *French Studies* 21, no. 3 (1967): 195–204.

Bainton, Roland H. "The Parable of the Tares as the Proof Text for Religious Liberty to the End of the Sixteenth Century." *Church History* 1 (1932): 67–89.

Banks, S. E. "Tilbury, Gervase of." *Oxford Dictionary of National Biography,* edited by H. C. G. Matthew and Brian Harrison. Oxford: Oxford University Press, 2004. Accessed April 21, 2016. http://www.oxforddnb.com/view/article/10572.

Baraut, Cebrià. "Els incis de la Inquisició a Catalunya I les seves actuacions al Bisbat d'Urgell (segles XII–XIII)." *Urgellia* 13 (1997): 407–38.

Barber, Malcolm. *The Cathars: Dualist Heretics in Languedoc in the High Middle Ages.* New York: Pearson, 2000.

——. "Northern Catharism." In *Heresy and the Persecuting Society in the Middle Ages: Essays on the Work of R. I. Moore,* edited by Michael Frassetto, 115–37. Boston: Brill, 2006.

Barbezat, Michael D. "Bodies of Spirit and Bodies of Flesh: The Significance of the Sexual Activities Attributed to Heretics from the Eleventh to the Fourteenth Century." *Journal of the History of Sexuality* 25, no. 3 (2016): 387–419.

——. "The Corporeal Orientation: A Medieval and Early Modern Framework for Understanding Deviance through the Object(s) of Love." In *The Routledge History Handbook to Emotions in Europe, 1100–1700.* New York: Routledge, forthcoming.

——. "The Fires of Hell and the Burning of Heretics in the Accounts of the Executions at Orleans in 1022." *Journal of Medieval History* 40, no. 4 (2014): 399–420.

——. "In a Corporeal Flame: The Materiality of Hellfire before the Resurrection in Six Latin Authors." *Viator* 44 (2013): 1–20.

Bartlett, Robert. *Trial by Fire and Water: The Medieval Judicial Ordeal.* Oxford: Clarendon Press, 1986.

Bautier, Robert-Henri. "L'hérésie d'Orléans et le movement intellectuel au début du XIe siècle: Documents et hypotheses." In *Actes du 95e Congrès national des societies savantes (Reims 1970) Section de philologie et d'histoire jusqu'a 1610.* Vol. 1: *Enseignement et vie intellectuelle (IXe–XVIe Siècle),* 63–88. Paris: Bibliothèque Nationale, 1975.

Bayless, Martha. *Sin and Filth in Medieval Culture: The Devil in the Latrine.* New York: Routledge, 2012.

BeDuhn, Jason. "The Metabolism of Salvation: Manichaean Concepts of Human Physiology." In *The Light and the Darkness: Studies in Manichaeism and its World,* edited by Paul Mirecki and Jason BeDuhn, 5–37. Boston: Brill, 2001.

Berlioz, Jacques. *"Tues-les tous, Dieu reconnaîtra les siens:" Le massacre de Béziers (22 juillet 1209) et la croisade contre les Albigeois vus par Césaire de Heisterbach.* Portet-sur-Garonne: Éditions Loubatières, 1994.

Bernstein, Alan. *The Formation of Hell: Death and Retribution in the Ancient and Early Christian Worlds.* Ithaca, NY: Cornell University Press, 1993.

——. "Named Others and Named Places: Stigmatization in the Early Medieval Afterlife." In *Hell and Its Afterlife: Historical and Contemporary Perspectives,* edited by Isabel Moreira and Margaret Merrill, 53–71. Farnham, UK: Ashgate, 2010.

——. "William of Auvergne and the Cathars." In *Autour de Guillaume d'Auvergne,* edited by Franco Morenzoni and Jean-Yves Tilliette, 271–92. Turnhout: Brepols, 2005.

Biget, Jean-Louis. *Hérésie et inquisition dans le Midi de la France.* Paris: Picard, 2007.

Biller, Peter. "Bernard Gui, Sex and Luciferanism." In *Praedicatores, inquisitores I: The Dominicans and the Medieval Inquisition,* edited by Wolfram Hoyer, 455–70. Rome: Institute of Dominican Studies, 2004.

——. "Through a Glass Darkly: Seeing Medieval Heresy." In *The Medieval World,* edited by Peter Linehan and Janet L. Nelson, 308–26. London: Routledge, 2001.

——. *The Waldenses, 1170–1530.* Aldershot, UK: Ashgate, 2001.

Binski, Paul. *Medieval Death: Ritual and Representation.* Ithaca, NY: Cornell University Press, 1996.

Blöcker, Monica. "Volkszorn im frühen Mittelalter." *Francia* 13 (1985): 113–49.

Blumenfeld-Kosinski, Renate. "Holy Women in France: A Survey." In *Medieval Holy Women in the Christian Tradition c. 1100–c. 1500,* edited by Alastair Minnis and Rosalynn Voaden, 241–65. Turnhout: Brepols, 2010.

Bossier, F. "L'élaboration du vocabulaire philosophique chez Burgundio de Pise." In *Aux origins du lexique philosophique européen: L'influence de la Latinitas,* edited by J. Hamesse, 81–116. Louvain-la-Neuve: Brepols, 1997.

Boureau, Alan. *Satan the Heretic: The Birth of Demonology in the Medieval West.* Translated by Teresa Lavender Fagan. Chicago: University of Chicago Press, 2006.

Bradbury, Jim. *The Capetians: Kings of France, 987–1328.* New York: Continuum, 2007.

Brooke, Christopher. *The Twelfth Century Renaissance.* London: Thames and Hudson, 1969.

Brown, Peter. *Augustine of Hippo: A Biography.* Rev. ed. Berkeley: University of California Press, 2000.

——. "St. Augustine's Attitude to Religious Coercion." *Journal of Roman Studies* 54 (1964): 107–16.

Brown, Warren C. *Violence in Medieval Europe.* London: Pearson, 2011.

Brundage, James A. *Law, Sex, and Christian Society in Medieval Europe*. Chicago: University of Chicago Press, 1987.

——. "Prostitution in the Medieval Canon Law." *Signs* 4 (1976): 825–45.

Brunn, Uwe. *Des contestataires aux "Cathares" Discours de réforme et propagande antihérétique dans les pays du Rhin et de la Meuse avant l'Inquisition*. Paris: Institut d'Études Augustiniennes, 2006.

Bruschi, Caterina, and Peter Biller, eds. *Texts and the Repression of Medieval Heresy*. Woodbridge, UK: York Medieval Press, 2003.

Butler, Judith. *Bodies That Matter: On the Discursive Limits of "Sex."* New York: Routledge, 1993.

Bynum, Caroline Walker. "Did the Twelfth Century Discover the Individual?" In *Jesus as Mother: Studies in the Spirituality of the High Middle Ages*, 82–109. Berkeley: University of California Press, 1984.

——. *Holy Feast and Holy Fast: The Religious Significance of Food to Religious Women*. Berkeley: University of California Press, 1987.

——. *The Resurrection of the Body in Western Christianity, 200–1336*. New York: Columbia University Press, 1995.

Caciola, Nancy. *Discerning Spirits: Divine and Demonic Possession in the Middle Ages*. Ithaca, NY: Cornell University Press, 2003.

Carpenter, David A. "Abbot Ralph of Coggeshall's Account of the Last Years of King Richard and the First Years of King John." *English Historical Review* 113 (1998): 1210–30.

Cassidy-Welch, Megan. "Images of Blood in the *Historia Albigensis* of Pierre des Vaux-de-Cernay." *Journal of Religious History* 35 (2011): 478–91.

Chenu, Christian. "Innocent III and the Case for War in Southern France in 1207." *Journal of Religious History* 35 (2011): 507–15.

Chiffoleau, Jacques. *Les justices du pape: Délinquance et criminalité dans la region d'Avignon au quatorzième siècle*. Paris: Publications de la Sorbonne, 1984.

Chiu, Hilbert. "Alan of Lille's Academic Concept of the Manichee." *Journal of Religious History* 35 (2011): 492–506.

Clanchy, M. T. *From Memory to Written Record: England 1066–1307*. 2nd ed. Malden, MA: Blackwell, 1993.

Clark, Anne L. *Elisabeth of Schönau: A Twelfth-Century Visionary*. Philadelphia: University of Pennsylvania Press, 1992.

——. "Holy Woman or Unworthy Vessel? The Representations of Elisabeth of Schönau." In *Gendered Voices: Medieval Saints and Their Interpreters*, edited by Catherine M. Mooney, 35–51. Philadelphia: University of Pennsylvania Press, 1999.

Clark, Stuart. *Thinking with Demons: The Idea of Witchcraft in Early Modern Europe*. Oxford: Clarendon Press, 1997.

Cohen, Esther. *The Crossroads of Justice: Law and Culture in Late Medieval France*. Leiden: E. J. Brill, 1993.

Cohen, Jeremy. *Christ Killers: The Jews and the Passion from the Bible to the Big Screen*. Oxford: Oxford University Press, 2007.

——. *Living Letters of the Law: Ideas of the Jew in Medieval Christianity*. Berkeley: University of California Press, 1999.

Cohn, Norman. *Europe's Inner Demons: The Demonization of Christians in Medieval Christendom.* Rev. ed. London: Pimlico, 1993.

Colish, Marcia. *Peter Lombard.* New York: E. J. Brill, 1994.

Copeland, Rita, and Stephen Melville. "Allegory and Allegoresis, Rhetoric and Hermeneutics." *Exemplaria* 3 (1991): 159–87.

Corner, David. "Coggeshall, Ralph of (*fl.* 1207–1226)." *Oxford Dictionary of National Biography,* edited by H. C. G. Matthew and Brian Harrison. Oxford University Press, 2004. Accessed March 9, 2017. http://www.oxforddnb.com/view/article/5816.

Costen, Michael. *The Cathars and the Albigensian Crusade.* Manchester: Manchester University Press, 1997.

Cotts, John D. *The Clerical Dilemma.* Washington, DC: Catholic University of America, 2009.

Coulton, G. G. *The Death Penalty for Heresy from 1184 to 1921 A.D.* London: Simpkin, Marshall, Hamilton, Kent, 1924.

Coxon, Sebastian. "Wit, Laughter, and Authority in Walter Map's *De nugis curialum* (Courtier's Trifles)." In *Author, Reader, Book: Medieval Authorship in Theory and Practice,* edited by Stephen Partridge and Erik Kwakkel, 38–55. Toronto: University of Toronto Press, 2012.

Croydon, F. E. "Abbot Laurence of Westminster and Hugh of St. Victor." *Medieval and Renaissance Studies* 2 (1950): 169–71.

Davenport, Tony. "Sex, Ghosts, and Dreams: Walter Map (1135?–1210?) and Gerald of Wales (1146–1223)." In *Writers of the Reign of Henry II: Twelve Essays,* edited by Ruth Kennedy and Simon Meecham-Jones, 133–50. New York: Palgrave Macmillan, 2006.

Davidson, Amy. "The Age of Donald Trump and Pizzagate." *New Yorker,* December 5, 2016. http://www.newyorker.com/news/amy-davidson/the-age-of-donald-trump-and-pizzagate.

De Lubac, Henri. *Exégèse medieval: Les quatre sens de l'écriture.* 2 vols. Paris: Aubier, 1959–64. Trans. Mark Sebanc. *Medieval Exegesis: The Four Senses of Scripture.* 2 vols. Grand Rapids, MI: 1998.

De Man, Paul. *Blindness and Insight: Essays in the Rhetoric of Contemporary Criticism.* 2nd ed. Minneapolis: University of Minnesota Press, 1983.

Derrida, Jacques. *Spectres of Marx: The State of the Debt, the Work of Mourning, and the New International.* Translated by Peggy Kamuf. New York: Routledge, 1994.

Dietz, Elias. "When Exile Is Home: The Biography of Isaac of Stella." *Cistercian Studies Quarterly* 41 (2006): 141–65.

Dinshaw, Carolyn. *Chaucer's Sexual Poetics.* Madison: University of Wisconsin Press, 1989.

——. *How Soon Is Now? Medieval Texts, Amateur Readers, and the Queerness of Time.* London: Duke University Press, 2012.

Dronke, Peter. *Women Writers of the Middle Ages: A Critical Study of Texts from Perpetua (203) to Marguerite Porete (1310).* Cambridge: Cambridge University Press, 1984.

Dubarle, A. M. "Les renards de Samson." *Revue du Moyen Age latin* 7 (1951): 174–76.

Duggan, Anne J. "Becket Is Dead! Long Live St Thomas." In *The Cult of St Thomas Becket in the Plantagenet World, c.1170–c.1220*, edited by Paul Webster and Marie-Pierre Gelin, 25–51. Woodbridge, UK: Boydell Press, 2016.

Easting, Robert. "Dialogue between a Clerk and the Spirit of a Girl *de purgatorio* (1153): A Medieval Ghost Story." *Mediaevistik* 20 (2007): 163–83.

Edwards, Graham Robert. "Purgatory: 'Birth' or Evolution?" *Journal of Ecclesiastical History* 36 (1985): 634–46.

Elliott, Dyan. *Fallen Bodies: Pollution, Sexuality, and Demonology in the Middle Ages.* Philadelphia: University of Pennsylvania Press, 1999.

——. *Proving Woman: Female Spirituality and Inquisitorial Culture in the Later Middle Ages.* Princeton, NJ: Princeton University Press, 2004.

Erikson, Kai T. *Wayward Puritans: A Study in the Sociology of Deviance.* London: John Wiley and Sons, 1966.

Evans, G. R. *Alan of Lille: The Frontiers of Theology in the Later Twelfth Century.* New York: Cambridge University Press, 1983.

"Executions by Year." Death Penalty Information Center. Accessed July 12, 2016. http://www.deathpenaltyinfo.org/executions-year.

Falkenstein, Ludwig. "Guillaume aux Blanches Mains, archevêque de Reims et légat du siège apostolique (1176–1202)." *Revue d'histoire de l'église de France* 91 (2005): 5–25.

Fanger, Claire. *Rewriting Magic: An Exegesis of the Visionary Autobiography of a Fourteenth-Century French Monk.* University Park: Pennsylvania State University Press, 2012.

Farkasfalvy, Denis. "The Use of Paul by Saint Bernard as Illustrated by Saint Bernard's Interpretation of Philippians 3:13." In *Bernardus Magister: Papers Presented at the Nonacentenary Celebration of the Birth of Saint Bernard of Clairvaux*, edited by John R. Sommerfeldt, 161–68. Spencer, MA: Cistercian Publications, 1992.

Ferruolo, Stephen C. *The Origins of the University: The Schools and Their Critics 1100–1215.* Stanford, CA: Stanford University Press, 1985.

Flanagan, Sabina. *Hildegard of Bingen: A Visionary Life.* 2nd ed. London: Routledge, 1998.

Foucault, *The History of Sexuality.* Vol. 1, *An Introduction.* Translated by Robert Hurley. New York: Random House, 1978. Reprint, New York: Vintage Books, 1990.

France, James. *Separate but Equal: Cistercian Lay Brothers, 1120–1350.* Collegeville, MN: Cistercian Publications, 2012.

Frassetto, Michael. "The Heresy at Orleans in 1022 in the Writings of Contemporary Churchmen." *Nottingham Medieval Studies* 49 (2005): 1–17.

Freccero, Carla. *Queer/Early/Modern.* Durham, NC: Duke University Press, 2006.

Freeman, Elizabeth. "Wonders, Prodigies and Marvels: Unusual Bodies and the Fear of Heresy in Ralph of Coggeshall's *Chronicon Anglicanum*." *Journal of Medieval History* 26 (2000): 127–43.

Frend, W. H. C. *The Donatist Church: A Movement of Protest in Roman North Africa.* Oxford: Oxford University Press, 1985.

Friedland, Paul. *Seeing Justice Done: The Age of Spectacular Capital Punishment in France.* Oxford: Oxford University Press, 2012.

Gallagher, Clarence. *Canon Law and the Christian Community: The Role of Law in the Church according to the Summa Aurea of Cardinal Hostiensis*. Rome: Università Gregoriana, 1978.

Gauthier, René-Antoine. *Ethica Nicomachea, Praefatio*. Leiden: E. J. Brill, 1974.

Geary, Patrick. *Living with the Dead in the Middle Ages*. Ithaca, NY: Cornell University Press, 1994.

Geremek, Bronislaw. *Les marginaux parisiens aux XIVe et XVe siècles*. Translated by Daniel Beauvois. Paris: Flammarion, 1976.

Gessler, J. "Mulier suspensa: à délit égal peine différente?" *Revue Belge de philology et d'histoire* 18 (1939): 974–88.

Given, James. "Chasing Phantoms: Philip IV and the Fantastic." In *Heresy and the Persecuting Society in the Middle Ages: Essays on the Work of R. I. Moore*, edited by Michael Frassetto, 271–89. Leiden: Brill, 2006.

——. *Inquisition and Medieval Society: Power, Discipline, and Resistance in Languedoc*. Ithaca, NY: Cornell University Press, 1997.

Graham-Leigh, Elaine. "Justifying Deaths: The Chronicler Pierre des Vaux-de-Cernay and the Massacre of Béziers." *Mediaeval Studies* 63 (2001): 283–303.

——. *The Southern French Nobility and the Albigensian Crusade*. Woodbridge, UK: Boydell Press, 2005.

Gransden, Antonia. *Historical Writing in England, c. 550 to c. 1307*. London: Routledge and Kegan Paul, 1974.

Gregory, Brad S. *Salvation at Stake: Christian Martyrdom in Early Modern Europe*. Cambridge, MA: Harvard University Press, 1999.

Grundmann, Herbert. "Der Typus des Ketzers in Mittelalterliche Anschauung." In *Kultur- und Universal Geschichte. Walter Goetz zu seinem 60. Geburtstag*, 91–107. Leipzig, 1927.

——. "Oportet et haereses esse. Das Problem der Ketzerei im Spiegel der mittelalterlichen Bibelexegese." *Archiv für Kulturgeschichte* 45 (1963): 129–64.

——. *Religious Movements in the Middle Ages*. Translated by Steven Rowan. Notre Dame, IN: University of Notre Dame Press, 1995.

Harrington, Joel F. *The Faithful Executioner: Life, Honor, and Shame in the Turbulent Sixteenth Century*. New York: Picador, 2013.

Hauck, Albert. *Kirchengeschichte Deutschlands*. 4 vols. Leipzig, 1887–1906.

Havet, Julien. "L'hérésie et le bras seculier au Moyen-Age jusqu'au treizième siècle." *Bibliothèque de l'Ecloe de Chartes* 41 (1880): 488–517.

Head, Thomas. "The Genesis of the Ordeal of Relics by Fire in Ottonian Germany: An Alternative Form of 'Canonization.'" In *Procès de canonisation au moyen âge: Aspects juridiques et religieux*, edited by Gábor Klaniczay, 19–37. Rome: École française de Rome, 2004.

——. *Hagiography and the Cult of the Saints: The Diocese of Orleans, 800–1200*. New York: Cambridge University Press, 1990.

——. "Saints, Heretics, and Fire: Finding Meaning through the Ordeal." In *Monks and Nuns, Saints and Outcasts: Religion in Medieval Society*, edited by Sharon Farmer and Barbara H. Rosenwein, 220–38. Ithaca, NY: Cornell University Press, 2000.

Hehl, Ernst-Dieter. "War, Peace, and the Christian Order." In *The New Cambridge Medieval History*. Vol. 4: *c. 1024–c. 1198.*, pt. 1, edited by David Luscombe and

Jonathan Riley-Smith, 185–228. Cambridge: Cambridge University Press, 2004.

Heidegger, Martin. *Being and Time.* Translated by John Macquarrie and Edward Robinson. New York: Harper and Row, 1962.

Hillgarth, J. N. "St. Julian of Toledo in the Middle Ages." *Journal of the Warburg and Courtauld Institutes* 21 (1958): 7–26.

Holmes, Robert L. "St. Augustine and the Just War Theory." In *The Augustinian Tradition,* edited by Gareth B. Matthews, 323–44. Berkeley: University of California Press, 1999.

Housley, Norman. "Crusades against Christians: Their Origins and Early Development, c. 1000–1216." In *Crusade and Settlement,* edited by Peter W. Edbury, 17–36. Bristol: University College Cardiff Press, 1985.

Hutton, Ronald. *The Triumph of the Moon: A History of Modern Pagan Witchcraft.* Oxford: Oxford University Press, 1999.

Iogna-Prat, Dominique. *Order and Exclusion: Cluny and Christendom Face Heresy, Judaism, and Islam (1000–1150).* Translated by Graham Robert Edwards. Ithaca, NY: Cornell University Press, 2002.

Kelly, Henry Ansgar. "Inquisition and the Prosecution of Heresy: Misconceptions and Abuses." *Church History* 58 (1989): 439–51.

——. "Inquisitorial Due Process and the Status of Secret Crimes." In *Proceedings of the Eighth International Congress of Medieval Canon Law (UCSD, 1988),* edited by Stanley Chodorow. Monumenta iuris canonici, Series C: Subsidia, vol. 4, 407–47. Vatican City: Biblioteca Apostolica Vaticana, 1992.

Kerby-Fulton, Kathryn. "Prophet and Reformer: 'Smoke in the Vineyard.'" In *Voice of Living Light: Hildegard of Bingen and Her World,* edited by Barbara Newman, 70–90. Berkeley: University of California Press, 1998.

Kieckhefer, Richard. *Magic in the Middle Ages.* Cambridge: Cambridge University Press, 1989. Reprint, Canto Classics, 2000.

——. "The Specific Rationality of Medieval Magic." *American Historical Review* 99 (1994): 813–36.

Kienzle, Beverly Mayne. *Cistercians, Heresy and Crusade in Occitania, 1145–1229.* Woodbridge, UK: York Medieval Press, 2001.

Knowles, David, C. N. L. Brooke, and Vera C. M. London, eds. *The Heads of Religious Houses.* Vol. 1: *England and Wales, 940–1216.* Cambridge: Cambridge University Press, 2001.

Koziol, Geoffrey. *Begging Pardon and Favor: Ritual and Political Order in Early Medieval France.* Ithaca, NY: Cornell University Press, 1992.

Kruger, Steven F. "The Spectral Jew." *New Medieval Literatures* 2 (1998): 9–35.

——. *The Spectral Jew: Conversion and Embodiment in Medieval Europe.* Minneapolis: University of Minnesota Press, 2006.

Kurpiewski, Christopher M. "Writing beneath the Shadow of Heresy: The *Historia Albigensis* of Brother Pierre des Vaux-de-Cernay." *Journal of Medieval History* 31 (2004): 1–27.

Ladner, Gerhart B. *The Idea of Reform.* Cambridge, MA: Harvard University Press, 1959.

Lambert, Malcolm. *Medieval Heresy: Popular Movements from the Gregorian Reform to the Reformation.* 3rd ed. Oxford: Blackwell, 2002.

Landes, Richard. *Relics, Apocalypse, and the Deceits of History: Ademar of Chabannes, 989–1034*. Cambridge, MA: Harvard University Press, 1995.

———. "Rodolfus Glaber and the Dawn of the New Millennium: Eschatology, Historiography, and the Year 1000." *Revue Mabillon: Revue international d'histoire et de literature religieuses* n.s. 7 (1996): 57–77.

Lansing, Carol. Epilogue to *The Albigensian Crusades* by Joseph R. Strayer, 175–239. Ann Arbor: University of Michigan Press, 1992.

———. *Power and Purity: Cathar Heresy in Medieval Italy*. Oxford: Oxford University Press, 1998.

Lazar, Moshe. "Theophilus: Servant of Two Masters. The Pre-Faustian Theme of Despair and Revolt." *Modern Language Notes* 87 (1972): 31–50.

Le Goff, Jacques. *The Birth of Purgatory*. Translated by Arthur Goldhammer. Chicago: University of Chicago Press, 1984.

Leclercq, Jean. *The Love of Learning and the Desire for God: A Study of Monastic Culture*. 2nd ed. Translated by Catherine Misrahi. New York: Fordham University Press, 1974.

Lemercier, P. "Une curiosité judiciaire au moyen âge: La grace par marriage subséquent." *Revue d'histoire du droit* 33 (1955): 464–74.

Lerner, Robert E. *The Heresy of the Free Spirit in the Later Middle Ages*. Berkeley: University of California Press, 1972.

Levine, Robert. "How to Read Walter Map." *Mittellateinisches Jahrbuch* 23 (1988): 91–105.

Lipton, Sarah. *Dark Mirror: The Medieval Origins of Anti-Jewish Iconography*. New York: Metropolitan Books, 2014.

Llewellyn, Kathleen M. "At Play in the Fields and Playing the Field: The *débat amoureux* in the *Pastourelle* and the *Heptaméron*." *Parergon* 27 (2010): 105–24.

Lowe, Kathryn A. "Lay Literacy in Anglo-Saxon England and the Development of the Chirograph." In *Anglo-Saxon Manuscripts and Their Heritage*, edited by Phillip Pulsiano and Elaine M. Treharne, 161–204. Brookfield, VT: Ashgate, 1998.

Mackey, Louis. *Peregrinations of the Word: Essays in Medieval Philosophy*. Ann Arbor: University of Michigan Press, 1997.

Maddern, Philippa C. *Violence and Social Order*. Oxford: University of Oxford Press, 1992.

Marrevee, William H. *The Ascension of Christ in the Works of St. Augustine*. Ottawa: University of Ottawa Press, 1967.

Martin, H. "Inventaires des biens et des livres de l'Abbaye des Vaux-de-Cernay aux XIIe siècle." *Bulletin de la societé de l'histoire de Paris et de L'Ile-de-France* (1886): 36–42.

Martin, Laurence W. "The Massacre at Béziers July 22, 1209: A Revisionist Look." In *Heresy and the Persecuting Society in the Middle Ages: Essays on the Work of R. I. Moore*, edited by Michael Frassetto, 195–225. Leiden: Brill, 2006.

McGinn, Bernard. *The Golden Chain: A Study in the Theological Anthropology of Isaac of Stella*. Washington, DC: Cistercian Publications, 1972.

———. *The Presence of God: A History of Western Christian Mysticism*. 5 vols. New York: Crossroad, 1992–2012.

———. *Three Treatises on Man: A Cistercian Anthropology*. Kalamazoo, MI: Cistercian Publications, 1977.

McGuire, Brian Patrick. "Friends and Tales in the Cloister: Oral Sources in Caesarius of Heisterbach's *Dialogus Miraculorum*." *Analecta Cisterciensia* 36 (1981): 167–247.

———. *Friendship and Community: The Monastic Experience, 350–1250*. Ithaca, NY: Cornell University Press, 2010.

———. "Written Sources and Cistercian Inspiration in Caesarius of Heisterbach." *Analecta Cisterciensia* 35 (1979): 227–82.

McNamara, Jo Ann. "The Herrenfrage: The Restructuring of the Gender System, 1050–1150." In *Medieval Masculinities: Regarding Men in the Middle Ages*, edited by Jo Ann McNamara, Thelma S. Fenster, and Clare A. Lees, 3–29. Minneapolis: University of Minnesota Press, 1994.

Merback, Mitchell B. *The Thief, the Cross and the Wheel: Pain and the Spectacle of Punishment in Medieval and Renaissance Europe*. Chicago: University of Chicago Press, 1998.

Merlo, G. G. *Eretici e inquisitori nella società piemontese del Trecento: Con l'edizione dei processi tenuti a Giaveno dall'inquisitore Alberto de Castellario (1335) e nelle Valli di Lanzo dall'inquisitore Tommaso di Casasco (1373)*. Turin: Claudiana, 1977.

Mills, Robert. *Suspended Animation: Pain, Pleasure and Punishment in Medieval Culture*. London: Reaktion Books, 2005.

Moore, R. I. "Afterthoughts on *The Origins of European Dissent*." In *Heresy and the Persecuting Society in the Middle Ages: Essays on the Work of R. I. Moore*, edited by Michael Frassetto, 291–326. Leiden: Brill, 2006.

———. "Heresy as a Disease." In *The Concept of Heresy in the Middle Ages (11th–13th Centuries)*, edited by W. Lourdaux and D. Verhelst, 1–11. Leuven: Leuven University Press, 1976.

———. *The First European Revolution, c. 970–1215*. Malden, MA: Blackwell, 2003.

———. *The Formation of a Persecuting Society*. Malden, MA: Blackwell, 1987.

———. *The Origins of European Dissent*. Oxford: Basil Blackwell, 1985.

———. "Principles at Stake: The Debate of April 2013 in Retrospect." In *Cathars in Question*, edited by Antonio Sennis, 257–73. Woodbridge, UK: York Medieval Press, 2016.

———. *The War on Heresy*. Cambridge, MA: Harvard University Press, 2012.

Morrison, Karl F. *I Am You: The Hermeneutics of Empathy in Western Literature, Theology, and Art*. Princeton, NJ: Princeton University Press, 1988.

Mowbray, Donald. *Pain and Suffering in Medieval Theology: Academic Debates at the University of Paris in the Thirteenth Century*. Woodbridge, UK: Boydell Press, 2009.

Munz, Peter. *Frederick Barbarossa: A Study in Medieval Politics*. London: Eyre and Spottiswoode, 1969.

Murray, Alexander. *Suicide in the Middle Ages*. 2 vols. Oxford: Oxford University Press, 2000.

Murray, Margaret Alice. *The Witch Cult in Western Europe: A Study in Anthropology*. Oxford: Clarendon Press, 1921.

Neufeld, Christine M. "Hermeneutical Perversions: Ralph of Coggeshall's 'Witch of Rheims.'" *Philological Quarterly* 85 (2006): 1–23.

Newman, Barbara. "Possessed by the Spirit: Devout Women, Demoniacs, and the Apostolic Life in the Thirteenth Century." *Speculum* 73 (1998): 733–70.

———. "'Sibyl of the Rhine': Hildegard's Life and Times." In *Voice of Living Light: Hildegard von Bingen and Her World*, edited by Barbara Newman, 1–29. Berkeley: University of California Press, 1998.

Newman, Martha G. *The Boundaries of Charity: Cistercian Culture and Ecclesiastical Reform, 1098–1180*. Stanford, CA: Stanford University Press, 1996.

Nirenberg, David. *Anti-Judaism: The History of a Way of Thinking*. London: Head of Zeus, 2013.

———. *Communities of Violence: Persecution of Minorities in the Middle Ages*. Princeton, NJ: Princeton University Press, 1996.

Nolan, Edward Peter. *Now through a Glass Darkly: Specular Images of Being and Knowing from Virgil to Chaucer*. Ann Arbor: University of Michigan Press, 1990.

Olsen, Glenn W. *Of Sodomites, Effeminates, Hermaphrodites, and Androgynes: Sodomy in the Age of Peter Damian*. Toronto: Pontifical Institute of Medieval Studies, 2011.

Oort, Johannes van. "Human Semen Eucharist among the Manichaeans? The Testimony of Augustine Reconsidered in Context." *Vigiliae Christianae* 70 (2016): 193–216.

Paterson, Linda M. *The World of the Troubadours: Medieval Occitan Society, c. 1100–c. 1300*. Cambridge: Cambridge University Press, 1993.

Patschovsky, Alexander. "Heresy and Society: On the Political Function of Heresy in the Medieval World." Translated by James Fearns. In *Texts and the Repression of Medieval Heresy*, edited by Caterina Bruschi and Peter Biller, 23–41. Woodbridge, UK: York Medieval Press, 2003.

Pegg, Mark Gregory. *The Corruption of Angels: The Great Inquisition of 1245–1246*. Princeton: Princeton University Press, 2001.

———. "Heresy, Good Men, and Nomenclature." In *Heresy and the Persecuting Society in the Middle Ages: Essays on the Work of R. I. Moore*, edited by Michael Frassetto, 227–39. Leiden: Brill, 2006.

———. *A Most Holy War: The Albigensian Crusade and the Battle for Christendom*. Oxford: Oxford University Press, 2008.

———. "The Paradigm of Catharism; or, the Historians' Illusion." In *Cathars in Question*, edited by Antonio Sennis, 21–52. Woodbridge, UK: York Medieval Press, 2016.

Peters, Edward. *Inquisition*. New York: Free Press, 1988.

———. *The Magician, the Witch, and the Law*. Philadelphia: University of Pennsylvania Press, 1978.

Power, Daniel. "Who Went on the Albigensian Crusade?" *English Historical Review* 128 (2013): 1047–85.

Putallaz, François-Xavier. "L'âme et le feu: Notes franciscaines sur le feu de l'enfer après 1277." In *After the Condemnation of 1277. Philosophy and Theology at the University of Paris in the Last Quarter of the Thirteenth Century. Studies and Texts*, edited by Jan A. Aertsen, Kent Emery Jr., and Andreas Speer, 889–901. Berlin: De Gruyter, 2001.

Reddy, William. *The Making of Romantic Love: Longing and Sexuality in Europe, South Asia and Japan, 900–1200 CE*. Chicago: University of Chicago Press, 2012.

———. *The Navigation of Feeling: A Framework for the History of Emotions*. Cambridge: Cambridge University Press, 2004.

Rider, Catherine. "Agreements to Return from the Afterlife in Late Medieval Exempla." In *The Church, the Afterlife and the Fate of the Soul. Papers Read at the 2007 Summer Meeting and the 2008 Winter Meeting of the Ecclesiastical History Society*, edited by Peter Clark and Tony Claydon, 174–83. Woodbridge, UK: Boydell Press, 2009.

Rigg, A. G. *A History of Anglo-Latin Literature*. New York: Cambridge University Press, 1992.

Roach, Andrew P. *The Devil's World: Heresy and Society 1100–1300*. Harlow, UK: Pearson, 2005.

Roach, Andrew P., and James R. Simpson, eds. *Heresy and the Making of European Culture: Medieval and Modern Perspectives*. Farnham, UK: Ashgate, 2013.

Rorem, Paul. *Hugh of St. Victor*. Oxford: Oxford University Press, 2009.

Rosenwein, Barbara H. *Emotional Communities in the Early Middle Ages*. Ithaca, NY: Cornell University Press, 2006.

———. *Generations of Feeling: A History of the Emotions, 600–1700*. Cambridge: Cambridge University Press, 2016.

———. "Worrying about Emotions in History." *American Historical Review* 107, no. 3 (2002): 821–45.

Roubach, Sharon. "The Hidden Apocalypse: Richard of Saint-Vanne and the Otherworld." *Journal of Medieval History* 32 (2006): 302–14.

Rubin, Miri. *Corpus Christi: The Eucharist in Late Medieval Culture*. Cambridge: Cambridge University Press, 1991.

———. *Gentile Tales: The Narrative Assault on Late Medieval Jews*. Philadelphia: University of Pennsylvania Press, 1999.

Ruff, Julius R. *Violence in Early Modern Europe 1500–1800*. Cambridge: Cambridge University Press, 2001.

Russell, Frederick H. *The Just War in the Middle Ages*. Cambridge: Cambridge University Press, 1975.

Russell, Jeffrey Burton. *Dissent and Order in the Middle Ages: The Search for Legitimate Authority*. New York: Twayne Publishers, 1992.

———. *Dissent and Reform in the Early Middle Ages*. Berkeley: University of California Press, 1965.

———. *Lucifer: The Devil in the Middle Ages*. Ithaca, NY: Cornell University Press, 1984.

———. *Witchcraft in the Middle Ages*. Ithaca, NY: Cornell University Press, 1972.

Sackville, Lucy J. *Heresy and Heretics in the Thirteenth Century: The Textual Representations*. Woodbridge, UK: York Medieval Press, 2011.

Sanchez, Pilar Jiménez. "Aux commencements du Catharisme: La communauté d'"apôtres hérétiques' denoncée par Evervin de Steinfeld en Rhénanie." *Heresis* 35 (2001): 17–44.

Schmitt, Jean-Claude. *Ghosts in the Middle Ages*. Translated by Teresa Lavender Fagan. Chicago: University of Chicago Press, 1998.

Siebert, Irmgard, ed. *Universitäts-und Landesbibliothek Düsseldorf, Katalogue der Handschriftenateilung*. 5 vols. Wiesbaden: Otto Harrassowitz, 2005.

Sinderhauf, M. *Die Abtei Deutz und ihre innere Erneuerung. Klostergeschichte im Spiegel des verschollenen Codex Thioderici*. Vierow: SH-Verlag, 1996.

Smalley, Beryl. *The Gospels in the Schools c.1100–1280*. London: Hambledon Press, 1985.

———. *The Study of the Bible in the Middle Ages*. Oxford: Blackwell, 1983.

Smith, Jonathan Riley. "Crusading as an Act of Love." *History* 65 (1980): 177–92.

Smith, Joshua Byron. *Walter Map and the Matter of Britain*. Philadelphia: University of Pennsylvania Press, 2017.

Southern, R. W. *Scholastic Humanism and the Unification of Europe*. 2 vols. Oxford: Blackwell, 1995–2001.

———. *Western Society and the Church in the Middle Ages*. London: Penguin, 1990.

Spackman, Barbara. "*Inter musam et ursam moritur*: Folengo and the Gaping 'Other' Mouth." In *Refiguring Woman: Perspectives on Gender and the Italian Renaissance*, ed. Marilyn Migiel and Juliana Schiesari, 19–34. Ithaca, NY: Cornell University Press, 1991.

Spinosa, Giacinta. "Plaisir de la connaissance comme émotion intellectuelle chez Hugues de Saint-Victor." *Quaestio* 15 (2015): 373–82.

Steiner, Emily. *Documentary Culture and the Making of Medieval English Literature*. Cambridge: Cambridge University Press, 2003.

Stock, Brian. *The Implications of Literacy: Written Language and Models of Interpretation in the Eleventh and Twelfth Centuries*. Princeton, NJ: Princeton University Press, 1983.

———. *Myth and Science in the Twelfth Century: A Study of Bernard Silvester*. Princeton, NJ: Princeton University Press, 1972.

Strayer, Joseph R. *The Albigensian Crusades*. New York: Dial Press, 1971. Reprint, Ann Arbor: University of Michigan Press, 1992.

Sullivan, Karen. *Truth and the Heretic: Crises of Knowledge in Medieval French Literature*. Chicago: University of Chicago Press, 2005.

Tarlazzi, Caterina. "Alan of Lille and the *Periesichen Augustini*." *Bulletin de Philosophie Médiévale* 51 (2009): 45–54.

Théry-Astruc, Julien. "The Heretical Dissidence of the 'Good Men' in the Albigeois (1276–1329): Localism and Resistance to Roman Clericalism." In *Cathars in Question*, edited by Antonio Sennis, 79–111. Woodbridge, UK: York Medieval Press, 2016.

———. "L'hérésie des bons homes. Comment nommer la dissidence religieuse non vaudoise ni beguine en Languedoc?" *Heresis* 36–37 (2002): 75–117.

Thomas, Keith. *Religion and the Decline of Magic: Studies in Popular Beliefs in Sixteenth and Seventeenth Century England*. Oxford: Oxford University Press, 1971.

Tierney, Brian. *The Crisis of Church and State: 1050–1300*. Englewood Cliffs, NJ: Prentice-Hall, 1964.

Trivellone, Alessia. *L'hérétique imaginé: Hétérodoxie et iconographie dans l'Occident médiéval, de l'époque carolingienne à l'inquisition*. Turnhout: Brepols, 2009.

Ullmann, Walter. "The Significance of Innocent III's Decretal 'Vergentis.'" In *Études d'histoire du droit canonique dédiées à Gabriel Le Bras*. Vol. 1, 729–742. Paris: Sirey, 1965.

Vanderputten, Steven, and Diane J. Reilly. "Reconciliation and Record Keeping: Heresy, Secular Dissent and the Exercise of Episcopal Authority in Eleventh-Century Cambrai." *Journal of Medieval History* 37 (2011): 343–57.

Van 't Spijker, Ineke. "'Ad commovendos affectus': Exegesis and the Affects in Hugh of Saint-Victor." In *Bibel und Exegese in der Abtei Saint-Victor zu Paris: Form und Funktion eines Grundtextes im europäischen Rahmen*, edited by Rainer Berndt, 215–34. Munster: Aschendorff Verlag, 2009.

Wailes, Stephen L. *Medieval Allegories of Jesus' Parables*. Berkeley: University of California Press, 1987.

Walsham, Alexandra. *Charitable Hatred: Tolerance and Intolerance in England, 1500– 1700*. Manchester: Manchester University Press, 2006.

Ward, Benedicta. *Miracles and the Medieval Mind: Theory, Record and Event 1000–1215*. London: Scolar Press, 1982.

Watson, Nicholas. "Desire for the Past." *Studies in the Age of Chaucer* 21 (1999): 59–97.

Waytz, Adam, Liane Young, and Jeremy Ginges. "Motive Attribution for Love vs. Hate Drives Intractable Conflict." *Proceedings of the National Academy of Sciences of the United States of America* 111, no. 44 (2014), 15687–92.

Zaleski, Carol. *Otherworld Journeys: Accounts of Near-Death Experience in Medieval and Modern Times*. Oxford: Oxford University Press, 1987.

Zerner, Monique, ed. *Inventer l'hérésie? Discours polémiques et pouvoirs avant l'inquisition*. Nice: Centre d'Études Médiévales, 1998.

——. "L'hérétique Henri dans les sources de son temps (1135–1145)." *Revue Mabillon* 86 (2014): 79–134.

Žižek, Slavoj. *How to Read Lacan*. New York: W. W. Norton, 2006.

Zuijdwegt, Geertjan. "'Utrum caritas sit aliquid creatum in anima': Aquinas on the Lombard's Identification of Charity with the Holy Spirit." *Recherches de Théologie et Philosophie Médiévales* 79 (2012): 39–74.

INDEX